S—

LEAVING MESA VERDE

AMERIND STUDIES IN ARCHAEOLOGY

SERIES EDITOR **JOHN WARE**

Leaving Mesa Verde

Peril and Change in the Thirteenth-Century Southwest

Edited by **Timothy A. Kohler**,
Mark D. Varien,
and **Aaron M. Wright**

The University of Arizona Press
Tucson

The University of Arizona Press
© 2010 The Arizona Board of Regents
All rights reserved

www.uapress.arizona.edu

Library of Congress Cataloging-in-Publication Data

Leaving Mesa Verde : peril and change in the thirteenth-
century Southwest / edited by Timothy A. Kohler, Mark D.
Varien, and Aaron M. Wright.
  p. cm. — (Amerind studies in archaeology ; v. 5)
  Includes bibliographical references and index.
  ISBN 978-0-8165-2885-1 (hard cover : alk. paper)
  1. Pueblo Indians—Colorado Plateau—
Migrations. 2. Pueblo Indians—Colorado Plateau—
Population. 3. Demographic archaeology—Colorado
Plateau. 4. Excavations (Archaeology)—Colorado
Plateau. 5. Colorado Plateau—Population—History—
To 1500. I. Kohler, Timothy A. II. Varien, Mark.
III. Wright, Aaron M. (Aaron Michael)
  E99.P9L39 2010
  304.609788′1—dc22   2010017032

Publication of this book is made possible in part by a grant
from the Board of Directors of the Amerind Foundation.

Manufactured in the United States of America on acid-free,
archival-quality paper containing a minimum of 30% post-
consumer waste and processed chlorine free.

15 14 13 12 11 10 6 5 4 3 2 1

CONTENTS

When asked about the fabled disappearance of the Ancestral Pueblo people from the Southwest's Four Corners region, Tewa anthropologist Alfonso Ortiz famously quipped, "The Anasazi didn't disappear, they're running bingo parlors in the Rio Grande Valley." Now, of course, the bingo parlors have morphed into casinos, but Ortiz's point remains the same. Alas, the mystery of Ancestral Pueblo disappearance was resolved many years ago by archaeologists, whose findings coincided with what the modern Pueblo people had been saying all along: that the countless pithouse and masonry ruins of the northern Southwest were the "footprints" of their ancestors.

But if we know who the people were who built Cliff Palace and other Ancestral Pueblo sites in the central Mesa Verde region, the questions of why they abandoned their ancestral homes on the Colorado Plateau at the close of the thirteenth century and precisely where they went when they left have been debated for years, and a consensus has been slow to emerge. Early explanations of Apachean invaders driving the Pueblos from their homes in the cliffs were challenged and laid to rest long ago, although warfare among Ancestral Pueblo peoples is now generally conceded and its effects carefully weighed against other factors, such as disease, habitat loss, drought, and crop failure. If Ortiz was right that Pueblo ancestors moved from the northern San Juan region of Colorado to the northern Rio Grande Valley of New Mexico in the early 1300s, we certainly don't see clear evidence of these migrants in the architectural forms and material culture of late prehistoric Rio Grande archaeology. In contrast, unambiguous evidence of Pueblo immigrants from the Kayenta region of northeastern Arizona is preserved in dozens (perhaps hundreds) of archaeological sites from central and southeastern Arizona. Why should immigrants from the western Plateau construct such obvious "site unit intrusions" while those from the eastern Plateau remain virtually invisible?

As recently as ten years ago, archaeologists were convinced that environmental conditions in the northern Southwest were never so severe that people would have been forced to migrate in order to survive. Research focused instead on various social factors that may have encouraged people to leave rather than continue to adapt in place. Recent research paints a more dire abandonment scenario, one in which famine, intense warfare, and social and political collapse may have figured in the final decision to leave and never return. These conclusions are supported by recent paleoclimatic studies that have recovered incontrovertible evidence of drought and changes in low-frequency weather patterns in the 1100–1200s that may have made it impossible for people to continue to farm many portions of the high, dry Colorado Plateau. All these facts may converge to help explain why there is so little direct evidence of Mesa Verde migrants in the Rio Grande Valley. Perhaps Mesa Verde populations declined so precipitously during the 1200s that there were few people left at the end of the century to pack up and move.

These and many other questions about the thirteenth-century depopulation of the northern Southwest were addressed in an advanced seminar at the Amerind Foundation in Dragoon, Arizona, in February 2008. The results of that seminar are assembled and synthesized in this groundbreaking volume. Organized and chaired by Tim Kohler of Washington State University (WSU) and the Santa Fe Institute, Mark Varien of the Crow Canyon Archaeological Center, and Aaron Wright of the Center for Desert Archaeology and WSU, the symposium brought together 14 scholars from across the country whose recent research in the northern San Juan region of southwestern Colorado and southeastern Utah bears directly on questions of depopulation, migration, paleoclimate change, and Pueblo social and ritual organization. In my judgment, this volume summarizes the results of some of the most sophisticated multidisciplinary research ever conducted in archaeology. Thanks in part to the extensive dendrochronological and climatological record assembled for the central Mesa Verde region, researchers are now able to date the archaeology and model the climate and environment of the northern Southwest with unparalleled precision, and more than a hundred years of intensive research in the northern San Juan region has created a prehistoric database that is perhaps unmatched anywhere else in the world. On behalf of the board and staff of the Amerind Foundation, I'd like to thank the organizers and authors of this volume for their inspiration and hard work in bringing these important research results to an interested public.

This volume brings us a step closer to understanding some of the more persistent puzzles of Southwest prehistory, but of course important questions remain. Perhaps the hardest things to know about the past are the social and ideological worlds of the people who inhabited deep prehistory, and without these key pieces of the larger puzzle, true understanding may continue to elude us. As this volume attests, archaeologists of the desert Southwest have become highly skilled at measuring changes in climate, demography, settlement patterns, technologies, foodways, and other aspects of prehistoric practice that leave discernable traces in the ground, but the decision to turn one's back on a landscape where all one's cultural stories are situated and where all one's ancestors are buried must have had immense psychological and ideological impacts on the people who finally decided to leave. Final answers about what these impacts were may be more easily grasped by the descendants of migrants than by archaeologists searching for clues in the soil.

John A. Ware

In this book, we seek to explain one of the classic problems in the archaeology of the Americas: the depopulation of the northern Southwest in the late AD 1200s. At the same time, we hope to contribute to migration studies more generally. The prehispanic history of the U.S. Southwest—even that of "sedentary farmers"—was marked by the recurrent movement of households and communities across local landscapes on generational timescales. Many of the relocations were apparently anticipated and socially nondisruptive. Against this background, though, several episodes stand out for the numbers of people affected, the distances moved, the permanence of the departures, the severity of the surrounding conditions, and the human suffering and culture change that accompanied them (Hegmon et al. 2008).

By any of these criteria, the thirteenth-century AD conclusion to the farming way of life in the northern Southwest must have been among the most challenging and remarkable experiences in the lives of Pueblo people across many generations. For more than two thousand years, Pueblo peoples had been planting corn, building houses, and burying their dead on the plateaus and in the canyons of what is today southwestern Colorado, southeastern Utah, and adjacent portions of Arizona and New Mexico. No human society—and more especially, no farming community that for generations had built up its villages and fields—leaves its homeland lightly. As we will see, even the incomplete record available to archaeologists reveals a traumatic side to this departure.

And yet, on long enough time scales, there would have been constructive and generative aspects to this crisis. One of them is obvious: human welfare can often be improved through migration from an environmentally poor area to an environmentally rich area. More subtly, as Boyd and Richerson point out, people also "tend to move to wealthier, safer, and more just *societies* from poorer, more violent, less just societies" (2009:331, emphasis added). If there is assimilation, then such movement (or "selective migration") can tend to increase the occurrence across societies of those group-beneficial values, institutions, or practices that made those societies more attractive.

Readers of this volume will see that there is always a tension between whether to view depopulation as a catastrophic historical event or as part of a longstanding southwestern (indeed, human) process leading ultimately to social and economic forms that were quite possibly more advantageous for individuals in a society. This cannot be resolved because it was both of those things, on differing temporal and experiential scales. Ultimately, it is less fruitful to regard the thirteenth and early fourteenth centuries as posing a dialectic between catastrophe and reorganization. Instead, we are coming to think of this era as having witnessed a competition between differing social and economic organizations in which selective migration was considerably hastened by severe climatic, environmental, and social upheaval. Moreover, as the chapters assembled here show, it is at least as true that emigration led to the collapse of the northern Southwest as that this collapse led to migration.

It cannot have escaped the attention of any of the fifteen archaeologists (and one geologist) who gathered at the Amerind Foundation near Dragoon in late February 2008 that our circumstances were markedly more comfortable and secure than those of the people we were studying. We were convening at the invitation of John Ware, executive director of the Amerind, to revisit in more detail and at greater leisure the content of a 2007 Society for American Archaeology symposium, organized by Aaron M. Wright and me and moderated by Mark Varien, entitled New Light on the Thirteenth-Century Depopulation of the Northern Southwest.

It was clearly time to revisit this problem, which as Varien shows in chapter 1 was a staple of southwestern archaeology in the first half of the twentieth century, but which has since been dealt with in a mostly oblique fashion. Many new paleoenvironmental data, and a great deal of archaeological survey and excavation, now permit us to be considerably more precise than we could be fifty years ago on the timing of the depopulation, the number of people affected by it, and the ways in which northern Pueblo peoples coped, and failed to cope, with the rapidly changing environmental and demographic conditions they encountered throughout the 1200s. Working from the other end, models are now providing insights into the processes behind the patterns we see, helping us to narrow the range of explanatory plausibilities.

We editors would like to thank the authors of this volume for their conscientious work. We have not reached consensus on all the issues raised here, but the outlines of what happened in the Southwest in the thirteenth century AD are markedly clearer for their efforts. We also thank John Ware and the staff of the Amerind for a delightful and productive seminar, as well as the National Science Foundation, which through BCS-0119981 helped underwrite both the Amerind seminar and some of the research reported in this volume. Finally, we thank Mark Hill, who at the time was a PhD candidate in anthropology at Washington State University, for his cheerful assistance during the initial compiling, editing, and formatting of the volume. May our efforts assist future research in this area, and may this and similar research eventually help humanity understand how to avoid collapses on possibly much larger scales.

—*T. Kohler, for the editors*

Leaving Mesa Verde

Depopulation of the Northern San Juan Region

Historical Review and Archaeological Context

Mark D. Varien

The northern San Juan region, an area defined in this volume as the drainages that empty into the San Juan River from the north, is one of the world's foremost archaeological areas. This is attested to by the extent of the public lands devoted to archaeological preservation and public interpretation. In southwestern Colorado, these include Mesa Verde National Park, the Ute Mountain Ute Tribal Park, and four national monuments—Yucca House, Hovenweep, Chimney Rock, and Canyons of the Ancients (CANM)—along with the Anasazi Heritage Center, headquarters for CANM and one of the premier interpretive and curation facilities in the Southwest. Public-land archaeological areas in southeastern Utah include Arches and Canyonlands National Park, Natural Bridges National Monument, Cedar Mesa–Grand Gulch Primitive Area, and Edge of the Cedars State Park. Northwestern New Mexico contains two prominent archaeological areas: Aztec National Monument and Salmon Ruins. The northern San Juan region has captured the imagination of the public and the attention of researchers since the late 1800s because of its incredible number of archaeological sites—more than one hundred per square mile in some areas—and their extraordinary preservation. Among these sites are multistoried pueblos and underground structures—some with roofs intact and murals decorating their walls—and abundant artifacts, many still on floors, as if the sites' residents had only recently left.

The subject of this volume is the depopulation of the region and the migration of its inhabitants to other areas. The volume begins by recognizing that depopulation and migration occurred throughout the Greater Southwest (fig. 1.1). Chapters 2, 3, and 6 examine population movement in this larger area to provide the context for these processes in the northern San Juan region (fig. 1.2). Depopulation also occurred in the context

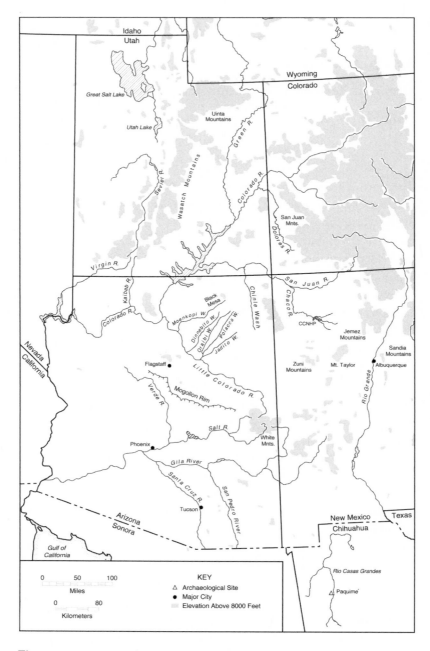

Figure 1.1. Portions of the Greater Southwest and adjacent areas, as referred to in this volume. (Courtesy Crow Canyon Archaeological Center)

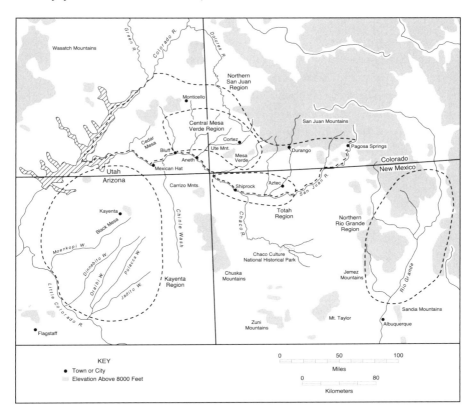

Figure 1.2. The northern San Juan and adjacent portions of the Southwest. (Courtesy Crow Canyon Archaeological Center)

of significant climate change, and chapters 4 and 5 present a large body of new research on the environmental setting that stimulated migration. Chapter 4 shows that thirteenth-century climate conditions were some of the worst ever for farmers in the northern Southwest, demonstrating that climatic variability remains an important factor in the migrations from both the losing and receiving ends. Chapter 5 uses high-frequency changes in both precipitation and temperature to provide annual estimates of maize-farming productivity, and these data are combined with models that examine the long-term use of meat obtained by hunting, wood collected for fuel, and water used for domestic needs. These reconstructions are used as the basis for developing a synthetic explanatory model for the depopulation of the central Mesa Verde region.

Chapters 7, 8, and 9 use archaeological data from the central Mesa Verde region to characterize the social upheaval that occurred during the thirteenth century. The emphasis shifts in the next three chapters to examine migration as a social process. Chapter 10 documents the cultural complex that was abandoned by Pueblo people when they left the central Mesa Verde region (CMV). Chapter 11 builds a case for the social identity of this group, arguing that they were Tewa speakers who moved to the Tewa basin in the Rio Grande Valley. Chapter 12 challenges the idea that people from the northern San Juan migrated in large numbers to the Rio Grande. Instead, this chapter argues, settlement change during the fourteenth century in the Rio Grande region is best understood as a local process augmented by a relatively small number of immigrants who had little effect on the local culture. The final two chapters, 13 and 14, provide big-picture syntheses of depopulation and migration in the northern Southwest.

As this summary illustrates, the volume makes an important contribution to understanding this fascinating historical problem. But it also addresses anthropological issues relevant to virtually all societies and to the world we live in today. In general, the volume clarifies processes that structure the collapse of settlement systems and the social reorganization that accompanies migration. Migration is seen as both a process and a historical event, and we show that the factors initiating this process may differ from those that hastened its conclusion.

The chapters in this volume show how demography, environment, and behavior are inextricably linked, but they also illustrate that these factors influence each other in complex ways that are nondeterministic, mediated by culture, and historically contingent. Several authors question how environmental and social conditions on the donor and receiving ends of a migration stream affect the visibility of immigrants in the archaeological record, and they use the northern San Juan region as a case study to tease out the general principles that structure these outcomes. The relationship between genes, language, and the creation of material culture is also examined, and this raises general, evolutionary questions about how the cultural stream of inheritance interacts with the processes of genetic and ecological inheritance. Examination of these issues clarifies why some societies are robust and resilient, while others become brittle and vulnerable to disaggregation and reorganization. Further, there is an effort to understand the tension between transformation that is accompanied by the generation of diversity on the one hand, and the persistence of structural regularities on the other, a distinction that is a key to understanding culture change. By addressing both historical and anthropological questions, the volume seeks to appropriately understand local and regional histories while clarifying the general processes that structure depopulation and migration in human society.

In this first chapter, I try to do more than simply introduce the volume. The chapter begins with a historical perspective on research into the depopulation of the northern San Juan region. Then, I present archaeological data that provide the context for a new consideration of this problem.

Explanatory Models and the Issue of Scale

The factors used to explain the depopulation of the northern San Juan region today were, for the most part, first proposed more than a century ago. The four most commonly cited factors are environmental change, human impact on the environment, warfare, and disease. I review each of these after making some general comments about the explanatory models themselves.

In reviewing the literature on the depopulation of the region, I was struck by the tendency in early models to identify a single factor that caused the depopulation. This style of argument reviews several factors, dismisses those deemed to lack explanatory power, and selects the single most salient factor. Unfortunately, the case for dismissing factors was typically more persuasive than the evidence given to support a specific theory. This reveals the limitations of these models: it is difficult to create a convincing argument that the depopulation was caused by a single factor.

The rejection of single-factor models is based on many observations, but most important is the issue of scale. In terms of spatial scale, the northern San Juan region is but one part of the Southwest that was depopulated (Duff 1998; Hill, this vol.). In terms of temporal scale, the depopulation of regions began in the AD 1200s and continued until at least the late 1400s. Linking these spatial and temporal scales, the depopulation can be seen as a phenomenon that *generally* cascades through time from north to south. By about AD 1500, population remained only in concentrated nodes in the central portions of this once vast and densely populated area (Duff 1998; Hill et al. 2004:695). As Hill and his colleagues note in chapter 2, depopulation of the northern San Juan region cannot be seen as an isolated event. Instead, it needs to be considered as one part of this larger reorganization of the prehispanic Southwest.

Three aspects of scale are most salient. First, depopulation was extensive in both space and time, and this suggests that the depopulation of adjacent regions was somehow related. A problem with single-factor explanations is that a cause deemed most important for one region is less important or even irrelevant to the depopulation of adjacent regions. This point is illustrated by Dean in chapter 12 in his comparisons of the Kayenta and central Mesa Verde regions.

A second point is that scale itself may be a factor that helps explain depopulation of the Greater Southwest: disruptions in one area may have caused the depopulation of adjacent regions. Davis (1964, 1965) made this point when she argued that interregional dynamics contributed to large-scale depopulation in the Southwest. Davis believed that environmental deterioration and Paiute pressures caused people to migrate from the northernmost portion of the Southwest. She argued that these emigrants entered the northern San Juan region, upsetting the balance that characterized settlement there—a balance that was already precarious because regional population levels had peaked. These perturbations produced increased movement among people in the northern San Juan, resulting in stylistic changes in artifacts and the formation of large villages in defensive locations. Ultimately, unrest led to the depopulation of the entire northern San Juan region (Davis 1965).

There is evidence, albeit scant, for interaction between the inhabitants of the last occupied villages in the northern San Juan region and people who lived north and west of this area (Kuckelman, ed., 2000, 2007; Ortman 2000a; Till and Ortman 2007). More generally, this idea resonates with much recent literature on extinctions, which recognizes that extinctions of single species can have effects that cascade across trophic levels through networks of interacting species (see review in Drossel 2001). It is therefore important to consider the timing of depopulation of areas north and west of the northern San Juan region, as Allison does in chapter 6.

The final point about scale is that it is also an important consideration *within* the northern San Juan region. There is a tendency to view Pueblo society in the region as a homogeneous cultural unit, but it was not. This is made clear by Glowacki (2006, this vol.). She documents considerable variation across the region in exchange relationships, settlement patterns, demographic histories, and the timing of depopulation. There is also evidence of conflict between the inhabitants of different subregions during the final period of occupation (Cole 2007; Kohler and Turner 2006; Kohler, Glaude et al. 2008). It is likely that the northern San Juan region was populated by groups with distinct histories speaking different languages, and it is therefore important to identify the specific area that is being considered when the depopulation of the larger northern San Juan region is discussed.

Explanatory Factors

Disease, human impact on the environment, warfare, and environmental change have all been used, singly and in combination, to explain the depopulation of the northern Southwest. Here, I present my assessment of their importance to current views, with disease receiving the least emphasis and environmental change the most attention. This is not an exhaustive synthesis. Rather, it highlights the points that merit debate—a "reader's guide" to issues to watch for in the following chapters.

Disease and Health

The question of disease is often raised, but it is rarely addressed with empirical data because most disease does not leave a trace on human skeletons. Human skeletons have, however, been used to assess the well-being of the people living in the central Mesa Verde region during the second half of the thirteenth century. These analyses indicate that the population enjoyed generally good health (Kuckelman, ed., 2007), although consideration of longer time scales shows significant deterioration in its status by Pueblo III times (Stodder 1987). Further, skeletal indicators reflect the health of individuals during their entire life, with an emphasis on their early years, and it is possible that people had declining health during the last years of their lives. There has also been no systematic evaluation of whether mortality increased during this period, and, if it did, how much the population may have declined as a result. This is important because it affects the estimates of the number of people who migrated from the region. Future research using ancient DNA may eventually supplement disease indicators macroscopically preserved on human bone and may help determine whether zoonoses—diseases spreading to humans from animals such as turkeys—could have further contributed to human mortality and depopulation.

Human Impact on the Environment

The second explanatory factor is human impact on the environment, with soil depletion, game depletion, and deforestation identified as the most likely problems. Resource depletion has only been systematically evaluated since the 1970s, when screening and sampling for floral and faunal remains became common. Analyses of these materials have conclusively documented that long-term occupation of the region did deplete resources; it is more difficult to assess if depletion was so severe that it forced depopulation.

Stiger (1979) linked resource depletion and depopulation by analyzing coprolites, botanical samples, and faunal remains from Mesa Verde National Park. He concluded that significant deforestation occurred, something he attributed to the practice of swidden agriculture. Deforestation has also been documented by subsequent studies. There was a shift from high-quality (e.g., pinyon and juniper) to low-quality (e.g., *Populus* spp. and rosaceous shrubs) fuel wood in the Dolores River valley during the eighth and ninth centuries (Kohler and Matthews 1988). But Varien and his colleagues (2007:287) use tree-ring and botanical evidence to argue that Pueblo I peoples engaged in more forest reduction than those who occupied this area in the twelfth and thirteenth centuries. Supporting this interpretation, research by Adams and Boyer (2002:134, 141–142) shows that pinyon and juniper remained the most common wood used for fuel during the thirteenth century, and they argue that the pinyon-juniper woodland was never absent or at a great distance from occupied sites. Clearly, deforestation occurred, as described by Duff and his colleagues in this volume and as suggested by computer simulation of wood consumption (Johnson et al. 2005)—but this deforestation was probably not extensive enough to be the primary cause for depopulation.

Meat from animals provided an important source of protein for Pueblo people, as well as being important in ritual activities and feasting (Driver 1996; Muir and Driver 2002, 2004; Potter 1997, 2000; Potter and Ortman 2004). Analysis of faunal remains demonstrates that, like wood resources, big game was depleted (Driver 2002). As this occurred, rabbits, hares, and turkeys became more important (Driver 2002; Munro 1994). Most recently, agent-based computer simulations have been used to evaluate the extent of overhunting, showing that large game would have been significantly depleted by about AD 900. This is near the time when archaeological data exhibit decreases in large game and increases in the relative proportions of rabbits, hares, and turkeys. As with wood resources, the depletion of animal resources almost certainly affected the lives of Pueblo people, but it is unlikely that this factor alone resulted in the depopulation of the region.

In chapter 7, Duff and his colleagues examine plant, animal, and pollen data to evaluate human impact on the environment. They isolate contexts dating to the mid- to late 1200s, documenting an environment altered by human use but conditions that could be interpreted as fairly good. Their reconstruction can be contrasted with the data presented by Kuckelman (2009, this vol.). She isolates remains that likely date to the final years of occupation—the late 1270s and early 1280s—and documents dramatically different conditions during these final years. The differences were likely due to many factors, including environmental change and a fundamentally different social landscape than was present in the preceding decades.

Warfare

Many of the first researchers working in the region believed that warfare caused people to leave in late 1200s (Blackburn 2006; Fewkes 1919; Morley 1908; Morris 1939; Nordenskiold 1979). This early research focused on late-thirteenth-century villages, which were interpreted as having a defensive character. These researchers also saw evidence for warfare in human remains that were not formally interred, and in trauma to human skulls and other bones. Some archaeologists have challenged this interpretation, but I consider the following characteristics, when taken together, to make a compelling case that warfare was a serious problem in the thirteenth century: (1) the relatively inaccessible location of

many sites, (2) the placement of sites and structures to provide views
of people entering the area, (3) the planned intervisibility among sites,
(4) the presence of site-enclosing walls and fortress-like walls with peep-
holes that concealed inhabitants while allowing them to see anyone
approaching the area, and (5) architecture that restricts access within sites
(Kuckelman 2002). Of course, aggregation itself, by providing safety in
numbers, is defensive. Nonarchitectural evidence further supports the
interpretation that warfare was prevalent. This includes (1) buffer zones
between clusters of sites; (2) artistic representations of warfare; (3) oral
traditions; (4) postmortem neglect of skeletons; (5) physical evidence of
violent death; and (6) physical evidence of scalping, trophy taking, and
anthropophagy (Kuckelman 2002).

Early interpretations identified hostile nomads as the enemy because
Navajos, Apaches, and Utes inhabited the region when Europeans first
arrived, and because American Indian oral history referred to conflicts
between Pueblo peoples and other groups. Ingersoll's 1874 story about
the battle at Castle Rock Pueblo was based on a second-hand account
of Hopi oral history and is the first published description of warfare in
the region (Ingersoll 1874). More than one hundred years later, Castle
Rock has become one of the best archaeologically documented cases of
warfare in the entire Southwest (Kuckelman, ed., 2000; Kuckelman,
Lightfoot, and Martin 2000, 2002; Lightfoot and Kuckelman 2001).

Some relatively recent researchers (e.g., Danson 1957; Jett 1964)
continue to advance the hypothesis that nomadic raiders forced Pueblo
people from the region. Today, however, most archaeologists cite two
reasons for dismissing this interpretation. First, the earliest well-dated
Apache, Navajo, and Ute sites do not overlap in time with Pueblo sites.
Second, it would have been logistically difficult for nomadic people,
who were fewer in number and who lacked horses, to muster a sufficient force to successfully attack Pueblo villages.

Still, I believe conflict with nomadic groups remains a possibility
because (1) we don't know when Utes first entered the area (their sites are
difficult to identify and date and therefore are understudied); (2) we likely
haven't found the earliest Athabaskan sites, since the earliest Navajo site
currently dates to 1541, and its inhabitants were already practicing corn
agriculture and had therefore been in the region for some time; (3) there
are a few non-Pueblo artifacts on the late thirteenth-century Pueblo

sites; (4) some Ute and Athabaskan oral histories tell of hostile interaction with Pueblo groups; and (5) even in small numbers, such groups could have complicated Pueblo life significantly if they prevented safe access to fields or hunting areas.

Although I can't therefore deny its possibility, conflict between Pueblo and Athabaskan groups remains a tenuous interpretation. Linton (1944) presented an early study that argued against non-Pueblo attackers, and Hester (1962) synthesized the evidence that Athabaskans did not enter the Four Corners area until after AD 1500. Wilshusen (2010) has recently summarized a large body of new evidence on Athabaskan entry into the region and the ethnogenesis of Navajo culture. He marshals multiple lines of evidence to argue that large numbers of Athabaskan speakers did not enter this region before about 1500. It is more difficult, however, to dismiss the possibility of interaction between Pueblos and other nomadic people, including Numic speakers (and it is equally difficult to ascribe ethnicity to remains left behind by these foragers).

There is increasing evidence of warfare *among* Pueblo people. Kuckelman and her colleagues have meticulously documented the evidence for warfare at Castle Rock Pueblo, Sand Canyon Pueblo, and other settlements in the region, and they believe that conflict was primarily among Pueblo groups (Kuckelman, ed., 2000; Kuckelman 2002, 2006, in press; Kuckelman, Lightfoot, and Martin 2000, 2002). Evidence for conflict in the northern San Juan region has also been reported by others (e.g., Billman et al. 2000; Cole 2007; Lambert 1999; LeBlanc 1999; Luebben and Nickens 1982; Turner and Turner 1999; White 1992).

Kohler and his colleagues (Cole 2007; Kohler and Turner 2006; Kohler, Cole, and Ciupe 2009) have recently shown that warfare was likely present at different levels of intensity between AD 600 and 1300, and they demonstrate that it increased during the thirteenth century. Kohler and Turner (2006) argue that there was conflict and raiding between Pueblo people in the Totah and central Mesa Verde regions that resulted in Totah people taking women from the Mesa Verde area as captives, an interpretation that appears to be supported by analysis of human skeletal remains from the Totah region (Martin 1997, 2008).

In sum, it's increasingly clear that warfare was present in the northern San Juan region, and that it escalated during the thirteenth century. Warfare is important for understanding the depopulation of the region for several reasons. First, escalating conflict may have constrained behaviors that people used to cope with environmental variability and local resource depression in earlier times. For example, it may have made it difficult for people to farm distant fields or maintain exchange rela-tionships with people living in distant communities. Second, escalat-ing conflict may have undermined other aspects of social life that were important to community and intercommunity social integration. Third, warfare would have increased mortality, reducing the number of people who actually migrated from the region. Finally, warfare would have pro-vided an additional motive for departure (Kohler et al. 2009).

Environmental Change

I now turn to environmental change and begin by briefly considering arroyo cutting. This doesn't appear to be of critical importance when considering depopulation of the central Mesa Verde region because dry farming was the primary agricultural strategy in this area, and dry farm-ing occurred on deep upland soils away from drainage channels that would have been affected by arroyo cutting. Stream and runoff irrigation, which depended on drainage channels that were not incised by arroyo cutting, was of secondary importance. This is not to say that arroyo cut-ting was absent, but it would have been less significant to farming suc-cess in the northern San Juan region than in some other parts of the Southwest—for example, the Kayenta region discussed in chapter 13.

In contrast, climate change has long been seen as a primary factor in the depopulation of the region. Here, I'll discuss three climatic factors: drought, colder than normal temperatures, and chaotic precipitation.

Douglass (1929) identified a drought between 1276 and 1299 and called it the Great Drought because it occurred at the same time as the depopu-lation of the Four Corners region. It's hard to point to a more influen-tial discovery in the Southwest; however, the explanatory power of this drought faded somewhat as it became clear that depopulation across the Colorado Plateau occurred both before and after it. Moreover, there were droughts at other times that were equally or more severe, and they did not cause complete depopulation. Van West's (1994) study quantified the relationship between precipitation and agricultural production and con-cluded that some people could have survived the Great Drought in the central Mesa Verde region. This raised two questions that an explanation relying on drought alone cannot answer: Why did everyone leave? And why didn't people return when the drought came to an end?

In spite of these unanswered questions, the issue of drought cannot be dismissed because drought obviously had significant negative impacts on agricultural production. Several chapters in this volume—those by Kohler, Wright, Berry and Benson, Kuckelman, and Duff and his colleagues—examine the relationship between drought, subsistence, and population movement in an attempt to clarify drought's role in the eventual depopulation of the region.

We now know that drought was not the only type of climate change that impacted Pueblo farmers during the thirteenth century, and it was quite possibly not the most significant. Recent research has documented the timing and effects of colder than normal temperatures. Woodbury (1961) was perhaps the first to draw attention to this issue, but it was Petersen (1988) who fully developed an argument for its significance by integrating pollen, tree-ring, and historical vegetation data. Assessment of temperatures is critical, because cooling could result in a growing season too short for maize to mature. Petersen (1988, 1994) argued for the occurrence of a cool, dry Little Ice Age (LIA): a long-term, spatially extensive, colder and drier than normal period (see Lamb 1977). Lamb's (1977) research was Europe specific and dated the LIA to the AD 1550–1850 period. In contrast, Petersen (1994) argued that the LIA's onset was much earlier in North America, beginning during the AD 1200s and lasting until the mid-1800s. Petersen concluded that it was impossible to farm in the northern San Juan region after AD 1275 because it was too cold and dry.

An important critique of Petersen's model focuses on chronology: the portion of his study that falls in the Pueblo period relied on only three dates. Wright (2006) has addressed this problem by collecting, dating, and analyzing new pollen cores, and he presents some of this exciting research in chapter 4.

Salzer (2000a, 2000b; Salzer and Kipfmueller 2005) examined bristlecone pines in the San Francisco Peaks of northern Arizona to clarify the timing and intensity of colder than normal temperatures. His work supports Petersen's interpretation that the thirteenth century suffered extended periods of cold temperatures, but it differs in two respects. Rather than seeing colder temperatures as continuous and centuries long,

Salzer documents episodic cooling in the AD 1195–1219 and 1225–1245 periods (Salzer and Kipfmueller 2005: table IV). Rather than seeing this as the early onset of the LIA in the western hemisphere, Salzer follows Lamb's (1977) nomenclature and chronology by viewing these colder periods as brief intervals within Lamb's Medieval Warm Period (AD 1000–1300) (Salzer and Kipfmueller 2005:481), and he associates part of the first cool period (AD 1215–1219) with a volcanic eruption (Salzer and Kipfmueller 2005:480). Wright reviews the chronological discrepancies between Petersen's and Salzer's research in more detail in chapter 4.

Identifying periods of colder than normal temperatures is important because it seems to solve the problem of scale that drought alone does not address. The colder periods cover extensive spatial and temporal scales, and if growing seasons became too short to grow maize, that would explain why Pueblo people left the northern San Juan region and never returned.

But questions remain. Could a global or regional cooling pattern have made farming untenable in low-elevation (i.e., about 5,400 ft), well-watered locales in the northern San Juan drainage—for example, the San Juan River and its tributaries—at the same time that Pueblo people successfully farmed high-elevation (e.g., about 7,200 ft) locales like the El Morro Valley, located just 120 mi south of the San Juan River? This seems unlikely to me. Regardless, it is clear that understanding the depopulation of the northern San Juan region requires integrating measures of precipitation and temperature and assessing their combined effects on farming, as attempted by Kohler in chapter 5.

The last type of climatic change I discuss is "spatial incoherence" in regional precipitation patterns identified by Dean and others (Dean 1996a; Dean and Funkhouser 1995). They analyzed a twenty-seven-station network of tree-ring chronologies and discovered that the bimodal winter-summer precipitation pattern that typically characterizes the northern San Juan region disintegrated between AD 1239 and 1488. This resulted in significant changes in the timing, strength, and dominance of winter storms and summer rains, undermining traditional farming practices. This is an important study because it documents the sort of big-scale climatic pattern that we might need to explain a large-scale demographic process. Moreover, the area affected by the spatial incoherence is approximately the same as the area that was depopulated, and, conversely, the unaffected area includes the places that continued

ten thousand people. Here, I focus on the final two decades of occupation by examining tree-ring cutting dates and structure abandonment.

Table 1.2 presents all the sites in southeastern Utah (as far west as Cedar Mesa) and southwestern Colorado that have more than ten cutting dates, along with dates from Aztec and Salmon Ruins in northwestern New Mexico. The table shows the total number of cutting dates, the earliest and latest cutting dates, and the latest noncutting date if it is later than the latest cutting date.

As can be seen, the latest dates are from the Great Sage Plain and Mesa Verde National Park in southwestern Colorado. This was the area with the highest population density in the northern San Juan region, and it was the last area to be depopulated. (Fourteen other sites from this area have 1270s dates, but they have fewer than ten cutting dates and are not included in this table.) The latest dates from sites surrounding this core area are all earlier, with no post-1270 dates from any dated site. Communities that occupied the canyons south of the Mancos River were abandoned by about AD 1250. The final depopulations of the Totah region and areas of southeastern Utah appear to be in the late 1260s or early 1270s, or about a decade earlier than Mesa Verde and the Great Sage Plain.

Table 1.3 examines the final decades in greater detail by compiling stem-and-leaf plots of cutting dates from key sites from the CMV. This shows that each site has many cutting dates from the 1260s and 1270s. Two points are worth emphasizing. First, there was considerable construction during this twenty-year interval, and the final abandonment of the region does not appear to have been a foregone conclusion. Second, this burst of construction occurred after migration was well underway.

Excavations at late-thirteenth-century sites support the interpretation that many structures were occupied into the 1270s, but these data also indicate that many people had emigrated before the final depopulation. This inference is based on many lines of evidence, especially stratigraphy indicating that roof timbers and artifacts were salvaged from structures at these late sites. For example, at least six of the ten tested kivas at Woods Canyon Pueblo showed evidence of planned abandonment before the final depopulation of the site. At Sand Canyon Pueblo, this is true for at least eleven of the twenty-four kivas that were excavated or tested.

Table 1.2. Earliest and latest cutting dates (and latest noncutting date if that is the latest date) from all sites in the northern San Juan region with more than ten cutting dates

Site location name	Number of cutting dates	Earliest cutting date	Latest cutting date	Latest date
Mesa Verde National Park				
Square Tower House	143	1182	1252	1270
Balcony House	101	1190	1280	
Long House	100	604	1280	
Spring House	98	1195	1280	
Cliff Palace	31	1190	1279	
Spruce Tree House	201	1167	1278	
Mug House	79	736	1277	
20 1/2 House	18	1205	1272	
Mesa Verde 16	13	1175	1271	
Badger House (Site 1452)	80	1239	1260	
5MT1253	100	1197	1255	
Farview House	15	890	1243	
Step House	92	574	1240	
Oak Tree House	40	1067	1209	
Great Sage Plain Sites				
Sand Canyon Pueblo	274	1196	1274	1277vv
Castle Rock Pueblo	69	1165	1268	1274vv
Shields Pueblo	68	744	1258	
Albert Porter Pueblo	10	1226	1250	
Saddlehorn Hamlet	19	1205	1237	1258vv
Mustoe Site	17	1065	1231	
Mitchell Springs Ruin	11	875	1211	
Pigge Site	14	1045	1201	
Knobby Knee Stockade	26	606	1201	
Ute Tribal Park/Toe of Ute Sites				
5MT9943	58	1086	1243	
Lion House	66	1094	1242	

(*Continued*)

Table 1.2. (*Continued*)

Site location name	Number of cutting dates	Earliest cutting date	Latest cutting date	Latest date
Ute Tribal Park/Toe of Ute Sites (*Continued*)				
Tree house	19	1197	1230	
Fortified House	19	1204	1230	
Eagle's Nest	24	1042	1219	
Hoy House	28	1023	1212	1227++vv
Site 5 (Morris)	20	1133	1209	
Southeast Utah				
Elk Ridge Group	15	1145	1267	
Moon House (M3)	79	1204	1266	
GG-TC1-2	11	1208	1265	
Lewis Lodge	17	897	1260	
NR-C17-2	10	1043	1259	
GG-C10-1	13	1218	1248	
Turkey Pen Site	11	1173	1244	1249++g
Totah/Middle San Juan				
Salmon Ruin	395	1068	1263	
Aztec West	?	?	1251	1254+v
Aztec East	?	?	1269	1270vv

The Final Depopulation

Ahlstrom (1985) argued that wood was continuously being brought into occupied sites, and that if a representative sample of wood exists, then site abandonment must have occurred shortly after the latest dated specimen. To assess the timing of the final depopulation, I use this assumption and all tree-ring cutting dates from the region dating between AD 1080 and 1280. This includes 2,322 cutting dates, with at least one cutting date in every five-year interval. I conducted a binomial probability analysis on this sample, and the probability of going five years without a cutting date was zero to at least ten significant digits. The latest tree-ring dates from the region are AD 1280. There were especially severe droughts in

Table 1.3. Stem-and-leaf Plots of cutting dates—and a noncutting date when that is the latest date from the site—from selected, well-dated sites in the core area of the northern San Juan Region (noncutting dates underlined)

Decade		Year
Balcony House		
1180s	118	4
1190s	119	078
1200s	120	333446
1210s	121	35
1220s	122	4
1230s	123	9
1240s	124	2222222223346667777777777788888888888
1250s	125	6
1260s	126	2289999
1270s	127	0112233333334444455555555555555555555556666889999 9999
1280s	128	0
Cliff Palace		
1190s	119	011
1200s	120	
1210s	121	1
1220s	122	
1230s	123	8
1240s	124	0178
1250s	125	
1260s	126	4578
1270s	127	1111123344444444559
Spruce Tree House		
1160s	116	7
1170s	117	
1180s	118	
1190s	119	67
1200s	120	03334
1210s	121	00013

(*Continued*)

Table 1.3. (*Continued*)

Decade		Year
Spruce Tree House		
1220s	122	111144
1230s	123	000000000001111122222233333455588888999999
1240s	124	0011111111112222223334445555666666666666777777 77888888888899999999
1250s	125	0000000000011111222333333444444444456
1260s	126	335778888889
1270s	127	1123334445778
Square Tower House		
1150s	115	0
1160s	116	
1170s	117	
1180s	118	255
1190s	119	
1200s	120	0223333333333333333333335
1210s	121	25
1220s	122	22
1230s	123	
1240s	124	01223333355
1250s	125	11
1260s	126	01114444566666666666666699
1270s	127	123378999
1280s	128	000000000000
Long House[a]		
1180s	118	34
1190s	119	7
1200s	120	0
1210s	121	
1220s	122	3599
1230s	123	0
1240s	124	011299
1250s	125	223334567778

(*Continued*)

Table 1.3. (*Continued*)

Decade		Year
1260s	126	11122333344446666777778
1270s	127	00002233444567889
1280s	128	0
Mug House[b]		
1200s	120	044445
1210s	121	3
1220s	122	48
1230s	123	129
1240s	124	113
1250s	125	000012235555889
1260s	126	0000122335566
1270s	127	67
Castle Rock Pueblo		
1160s	116	5
1170s	117	0
1180s	118	
1190s	119	88
1200s	120	
1210s	121	
1220s	122	9
1230s	123	69
1240s	124	88
1250s	125	235555666666
1260s	126	00111111111111133334556666666666666666666666888
1270s	127	**4**
Sand Canyon Pueblo		
1190s	119	689
1200s	120	011122233333333333333333333333333444444456
1210s	121	0000122244556788935
1220s	122	000000000444423444444458
1230s	123	12344555555555555555555678888

Table 1.3. (*Continued*)

Decade		Year
Sand Canyon Pueblo		
1240s	124	00000222222222222222222222222222222229999999999
1250s	125	000000000000000000011111111222477777
1260s	126	000000001111111111111111111111111222222222222222244
		4444466679
1270s	127	0011111447

[a] There are many earlier dates from Long House, including twenty-five dates in the 600s (and a big cluster at 646–648), three scattered in the 1000s, and three between 1110 and 1141.

[b] There are earlier dates at Mug House, including 736, 803, 831, 987, and scattered dates between 1011 and 1108.

1280, 1283, and 1284. I therefore believe that the depopulation of the entire region was complete by AD 1285.

Settlement Patterns: Depopulation in the Context of Dramatic Change

As population declined in the central Mesa Verde region during the thirteenth century, there were also two dramatic changes in settlement patterns: increased aggregation and a shift from upland to canyon settings for the location of these aggregated sites. Table 1.4 summarizes these data. I use data from the VEP study area to carefully examine these changes, link these observations to the demographic data presented above, and ask what this reveals about the depopulation of the entire northern San Juan region.

Table 1.4 distinguishes settlements called "community centers" from smaller sites in the VEP study area. Community centers are defined as settlements with nine or more pit structures, settlements with fifty or more total structures, or sites with public architecture. Table 1.4 shows that the percentage of the total population living in aggregated settlements increased during each period, leading us to argue that aggregation was a fundamentally historical process (Varien et al. 2007).

In each period, centers were mostly settlements that had been founded in earlier periods, but in each period there were also centers

Table 1.4. Changing size and location of settlements in the VEP area during the AD 1140–1280 period

Period	Percent of households in centers	N Centers	N Centers founded	N Centers abandoned	Largest center (households)	Mean center size (households)	N Centers in canyon setting
1140–1180	26	26	7	2	118	13.6	5
1180–1225	32	38	13	1	132	15.3	13
1225–1260	39	60	25	3	134	16.1	33
1260–1280	71	47	2	15	115	17.7	26

that were newly founded. It is clear from these data that most centers were not short-term occupations, but rather settlements that persisted for decades and even centuries. The largest number of new centers was founded during the period when population decline began, AD 1225 to 1260, and it can be seen that many of these newly founded centers were located in canyon settings.

In contrast, few centers were founded during the final twenty years of occupation, something consistent with the interpretation that population decline began during the previous period. The final twenty years was also the era when the percentage of people living in aggregated sites increased dramatically, to a high of 71 percent. In part, this is due to households abandoning small farmsteads after AD 1225. While some households at these small sites likely moved into larger villages, many apparently left the region. There was a decline in the total population that lived in centers as they, too, were gradually abandoned, although some centers that did persist actually grew in size during the final period of occupation.

To summarize these data, dramatic change characterized the thirteenth century in the VEP study area. This included fluctuations in population size, especially during the AD 1225–1260 period. Population peaked at the beginning of this period, but it had declined substantially by the end of the period. This demographic change was accompanied by the founding of many new aggregated villages, which were increasingly located in canyon settings. Moving to the canyons enabled the inhabitants of these villages to secure water sources and live closer to the stone used for building (Lipe and Ortman 2000). In some cases, a canyon setting provided a more defensible site location, and these settings may have been important ideationally (Lipe and Ortman 2000; Ortman and Bradley 2002).

The interpretation that population decline began sometime after AD 1225 and continued until about AD 1285 is an extremely important observation. This means depopulation occurred over a period of many decades and during a period when settlement patterns were radically transformed. Pueblo people in the northern San Juan region had a decision to make during this era: Should I stay or should I go? Those who remained increasingly chose to live in larger villages, and smaller sites were abandoned. I believe we can model depopulation of the region as a decades-long process that occurred during an episode of dramatic culture change. I further suggest that the early migrations were the movement of small, kin-related groups. In contrast, the final migrations were likely undertaken by larger groups that were segments of communities or what remained of whole communities.

Who Moved Where? Tracking the Movement of San Juan Tradition People

Another question is central to the discussion of the depopulation of the northern San Juan region: Where did people go? Traditionally, this issue has been examined by looking for site-unit intrusions: sites outside of the northern San Juan region that are interpreted as having been built by immigrants because their architecture and pottery are similar to that found in the northern San Juan. Davis (1964) took this approach in her dissertation, although she concluded that her initial proposal of tracking traits from Mesa Verde to other areas was far too simplistic. She came to recognize that general Mesa Verde–style pottery was produced over a large area that included broad regions north and south of the San Juan River; Roney labels this the "McElmo/Mesa Verde" pottery tradition and illustrates its distribution (Roney 1995:174–175). Similarly, Davis came to realize that she was trying to trace what she called "San Juan tradition people" rather than tracking people who specifically moved from Mesa Verde Proper or even the northern San Juan (Davis 1964:140).

Davis reconstructed a trail of San Juan traits extending from the Mesa Verde region to Chaco Canyon, then east-southeast along Chacra Mesa and down into the eastern Puerco River drainage. At this point, her trail divides: one fork goes east into Jemez country and another goes south into Laguna and Acoma territory. This includes settlements as far south as Gallinas Springs (Davis 1964).

The Southeastern San Juan Basin

The information first presented by Davis for the southeastern San Juan basin has been expanded and summarized by Roney (1996) and Durand and Baker (2003). They argue that all of the major communities in this area have likely been identified. Table 1.5 is compiled from their reports.

Table 1.5. Pueblo III settlements in the eastern San Juan basin, sorted by peak date

Name of site-community	Number of sites	Number of rooms	Number of pit structures	Largest site (structures)	Peak date
Ojito	13	85	9	15	1130–1200
Coor Ridge	27	222	33	40	1130–1200
Jones Canyon/Headcut Reservoir	50	?	?	?	1150–1230
Torreon	18	175	5	50	Late 1100s
Guadalupe	82	581	?	39	1200–1250
Salado	66	914	?	60	1200–1250
Prieta Vista	?	100	1	27	1220–1240
Cuervo	24	200	44	110?	1220–1250
Chaco Canyon	?	?	?	?	1220–1240
Canada de las Milpas	50	400		48	1230–1260
Mesa Portales		50+		50 (Ojo Jorido)	1200–1300
Chacra Mesa	67	546	lots	65	1200–1300
Mesa Pueblo	1	25	1	25	1240–1280
Total	398	3,298	93+	N/A	

Source: Roney 1996

The room counts for communities in table 1.5 are not momentized, so the size of these communities at any point in time was smaller than the numbers presented here. With the exception of Prieta Vista, all of these communities had occupations in the period preceding their peak population. Some of the population growth during the peak period was probably due to migration, but it is likely that these communities also included people who had lived in the area for some time. This means that the number of immigrants was limited in size.

Table 1.5 lists thirteen communities. Four exhibited their peak occupation during the AD 1100s, and these might include migrants who left the northern San Juan during the drought of the mid- to late 1100s. Again, the number of immigrants—regardless of their origin—would have been few in number. These twelfth-century sites declined in size during the late twelfth and thirteenth centuries, and people from these sites may have contributed to the growth of sites and communities that grew during the thirteenth century.

Six of the thirteen communities experienced peak population during the early to middle 1200s, a time of demographic decline in the northern San Juan region. Given the relatively small size of these communities, in-migration from the northern San Juan would have had to have been by relatively small social groups. These communities were, in most cases, smaller than individual thirteenth-century villages in the central Mesa Verde region. Indeed, the entire settlement system in the southeastern San Juan Basin, even if it were entirely composed of northern San Juan immigrants, is not nearly large enough to account for the number of people who likely moved from the central Mesa Verde region, much less the northern San Juan region and the even larger area encompassed by the San Juan tradition.

Finally, although these communities do include larger focal sites, these centers do not resemble villages from the northern San Juan region. Instead, focal sites in the southeastern basin have a distinctive "ladder-type" construction (Fowler, Stein, and Anyon 1987:100; Roney 1996:150–156; Wozniack and Marshall 1991: fig. 8.9). These pueblos were typically E- or F-shaped buildings that enclosed or partially enclosed plazas. Roomblocks were built by constructing long rows of parallel walls that were subdivided with cross walls. There appear to be relatively few kivas/pit structures associated with these roomblocks. This village

Table 1.6. Site intrusions in southwestern New Mexico

Site name	Total number of structures	Structure estimate for founding group	Period of occupation
Gallinas Springs	400–500	100–200	1250–1400
Pinnacle Ruin	100–150	75–100	1250–1400
Roadmap Site	75	50	1250–1400

Sources: Compiled from Lekson et al. 2002 and personal communication with Karl Laumbach and Peggy Nelson, 2008.

layout is much different than the kiva-dominated villages located in the core of the northern San Juan region (Lipe and Ortman 2000; Lipe, this vol.).

Southwestern New Mexico

Southwestern New Mexico is another area in which site intrusions from the northern San Juan region may be located. This includes sites described by Davis and recently investigated by Laumbaugh and Lekson (Clark and Laumbaugh 2009; Lekson et al. 2002). Table 1.6 lists the sites most often mentioned: Gallinas Springs, Pinnacle Ruin, and the Roadmap site.

All of these sites have founding occupations that date to the mid-1200s, and the carbon-painted pottery interpreted as intrusive has designs that resemble McElmo rather than Mesa Verde Black-on-white. These data suggest that relatively larger groups emigrating from the area encompassed by the San Juan tradition may have planned relatively late, long-distance moves.

Summary: Who Moved Where?

It is probable that archaeologists will identify a few more settlements that qualify as site intrusions built by people who likely migrated from the northern San Juan, but those discussed above are currently the best-known examples showing this phenomenon. When taken together, these sites do provide interesting insights into migration processes. Settlements in the southeastern San Juan basin suggest that migration into that area was by relatively small social groups over an extended period of time. In that area, immigrants likely joined existing populations, and the settlements exhibit material culture that reflects a population with a mixed identity. For example, the pottery appears to have been made by people from the north, but the buildings do not resemble northern villages. Settlements in southwestern New Mexico appear to have been founded later in time and likely represent planned, long-distance moves by larger social groups. These emigrants were from somewhere in the area encompassed by the San Juan tradition and were people who moved to the underpopulated areas of southwestern New Mexico.

But the most salient point of this summary is that there would have to be many, many more site intrusions to account for the number of people who left the northern San Juan and the larger area encompassed by the San Juan tradition. It seems likely to me that immigration recognized by site intrusions will never account for all the people who left these northern areas. Instead, it appears that when most people left, they abandoned traits that characterized their occupation of the northern San Juan, something discussed in detail in chapters 9 and 11.

Conclusions

The depopulation of the northern San Juan region is interesting because it is both a historical and an anthropological problem. Most archaeologists have addressed the historical question and tried to identify the factors that caused the depopulation. With regard to this historical research, a key question is whether the climate deteriorated to the point at which farming was literally impossible. Several chapters in this volume address this issue and paint a bleak picture of settlement during the late AD 1200s. Kohler suggests that the recently produced and already low estimates of potential maize production for some of the 1200s might be too high. Although his reconstruction of maize yields indicates that occupation of the region would have been possible for a reduced number of people, there is some (unknown) chance that production could have been reduced to zero or near zero in some years.

Another historical question carefully considered in this volume is where these emigrants went. There is no consensus on the answer to this question. Ortman argues that people from the central Mesa Verde region were Tewa speakers who migrated to the Tewa basin near present-day Española, New Mexico. Boyer and his colleagues argue this is unlikely, suggesting that the best evidence for thirteenth-century immigration is farther south into areas today inhabited by Keres speakers. Although they disagree, both chapters present interesting arguments, and these opposing views will undoubtedly shape future research that tries to resolve this question.

But even if we solve these historical puzzles, questions remain about how the migrations occurred as a social process. Previous research has done comparatively little to examine these social dynamics, but Cameron, Glowacki, Kohler, Lipe, and Ortman all examine migration as a social process and usher in a new era of research that will shape future work on this topic.

Integrating these historical and anthropological perspectives allows this volume to achieve two of its primary goals: markedly improving our understanding of one of the most interesting episodes in Pueblo history, and using what is learned from this historical account to clarify the causes and consequences of human migrations.

2

Depopulation of the Northern Southwest

A Macroregional Perspective

J. Brett Hill, Jeffery J. Clark, William H. Doelle, and Patrick D. Lyons

Our objective in this chapter is to provide a macroregional context for the depopulation of the northern Southwest. We propose to do this through the use of the Coalescent Communities Database (Wilcox et al. 2003), which allows us to illustrate demographic trends throughout the Greater Southwest in the late prehispanic period. This also allows us to discuss some of the subtleties and complications of regional depopulation by comparing the northern Southwest—the primary focus of this volume—to the Hohokam region of southern Arizona.

The Coalescent Communities Database (CCD) comprises information on location, size, and occupation span for all recorded archaeological sites in the Greater Southwest dating between AD 1200 and 1700 with more than twelve rooms. It was initially developed with major input from David Wilcox of the Museum of Northern Arizona, William Doelle of the Center for Desert Archaeology, and James Holmlund of Western Mapping, Inc., but significant contributions have been provided by numerous scholars who are experts in local areas. In 2003, the database was transformed from a series of separate tables and lists into a unified relational database containing information on approximately three thousand sites. It has since grown to include more than four thousand sites in an area that spans the region from Utah and Colorado in the north to Sonora and Chihuahua in the south. Information for some areas remains less thoroughly developed than for others, but we believe that the CCD currently represents the most complete single compilation of site data in the Southwest for this time period. For this chapter, it has been updated to include the Village Ecodynamics Project data for the central Mesa Verde region—also used by Varien and Kohler in their chapters in this volume—as well as recent data for the Paquimé area provided by Minnis and Whalen. It thus offers a valuable perspective on demographic change that characterized the Greater Southwest during this interval, as well as on the causes for and consequences of that change.

Depopulation of the northern Southwest during the AD 1200s and the role of climate in this process are two foci of this volume and have been prominent subjects in southwestern archaeology for generations (see Gumerman, ed., 1988; Varien, this vol.). Compared to the northern San Juan region, other areas have received less research and show weaker correlations between demographic and climatic change, but there are other important episodes of local demographic decline with potential climatic involvement. In fact, local episodes of demographic growth and decline were ubiquitous in the Southwest, and frequently climate has been implicated in a causal role. Yet the relationship between local depopulation and climate has proven to be complex, and use of climate change as the sole factor in explaining depopulation has generally proven to be unsatisfactory. Before discussing causal relationships, we begin by establishing the frequency of demographic upheaval in the Greater Southwest.

The Coalescent Communities Database and Demographic Change

Many have contributed to a growing awareness that demographic change was a fundamental characteristic of the Southwest, but a recent publication by Wilcox and colleagues (2007) on panregional trends exemplifies attempts to quantify this process. They use analyses of room counts in the CCD to illustrate the numerous instances of rising and declining local systems in the Southwest, drawing special attention to settlement histories in the areas near Zuni, Jemez, the Galisteo basin, and the Chama River valley just above its confluence with the Rio Grande. We examine demographic changes throughout the Greater Southwest in a spatial context, thereby shedding light on the geographic factors structuring these fluctuations. Our procedures for estimating ancient population from architectural data in the CCD are described in detail elsewhere (see Hill et al. 2004).

One important assumption affecting our regional population estimates is that all major residential sites are considered. The development of the CCD was based on the inference that by the year AD 1200, most people in the Southwest were living in settlements of more than twelve surface rooms and that after more than a century of research, the majority of such sites have been documented. Trends in site size indicate that through time, more people lived in the larger sites, which have a better chance of having been identified and recorded. A consequence of this is that our population estimates are likely to be too low in the earliest intervals, when relatively more people were still living in small, dispersed sites not included in the CCD. Furthermore, some areas of the Southwest are not as well known to the CCD authors and consequently have not received as detailed attention. Despite these caveats, we think the CCD illustrates broad demographic trends at a macroregional scale that are amenable to further analysis.

Demographic Change in the Greater Southwest

Analysis of the CCD demonstrates that depopulation was an ongoing process between AD 1200 and 1500. This is illustrated by two maps showing the distribution of population (as estimated in the CCD) during the AD 1250–1300 and 1450–1500 periods (figs. 2.1a, b). During these two and a half centuries, the Greater Southwest changed from an area where virtually every major river valley from the Colorado Plateau to the Sonoran desert was inhabited to one where population was concentrated in a few small areas in the north-central and eastern portions of the previous distribution.

We examine this dramatic population change by modeling sequential fifty-year intervals and producing a time-series analysis of population distribution over the Southwest (see also Hill et al. 2004). We are less concerned here with the overall population distributions than with the shifts in demographic centers of gravity. The resulting simplified perspective illuminates essential demographic trends and allows easier consideration of their relation to climate on a large scale.

To illustrate these demographic centers of gravity, the time-series maps display only the upper quartile of population density. In other words, these maps resemble ordinary population-density maps, with the exception that all but the highest-density contours are removed from them. Density calculations are made for a 36 km search radius, a distance

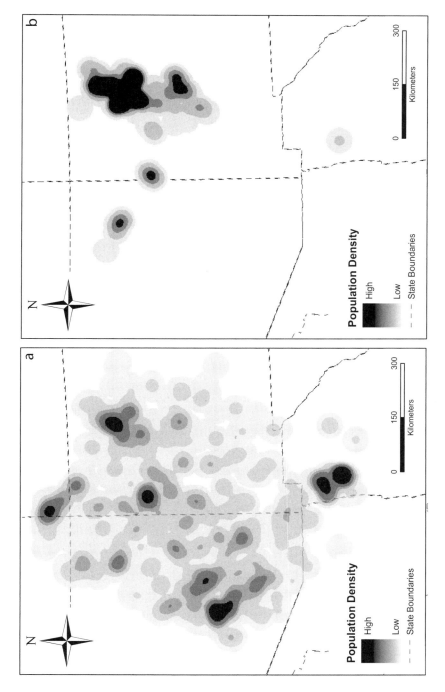

Figure 2.1. Population distribution in the Greater Southwest during (a) the AD 1250–1300 period, and (b) the AD 1450–1500 period.

reflecting an approximately one-day walk from sites, and represent numbers of persons, ranging from approximately 1 to 12 persons/km^2.

Figures 2.2 through 2.4 depict these distributions for fifty-year intervals from AD 1200 to 1500 for the entire Southwest, showing how depopulation in the region progressed over time. In the first interval (fig. 2.2a), we see widely distributed population with demographic centers located in multiple areas, including dominant centers in the central Mesa Verde region and the Phoenix basin. Smaller centers are evident in the northern Rio Grande, Paquimé, Zuni, Tonto basin, middle San Juan, and upper Tularosa areas.

Substantial change is already apparent by the late 1200s, when the northern San Juan region was in decline and the Zuni and northern Rio Grande areas took dominant positions (fig. 2.2b). Declines in the northern Southwest were also complemented, probably not coincidentally, by growth in the Tonto basin and Paquimé area, as well as the appearance of centers in the Hopi, Safford, and Santa Cruz areas.

By the early 1300s, the northern Rio Grande, Phoenix basin, and Paquimé areas were the largest centers (fig. 2.3a). The central Mesa Verde region and middle San Juan centers were almost completely depopulated, while the Zuni area declined, the Hopi area grew, and a new center appeared in the Chupadera Mesa area. In the southern Southwest, new centers emerged in the Verde and Animas valleys, the Santa Cruz Valley disappeared as a population center, and density in the Tonto basin began to decline in favor of increases in the surrounding upland areas of Globe and Grasshopper.

In the late 1300s, northern Rio Grande population density increased in the Chama, Galisteo basin, and Jemez areas, while the Zuni area population continued to decline (fig. 2.3b). In the southern Southwest, the Tonto basin and Animas population centers disappeared. In contrast, upland areas—including Perry Mesa, Globe, Grasshopper, and Point of Pines—grew in prominence.

By the early 1400s, Zuni had also disappeared as an area of high population density in the northern Southwest (fig. 2.4a), and the only population centers that remained were concentrated along the Rio Grande, with the appearance of a small center in the Rio Abajo, and a continued presence at Hopi. In the southern Southwest, all centers were depopulated except Paquimé and a greatly diminished Phoenix basin. By the

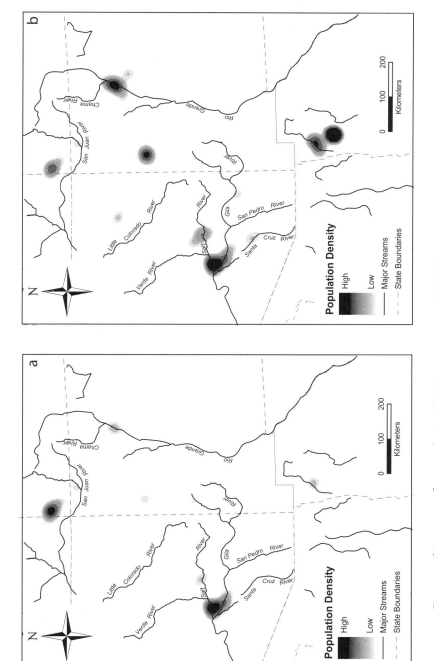

Figure 2.2. Demographic centers of gravity during (a) AD 1200–1250, and (b) AD 1250–1300.

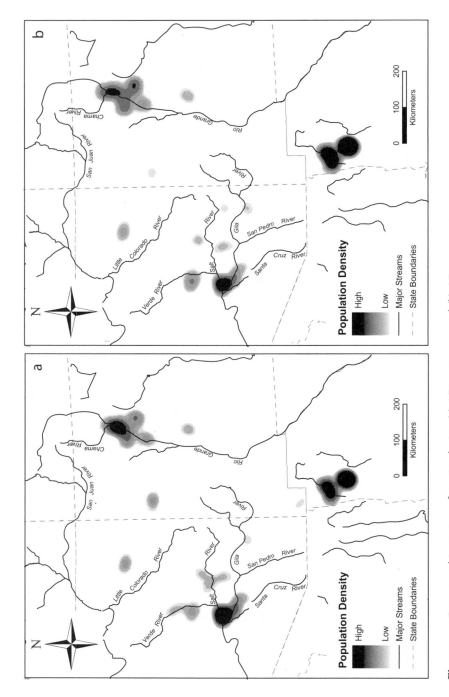

Figure 2.3. Demographic centers of gravity during (a) AD 1300–1350, and (b) AD 1350–1400.

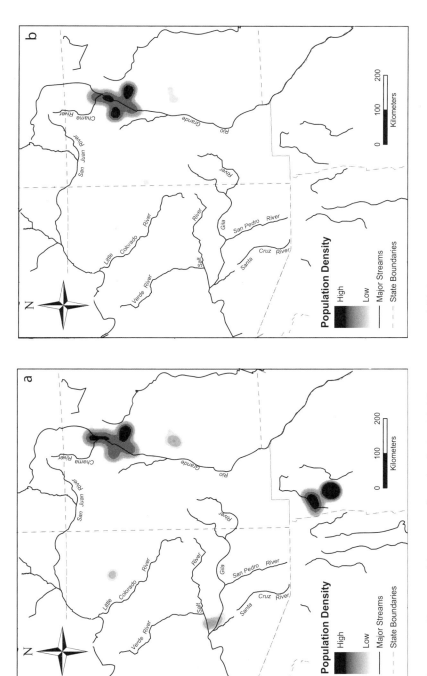

Figure 2.4. Demographic centers of gravity during (a) AD 1400–1450, and (b) AD 1450–1500.

late 1400s, major population concentrations had taken on a distribution similar to what Europeans encountered when they first entered the area, with population concentrated in the northern Rio Grande, Zuni, and Chupadera Mesa areas (fig. 2.4b). Of course, there were also substantial populations in places like Hopi and Acoma, but they were not large enough to be included in the upper-quartile density threshold used in these analyses. Despite intensive investigation, we are unable to document significant settled populations in the southern Southwest from the mid-1400s to the mid-1600s. Some areas of the southern Southwest undoubtedly did remain occupied by the descendants of the Hohokam, who are largely invisible archaeologically but may have taken up different adaptive strategies that greatly reduced their archaeological visibility (see Ravesloot, Darling, and Waters 2009).

Among the many particular observations that might interest researchers working in the areas described here, we suggest two broadly useful conclusions: (1) demographic change and shifting centers of population characterized the period between AD 1200 and 1500, and (2) depopulation of some areas appears to be closely coincident with population growth in others, raising the issue of migration. No less than four major centers are observed and at least sixteen smaller centers are identified. Of particular note with regard to migration was growth in northern Rio Grande areas coincident with the depopulation of the central Mesa Verde and middle San Juan regions. The details and mechanisms of migration between these areas is a subject for other researchers (see especially Ortman, this vol., and Boyer et al., this vol.), but these analyses support a substantial southward movement. It is also interesting that the population movements we infer from these maps do not conform to the boundaries of the Pueblo, Mogollon, and Hohokam "traditions" as historically conceived by archaeologists, but instead suggest considerable movement of people across these boundaries.

These macroregional analyses show that the Paquimé area, the Phoenix basin, and the northern Rio Grande were the largest and longest-enduring demographic centers, with each in one of the top three positions for several centuries. Extending analyses into earlier time periods would likely include the Mesa Verde area among these long-lived centers. At their peak densities, the Paquimé area, Phoenix basin, northern Rio Grande, and Mesa Verde centers have approximately 12.2, 10.7, 5.2, and 4.3 persons per square kilometer, respectively. Recent analysis by the Village Ecodynamics Project using other methods estimates nearly 11 persons/km^2 for the Mesa Verde area at its occupation peak (Varien et al. 2007).

In these analyses, we defined at least twenty different population centers emerging and declining during a three-hundred-year period. Obviously, these centers exhibited a range of sizes and population dynamics, and it is not our intention to argue that the same processes were responsible for demographic change in all of them. On the contrary, they were quite variable in nature and undoubtedly a variety of climatic, geographic, and social factors affected their growth and decline.

A critical question for many studies of depopulation and migration is the role of climate change. We distinguish climate from weather, acknowledging that some climatic variation may have been of relatively short duration but can probably be distinguished from individual weather events (see also Wright, this vol.). Clearly, the Great Drought (AD 1276 to 1299) is an example of climatic fluctuation that seems to have played some part in the collapse of the northern San Juan region, and the decline of other areas has also been associated with drought and/or flood. Other types of climatic shifts identified by researchers such as Dean (1996a) and Graybill and colleagues (2006) also appear to have been important factors in many of the demographic shifts illustrated in our analyses, providing both push and pull mechanisms for migration.

On the other hand, it is too simplistic to posit a monolithic cause-and-effect relationship between climate and population movement, particularly depopulation well below regional carrying capacities. Instead, we believe climate variably affected populations in different environmental settings that practiced different subsistence strategies. Further, it is rare that archaeologists anywhere can conclude that environmental change rendered an area completely unfit for human occupation, and yet depopulation was often nearly complete. Consideration of factors including population density, length of occupation, socioeconomic organization, intercommunity relations, and anthropogenic environmental degradation is necessary to fully unravel the relationship between climatic downturns and depopulation. It is likely that the relationship among multiple factors structured the effects of climate on demography. Our understanding of the process of depopulation in the Hohokam area provides a useful illustration of the multidimensional, nonlinear relationship between climate and demography.

The Hohokam: A Case Study of Climate Change and Depopulation

Some researchers have noted direct relationships between the hydrological cycles of the Salt and Gila rivers and Hohokam population dynamics (e.g., Graybill et al. 2006; Nials et al. 1989; Waters and Ravesloot 2001). We and others have noted problems associated with these interpretations (Hill et al. 2004; Howard 1991), but it is not our intention to suggest that climate was unimportant to demographic change. Rather, we argue that climate was very important—just not as a "prime mover." In fact, we believe that the Great Drought that affected the northern San Juan region had an important causal role in the Hohokam collapse a century later. We have argued in detail elsewhere (Hill et al. 2004; Hopi Dictionary Project 2008; Lyons, Hill, and Clark 2008) that unfavorable climatic conditions hundreds of miles away from the Hohokam contributed to demographic stress among the Hohokam, and we continue to develop that argument here.

The Hohokam world was oriented around the major river valleys of southern Arizona, including the Salt and Gila, and their major tributaries, including Tonto Creek and the Santa Cruz, San Pedro, and Verde rivers. Significant changes in land use and population were correlated with Pueblo immigration to these areas between AD 1250 and 1350 (Clark 2001; Clark, Woodson, and Slaughter 2004; Doelle 2000; Doelle and Wallace 1991; Elson 1998; Fish and Fish 1992; Fish and Nabhan 1991; Fish, Fish, and Madsen 1990; Neuzil 2008; Woodson 1999). The presence of Pueblo migrants is most clearly documented in the Tonto and Safford basins and the lower San Pedro Valley, along the eastern perimeter of the largest Hohokam concentrations in the Phoenix basin. Evidence for migrants includes new domestic and ritual architectural styles such as stone masonry construction, kivas, slab entryboxes, and mealing bins (Clark 2001; Di Peso 1958a; Neuzil 2008; Woodson 1999). New ceramic technology and styles such as coil-and-scrape corrugated pottery, perforated plates, Maverick Mountain series pottery, and Salado polychrome appeared that were unlike existing Hohokam traditions but were locally made and bear close resemblance to traditions in the northern Southwest (Clark 2007a; Crown 1994; Lyons and Lindsay 2006). As in the northern Rio Grande, their arrival was associated with intensified aggregation around existing irrigation-farming communities and the abandonment of many upland sites believed to be associated with dry farming (Luchetta 2005). This transition was accompanied by increased social tension, as evidenced by more defensive site construction and locations (Oliver 2001; Wallace and Doelle 2001; Wilcox, Robertson, and Wood 2001), which may have been a contributing factor in the shift from dispersed to aggregated settlement.

Thirteenth- to fifteenth-century occupation on the middle Gila is well documented in some areas (Crown 1987; Doyel 1974; Neuzil 2008), while other areas, such as the Gila River Indian Community, remain relatively unknown. Northern immigrants have not been definitively identified in the middle Gila River valley west of the Safford basin, but the evidence suggests that some sites were abandoned early, while others represent coalescent settlements occupied by remnant late Classic–period groups from a variety of cultural backgrounds.

"Core Decay" in the Lower Salt Valley

The Phoenix basin, as the "Hohokam Core," may have been one of the last areas entered by Pueblo migrants (Haury 1945; Clark 2007c), and demographic decline in the Phoenix basin has usually been attributed largely to internal factors (Abbott and Foster 2003; Gregory 1991; Henderson 1995; Kwiatkowski 2003; Rice 1998; Sheridan 2003), some of which may have been exacerbated by immigration. Evidence for immigrant groups includes perforated plates (Lyons and Lindsay 2006), evidence for local Roosevelt Red Ware production (Clark 2007c; Crown 1994), and Phoenix Red pottery (Di Peso 1958a; Nelson and LeBlanc 1986; Wilson 1998), which have been recovered from large, aggregated sites dating to the late fourteenth and early fifteenth centuries (Abbott 2000; Abbott and Gregory 1988; Brunson 1989; Crown 1981; Crown et al. 1988; Haury 1945; McDonnell, Doyel, and Large 1995).

Evidence from burials at large sites such as Pueblo Grande indicates that aggregation and agricultural intensification in the Phoenix basin led to a severe decline in health and life expectancy during the fourteenth century (Abbott 2003; Fink 1991; Fink and Merbs 1991; Hartman 1988:242–243; Martin 1994; Sheridan 2003; Van Gerven and Sheridan 1994). Moreover, Wilcox and others have argued that compounds and intervisible platform mounds and towers were built from the thirteenth century through the fifteenth century for the purpose of creating a defensive settlement system (Hinsley and Wilcox 2002; Wilcox, Robertson, and Wood 2001).

Recent geographic information system analyses of demography and irrigation agriculture on the lower Salt indicate a process of "core decay," in which the fields associated with core areas close to the intakes of large canal systems were degraded through the fourteenth and fifteenth centuries (Hopi Dictionary Project 2008). To offset this degradation of core settlement fields, agricultural efforts were expanded at sites, some occupied by Puebloan immigrants, located at the distal ends of the irrigation systems during the late fourteenth and early fifteenth centuries. This redirection and concomitant demographic shift would have dramatically changed the efficiency and organization of agricultural production, requiring more costly system maintenance as the distance between settlements and critical irrigation features increased. Moreover, long-established social relationships among local and immigrant populations were altered as the relative prosperity of central and distal communities was reversed.

The relatively early abandonment of large, centrally located sites appears related to the intensity of land use and consequent degradation in their vicinity. During the early fourteenth century, the largest sites controlled the intakes of the largest canal systems in the valley. By the late fourteenth century, all large sites in the central area had fallen into decline. In contrast, occupation remained relatively stable for several more decades at those sites more distant from canal intakes. These distal settlements would not have been able to support significant populations without continued use of the irrigation systems along which they were established. Their relative success during their last decades of occupation appears to have been related to the ability of their inhabitants to practice more extensive irrigation, shifting canal and field locations across the landscape in a way that was not possible near canal intakes.

This model has important implications for social and economic life in the region and beyond. First, the cost of practicing irrigation agriculture under these conditions continued to increase, while overall productivity decreased. Health, nutrition, and other quality-of-life measures also declined. Ability to respond to system damage from flooding and incision of canal intakes diminished as cultivation focused on places farther from these overexploited central areas that were experiencing population decline. These already stressed systems would have been more susceptible to hydrological problems and climatic variation than previous systems. An essential dilemma arose: without regular maintenance of central irrigation features, the system as a whole could not have functioned, even though fields in the vicinity of these features were in declining use. The magnitude of this dilemma increased as people moved their efforts farther down-canal from the intakes. Ultimately, the costs of maintenance outweighed the benefits, leading to a systemwide collapse.

In addition to material effects, the process of core decay had significant social effects. Labor demands would have increased as system maintenance became more difficult, possibly changing local attitudes toward immigrants and the relative power of lower-status individuals. As the higher-status residents of central villages near canal intakes confronted local environmental degradation and were forced to focus their subsistence efforts on distal locations, they would have come into conflict with lower-status people already controlling these areas. Those cultivating distal locations would have included relative newcomers to the lower Salt River from Hohokam hinterlands and farther west and north (Abbott 2003; Haury 1945; Lyons 2003; Lyons and Lindsay 2006). Conflict between the traditionally powerful central communities and newly empowered distal communities would have led to social and ideological upheaval during an interval when cooperation was essential to maintain increasingly labor-intensive irrigation systems. Archaeological evidence for this upheaval is consistent with—and sheds new light on—O'odham oral tradition, in which ethnographic accounts tell of a conflict between O'odham ancestors and the seemingly incongruous Pueblo chiefs who came to live in lower Salt River irrigation communities (Bahr 1971; Bahr et al. 1994).

Discussion

The complex demographic process described here can be summarized as a series of cascading and mutually amplifying feedback cycles.

Undoubtedly, many long-term processes set the stage for an unsustainable progression of demographic change, but one important early catalyst for upheaval seems to have its roots in the environmental crisis of the northern Southwest during the late thirteenth century. This crisis and resultant social tension caused populations there to immigrate to the valleys of southern Arizona, where they came into contact with the Hohokam, who had long-established and stable agricultural traditions. The Hohokam communities utilized a variety of both upland and valley-bottom settings, with large villages surrounded by dispersed farms and hamlets.

The arrival of Pueblo immigrants in this setting contributed to the abandonment of dispersed settlements and aggregation into valley-bottom villages near optimal areas for irrigation and agricultural intensification. Population aggregation and diminished economic diversity caused a deterioration of health and reproductive success among the Hohokam. This aggregation and agricultural intensification resulted in environmental degradation around these villages, leading in turn to heightened social tension and the eventual depopulation of these central sites.

A fascinating question raised by this model relates to why Hohokam populations remained aggregated in large settlements focused largely on irrigation rather than reverting to dispersed settlements and diversified subsistence strategies that were more sustainable over the long haul. Aggregation continued, even as settlements failed and immigrant-local tension abated, resulting in densely populated areas surrounded by depopulated buffer zones—a process we have called the "aggregation trap." Social tensions between locals and migrants contributed to initial population aggregation in some regions, which required agricultural intensification and new leadership institutions. Intensification of irrigation agriculture increased labor demands, leading to further aggregation and dependence on irrigation agriculture. Leaders may have also wanted to keep groups aggregated to facilitate their control. The specific social and economic mechanisms at play here present valuable directions for future research and may illustrate the aggregation trap as a more broadly useful concept.

In this model, a clear relationship between climate and depopulation can be discerned, but with a couple of significant caveats. First, the climatic downturn that appears to have precipitated the problem occurred in a distant region rather than in the Hohokam heartland. Second, the effects of climate change were strongly mediated by other social and ecological factors. We give special attention to this second point because we believe it has important implications for demography, ecology, and larger questions relating to the connections between society and the natural environment.

An important point to bear in mind in any discussion of human ecology is that environmental change is not, in itself, a crisis. Environmental crises are instead crises in the relationships among humans and their environment (van der Leeuw 2008). In one sense, this is manifestly obvious. For example, recent hurricanes in the southeastern United States have had more disastrous outcomes in part because they affected larger population concentrations than those in earlier generations. A similar process seems to have played out in the fourteenth-century lower Salt River valley, where larger population aggregations and localized anthropogenic degradation at core irrigation sites rendered the entire system more vulnerable to environmental change than had been the previously more dispersed and diversified populations.

In an important way, however, the implications are somewhat subtler, and it is for this reason that the rich archaeological record of environmental crises may be of value in understanding the larger connections between society and nature. Environmental change does not simply affect people; it also affects the way people affect each other. The social and cultural relations present may either mitigate or magnify the impacts of environmental change on populations. In some cases, people may be able to survive a drought or a flood but not the ensuing sociopolitical upheaval. Many instances in the archaeological record suggest that conflict is a common result of environmental degradation. The amplification of environmental change in the social realm may help explain why it often results in such complete depopulation rather than merely diminished productivity.

A rich O'odham oral tradition has been recorded that recounts the final days of the Hohokam. A thorough reading of the accounts (Bahr et al. 1994; Bahr, ed., 2001; Russell 1908; Underhill 1946) finds numerous references to drought, flood, famine, and disease, but these are precursors and even secondary features of an essential narrative that relates the story of epic conflict among gods and their respective followers.

In stories that may have originated with those who witnessed Hohokam collapse, overpopulation and environmental degradation created significant hardships, but the ultimate fate of "the finished ones" was a deadly battle. It seems probable that areas such as the lower Salt River valley could have continued to support substantial numbers of people, but the breakdown of various integrative institutions resulted in the nearly complete depopulation of this area for centuries afterwards.

It is unlikely that processes occurring in the northern Southwest followed this pattern precisely, but general lessons about the complex relationships between society and climate may be applicable. Previous attempts to quantify the effects of drought in the northern Southwest have similarly concluded that some people could have continued to occupy this region (e.g., Van West 1994). Likewise, clear evidence for conflict suggests the effects of drought were not limited to declining economic production (Kuckelman, Lightfoot, and Martin 2002; Kuckelman, this vol.). From our vantage point, it seems likely that the effects of environmental degradation, demographic growth, and increased population aggregation were magnified through the lens of social interactions, compounding difficulties well beyond the potential economic hardships induced by climatic variability.

Conclusions

Several issues raised in this chapter might be useful to archaeologists working elsewhere in the Southwest. First, the rise in northern Rio Grande populations was coincident with population decline in the northern San Juan region. This does not in itself demonstrate migration, but it does offer supporting evidence of both source and destination areas for migration. A similar relationship is well documented for migration between northern and southern Arizona that took place during the same time period.

Second, the material evidence linking migrants to their present and former identities varies considerably, depending on the social and natural environments they enter (e.g., Clark 2001; Neuzil 2008; Wilcox, Robertson, and Wood 2001). Lyons, Hill, and Clark (2008) have noted elsewhere the relatively low visibility of immigrants into the Tonto basin, where the identity of an immigrant minority was not overtly displayed in an already saturated socioecological environment. Similar factors may affect the visibility of northern San Juan migrants as they entered the northern Rio Grande.

Third, the frequency of significant demographic change in the prehispanic Southwest indicates that it was the norm for this region. Some have referred to the unparalleled or unique depopulation of the northern Southwest, but we would argue that such movement appears to be the rule rather than the exception in many regions. Other areas, such as southern Arizona, experienced depopulation on at least as large a scale as the northern San Juan region. In this chapter, we have shown the emergence and decline of more than twenty different demographic centers of varying size throughout the region between AD 1200 and 1500. This observation is not intended to diminish the importance of depopulation in the northern San Juan region, but to draw attention to some of the general processes that may be concluded from it. We would argue that portraying the northern San Juan region as an isolated or unique phenomenon in the Southwest undervalues its importance as an exemplar for the study of relationships among humans and their environments in the Southwest and beyond.

Fourth, a problem with archaeological studies of depopulation is the perception that people must have either died in place as the result of some catastrophic event or emigrated. Although both of these have undoubtedly occurred, time depth and the implications of biological and cultural reproduction render archaeological demography more complex. Small generational changes in fertility and mortality over the span of decades and centuries can dramatically alter the size of populations. In the Hohokam region, we argue, gradual population decline resulted in a greatly reduced terminal population (Hill et al. 2004). The population numbers and time spans associated with the northern San Juan region abandonment were not as great, but the actual numbers of people who left the area in the late 1200s remains uncertain and subject to similar processes of gradual decline throughout the final decades of occupation. Changes of less than 1 percent per year could have reduced total population by 30 to 40 percent over a few decades. Such declines may greatly reduce the size and archaeological signature of a migrant population—as in fact is argued for the northern Rio Grande in chapter 12 of this volume.

Fifth, we believe our case study indicates that the relationship between climate and demography is usually complex. It is unlikely, given the differences between the northern San Juan and Hohokam regions, that the details of the process were identical. But we are struck by the evidence for similarities presented in this volume, including previous episodes of environmental degradation, migration, aggregation, and conflict. It seems quite likely that a similarly complex interplay of social, economic, and ecological factors was responsible for demographic collapses in both areas, rendering cause-and-effect connections multidimensional and nonlinear. In the Hohokam case, explanations based solely on local climate episodes, such as the floods of the late AD 1300s, are inadequate by themselves in explaining systemic and irreversible collapse. Rather, these important natural events occurred in a social system that had already witnessed a century of demographic upheaval related to separate climatic events in a distant area. It seems likely that the problems of correlating climate and depopulation in the northern San Juan region are due to similarly complex processes operating on a macroregional scale.

3

Tree-Ring Dates and Demographic Change in the Southern Colorado Plateau and Rio Grande Regions

Michael S. Berry and Larry V. Benson

In this chapter, tree-ring dates from the southern Colorado Plateau, Mogollon Highlands, and Rio Grande areas (fig. 3.1) (hereafter referred to as the study area) are used to estimate regional-scale timber-harvesting and construction activities between AD 600 and 1600 (the Basketmaker III through Pueblo IV periods). Within that time span, we focus our attention particularly on the AD 1045–1300 period, a time when anomalously wet periods alternated with megadroughts (fig. 3.2). Tree-ring-date distributions (histograms) for eight archaeological subregions within the study area have been created using a database of more than twenty-four thousand tree-ring dates from archaeological sites. These dates, in turn, are compared with the paleoclimatic record for the study area as a whole (fig. 3.2).

The Sample: Bias and Interpretation

More than twenty-five years ago, Berry (1982) used the then-available tree-ring data from the Quadrangle Series of the Laboratory of Tree-Ring Research to generate a histogram of contemporaneously occupied sites for each ten-year increment during the period from AD 600 to 1450. Berry argued that fluctuating southwestern tree-ring date distributions indicated changes in relative population size and consequent population movement. He inferred that these phenomena resulted from periodic droughts. He further argued that the stages of the Pecos classification system could be interpreted as temporally discrete episodes separated from one another by drought events. The modeling of paleoclimates for the Southwest has evolved significantly since then, but our current understanding lends support to Berry's model of demographic shifts, especially during the mid-twelfth century and the thirteenth-century megadroughts.

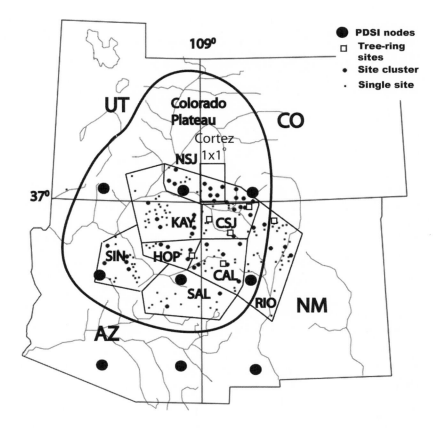

Figure 3.1. The location of tree-ring dated sites in the southern Colorado
Plateau and Rio Grande areas.

KAY   Kayenta region
NSJ   northeastern San Juan Basin
CSJ   central San Juan Basin
SIN   Sinagua region
HOP   Hopi region
CAL   Cibola-Acoma-Laguna region
RIO   Rio Grande region
SAL   Salt River region (Mogollon Highlands)

Large filled circles indicate location of PDSI nodes; open squares indicate
locations of tree-ring sites; medium-sized filled circles indicate site clusters;
small filled squares indicate single sites.

The rectangle encloses the Cortez rectangle, which ranges from 109° to 108° W
and from 37° to 38° N.

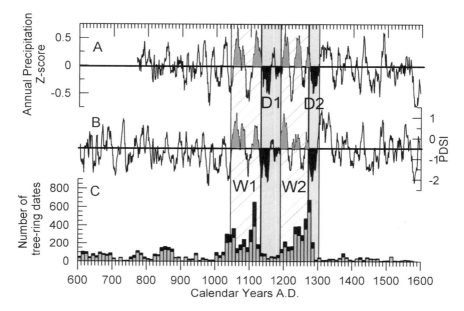

Figure 3.2. (A) The mean of six normalized precipitation data sets from the Four Corners area. (B) The mean of nine PDSI data sets from the southern Colorado Plateau. (C) "Death" (grey rectangles) and "v" (black rectangles) date distributions for the southern Colorado Plateau. The tree-ring-based climate data sets were smoothed with an eleven-year running average. W1 and W2 refer to two wet periods (grey-shaded areas), and D1 and D2 refer to the mid-twelfth- and late-thirteenth-century megadroughts (black-shaded areas).

Criticisms of Berry's model revolved around the issue of potential sampling bias. It was argued that such variables as differential preservation, archaeological interest, systematic neglect, a penchant for burning structures at various times, a penchant for not burning structures at other times, etc., had the combined potential of rendering meaningless the patterning of the tree-ring sample. As a consequence, the model, as well as the attendant notion of climatically induced demographic shifts, was largely ignored. Indeed, despite the focus of the current volume, none of our fellow contributors cited Berry's 1982 work. We therefore anticipate that many archaeologists working in the Southwest today may similarly dismiss the representativity of the data we present herein. However, confronted with the very large sample of chronometric data currently available that suggests a punctuated set of temporally discrete occupations, we have opted to consider the likelihood that these data are, in fact, representative of prehistoric reality and worthy of further inquiry, even as we acknowledge the occurrence of certain potential sources of bias.

A much more robust sample of more than twenty-four thousand tree-ring dates is now available from structures in the study area that fall between AD 500 and 1600, yet the fundamental temporal distribution presented by Berry (1982:105) has not significantly changed. Of the total number of dates, 8,515 are "death" or cutting dates and another 3,068 are "v" dates, which are accurate to within a few years of the timber-harvest date. During the time period of interest for the current analysis (AD 1045–1300), the tree-ring database contains 6,984 "death" and "v" dates collected from 413 archaeological sites. In the following sections, we rely solely on "death" and "v" dates (referred to collectively as tree-ring dates) for interpretation. We have eliminated from consideration "vv" dates, the temporal placements of which are earlier than the cutting event of interest by an unknown amount of time. We acknowledge that, in rare cases, a clustering of "vv" dates can inferentially indicate a probable construction event. Such cases are in the minority, and a site-by-site analysis is not the focus of the current chapter, since this is, after all, a regional analysis. As a result, we may overlook a few individual sites of possible interest. We have also excluded dates with a "++" modifier because they likely indicate the use of dead timbers. We point out, however, that histograms generated with "vv" or "++" dates are not markedly different from the temporal patterns we have constructed using only "death" and "v" dates. When the "too old" dates were included, high points remained high, and low points, as might be expected, were partially filled in (fig. 3.3D).

In the discussions that follow, we make no assertion of a direct correlation between tree-ring date fluctuations and population *size*. We do, however, interpret these fluctuations as a relative measure of construction activity. Diminished construction activity, as measured by the lack of cutting dates, most likely indicates declining populations, whereas increasing populations were likely accompanied by accelerated construction activities, with a concomitant increase in tree-ring dates. Of particular interest are those cases wherein diminished construction activity in one area is coupled with accelerated construction in an adjacent area,

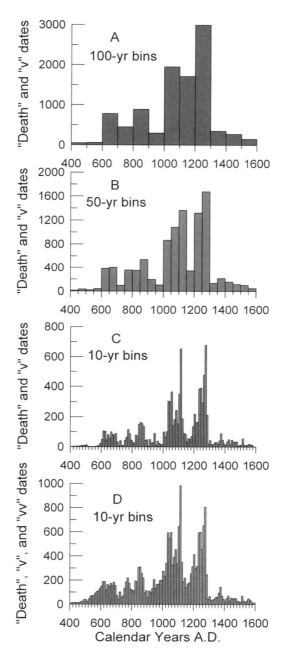

Figure 3.3. Cutting-date histograms for study area demonstrating the effect of bin size and tree-ring date accuracy on tree-ring date distributions. A–C were created using "death" and "v" dates; D was created using "death," "v," and "vv" dates.

leading to the inference that this pattern probably reflects population movement (e.g., Ortman, this vol.). However, we make no attempt to quantify the populations involved. That would require a much more in-depth analysis incorporating room counts, room size, site-specific room contemporaneity, and a host of other variables. (Such population esti-mates have been undertaken, for example, for a subregion of the South-west by the Village Ecodynamics Project [Ortman, Varien, and Gripp 2007; Varien, this vol.].) No quantitative population analyses have yet been conducted for the entire study area considered in the current chap-ter, and such an effort is clearly beyond the scope of this chapter.

Analytic Methods

To facilitate analysis, the senior author developed a computer applica-tion, TRGraph, that features data input, data querying, mapping, and histogram functions. The underlying database is Microsoft Access,[1] but other formats can be imported. The user interface is written in Borland C++ Builder, Version 6.0. The mapping function allows the user to place a polygon around a geographic area of interest and generate a histogram of tree-ring dates from archaeological sites within that particular polygon. The Structured Query Language (SQL) interface allows the user to query the database on a wide variety of criteria and display the results in both map-distributional and histogram formats. The queried data can then be exported to a spreadsheet such as Microsoft Excel for further analyses.

Histogram Bin Size and the Inclusion of "vv" and "++" Dates

Figure 3.1 indicates the overall study area, with eight archeological subdivisions enclosed in polygons. Figure 3.3 illustrates the effects of both bin size and the inclusion of "vv" and "++" dates on the depiction of tree-ring dates from the study area. If the bin size is decreased to ten-year increments (compare figs. 3.3A–C), the fine structure in the distribution of tree-ring dates becomes visible. Inclusion of "vv" and "++" dates (fig. 3D) tends to blur the fine structure, with the "vv" dates filling in minima in the tree-ring date distributions (compare fig. 3.3C with 3.3D). The lesson here is that using too large a bin size (e.g., of twenty-five or fifty years) will tend to smooth substantial variability, masking significant tree-ring minima of decadal duration. Given the effect of "vv" and "++" dates on the histograms, all plots that follow omit "vv" and "++" dates and display only tree-ring dates that fall within ten-year intervals.

Using intervals larger than ten years for plotting the number of tree-ring dates is quite similar to the problem of temporal interpretations that rely primarily on ceramic "dating," which has an inferential accuracy of between twenty-five and two hundred years (Blinman 2000; Breternitz 1966). Consequently, ceramic dating will similarly mask decadal-scale occupational variations. Ceramic dating is based on the proposition that a given relative frequency of ceramic types at a tree-ring-dated site, if found in similar proportions at an undated site, implies contemporaneity. Such an inference, of course, represents a hypothesis to be tested, not an empirical fact. The pitfalls of reliance on ceramic dating when dealing with decadal change need no further elaboration.

Tree-Ring-Based Reconstructions of Climate Change

One of the questions we seek to answer is whether the distribution of tree-ring dates from archaeological sites bears a significant relationship to records of climate change in the study area. Tree-ring-based reconstructions of the Palmer Drought Severity Index (PDSI) (fig. 3.2B) averaged over nine nodes within the study area (fig. 3.1) are based on an expanded tree-ring data set (Edward Cook, Lamont-Doherty Earth Observatory, personal communication, 2007) that improves the accuracy of the gridded network of PDSI reconstructions originally created by Cook and colleagues (2004). The 2004 tree-ring network used for PDSI reconstruction over North America was originally composed of 835 annually resolved records. Cook's 2007 revised network containing 1,825 records is now available and has been used in this chapter. PDSI data were calibrated using a point-by-point regression of prewhitened instrumental PDSI data against tree-ring records for the period 1928–1978 (see Cook et al. 2007 for a discussion of the calibration procedure).

Tree-ring-based reconstructions of precipitation (fig. 3.2A) used here are derived from data sets published by Grissino-Mayer (1996) and Dean and Funkhouser (2004), as well as recently published data sets from the University of Arizona Tree-Ring Laboratory (Benson, Peterson, and Stein 2007) (see fig. 3.1 for locations of the tree-ring sites). Each of the climate-proxy records was normalized (Z-scored) before stacking (averaging of data sets), and the normalized records of the precipitation and PDSI data sets were plotted using an eleven-year running average, which is comparable to the ten-year increments used in the tree-ring-date histogram for the study area (fig. 3.3C).

In order to apply regional and overall tree-ring-date distributions to the estimation of timber harvesting, construction, and population changes over time, we made the following assumptions:

- Although regional sample sets of archaeological tree-ring dates used in this chapter clearly do not represent random selection, there is no reason to suspect intentional systemic bias. Moreover, the very large sample size lends confidence to the representativeness of the tree-ring-date distributions.

- Given that many, and perhaps most, pithouses and small sites were occupied from ten to forty years (Ahlstrom 1985; Cameron 1990; Cordell 1997; Crown 1991; Gilman 1987; Hantman 1983; Matson, Lipe, and Haase 1988; Nelson and LeBlanc 1986; Powell 1983; Schlanger 1987; Varien and Ortman 2005; Varien et al. 2007), timber harvesting and construction activities should have persisted even when populations were static or slightly decreasing. It follows, therefore, that tree-ring date minima indicate times when populations probably declined (either as people migrated from the region in question or as death rates exceeded birth rates).

- When maxima in tree-ring-date distributions are based on large samples, the maxima can be assumed to indicate times of intensified timber harvesting and construction. We assume that population increases were primarily responsible for increases in construction.

- Tree-ring dates used in this study are probably accurate within one to five years and serve to precisely define temporal changes in timber harvesting and construction activities. Thus, they have a significant advantage over ceramic dating or radiocarbon-based models of construction activity.

Results

In the following section, we show that tree-ring-date patterns from the eight archaeological regions that comprise the study area reflect demographic change in response to climatic change. In general, when we speak of demo-graphic change, we are referring—nonquantitatively—to fluctuations in human populations, human aggregation in response to subsistence stress and violence, and human immigration and emigration as reflected in the tree-ring record of construction activity.

A Comparison of Tree-Ring Dates from the Study Area with Tree-Ring-Based Reconstructions of Climate Change

Figure 3.2 indicates two composite records of climate change for the study area. Figure 3.2A shows the mean of six normalized (Z-scored) records of precipitation from northwestern New Mexico and east-central Arizona (fig. 3.1). The stacked (averaged) record of PDSI for nine nodal sites (fig. 3.1, large filled circles) is shown in figure 2B. The PDSI value is a measure of soil-moisture content and is a function of air temperature, precipitation, and soil moisture (Palmer 1965). Negative PDSI values indicate dry conditions, whereas positive values indicate wet condi-tions. This index was specifically designed to evaluate drought impacts on agriculture. PDSI values range from -6 (extreme drought) to $+6$ (extreme wet) and were calibrated using data for the period 1928–1978, which was a wet period relative to the mean value for the past two thou-sand years (Cook et al. 2004). Therefore, we have plotted the stacked PDSI values relative to a PDSI value (-0.5), which is the mean value for the six site records during the past two thousand years. For the period in which they overlap (AD 765 to 1600), the two stacked records are nearly identical (figs. 3.2A, B). Therefore, in what follows, we have chosen to use only the longer PDSI record.

A Comparison of the PDSI and Tree-Ring-Date Records

Figure 3.2 (B, C) indicates that prior to AD 1000, when the tree-ring datasets are relatively sparse, tree-ring date minima and maxima are not always associated with a particular degree of wetness/dryness. On the other hand, when a high density of tree-ring dates is achieved—certainly between AD 1045 and 1300, when populations were at rel-atively high levels across the study area (Dean, Doelle, and Orcutt 1994:73)—the number of construction dates during minima and maxima

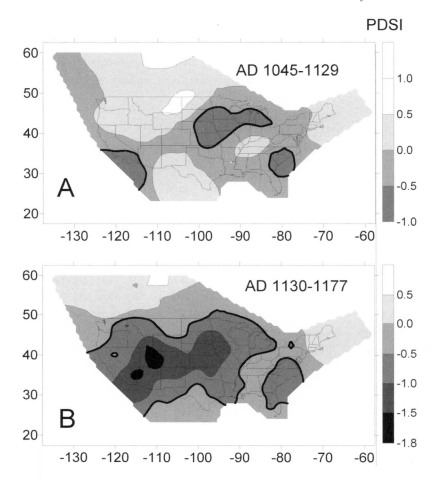

Figure 3.4. PDSI contour maps for (A) the AD 1045–1129 wet period,
(B) the middle-twelfth-century drought, (C) the AD 1193–1269 wet period,
and (D) the late-thirteenth-century drought. An average PDSI value of −0.5
(calculated for the period AD 1–2000) has been used to distinguish drought
conditions (PDSI < −0.5) from relatively wet conditions (PDSI > −0.5).
PDSI values are given in the scale to the right of each contour map.

frequently have a clear relation to climate change. For example, the very
pronounced timber-cutting maxima between AD 1030 and 1130 and
between AD 1190 and 1290 are associated with two of the wettest periods in the PDSI record (W1 and W2). In contrast, the timber-cutting

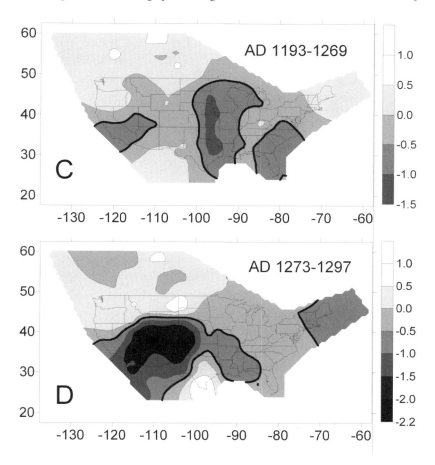

Figure 3.4. (*Continued*)

minimum between AD 1130 and 1200 and the rapid decline in tree-ring dates after AD 1290 were each prefaced by severe decadal-scale mega-droughts, the middle-twelfth and late-thirteenth-century droughts, D1 and D2, which occurred between AD 1130 and 1177 and between AD 1273 and 1297, respectively (figs. 3.2B, C).

These megadroughts impacted much of the contiguous United States, with the southern Colorado Plateau being a region of severe drought during both periods (fig. 3.4B, D). For the most part, the southern Colorado Plateau was free of drought during the two wet periods (AD 1045–1129 and 1193–1269), although areas to the east and west of the southern Colorado Plateau were mildly drought stricken (figs. 3.4A, C). Importantly, Cook et al. (2007) concluded that the twenty-three-year period from AD 1140 to 1162, which falls within the middle-twelfth-century drought, represents the single greatest megadrought experienced by North America since AD 1.

A Comparison of the Timing of Major Climate Oscillations with Regional Tree-Ring-Date Distributions

The eight archeological subregions delineated in figure 3.1 reflect generally accepted southwestern culture areas (Adler 1996a). Figures 3.5A–D and F–I display tree-ring date distributions for these archaeological subregions. Date distributions for the Cortez 1° × 1° area (fig. 3.5E) are also included because of their relevance to interpretations generated by the Village Ecodynamics Project (Kohler et al. 2007)—interpretations that lead to different conclusions from those we reach in this chapter. The tree-ring data from each of these subregions are considered below. We shall discuss the relationship between the construction histories in each subregion and (1) the two wet periods, AD 1030–1130 and AD 1190–1290 (W1 and W2, respectively); and (2) the two megadroughts, AD 1130–1177 and AD 1273–1297 (D1 and D2, respectively). Where relevant, construction activity during the AD 1140–1162 segment of D1 will be examined. This period, as noted above, represents the single greatest megadrought experienced by North America since AD 1, and close examination of the contemporaneous construction activity yields insight into critical transitional events. We will, admittedly arbitrarily, set the analytical threshold at sites having more than two dates for this period as substantial evidence of construction.

The Northern San Juan Subregion.   The tree-ring sample for the northern San Juan subregion consists of 3,601 dates from 234 archaeological sites. The archaeological record indicates that timber harvesting accelerated during the W1 wet period (AD 1045–1129) (fig. 3.5A). During the succeeding D1 megadrought (AD 1130–1177), timber harvesting decreased sharply. Only five sites evidence substantial construction during the most intensive period of D1 (AD 1140–1162). These include the Eagle's Nest ($n = 11$), Hoy House ($n = 11$), Lion House ($n = 24$), and

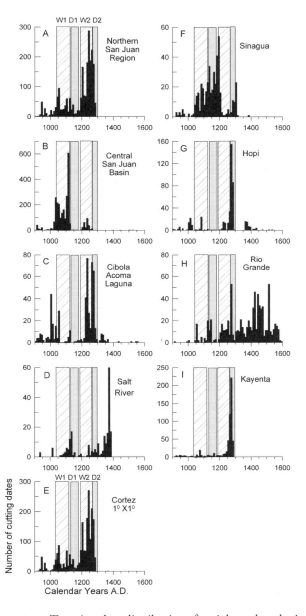

Figure 3.5. Tree-ring date distributions for eight archaeological regions and the Cortez 1° × 1° rectangle. The two vertical hachured rectangles indicate two climatically wet periods (W1 and W2), and the two grey rectangles indicate two mega-droughts (mid-twelfth- and late-thirteenth-century droughts, D1 and D2). The number of tree-ring dates incorporated into each histogram is shown on the vertical scales.

Morris' Site 5 ($n = 7$) (all located in Johnson Canyon, immediately
south of Mesa Verde National Park on the Ute Mountain Ute Reserva-
tion), as well as Knobby Knee Stockade ($n = 4$) (located south of Ruin
Canyon, in southwestern Colorado).

Accelerated timber harvesting appears in the archaeological record
once again at the beginning of the W2 wet period (AD 1193), only to
terminate during the late-thirteenth-century drought (fig. 3.5A). The
late-thirteenth-century cessation of timber harvesting is consistent with
Lipe's (1995) previous analysis of tree-ring dates from the northern San
Juan drainage, which showed that tree-ring dates later than AD 1280
were absent from the subregion.

The Central San Juan Basin Subregion.   The tree-ring sample for the
central San Juan basin consists of 2,697 dates from 38 sites. The history
of timber harvesting in this subregion (fig. 3.5B) is somewhat similar
to that in the northern San Juan subregion, but with a few significant
differences. Although both subregions show diminished construction
during the D1 and D2 megadroughts, low levels of timber harvesting
persisted during the D1 drought in the northern San Juan subregion,
whereas harvesting all but ceased in the central San Juan basin. Indeed,
no sites date convincingly to the AD 1140–1162 period of the D1 drought
in the central San Juan basin.

However, tree-ring dates during the W1 wet period in the central
San Juan basin (fig. 3.5B) are far more numerous than in the northern
San Juan subregion (fig. 3.5A). This situation is reversed during the W2
wet period, with the northern San Juan evidencing much greater construction activity than that seen in the central San Juan basin. The ter-
mination of the Chaco phenomenon during the D1 drought is perhaps
the event of greatest cultural significance in this subregion.

The Cibola-Acoma-Laguna Subregion.   The tree-ring sample for the
Cibola-Acoma-Laguna subregion consists of 686 dates from 39 sites. Some
timber harvesting occurred prior to and during the first part of the W1 wet
period (fig. 3.5C). During the succeeding D1 drought, minimal timber
harvesting is indicated in the archaeological record for this subregion. Two
sites on Cebolleta Mesa, each with a single date, yield weak evidence of
construction during the AD 1140–1162 segment of the D1 drought.

Timber harvesting markedly increased during the W2 wet period, only to cease with the onset of the D2 megadrought. Timber harvesting again resumed between AD 1310 and 1370, after the D2 drought (fig. 3.5C).

The Mogollon Highlands Subregion. The tree-ring sample for the Mogollon Highlands (Salt River) consists of 322 dates from 17 sites. Timber harvesting in this subregion accelerated during the middle of the W1 wet period, only to decline during the D1 drought (fig. 3.5D). Construction during the AD 1140–1162 portion of D1 is evidenced at Carter Ranch ($n = 3$). During the later stage of the W2 wet period, timber harvesting increased in the Mogollon Highlands. During the D2 drought, construction occurred at the Pinedale Ruin ($n = 3$). Similar to the situation in the Cibolla-Acoma-Laguna subregion, timber harvesting in the Mogollon Highlands surged again after the D2 drought, beginning at AD 1330.

The Sinagua Subregion. A total of 466 dates from 45 sites comprises the sample from the Sinagua subregion. Timber harvesting in this subregion differed markedly from that documented for the central and northern San Juan subregions. As was the case for the central San Juan basin, harvesting increased in the Sinagua subregion during the W1 wet period. However, in contrast to the central San Juan basin, harvesting continued in the Sinagua subregion throughout the D1 and D2 droughts. For the AD 1140–1162 segment of the D1 drought, Wupatki ($n = 35$) is the only site evidencing construction. During the D2 drought, construction occurred at Kinnikinnick Pueblo ($n = 17$) and the Pollack site ($n = 3$) in the southern portion of the subregion. The continued construction in the Sinagua subregion strongly indicates that this subregion acted as a refugium during the two megadroughts (Berry 1982; Plog 1989).

The Hopi Subregion. The tree-ring sample for the Hopi subregion consists of 544 dates from 19 sites. Substantial increases in construction are not indicated by tree-ring dates in this subregion during the W1 wet period (fig. 3.5G). Instead, construction dates began to increase at about AD 1220, during the middle part of the W2 wet period. The number of construction dates increased sharply at about AD 1250, that is, toward the end of the W2 wet period. Thereafter, the subregion witnessed a rapid decline in construction dates during the onset of the late-thirteenth-century megadrought. Construction activity does not reappear in the archaeological record until AD 1360. As a caveat, little timber exists in the Hopi subregion, and the dates from this area may reflect the use of recycled material in some instances. Thus, it is possible but not demonstrable that older timbers may have been used in construction that post-dates the D2 drought. However, it is just as feasible that the dating is representative of actual construction activity, thus casting doubt on the widely held notion that the Hopi mesas were continuously occupied from some time in the distant past through the modern era.

The Rio Grande Subregion.   The tree-ring sample for the Rio Grande subregion consists of 722 dates from 53 sites. In this subregion, construction dates were sparse during the W1 wet period. A very small number of tree-ring construction dates are documented for the latter part of the D1 drought (fig. 3.5H). Construction dates during the AD 1140–1162 period of the D1 drought are from the Arroyo Negro site ($n = 20$). During the following W2 wet period, a large number of tree-ring construction dates are documented in the Rio Grande subregion. In contrast, there are few tree-ring construction dates for the D2 drought. The latter are from a group of sites in the Cochiti Dam pool area ($n = 44$) and at Pindi Pueblo ($n = 13$). Tree-ring construction dates increase markedly between AD 1300 and 1580. This latter phenomenon may indicate an expansion of an empirically underrepresented, preexisting Rio Grande population (Boyer et al., this vol.) or the impact of immigration from areas outside the Rio Grande (Lipe, this vol.; Ortman, this vol.).

The Kayenta Subregion.   The tree-ring sample for this subregion consists of 885 tree-ring construction dates from 53 sites. Construction dates in the Kayenta subregion (fig. 3.5I) began with an increase in the latter part of the W2 wet period and peaked during the initial portion of the D2 drought, then abruptly terminated during the last phase of the late-thirteenth-century drought. This pattern is consistent with other data indicating that most of the Kayenta population was moving south during the latter part of the thirteenth century (Dean, Doelle, and Orcutt 1994; Dean 1996b; Dean, this vol.).

The Cortez Subregion. In addition to our eight cultural subareas, we have plotted the tree-ring construction date distribution for the general Cortez area (Cortez 1° × 1° rectangle). This area is congruent with that bounded by the Village Ecodynamics Project Study Area (Kohler et al. 2007), a region central to many studies presented in this book. The tree-ring sample for this subregion consists of 885 dates from 79 sites.

In a study of the occupation histories of 3,176 habitation sites in this area, Varien and others (2007) identified two population cycles, one peaking in the late AD 800s and the other peaking in the middle AD 1200s (Varien et al. 2007: fig. 4; table 1.1, this vol.). Varien and colleagues created "momentary" population estimates for 14 periods between AD 600 and 1280, each of which has a time span ranging from 20 to 125 years, with most of the time spans being 40 years or greater in duration. Varien and his colleagues concluded that "formation of aggregated settlements . . . is positively correlated with increasing population . . . but it does not correlate with climate variation averaged over periods" (Varien et al. 2007:273).

This conclusion is inconsistent with the distribution of tree-ring construction dates displayed in figure 3.5E. These data clearly indicate a construction minimum during the middle-twelfth-century drought (D1), implying a reduction in the population of the Cortez subregion. Kohler and colleagues (2007:83)—although acknowledging "that in general tree harvesting tended to decline during periods with a greater proportion of drought years and increase during periods with fewer drought years"— suggested that their study area "served as a potential refugium during drought."

We suggest that the relatively large bin size used by Varien and colleagues (2007) when constructing their population estimates obscured decadal-scale variability in timber harvesting and construction, thereby essentially masking the substantial impacts of the D1 drought. Moreover, we submit that the minimum in tree-ring construction dates during the D1 drought indicates a significant reduction in population within the Cortez subregion.

As discussed in the northern San Juan subregion summary, the primary evidence for occupation during the D1 drought is from the Johnson Canyon area south of Mesa Verde National Park. Excavations in the Johnson Canyon area that produced evidence of occupation during the D1 drought were accomplished during the 1970s (Nickens 1975). Despite the subsequent energetic and highly productive efforts of the Crow Canyon Archaeological Center, *no additional D1 sites have been tree-ring dated to this period.* Clearly, the tree-ring construction record from archaeological sites and the climatic data do not support the assertion that the northern San Juan subregion, as a whole, served as a drought refugium.

Regional Construction Trends

We are certainly not the first to suggest a relationship between droughts, population decline, and migration in the Southwest (see Berry 1982; Brown, Windes, and McKenna 2008; Clark 2001, 2007a; Crown, Orcutt, and Kohler 1996; Dean 1996b; Dean, Doelle, and Orcutt 1994; Douglass 1929; Fowler and Stein 1992; Gumerman and Dean 1989; Hill et al. 2004; Judge 1989; Kintigh et al. 2004; LeBlanc 1989; Lekson 1986; Matson, Lipe, and Haase 1988; Plog 1989; Reid 1989; Rose, Dean, and Robinson 1982; Stanislawski 1963; Stein and Fowler 1996; Varien et al. 1996; Varien et al. 2007). While there is merit in all the previous studies, the chronometric support for the various arguments is uneven. Some studies are, indeed, based on tree-ring data, but others rely on radiocarbon dating or assumptions based on ceramic temporal placement. In the current study, we have opted to restrict analyses to tree-ring-dated sites in a large but geographically bounded region of the Southwest in order to minimize reliance on imprecise absolute dating methods (radiocarbon, paleomagnetic dating, thermal luminescence, etc.) or conjectural inference (ceramic dating).

We have shown that tree-ring dates from eight archaeological subregions on the southern Colorado Plateau (fig. 3.1) provide a coherent history of timber harvesting and construction activities when their distributions over time are binned at ten-year intervals. The data indicate that

- A wet period between AD 1045 and 1129 (W1) was associated with an overall increase in tree-ring dates throughout most of the study area (figs. 3.2C, 3.5).
- The mid-twelfth-century megadrought (D1) was associated with tree-ring date minima in every archaeological subregion except the

Sinagua, which appears to have been a refugium for people abandoning other areas (fig. 3.5F). The Wupatki basin of the Sinagua subregion is an arid landscape, seemingly an unlikely refugium candidate. Stone and Downum (1999:113) provide the following explanation:

> The ashfall left by the eruption of Sunset Crater Volcano in AD 1064 created a bonanza for the prehistoric inhabitants of the area around Wupatki National Monument in northern Arizona. . . . This natural mulch apparently improved soil conditions enough to attract more than 2,000 immigrants during the following century. . . . A recent survey recorded more than 2,000 small sites on the 55 km² monument, but the most striking feature of the cultural landscape are the numerous large pueblos that arose in the twelfth century. These include 10 pueblos of more than 20 rooms each, apparently organized into settlement districts or clusters centered on Wupatki Pueblo (150+ rooms) and the Citadel (50+ rooms).

As shown in figure 3.5F, increased construction activity followed immediately on the heels of the ashfall and continued through AD 1220. Given that the vast majority of Colorado Plateau sites experienced tree-ring minima during the D1 drought, the significance of the Wupatki basin as a drought refugium has yet to be fully recognized.

To a lesser extent, the early part (AD 1130–1150) of the D1 drought was accompanied by some timber harvesting in the Johnson Canyon area of the northern San Juan subregions, the Mogollon Highlands, and the Rio Grande (figs. 3.5A, D, H).

- A wet period between AD 1193 and 1269 (W2) was associated with a sharp increase in tree-ring dates in the northern San Juan, Cibola-Acoma-Laguna, Hopi, Rio Grande, and Kayenta subregions (figs. 3.5A, C, G, H, I). Increases in timber harvesting and construction also occurred during this period in the Mogollon highlands and Sinagua subregion (fig. 3.5D, F).

- The late thirteenth-century megadrought (D2) was associated with an apparent cessation of tree harvesting and construction activities in the northern San Juan subregion, the central San Juan basin, and the Cibola-Acoma-Laguna, Sinagua, Hopi, and Kayenta subregions (fig. 3.5A, B, C, F, G, I). Tree harvesting and construction in the

Cibola-Acoma-Laguna, Mogollon Highlands, Hopi, and Rio Grande subregions continued after AD 1300 (figs. 3.5C, D, G, and H). The Sinagua subregion witnessed construction activity during D2 for entirely different reasons from those behind its refugium status during D1. Sites in the southernmost portion of the Sinagua area occur at 7,000 ft in elevation on Anderson Mesa. Taking advantage of an extended growing season during warm droughts and orographic rainfall in high-elevation environments was a fairly common drought strategy in the Southwest (Berry 1982).

We invoke Occam's razor in suggesting that tree-ring-date distributions in the southern Colorado Plateau reflect demographic responses to climate change after regional populations achieved a certain density. That is, at higher population densities than previously achieved, people were increasingly vulnerable to a combination of anthropogenic reduction of local resources (Duff et al., this vol.) and regional climate change. In addition, larger local populations provided more samples for the documentation of trends in construction. In terms of the data presented here, that population density was achieved in the study area on or before approximately AD 1000, at which time populations were expanding into areas that were marginal with respect to dryland production of maize under "normal" climatic conditions. Although tree-ring date distributions are not quantitative measures of population change, their minima and maxima are critically informative of major decreases and increases, respectively, in subregional populations.

Concluding Remarks

So, how best to interpret the rapid acceleration of tree-ring dates that followed major drought intervals? More than six decades ago, well before the existence of the sophisticated databases upon which the current analyses rely, famed geographer Carl O. Sauer (1954:553) may have said it best: "It seems to me most appropriate to re-examine the cultural scene of the Southwest, both vertically and horizontally, as a deep and wide zone of interpenetration of peoples and institutions, mainly originating elsewhere." How else to explain the linguistic and cultural variation of the Southwest overlain upon the common factor of maize dependence? We suggest that the rapid responses of building activity, following the two megadroughts, are not solely attributable to *in situ* population increase on the part of residual populations that may have persisted during droughts in extant structures. In situ survival of remnant populations may well explain the observed continuity of certain classes of material culture (e.g., ceramics, textiles, lithics, etc.), but the accelerated building rates immediately following the return to favorable climatic circumstances may well reflect influxes from adjacent regions of populations—perhaps including hunter-gatherers attracted to a new lifeway—to regions that once again possessed robust agriculture potential. Each such influx would have contributed linguistic, cultural, and genetic variability to, in Sauer's terms, the deep and wide southwestern cultural scene.

This leads to a consideration of "pushes" and "pulls" in the explanation of prehistoric migrations—a topic frequently raised in this volume. While we do not deny the possibility that environmental and cultural "pulls" exerted influence over the outcome of certain migrations, we have concentrated on the climatic "pushes" that instantiated population movement. We have taken this approach primarily because climatic variability and the corresponding maxima/minima are empirically attainable. Conversely, the "pulls" or attractors, especially the cultural variety, rely upon secondary or tertiary levels of abstraction that have little probability of empirical support or refutation. We are not saying that such conjectural modeling is a waste of time. Those engaging in such conjecture, however, are obliged to provide a possible roadmap to connect with the empirical world of archaeological data. For example, the scenario briefly suggested above of hunter-gatherers enjoining a maize-dependent lifeway is eminently testable through the use of $^{12}C/^{13}C$ isotopic analyses in conjunction with chronometric data (Coltrain 1993, 1997; Coltrain and Leavitt 2002; Coltrain and Stafford 1999; Decker and Tieszen 1989; Ezzo 1993; Martin 1999; Matson and Chisholm 1991; Spielmann et al. 1990; Wolley 1988).

In conclusion, we have presented a geographical and temporal substrate for the understanding of southwestern prehistoric phenomena. Unless or until the patterns we have demonstrated are overturned through the recovery of additional data, we recommend that southwesternists involved in regional modeling at various levels of abstraction be cognizant of, and account for, the constraints imposed by these geotemporal patterns. To do otherwise will likely lead to dubious inferences.

Acknowledgments

The authors thank Scott Ortman and Mark Varien for access to tree-ring data from the northern San Juan region, Jeffrey Dean for access to tree-ring data from the Tree-Ring Laboratory at the University of Arizona, and Keith Kintigh for access to tree-ring data from the El Morro area. Some tree-ring data for the Chaco Canyon area were downloaded from the Chaco Digital Initiative (http://www.chacoarchive .org/). We also express our appreciation for the comments of Scott Ortman on an earlier version of the manuscript and for the insights of Jeffrey Dean and Tom Windes on the application of existing tree-ring data to archaeological questions. Two anonymous reviewers provided valuable suggestions for the improvement of the chapter. Finally, thanks are due to Claudia F. Berry for a critical reading of the manuscript and the myriad attendant improvements in style and substance.

Note

1. Any use of trade, product, of firm names in this chapter is for descriptive purposes only and does not imply endorsement by the U.S. government.

4

The Climate of the Depopulation of the Northern Southwest

Aaron M. Wright

In this chapter, I examine the climate of the northern Southwest between AD 1000 and 1400, a period with major cultural and demographic transitions, including the complete depopulation of the northern San Juan region and the "Northern Periphery" (see Allison, this vol.) during the thirteenth century. My goal is to present an up-to-date synthesis of southwestern climatic variability, highlighting its potential relevance for understanding the demographic, social, economic, and ritual transformations discussed elsewhere in this volume. Ultimately, the interplay of environmental and social factors underlies the multifaceted, complex history of Ancestral Pueblo society and movement during the late prehispanic period.

The paleoclimate of the northern Southwest, the heartland of Ancestral Pueblo peoples, is one of the best known in North America. This is partly because a deteriorating climate has long been posited as a prime motivator for regional depopulation (e.g., Douglass 1929; Hewett 1908; Kidder 1924). Moreover, the number of trees from local archaeological sites, on which most southwestern climatic reconstructions are based, is by far the greatest of any region in western North America. As a result, the regional paleoclimate is well known and the impacts of climatic variability on local farmers thoroughly studied, although new dendrochronological research and analyses of other proxies continue to provide new insights on climate at various temporal and spatial scales. This chapter couples some of these previous climatic data with the results of new studies to provide an up-to-date picture of temperature and precipitation variability to better understand the conditions facing farmers in the late prehispanic central Mesa Verde region.

Since the impact of climatic downturns on subsistence is often invoked as a causal force in the depopulation of the northern Southwest, this chapter also considers the climatic conditions of regions that might have come to host migrants from the north. Cordell and colleagues (2007) have considered the precipitation differences between the northern Rio Grande and central Mesa Verde regions. This chapter expands their approach by considering temperature as well as precipitation, and it broadens the geographic scope to include regions often neglected as potential migrant destinations.

I begin by reviewing known climate processes and patterns across the northern Southwest. Recent research and modeling have greatly enhanced current understandings of both high- and low-frequency processes, some of which account for the well-known droughts that occurred during the late prehispanic period. The climatic requirements for maize farming in the northern Southwest are then addressed to show that fluctuations in precipitation and temperature patterns—some of great magnitude and extreme duration—were relevant to Ancestral Pueblo farming practices. Precipitation and temperature reconstructions for various regions across the northern Southwest and Mogollon Rim are then presented. Finally, I can then compare regional climatic conditions to gauge the influence climate may have had on attracting Mesa Verdean migrants into other regions.

Understanding Southwestern Climate

The following discussion distinguishes between environment and climate, the latter being more specific and my chief concern here. Although climatic variability is continuously scalar through both space and time, for analytical purposes archaeologists have come to address southwestern climate in terms of high- and low-frequency processes and variability (e.g., Dean 1988; Dean et al. 1985; Dean, Doelle, and Orcutt 1994; Euler et al. 1979). Short-term climatic variability, such as fluctuations in seasonal and annual climate, is referred to as high frequency and tends to be more localized than low-frequency variability. High-frequency variability—for example, early and late frosts, droughts, and floods—is archaeologically important because such occurrences can, among other things, be detrimental to crops and significantly influence the distributions of annually derived wild resources. Low-frequency climatic variability refers to those patterns that are realized in periods of twenty-five years or more. Such fluctuations are dictated largely by extraregional, and sometimes global, processes. Low-frequency variability can have long-term effects on regional ecosystems and can induce significant environmental changes. However, low-frequency environmental change can also be human-induced (e.g., Redman 1999), for example through deforestation (e.g., Kohler 1992; Kohler and Matthews 1988) and overhunting (e.g., Driver 2002). It is traditionally hypothesized that, unless a population has overexploited a local environment or has reached some threshold of resource availability, demographic shifts should respond more closely to low-frequency than to high-frequency climatic and environmental variability (e.g., Dean et al. 1985).

Precipitation Variability

Southwestern precipitation is driven by dynamic and complicated relationships between mid-latitude and subtropical jetstreams. Their shifts, and fluctuations in sea-surface temperatures (SSTs), account for the majority of precipitation variability. Rain-shadow effects around major geological uplifts, differences in ground and atmospheric temperatures, and differing rates of evapotranspiration also contribute to regional moisture variability but at more localized scales (Scott 1991). In turn, annual precipitation in the Southwest is extremely variable through time and space. For example, mean annual precipitation rates vary between 12.7 and 50 cm across most of Arizona, New Mexico, western Colorado, and eastern Utah (Sheppard et al. 2002:221), with rates being considerably higher in mountainous regions such as the La Salles and southern Rockies, as well as the Mogollon Rim (Sheppard et al. 2002: fig. 2; see also Daly, Neilson, and Phillips 1994).

Seasonal precipitation rates vary considerably across the Southwest as well. As Sheppard and others (2002: fig. 3) show, the current distribution of precipitation follows three broad spatial patterns. Throughout most of Arizona, precipitation arrives in an annually bimodal pattern during winter (November–March) snows and rains and summer (July–September) monsoons. Precipitation across most of New Mexico is delivered more unimodally, with a peak during the summer monsoon. In both Arizona and New Mexico, the monsoon provides most of the precipitation, accounting for as much as 50 percent of the annual mean. Winter precipitation accounts for approximately 30 percent (Barry and

Chorley 2003). North and west of the Four Corners region, in areas once inhabited by Virgin and Fremont peoples, precipitation rates are low but relatively evenly distributed throughout the year. The northern San Juan region, which is uniquely situated near where these three patterns merge, experiences unpredictable season-to-season variability in precipitation because the boundaries around these established regimes are somewhat diffuse and unstable, subject to shifting in any direction.

Winter precipitation in the Southwest is controlled largely by the polar jetstream, which carries moist air from the west. The latitude at which this jetstream enters the Pacific Coast varies annually, however, and as a result, rates of winter precipitation can be highly variable in the Southwest. Summer precipitation is brought to the Southwest by the North American monsoon between late July and September. The monsoon is driven mainly by air currents bringing moisture from the equatorial Pacific Ocean and the Sea of Cortez into the Sonoran desert and northern Southwest (Sheppard et al. 2002). Moist air moving in from the Gulf of Mexico also contributes to the southwestern monsoon (Adams and Comrie 1997; Higgins, Chen, and Douglas 1999; Poore, Pavich, and Grissino-Mayer 2005). This is caused by the Bermuda high-pressure system (Allen 2004:22), which extends from the Atlantic Ocean to the central United States. The teleconnections between Pacific and Atlantic ocean airflows and their combined impact on summer precipitation, however, are still poorly understood (Sheppard et al. 2002).

The processes causing southwestern precipitation variability operate at both high and low frequencies. The El Niño-Southern Oscillation (ENSO) phenomenon is a relatively high-frequency process. El Niño events result from increased SSTs in the equatorial eastern Pacific Ocean, combined with an associated easterly translocation of an equatorial center of atmospheric convection to the central Pacific Ocean (Southern Oscillation) (Sheppard et al. 2002). Southwestern regions generally experience cooler and wetter than average winters during El Niño events (Andrade and Sellers 1988; Kiladis and Diaz 1989; Woodhouse 1997). These cool and wet periods may last from two to ten years and can be contrasted with La Niña conditions (Barry and Chorley 2003; Quinn and Neal 1992), which are typically three to four years in length. La Niña events, associated with decreased SSTs in the eastern equatorial Pacific, are expressed in the Southwest as warmer and drier than average winters (Kiladis and Diaz 1989; Molles and Dahm 1990).

These relatively high-frequency ENSO-related phenomena are linked to low-frequency processes, such as the Pacific Decadal Oscillation (PDO) (Goodrich 2007), in a complex manner. Both the PDO and the Atlantic Multidecadal Oscillation (AMO) influence the climatic regime of the Greater Southwest (McCabe, Betancourt, and Hidalgo 2004; McCabe, Palecki, and Betancourt 2007). The PDO, an index of Pacific Ocean SSTs, is similar in spatial extent to ENSO-related events (Mantua et al. 1997); however, it ranges from fifty to seventy years in duration (MacDonald and Case 2005). The Southwest tends to have higher rates of precipitation and lower temperatures during warmer than normal Pacific SSTs (positive PDO) and vice versa (Benson et al. 2007; Sheppard et al. 2002). Winter precipitation throughout western North America is positively correlated with the PDO (Brown and Comrie 2002; Mantua et al. 1997; Ni et al. 2002). The AMO is an average measure of Atlantic Ocean SSTs between 0 and 70° longitude (Kerr 2000), and it has expressed a cyclity of sixty-five to eighty years in length since AD 1856 (Benson et al. 2007). Although research on the PDO, the AMO, and their interrelationships is in its infancy, atmospheric modeling efforts suggest that the western U.S. megadroughts—unusually long periods of below-average precipitation (Herweijer et al. 2007; Stahle, Stahle, and Cook 2000; see also Berry and Benson, this vol.)—are associated with positive AMO and negative PDO phases (Fye, Stahle, and Cook 2003; McCabe, Palecki, and Betancourt 2004; Schubert et al. 2004).

Temperature Variability

Our knowledge of temperature processes and patterns is unfortunately less refined. Since these data have only been collected for little more than a century—and since we don't fully understand anthropogenic impacts to temperature through greenhouse gases and mass deforestation (Mann, Bradley, and Hughes 1998; Trenberth and Hoar 1996, 1997; see also Cook et al. 1995)—extrapolation of modern processes into the past is problematic. This problem also holds true for attempting quantitative reconstructions of annual temperature highs and lows from tree rings because it is not known how ring growth may have differed in response to temperatures before and after the onset of industrialization and the introduction of associated greenhouse gases into the atmosphere. Thus, calibrations with modern temperature data, while likely accurate, are less certain than for precipitation.

Temperature fluctuations are indirectly connected to ENSO (high-frequency) and PDO (low-frequency) processes by virtue of temperature's typical correlation with precipitation (i.e., warm and dry conditions tend to co-occur, as do cool and wet conditions), whereas spatial variability is dictated mostly by the landscape's orographic characteristics. Some additional temperature-related processes at low and high frequencies and of differing spatial scales are known (e.g., Crowley 2000); however, of relevance to understanding human response to temperature change in the late prehispanic Southwest, these would be limited to variations in solar irradiance (i.e., sunspot minima) (e.g., Eddy 1977; Hoyt and Schatten 1997) and the effects of volcanic emissions (e.g., Salzer 2000a).

The variable nature of both precipitation and temperature can have substantial impacts on either farmers or hunter-gatherer groups. The following discussion highlights the importance of these climatic variables in relation to success of southwestern dry-farming practices.

Corn and Climate in the Mesa Verde Region

Maize (*Zea mays*) was the most important dietary resource for most Ancestral Pueblo peoples after 400 BC (Matson 1991) and may have provided 70 to 80 percent of the average Mesa Verdean caloric intake during the thirteenth century (Decker and Tieszen 1989), although other domesticates (i.e., beans and squash), wild plants, and animals provided important dietary contributions. However, the productivity of these food sources in the Southwest, especially domesticates, is highly dependent on climatic factors. The following reviews what we currently know regarding the climatic requirements of maize.

Basing his conclusions on historical Hopi farming, Hack (1942:23) suggested that maize agriculture in the northern Southwest requires at least 12 in (31 cm) of annual rainfall. Since the climatic and environmental requirements for maize vary from place to place, Petersen (1988:11) increased Hack's estimate to a minimum of 14 in (36 cm) for the central Mesa Verde region. Milo (1991), however, considers annual precipitation to be a poor measure when considering the growing-season requirements for maize, and suggests that precipitation measures should therefore be distinguished for each precipitation mode in the biseasonal pattern. Adams and Petersen (1999:23) have also highlighted the importance of the biseasonal distribution of precipitation for dry farming in the central Mesa Verde region, where soil moisture from winter precipitation is necessary for plant germination and summer rainfall is critical for maturation. Yet, as Adams (2008) has recently pointed out, the paleoclimatic reconstructions upon which southwestern archaeologists rely do not distinguish between these seasonal patterns. Therefore, although the Southwest has one of the most refined paleoclimatic records, our estimates of the impacts of changing precipitation and temperature regimes will be imperfect so long as we cannot reconstruct precipitation regimes at a seasonal scale. Given the intricate relationships among moisture, soil nutrients, and temperature involved in maize growth and reproduction (Adams et al. 2006), it should be emphasized that annual precipitation reconstructions only serve as a somewhat unsatisfying proxy for a region's agricultural potential.

Since Douglass' (1929) discovery of the late-1200s "Great Drought," discussion of agricultural productivity in the face of climatic downturns in the northern Southwest has centered largely on the effects of precipitation shortfalls. Rainfall, however, is not the only climatic variable critical to maize agriculture. Petersen (1988) has argued that maize productivity in the central Mesa Verde region would have also been affected by temperature, probably more so than in lower areas to the south and west. This is because the Mesa Verde region is the northernmost or highest of the prehispanic Southwest, where farming was common. Its high elevations and the effects of other orographic features (i.e., cold-air drainage patterns) cause shorter growing seasons, lower temperatures, and a higher probability of detrimental early and late frosts than occur in many other areas of the Southwest. Earlier researchers (e.g., Berlin et al. 1977:59; Martin and Byers 1965:135; Petersen 1988; Smiley 1961:703; Woodbury 1961:708–709) also suggested that reduced temperatures may have contributed to the depopulation of the Mesa Verde region during the 1200s, and more recent investigations (e.g., Dean and Van West 2002; Kohler, this vol.; Kohler et al. 2007; Salzer 2000b; Van West and Dean 2000; Wright 2006) have given increased attention to the role of temperature in agricultural productivity during this turbulent period.

Temperature variability can impact maize farming in several ways. For example, early-season cold spells can delay germination and the development of roots, while prolonged episodes of cool temperatures inhibit overall plant development by extending the time required for germination and growth. Frosts can kill plants by creating ice crystals that dehydrate or damage the cellular structure of the plants. Given these problems, modern maize is rarely grown where mean growing season temperatures are below 19° C (66.2° F) (Shaw 1988; Tivy [1990] suggests that normal plant growth occurs when temperatures range between 10 and 40° C [50 and 104° F]). Although little is known about the growing season requirements of many aboriginal varieties of maize (Adams et al. 2006), Zuni blue-flour corn (Muenchrath et al. 2002:20) and Hopi maize (Bradfield 1971; Hack 1942) have matured within spans of 95–130 and 115–130 days respectively. A study by Adams and colleagues (2006), albeit using nonindigenous technologies, resulted in a range of 111–144 frost-free days required for a variety of aboriginal maize cultivars grown outside Farmington, New Mexico. These ranges in the requisite number of frost-free days among maize varieties suggest that there is a complex relationship between plant genetics, local environment, precipitation, soil chemistry, farming practices, and temperature when considering the productivity of maize agriculture (see Bellorado 2007). In the northern Southwest, a longer growing season helps ensure successful harvests, especially in regions where other environmental and climatic requisites are deficient.

In overview, then, variable precipitation and temperature regimes affect the timing of maturation and overall productivity of maize and other domesticates—as well as the accessibility of wild plants. As a result, climate, in conjunction with many other environmental and social variables not reviewed here, sets parameters around the potential productivity of prehispanic southwestern farming practices. Did climate-induced subsistence stress encourage or require prehispanic Mesa Verdeans to vacate their communities in the 1200s with no clear intention of returning?

Paleoclimate across the Northern Southwest

This section uses data from previous tree-ring studies and a new strati-graphic pollen sequence to model variability in southwestern precipi-tation and temperature from AD 1000 to 1400, including places that potentially received immigrants from the Mesa Verde region. Table 4.1 lists the seven climate divisions used in this study, which correspond roughly to archaeological culture areas. Although climatic variability is scalar—with regard to both space and time—the spatial scale repre-sented by these seven divisions allows an assessment of climatic variability

Table 4.1. Regional climate divisions and reconstructed annual precipitation in inches, AD 1000–1400

Climate region	Tree-ring stations[a]	Reconstructed annual tree-year precipitation		
		Mean	Range	Standard deviation
Central Mesa Verde	11 Mesa Verde	18.18	5.75–30.36	4.34
Western Mesa Verde	1 Natural Bridges	9.24	4.83–14.11	1.74
Northern Rio Grande	18 Jemez 19 Chama 21 Santa Fe	15.89	10.86–21.25	1.94
Cibola-Puerco	9 Puerco 13 Cibola El Malpais	12.97	8.23–17.37	1.65
Kayenta	2 Navajo Mountain 3 Tsegi Canyon 8 Hopi/Black Mesa	14.29	7.59–23.42	2.25
Mogollon Rim	6 Central Mountains North 14 Quemado	13.90	9.49–18.39	1.57
Below Rim	7 Central Mountains South 24 Reserve	15.64	8.98–21.78	2.34

[a] Data courtesy of the Southwest Paleoclimate Project of the University of Arizona's Tree-Ring Laboratory (Dean and Robinson 1977, 1978) except for the El Malpais tree-ring chronology (Grissino-Mayer 1996).

in relation to our current knowledge of regional demography (Berry and Benson, this vol.; Hill et al., this vol.). This approach affords the presentation of a tremendous amount of climatic variability at a spatial scale compatible with the archaeological record.

Precipitation

With the exception of the El Malpais reconstruction (Grissino-Mayer 1996), the raw precipitation data presented here originate from the Southwest Paleoclimate Project of the Laboratory of Tree-Ring Research at the University of Arizona (Dean and Robinson 1977, 1978). These data reflect estimates of total annual tree-year (August through July) rainfall in inches for each climate division. Rainfall estimates are produced by regressing local ring-width index series on recorded meteorological data for each tree-ring station; these equations allow rainfall estimates to be applied to ring widths that pre-date the collection of historical climate data. Precipitation data for each climate division were calculated by averaging the total number of tree-ring stations within that division (table 4.1). This obscures some spatial variation, but it provides a more representative measure of a division's paleoclimatic record. The northern San Juan region is here divided into the central and western Mesa Verde regions, each with a unique precipitation record. This permits an evaluation of large-scale spatial variability across the region and provides a means to assess the influence climate may have had on the thirteenth-century concentration of population into the central Mesa Verde region (Glowacki 2006, this vol.; Varien 1999).

Figure 4.1 presents precipitation data for each climate division, plotted around regional means (thin, straight lines) for the AD 1000–1400 period. Each figure segment presents both the high-frequency variability (annual rainfall estimates represented by the thin, light lines) and the low-frequency trends (plotted with heavier, darker lines). The low-frequency component was calculated by smoothing the annual estimates with a ten-year running mean.

Temperature

Figure 4.2 presents four temperature reconstructions for the northern Southwest, with each record standardized via Z-scores and plotted around each record's mean (thin, straight lines). The thin, wavy lines in

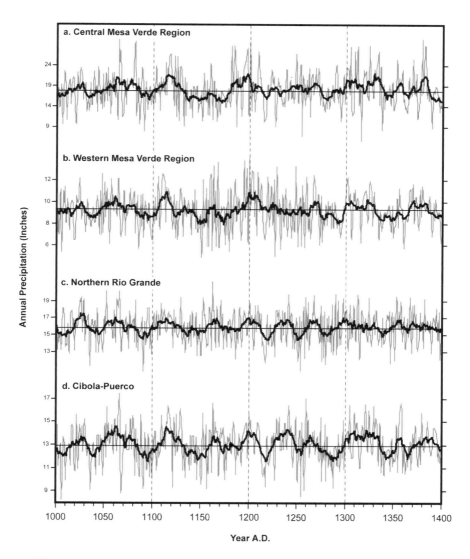

Figure 4.1. A comparison of reconstructed annual tree-year (August through July) precipitation, in inches, for each region, AD 1000–1400. Thin straight lines show regional means, thin jagged lines represent annual values, and heavy jagged lines approximate long-term trends as calculated by a ten-year running mean.

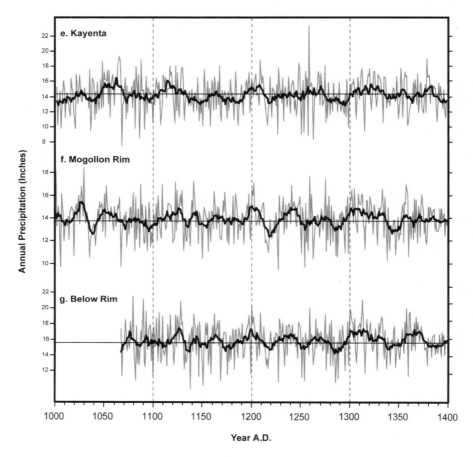

Figure 4.1. (*Continued*)

figure 4.2 represent annual (high-frequency) tree-year variability in temperature. The heavier, darker lines approximate long-term trends (low-
frequency variability) as calculated by a ten-year running mean of the
annual data (with the exception of the Beef Pasture record). Included
in figure 4.2 are two high-frequency temperature reconstructions, both
based on high-elevation bristlecone pine (*Pinus aristata*) chronologies;
one from the San Francisco Peaks (Salzer 2000a; Salzer and Kipfmueller 2005), located approximately 335 km southwest of the central Mesa
Verde region near present-day Flagstaff, Arizona (fig. 4.2c), and another
from Almagre Mountain (Graybill 1983) on the Colorado Front Range,

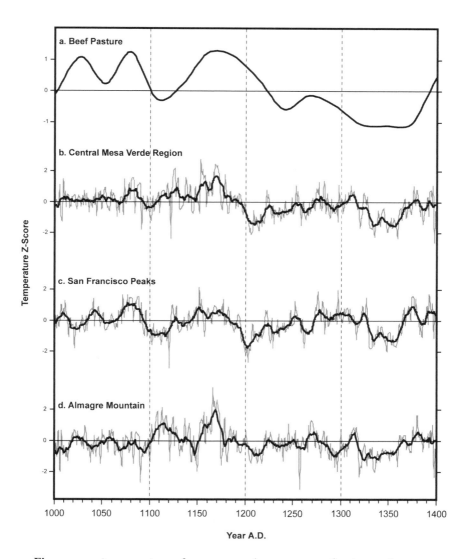

Figure 4.2. A comparison of reconstructed temperatures for the northern Southwest at various temporal scales using different proxies, AD 1000–1400. For standardization, data from each record have been converted to Z-scores and plotted around each record's mean (thin, straight line). (a) Beef Pasture— ratio of ponderosa pine pollen to spruce pollen (after Wright 2006); (b) central Mesa Verde region—scores on first principal component of c and d (after Kohler et al. 2007:65); (c) San Francisco Peaks—bristlecone pine ring-width index (after Salzer 2000a); (d) Almagre Mountain—bristlecone pine ring-width index (Graybill 1983). Thin wavy lines in b, c, and d represent annual values, whereas heavy wavy lines approximate long-term trends as calculated by a ten-year running mean.

approximately 350 km east-northeast of the central Mesa Verde region (fig. 4.2d). The central Mesa Verde region is located almost exactly between these two mountainous areas, where the bristlecone-pine chronologies were developed, so neither record fully approximates historical temperature changes in southwestern Colorado. To overcome this, the Village Ecodynamics Project (VEP) developed a unique temperature reconstruction for the central Mesa Verde region (Kohler et al. 2007:65), also presented in figure 4.2b. This was accomplished by extracting the first principal component of these two bristlecone-pine records; annual scores on this component for the historical era proved to be highly correlated with various local measures of temperature in and near the central Mesa Verde region.

Figure 4.2a presents a pollen-based low-frequency temperature reconstruction from Beef Pasture reported in Wright (2006). This proxy is different from that in Petersen's (1988) study. Wright's (2006) temperature reconstruction is based on the ratio of ponderosa pine (*Pinus ponderosa*) pollen to that of Engelmann spruce (*Picea engelmannii*) from a subalpine fen. In contrast, Petersen's (1988:100) reconstruction relied on a twenty-year smooth of the Almagre Mountain tree-ring series to infer low-frequency temperature changes between AD 500 and 1970 (fig. 2d presents a ten-year smooth of a very similar Almagre series).

There are currently no other temperature reconstructions from the Greater Southwest of comparable temporal resolution. As a result, temperature change cannot be reliably gauged for areas beyond the San Juan and San Francisco Peaks regions and the Rocky Mountain Front Range. The lack of temperature data for regions below the Mogollon Rim is problematic; however, given these regions' lower elevations, temperature was probably less limiting for local agricultural productivity than it was further north. Of greater concern is a lack of data for the northern Rio Grande region. Many of the settlements in this area were situated at elevations comparable to those in the central Mesa Verde region, and temperature was likely a limiting factor for agricultural productivity in both regions. Considering that air currents from the Atlantic Ocean conditioned the climate of this region more than in areas west of the continental divide, it is quite possible that temperature variability in the northern Rio Grande region is better proxied by the Almagre Mountain reconstruction. Until a more local temperature reconstruction is developed, however, a comparison of temperature oscillations in the Mesa Verde region with those of the northern Rio Grande is not possible.

Climate Variability in the Mesa Verde Region

Figures 4.1 and 4.2 demonstrate the cyclical variability that characterizes southwestern climate at both high- and low-frequency scales. It is assumed that the higher-frequency peaks and dips (those of one- to five-year duration) represent short-term climate cycles, such as ENSO-related phenomena. While relevant to agricultural productivity models (see Kohler, this vol.), the high-frequency component is not emphasized here. Instead, this chapter focuses on lower-frequency paleoclimatic variability in the northern Southwest and its potential relationship to demography. To examine this relationship, prolonged periods of drought and reduced temperatures for the seven climate divisions between AD 1000 and 1400 are presented. As done by Herweijer and colleagues (2007:1355), prolonged droughts are defined here as ten or more years of below-average precipitation where interannual reversals toward above-average precipitation are nonsuccessive. Following this guideline, the dark lines in figure 4.3 reflect prolonged droughts in each region. As shown, the central Mesa Verde region experienced five such droughts during the three centuries prior to regional depopulation (1030–1046, 1090–1101, 1130–1158, 1164–1178, and 1273–1288). On the other hand, this region also experienced five periods of prolonged wet conditions during these three centuries (1047–1066, 1069–1080, 1102–1129, 1179–1197, and 1252–1272).

Each of the prolonged droughts witnessed in the central Mesa Verde region, as well as in many of the other reconstructions (fig. 4.3), represent local expressions of the "medieval megadrought" (Cook et al. 2004), an era of above-average aridity across much of North America that exhibited twenty- to forty-year periods of persistently dry conditions (Herweijer et al. 2007:1355) (the last drought considered here, that of 1273–1288, is usually dated to 1276–1299 [Douglass 1929]). Yet, droughts, or our conception thereof, can result from multiple factors with different impacts. For example, a drought can be characterized by reduced interannual variation, or a "leveling out," where the mean is minimally affected but the magnitudes of year-to-year fluctuations are greatly reduced. As Dean and Van West (2002:88) have suggested,

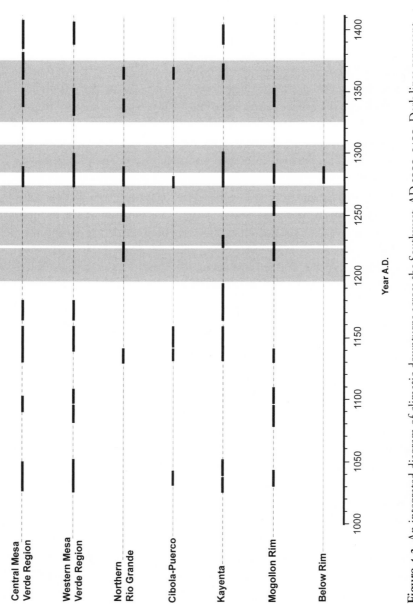

Figure 4.3. An integrated diagram of climatic downturns across the Southwest, AD 1000–1400. Dark lines represent periods of prolonged drought, and shaded regions correspond to prolonged below-average temperatures in the northern Southwest.

droughts of the early 1000s in the Mesa Verde region would meet these criteria (see fig. 4.1a). Such conditions may have actually had favorable effects on agricultural practices, given the increased predictability and reliability afforded by reduced interannual variation. Another form of drought could be characterized as successive years of prolonged shortfalls, where mean precipitation decreased as a result of either an increased number of dry years or fewer wet years. The mid-1100s and late 1200s droughts in the central Mesa Verde region would be characterized as such because these resulted from successive years of below-average conditions (fig. 4.1a). In effect, there were few "recovery" years during these droughts, when conditions became favorable and could have counter-balanced the negative impacts of dry years.

Since most of the lower-frequency precipitation highs and lows in the central Mesa Verde region occurred in many other regions as well (figs. 4.1 and 4.3), these oscillations were seemingly intense in nature and broad in scale and were thus likely associated with major climate processes, such as the PDO. MacDonald and Case (2005) have modeled the annual PDO index from AD 1000 to the present era. During the post-1850 era, lows in the PDO index tend to be expressed as below-average precipitation and above-average temperatures in the Southwest, with PDO highs producing the opposite conditions. Based on their reconstruction, PDO lows occurred approximately during the following periods: 1020–1050, 1110–1160, 1215–1240, and 1280–1305 (MacDonald and Case 2005:fig. 2). As would be expected, the prolonged droughts of the early 1000s and mid-1100s generally correspond with the modeled PDO index. The Great Drought of the late 1200s was also correlated with a PDO low; however, this drought was not as persistent or severe in the central Mesa Verde region as it was in other regions (figs. 4.1 and 4.3). Likewise, the prolonged wet periods of 1069–1080, 1179–1197, 1252–1272, and 1330–1339 correspond to peaks in the modeled PDO index.

Regarding temperature, each of the records in figure 4.2 shows that conditions across the northern Southwest can be broadly characterized as above average during the 1100s and below average during the 1200s. The San Francisco Peaks record shows a brief turn toward cold conditions near 1150, but the century could be characterized as warmer than average. This prolonged warmth is strongly expressed in the other three indices as well as in the local Mesa Verde reconstruction developed by Dean and Van West (2002: fig. 4.2). In contrast, the 1200s and 1300s register largely as below average in all four records, with major lows occurring during the early and late 1200s and mid-1300s. This period of prolonged cooler than average conditions corresponds with a global-scale downturn in solar irradiance between AD 1200 and 1700, as evidenced by atmospheric carbon isotope ratios, that was likely caused by a triple-event sunspot minimum (Damon et al. 1978; Stuiver and Brazunias 1988).

Using the VEP temperature reconstruction as the default proxy, the duration of the prolonged warm and cool spells evident in figure 4.2 can be quantified in a fashion similar to that used to identify prolonged droughts. Ten or more years of above-average temperature, where deviations toward below-average conditions are minimal, were experienced by the Mesa Verde region three times (1072–1089, 1105–1129, and 1152–1180). In contrast, the Mesa Verde region experienced five periods of prolonged cool temperatures (1195–1223, 1226–1252, 1257–1273, 1284–1307, and 1326–1375), four of which occurred during the region's last century of residence by Ancestral Pueblo farmers. These periods are shown as shaded gray bars in figure 4.3. From a high-frequency perspective, then, seventy-nine of the one hundred years in the thirteenth century exhibited below-average temperatures.

Climate and Mesa Verdean Demography During the 1200s

Like the influence of climatic variability on Mesa Verdean subsistence, the demographic trajectory of the northern San Juan has been a matter of debate for some time (e.g., Dean, Doelle, and Orcutt 1994; Duff and Wilshusen 2000; Rohn 1989; Wilshusen 2002). For the Mesa Verde region at least, recent fine-scale settlement pattern analyses (e.g., Glowacki 2006; Mahoney, Adler, and Kendrick 2000; Ortman, Varien, and Gripp 2007; Varien et al. 2007) have seemingly clarified much of the picture. It now appears that a pattern of potential regionwide population decline in conjunction with population concentration in the central Mesa Verde region occurred during the 1200s (a demographic process similar to that referred to as "coalescence" by Hill and colleagues [2004] among the Hohokam). In turn, it appears that this central region came to host many migrants from peripheral areas of the northern San Juan during the decades leading up to final depopulation in the late 1200s (Glowacki 2006, this vol.; Kohler, Varien et al. 2008; Wright 2006).

The 1200s convergence into the central Mesa Verde region may have had a climatic underpinning (Wright 2006). The central Mesa Verde region receives, on average, twice as much annual precipitation as the western region (table 4.1, fig. 4.4). Moreover, the Great Drought was more pronounced in the western Mesa Verde region than in the central area (figs. 4.1 and 4.3). Another important factor is the effect of increased interannual variability in precipitation in the western Mesa Verde region between AD 1150 and 1280 (fig. 4.1). Although the long-term trend falls largely around the regional mean, the high variability was atypical for this region and may have elicited unusual or extreme responses by local farmers, such as the choice to vacate their communities and move into the central region and elsewhere.

Van West's (1994, 1996) detailed maize-productivity model for the central Mesa Verde region showed that local soils provided some of the most productive dry-farming lands in the northern Southwest (see also Varien, Van West, and Patterson et al. 2000). Perhaps the productive soils and higher precipitation rates in the central Mesa Verde region were attractive to farmers in the peripheral and less agriculturally viable regions of the northern San Juan. As argued by Kohler (this vol.; Kohler, Varien et al. 2008), this region may have become a "refugium" from the effects of deteriorating farming climates on the peripheries. Population growth in the central region would have placed added demand on local productivity, however. Combining this with the prolonged below-average temperatures (fig. 4.2), the unpredictable nature of post-1150 rainfall, violence (Kuckelman, this vol.), and changing social and ritual institutions (Glowacki, this vol.), we can see that local residents and immigrants to the central Mesa Verde region were likely faced with a cascade of social and economic ills. Those remaining in the central region either perished entirely—a rather unlikely scenario—or decided to leave this once-vibrant and productive landscape, a decision that Glowacki (this vol.) cogently characterizes as an option of last resort.

By 1300, the majority of the northern Southwest was depopulated. Identifying where these people went is no easy task, however, as several chapters later in this volume will discuss. It is reasonable to assume that population concentrations after 1300 subsumed many of these migrants, especially where there were noticeable population increases after 1250. Such population increases occurred in the northern Rio Grande, along the Mogollon Rim, and in portions of southern and central Arizona (Hill et al., this vol., figs. 2.4 and 2.5). All of these regions are beyond the northern Southwest, and we may suspect that emigrants from the north contributed to these population increases. To explore whether better farming conditions may have attracted migrants into these probable host regions, the following section compares the climatic conditions of these destinations to those of the central Mesa Verde region.

A Comparison of Southwestern Climate Patterns

To this point, four hundred years of climatic variability in the northern Southwest has been presented. This section emphasizes variability in the thirteenth century to determine whether other regions may have offered more productive alternatives than did farming in the central Mesa Verde region. I focus on four variables believed to affect farming prospects: drought, interannual variability, seasonal precipitation patterns, and temperature oscillations.

Addressing drought, figures 4.1 and 4.3 reveal that many of the long-term precipitation trends witnessed in the Mesa Verde region, both favorable and unfavorable, occurred in other regions in the Southwest because these were linked to broad-scale low-frequency processes. Figure 4.3 charts each of the prolonged droughts in the various regions. It reveals that some droughts were localized, witnessed in only a few regions (e.g., the late 1000s); of course, these provide plausible motivations for interregional migration. The more severe droughts of the early 1000s, mid-1100s, and late 1200s, however, affected most of the regions under consideration, with the Great Drought being largest in spatial scope. Since these droughts were so broad in scale, it is difficult to conceive of farmers simply migrating from one drought-stricken region to another in an effort to buffer poor conditions. Thus, it appears that farmers did not migrate out of the northern San Juan solely to places known to have more annual rainfall.

Since migrants leaving the northern Southwest during the late 1200s would have entered regions also afflicted by drought, we should consider how variable the rainfall in each region was. Here, a quantitative regional comparison can shed some insights. That presented in figure 4.1 is somewhat misleading, however, because each reconstruction is scaled differently to accentuate local variability. When scaled uniformly, the long-term trends for each region would appear as nearly straight lines in comparison to that of the central Mesa Verde region. This is due to the magnitude of interannual precipitation variability in the central Mesa Verde region. Figure 4.4 shows not only that the central Mesa Verde region received more precipitation on average (18.18 in) than any other region, but also that its range of variation is twice as great. (Figure 4.4 considers data for the AD 1000–1400 period, but the medians, ranges of variation, and interregional differences are nearly identical when the dataset is limited to the 1200s.) While precipitation in the central Mesa Verde region was more plentiful than in the other regions considered here, its unpredictability may have been a factor inducing farmers to leave. Although these northern migrants moved to regions that tended to have less rainfall, its annual distribution was seemingly more predictable.

Another, perhaps more important, variable is the evidence for a major and long-lasting disruption to seasonal rainfall patterns that began in the 1200s. Based on a principal component analysis (PCA) of the twenty-seven tree stations of the Southwest Paleoclimate Project, Dean (1996a; Dean and Funkhouser 1995) observed a breakdown in spatial coherence across the Southwest between approximately AD 1250 and 1450. For most years, the PCA divided these stations into groups that conform to the general distribution of the historically observed unimodal and bimodal precipitation regimes in the Southwest (Dean and Funkhouser 1995:fig. 7). The PCA results for the 1250–1450 period, however, were considerably different (Dean and Funkhouser 1995: fig. 9) and likely signify a breakdown in this dominant and once-stable precipitation pattern across the northern Southwest.

It is unclear how this disruption manifested itself, since a climatic transition of this nature has not been observed historically. Possibly it represents a weakening of the summer monsoon. Such a major and prolonged alteration to long-established conditions, especially considering the importance of summer rainfall to maize farming, would have entailed significant impacts on farmers in afflicted regions. This disruption,

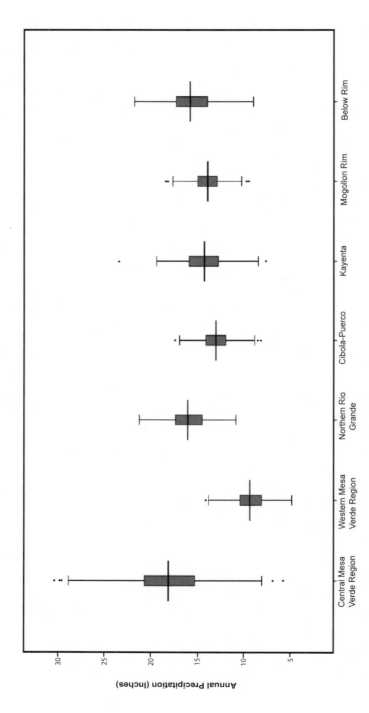

Figure 4.4. Boxplots showing median, range, and standard deviation of reconstructed annual tree-year (August through July) precipitation, in inches, for each region, AD 1000–1400.

however, did not affect regions east of the Continental Divide, specifically the northern and central Rio Grande regions and their tributaries (Dean and Funkhouser 1995:94). Therefore, if a stable and predictable precipitation regime was a significant influence on where northern migrants relocated, we should expect at least a partial population increase—as a gauge of in-migration—in these regions after AD 1250 (see also Ahlstrom, Van West, and Dean 1995). The demographic measures presented by Hill and colleagues (this vol., figs. 2.4 and 2.5) show, in fact, that populations increased at various centers within these regions. This suggests that at a gross scale, demographic transitions in the late prehispanic northern Southwest were correlated with expectations from the precipitation data, but that the critical factor may have been the timing and reliability of precipitation rather than annual rainfall rates.

A final climatic transition that has often been given less weight but likely had an impact on farming in the northern Southwest is the major cooling episode that spanned the thirteenth and fourteenth centuries (figs. 4.2 and 4.3). More than drought, it was this period of below-average temperatures that lowered agricultural productivity in the central Mesa Verde region during the AD 1200s, as revealed by Kohler's reconstruction for the VEP (Kohler, this vol.; Kohler, Varien et al. 2008; Varien et al. 2007). Although the exact spatial extent of this cooling within the Southwest is unknown, it is correlated with a major downturn in solar irradiance, suggesting it was a global occurrence. Thus, it is quite likely that temperatures in the northern Rio Grande and elsewhere were also reduced during this period. Extreme cooling may have made farming nearly impossible at higher elevations during this time. It is difficult to quantify the impact that such cooling would have had, since temperature reductions of that magnitude have not occurred since the inception of modern meteorological records. Whether or not this cooling was somehow related to the aberrant precipitation regime observed by Dean (1996a; Dean and Funkhouser 1995), the combined effect of these disruptions and the Great Drought may have necessitated a major transition in Ancestral Pueblo lifeways and worldviews, such as the depopulation of vast regions of the northern Southwest and loss of some long-established visible expressions of cultural identity (e.g., Clark 2001; Lipe, this vol.), during this process.

Discussion and Concluding Thoughts

The comparison of absolute rates of precipitation among regions (figs. 4.1 and 4.4) prompts several inferences regarding the influence of precipitation variability on thirteenth-century Mesa Verdean farmers. First, although medians in each region's annual precipitation varied slightly, rainfall regimes outside the central Mesa Verde region exhibited considerably less variation than in the central Mesa Verde region (fig. 4.4). The central Mesa Verde region's unusually high range in annual precipitation underscores the unpredictable nature of local rainfall. More than drought, the region's highly variable rainfall patterns may have provided an incentive to emigrate, especially in conjunction with the increasingly aggregated and violent village conditions that characterized the thirteenth-century central Mesa Verde region.

Figure 4.4 also shows that, except in the western Mesa Verde region, annual rainfall would have generally been sufficient for dry farming in most regions and years, using the 12 and 14 in requirement for maize previously discussed. Even during the major prolonged droughts of the 1100s and 1200s, as calculated here, yearly precipitation rates rarely fell below 12 in, except in the western Mesa Verde and Cibola-Puerco regions (fig. 4.1). Thus, it appears that even though droughts likely caused problems, annual precipitation rates were usually high enough to meet the minimum requirements for maize dry farming, even during arguably dry years.

Applying the annual rainfall requirements for maize across regions, however, likely fails to capture each region's unique environmental characteristics, not to mention the diversity of farming practices employed. Our current inability to tease apart seasonal precipitation records from tree rings adds to the difficulties. The timing of rainfall is as critical to agriculture as the rainfall annual quantity. Therefore, long-term disruptions of seasonal patterns, which are not readily visible in the annual reconstructions, may be more relevant to understanding prehispanic southwestern demography than is drought alone. Such breakdowns in established regimes would have had major impacts not only on agricultural productivity but also on peoples' relationships to one another, as well as on their worldviews.

The regional comparisons presented here provide a first step toward understanding possible climatic "pushes" and "pulls" that may have influenced migration from the northern Southwest. An unprecedented disruption to the bimodal seasonal precipitation pattern and a prolonged period of cool temperatures across the northern Southwest began during the 1200s and persisted for several hundred years. When this is coupled with the better-known Great Drought of the late 1200s, the northern Southwest may have become a rather difficult landscape to dry farm. During these poor conditions, many people moved out of the northern San Juan and Kayenta regions and into large communities along perennial rivers and in lower regions with different precipitation regimes. In particular, the northern Rio Grande, the upper and middle Gila River, and their tributaries—places where we have the clearest (albeit variable) evidence for Puebloan migrants from the Kayenta and northern San Juan regions—experienced significant increases in population. These places would have provided warmer conditions, more reliable water supplies, and possibly more secure social conditions, because their regions were seemingly immune to the breakdown in the bimodal precipitation pattern and had less-variable precipitation regimes. The lower elevations of some of these places contributed to adequate growing seasons despite the cooling temperatures. Therefore, it appears that climate did play some part in the depopulation of the northern Southwest, as well as attracting northern migrants into certain areas. The exact role of climate in this process, however, remains unclear.

Whether or not the climate was so poor that it rendered vast regions of the northern Southwest too dry and cold to farm—a key question we can't yet answer with certainty—significant and long-term breakdowns in established patterns could have been catalysts for a number of social changes that swept the Southwest during this time. Although Glowacki (this vol.) reviews the interplay between climate change and social transformation in the Mesa Verde region in greater detail, the effects of climatic variability on social institutions may have been more direct than we often consider. For example, it is quite likely that there was an ideological aspect to the depopulation of the northern Southwest (Glowacki, this vol.; see also Lipe 1995). If ritual practices, social institutions, and their leaders were responsible for ensuring rainfall and successful harvests—as is often the case among pre-industrial agriculturalists, and historical southwestern indigenous peoples specifically—then a major climatic disruption may have entrained serious social repercussions. The new ideological institutions that spread through the Southwest during the late 1200s and 1300s (i.e., southwestern [Crown 1994] and kachina [Adams 1991; Schaafsma 1992; Schaafsma and Schaafsma 1974] cults) likely contributed to the successful integration of migrants into local settings (e.g., Duff 2002:175–183), particularly those in the northern Rio Grande, along the Little Colorado River, and in south-central Arizona. Perhaps the attraction and success of these new ritual and ideological systems, which clearly emphasized water symbolism if not rainfall itself, was due in part to the fact that they occurred in the regions least affected by the Great Drought and by the breakdown in the bimodal precipitation pattern.

In conclusion, the data presented here suggest that perturbations in annual rainfall rates, such as the Great Drought, cannot alone account for the migration from the northern Southwest and into particular regions during the thirteenth and fourteenth centuries. If this demographic shift was related to climate in some manner, the perturbation must have been similarly long-term and spatially extensive, and possibly more severe than anything observed recently. The major cooling episode and a breakdown in seasonal precipitation patterns between AD 1200 and 1400 may have been just such catalysts, as northern migrants ultimately moved to the places that were least affected by these perturbations. Since there is no historical analog for these poor climatic conditions, current agricultural productivity models may underestimate their effects, as Kohler argues in the next chapter. Moreover, climate is only one component in the complexity of understanding farming potential. Development of agricultural paleoproductivity models like that of the VEP (Kohler et al. 2007) for recipient regions, which could consider a whole suite of social, environmental, and climatic variables, would greatly aid in evaluating the importance climate and farming potential had for migration decisions. At this point, we can conclude that a cascade of related climatic downturns and changing social conditions contributed to the depopulation of the northern Southwest and to the formation of large, nucleated villages in the post-1300 era.

Acknowledgments

A first draft of this chapter, co-authored with John G. Jones, was delivered at the seventy-second annual meeting of the Society for American Archaeology in the symposium "New Light on the Thirteenth-Century Depopulation of the Northern Southwest." The final product was greatly enhanced by insights provided by the Amerind seminar participants, especially those of Jeff Dean, Larry Benson, and Tim Kohler. Additionally, I thank Jeff Dean and the Southwest Paleoclimate Project of the University of Arizona's Laboratory of Tree-Ring Research for providing the tree-ring precipitation reconstructions presented here. The Beef Pasture pollen study, funded by a grant of the National Science Foundation (BCS-0119981) to Tim Kohler, was undertaken during my graduate enrollment at Washington State University. I thank Tim Kohler, John Jones, and Andrew Duff for their assistance with the project.

5

A New Paleoproductivity Reconstruction for Southwestern Colorado, and Its Implications for Understanding Thirteenth-Century Depopulation

Timothy A. Kohler

> In complex systems, we accept that processes that occur
> simultaneously on different scales or levels are important,
> and the intricate behaviour of the whole system depends on
> its units in a nontrivial way.
> —Vicsek 2002:131

With its well-known and high-resolution archaeological record, the northern San Juan region is a place where we can hope to make relatively firm statements about the causes of human behavior. And as Varien recounts in the first chapter of this volume, no event or process in this region has attracted more popular and scientific attention than its thirteenth-century depopulation. This would then appear to be one region—and one process—for which the data are so strong that archaeologists would long ago have agreed on the causes of the thirteenth-century population collapse. This volume is simultaneously evidence that this has not been the case, and an argument that new data and approaches are putting that old goal firmly in our sights.

In this chapter, I take what might be called a complex adaptive-systems perspective on the thirteenth-century depopulation. By this I mean several things. First, social and natural processes governed by evolutionary logics are expected to interact, and neither is given unexamined explanatory preference. Second, there is a commitment to examining these processes in as disaggregated a way as possible, with the expectation that systems-level novelty frequently arises from the interactions of constituent entities. Here, I use agent-based modeling to leverage our insight on human environmental impacts. Third, we expect that even though human societies and their dynamics will have some special properties because of their greater use of symbolic systems and the Lamarckian nature of culture change, nevertheless their organizational and dynamic commonalities with other living systems remain significant. I would also include in this approach much of what Bintliff (2007) has recently characterized as the key tendencies of a "chaos-complexity" approach to understanding change and stability in human societies.

I begin by reviewing results of the Village Ecodynamics Project (VEP), focusing on our estimates for maize production from AD 600 to 1300 (Kohler et al. 2007), a regional reconstruction of low-frequency climate change (Wright 2006), and local estimates of momentary human population through time (Ortman, Varien, and Gripp 2007; Varien et al. 2007). These data can be complemented by estimates of the human impact on forest and game resources as modeled by the VEP agent-based simulations (see Kohler et al. 2007). After this review, I integrate the most relevant data from the thirteenth century into a longer-term perspective. I then add a more general discussion of inferred changes in social organization in the late Pueblo II and Pueblo III (PII, PIII) periods that seem to me to have been leading toward a society whose organization was less robust and more brittle (as these terms are defined below).

A complete understanding of these large-scale population movements would ideally begin from four time-series of information for both the population source and the sink areas. These are (1) paleoproductivity data that are sensitive to high-frequency changes in both precipitation and temperature, (2) proxy climatic series that can help us put that high-frequency variability into a low-frequency perspective, (3) temporally sensitive estimates of local prehistoric population size, and (4) models that specify how population size relates to access to critical environmental resources such as fuelwood and animal protein (Johnson 2006; Johnson et al. 2005). Any credible explanation will need to consider whether differential per-capita subsistence opportunities were influential in decisions to migrate, rather than simply making assumptions about what was important.

Unfortunately, southwestern archaeologists and paleoclimatologists are still a long way from being able to provide all of these series (though Wright, this volume, reviews the available climatic data in the central Mesa Verde region as well as in possible regions receiving population from the central Mesa Verde in the AD 1200s). We can, however, fulfill these requirements reasonably well for the portion of the central Mesa Verde (CMV) region studied by the VEP (figs. 1.1, 1.2), as we'll see below. In the absence of comparable data from other areas, however, we cannot perform the comparative evaluations of different areas that presumably informed the movements of Pueblo peoples.

One approach to doing the best we can while waiting for these series to become available would be to tell our story from the CMV and try to fill in the "other sides of the story" with what hints we can glean from available archaeological and paleoclimatic data for possible destination areas for the central Mesa Verde populations. This is, in part at least, the strategy of Cordell and colleagues (2007).

These authors begin by proposing that the shape and size of ceramic style zones (e.g., as depicted by Roney 1995) provide evidence for social interactions among communities that are often at some distance from each other. Following arguments by Rautman (1996) and others, they suggest that if these networks evolved to buffer risks, then they ought to straddle areas that are climatically as uncorrelated as possible.[1]

For the three centuries from AD 900 to 1200, correlations among five tree-ring series selected to be representative of the Kayenta, Mesa Verde, Cibola, Chama, and Santa Fe areas allow them to show that using this logic, Mesa Verde ought to be linked with Santa Fe (and ought *not* to be linked with Kayenta, for example). Since they follow Roney (1995) and others in identifying significant similarities between Mesa Verde ceramics and northern Rio Grande ceramics, including Santa Fe Black-on-white but particularly Galisteo Black-on-white, they see significant support for their proposal that Mesa Verde and Santa Fe were part of a single exchange network/style zone. By inspecting the hundred-year running mean Z-scores for the Mesa Verde and Santa Fe series, they further suggest that there was a gradient of attraction towards the south, concluding that "for the 1200–1500 period, the precipitation regime near Santa Fe was not only different from that at Mesa Verde but was also generally better (above average)" (Cordell et al. 2007:394). (My own reading of their figures suggests that the period in which the Santa Fe precipitation series is markedly more favorable than the Mesa Verde precipitation series is limited to the fifteenth century, although in the critical late thirteenth century, the Santa Fe Z-scores are slightly more positive than those in Mesa Verde.)

Although attempts such as that by Cordell and colleagues (2007) are essential, in this chapter I restrict myself to outlining the VEP approach to estimating paleoproductivity series that are sensitive to high-frequency changes in both precipitation and temperature. Then, instead of trying to draw large-scale conclusions that link the VEP area and possible population-receiving areas to the south, I will build a more local model that brings together the four strands identified above—paleoproductivity, low-frequency climate change, population size, and the access to critical natural resources—with some cross-scale discussions of the characteristics of robustness in living systems in general. The resulting model provides a synthetic hypothesis for the AD 1200s depopulation of the entire northern Southwest, from the perspective of the central Mesa Verde region.

High-Frequency Maize Production Estimates in the CMV

Burns

Burns (1983) was responsible for the first temporally precise reconstruction of potential maize yields in the Pueblo Southwest. He chose the CMV both because of its dense prehispanic farming occupation and because there he was able to find local historical records of dry-farmed maize (fig. 5.1) and beans from the 1920s through about 1960. These twentieth-century agricultural production records were not without problems for his purposes. For example, no yields were published for a few years. The period between 1930 and 1960, for which the production data were best, also witnessed great change in agricultural technology, which complicated the identification of the response of maize to annual precipitation records.

Burns therefore removed what he called a "technology trend" by regressing historic-yield data on pounds of fertilizer applied per harvested acre, which increased dramatically following World War II as manufacturers of explosives sought to develop other markets for similar compounds (Pollan 2006:41–47). Burns considered fertilizer use to be closely correlated with other uses of technology that had similar effects in boosting yields (e.g., the use of mechanized equipment, pesticides, and herbicides; as well as hybrid varieties and closer planting intervals

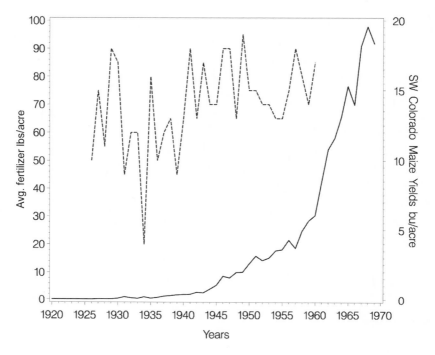

Figure 5.1. The solid line shows the average pounds of fertilizer applied per harvested acre in Colorado, 1920–1969. The dashed line shows southwestern Colorado maize yields, 1926–1960 (values for 1944–1947 are estimates). Data from Burns (1983:321–323).

among plants). Figure 5.1 shows the increase in fertilizer from 1931 to 1960, the period Burns used for calibration.

With the "technology trend" removed (Burns used the residuals from the regression of production on current and lagged fertilizer use for the remainder of his analyses), he used as independent variables several tree-ring series, both lagged and unlagged, to achieve a reasonably good fit with the historic-yield data, which he was then able to retrodict for the years preceding the historically available yield data. Using five tree-ring vectors as independent variables, he reconstructed an average yield of 12.87 bu/ac for dry-farmed maize in southwestern Colorado between AD 652 and 1968 (adjusted for removal of the technology trend) ($s = 1.92$; Burns 1983:371), or 795 kg/ha ($s = 120.5$, $R^2 = 0.33$, adjusted

$R^2 = 0.20$; Burns 1983:335). Of course, these potential yields refer only to those portions of southwestern Colorado farmed historically.

Van West

Better known to contemporary audiences than Burns's study is Van West's work in the same area beginning in the late 1980s (a slightly condensed version of her dissertation was published in 1994). Van West used the same historic-production series discovered by Burns, but she limited her focus to those values from Montezuma County. In other ways, her analysis proceeded quite differently from that of Burns; for example, she used a different (though overlapping) set of tree-ring data as independent variables, as well as using Palmer Drought Severity Index (PDSI) values as intermediary predictors for maize production. (See Berry and Benson, this volume, for more discussion of the Palmer Drought Severity Index.) Her method for removing the technology trend from this 1931–1960 series was simply to add "year" as another independent variable, along with the PDSI value as estimated from climatic and soils data for the historical period, assuming that the technology inputs (for example, increasing use through the 1931–1960 period of hybrid seed and mechanized equipment) have an approximately linear and positive effect throughout this period. Her reconstructed values for maize from the historical period can be correlated with the actual values from 1931 to 1960 at a value of $R^2 = 0.49$ (adjusted R^2 not reported) (Van West 1994:101). Although this fit is much higher than that reported by Burns, the values are not comparable, because Van West's R^2 value includes the fit attributable to the temporal (technology) trend, whereas Burns's measure does not.

Van West's most important innovation, though, was to employ a geographic information system to spatialize the annual predictions, allowing her to create separate reconstructions for various combinations of soil depths and elevations. Her completed reconstruction, averaged across the VEP area, is shown in figure 5.2a. This has earned a number of discussions in the literature (e.g., Van West and Lipe 1992; Van West and Kohler 1995). Van West's production estimates (average = 626.7 kg/ha, $s = 103$, for AD 900–1300) were lower than those of Burns, but this is mostly due to the fact that her reconstruction extended to some of the less-productive lands in her study area, which were not historically

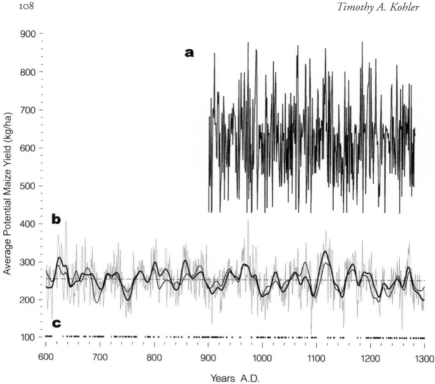

Figure 5.2. (a) Van West's (1994) potential production estimates for maize in the VEP study area. (b) VEP estimates for the same area. The light-gray rough line shows the annual estimates using the Almagre series proxy for temperature. The heavy smooth line is a seven-year smooth using a spline function for these same data. The light-gray straight dashed line at 256 kg/ha is the mean value for this same series. Finally, the remaining line shows the seven-year spline smoothing for this production series using the scores on the first principal component of the Almagre and San Francisco Peaks series as the temperature proxy. (c) Dots mark years in which the value for the Almagre indexed series is lower than any of the values for that series for 1931–1960, which was used in establishing the relationship between production and climate in the historical period.

farmed. Even so, her reconstruction implied that this area could always have supported thousands of people, even in the late AD 1200s. This research coincided with a generally declining popularity for models of human behavior in which environmental factors held a causal role, and it led to increased interest in models to explain the depopulation of the northern Southwest that featured social advantages in probable destination areas or social disadvantages to remaining in place.

The VEP

Village Ecodynamics Project research into paleoproductivity estimates began around 2002 with a desire to extend Van West's reconstructions back to AD 600, to fill in a few areas for which she did not have soils data, and to see whether giving temperature a more explicit role in the reconstruction improved the fit of the reconstruction to the available historical-production data. These efforts are also explained in work by Kohler and colleagues (2007:64–67) and Varien and others (2007), and they will be laid out in more detail in an anticipated VEP final report. Here, I give an abbreviated version of how this new reconstruction was built:

- After assessing the goodness of fit between various aspects of instrumented VEP-area temperature records and many high-elevation western tree-ring series, we chose two bristlecone-pine ring-width series to provide the temperature signal: Graybill's Almagre series (Graybill 1983), to the northeast, and Salzer's San Francisco Peaks series (Salzer and Kipfmueller 2005), to the southwest. We used the scores on the first principal component extracted from these two series in one reconstruction, and the Almagre series by itself in another.
- Like Van West, we produced separate PDSI reconstructions for various combinations of soil depth and elevation, using instrumented data for the historical period, and then assessed the correlation between these PDSIs and the Mesa Verde Douglas fir–indexed series, which turned out to be significant and positive in each case.
- Like Van West, we were then able to retrodict each of these PDSI sequences back in time—in our case to AD 600—after which we pooled the PDSI values for those soils used to dry farm corn and pintos in the historical period.
- Then, we regressed historic-period maize and bean yields for those soils on these PDSIs, on our two proxies for growing season length/ growing season temperature, and on year as a proxy for the technology trend, achieving relatively high measures of goodness of fit (for maize

and principal component score proxy, $R^2 = 0.59$, adjusted $R^2 = 0.54$; for maize and the Almagre proxy, $R^2 = 0.62$, adjusted $R^2 = 0.58$).

- We then adjusted these predictions appropriately for the other soils in the study area, imposing some limits on how much production can be achieved at very high elevations with very short growing seasons using a function that takes into account both how high the location is and how cold it was (according to our temperature proxies) in any particular year. This correction has an effect only on areas between 2100 m (6890 ft) and 2395 m (7860 ft) in elevation, and then only in cold years. We model no maize production coming out of areas above 7,860 ft.

- Finally, we apply two additional downward corrections. The first renorms production to be more similar to what we suspect was achieved with aboriginal varieties and planting densities, as opposed to those in use from 1931 to 1960, and the second removes some production for those soils that the soil survey considers as having severe restrictions for hand planting.

After these steps, we end up with a potential maize-production series (fig. 5.2b) that is considerably lower than that of Van West. The mean production for the seven-hundred-year period is about 4 bu/ac or 253.8 kg/ha ($s = 45.8$) for the reconstruction using the scores on the first principal component of the Almagre and San Francisco series as the temperature proxy, or 256.2 kg/ha ($s = 47.3$) using just the Almagre series as the temperature proxy. Our estimates of production are particularly lower than West's for the period from the very late 1100s through around 1240, a generally cold period (Wright, this vol.).

Even though I believe that this is the most accurate reconstruction ever made for potential production of a cultivated crop in a prehistoric sequence, it is nevertheless plagued by three main difficulties. First, our training (calibration) period from 1931 to 1960 was relatively warm compared to the previous fifteen hundred years. In figure 5.2c, black dots mark the years in which the Almagre series suggests colder temperatures than anything from 1931 to 1960. (We would see similar patterns if we were looking at the scores on the first principal component of the Almagre and the San Francisco peaks series.) These cold years are especially clustered in the early 900s, around 1000, in the late 1100s and early 1200s, and in the late 1200s.

For these years, we are forced to extrapolate our production estimates beyond the limits of our sample data. As anyone with a first course in regression knows, this is a bad idea, but we can't see any alternative— and since we are using *linear* regression, we are implicitly assuming that maize response to growing seasons that are shorter and colder than anything seen in our area between 1931 and 1960 will simply be lower in a linear fashion. Maize growth, however, stops entirely at temperatures of around 5° C, and at 0° C or just slightly less, the plant dies, severely and nonlinearly reducing its yield (Hunt et al. 2003: figs. 4–7). Because of this effect, our linear estimates are probably optimistic for the years marked by dots on figure 5.2, but we can't know by how much.

The second main reason our reconstruction might be in error in some periods is that it is based on tree rings and so likely underestimates the effects of low-frequency variability (Cook et al. 1995). Figure 5.3 superimposes Wright's pollen-based (and therefore low-frequency) standardized reconstructions of temperature (T) and winter precipitation (W) on our spline-smoothed high-frequency maize-production estimates from figure 5.2b. We don't know how to appropriately combine these low- and high-frequency data, but we think that their juxtaposition can at least be used to help understand the probable direction of error for the high-frequency series. Thus, we may be underestimating production in the mid-700s and even in the infamous mid-1100s, when both low-frequency trends are favorable. On the other hand, we suspect that we are overestimating production from the early 800s through the late 900s, when long-term trends in both temperature and winter precipitation bottom out, and also in the mid- through late 1200s. Differences in spatial scale for these estimates have to be kept in mind. The high-frequency reconstructions are tuned to the VEP landscape and may not be extrapolatable very far from there. The temperature (and perhaps to a smaller extent, the winter precipitation) trends reconstructed from pollen are probably reflecting widespread conditions in the northern Southwest, since temperature data have greater spatial coherence than precipitation data (Jones and Thompson 2003).

The third problem with our paleoproduction series is that tree rings always underestimate lows in their limiting factors, partly because of tree death, but mostly because of threshold effects. (They may underestimate highs as well, though that is less of a concern here.) As Dean said

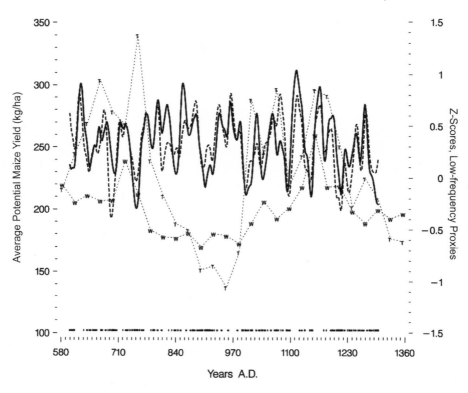

Figure 5.3. Standardized pollen ratios from Beef Pasture: winter-precipitation proxy (W) using sedge-to-cheno-am pollen ratios, and temperature proxy (T) using ponderosa pine pollen to spruce pollen ratios, both from Wright (2006:75–83), plotted against spline-smoothed VEP paleoproduction estimates as in figure 5.2b, and Almagre index "underflows" as in figure 5.2c.

during the Amerind seminar at which this chapter was discussed, "You can't go lower than a missing ring!" So if a tree species in a particular area fails to put on any rings when annual precipitation is below, say, 20 cm, then a reconstruction based on that species in that area will not discriminate between the effects on maize production of 19 cm versus 0 cm in annual precipitation.

Together, these three problems practically guarantee that there were years in which the production was in fact below (and possibly far below) what we reconstruct in figure 5.2b. Overestimates are especially likely at (1) local minima in the high-frequency reconstruction; (2) periods when

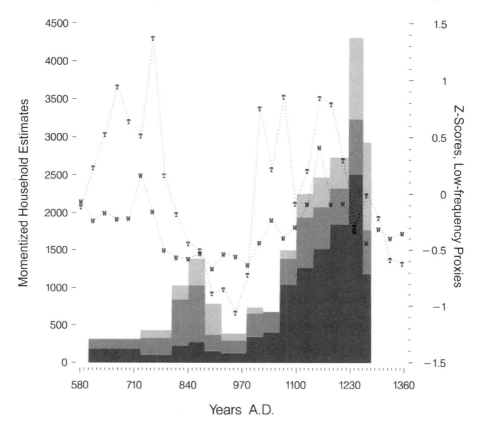

Figure 5.4. Grayscale histograms showing three estimates of momentary population for the VEP areas (see Varien et al. [2007] for derivation). Dotted lines marked with T and W display low-frequency pollen-based proxies for temperature and winter precipitation, respectively, from figure 5.3.

one or both low-frequency proxies are low; and (3) in the years marked by dots, when production was likely more temperature limited than we estimate.

VEP Demography

So how do these data align with our local demographic reconstruction? Figure 5.4 displays what we believe we know about the paleodemography of the VEP area through time, as documented in detail by Ortman and others (2007) and Varien and colleagues (2007). We favor the reconstruction provided by the middle bars, for which the other two reconstructions provide informal confidence intervals. All three series identify two cycles of population increase and decrease, with a Pueblo I (PI) population peak, followed by a population trough and then by a rapid recolonization in the late PII period. The sharp population peak that we reconstruct in the PIII period between 1225 and 1260 was not recognized prior to the VEP's paleodemographic work. Note also that a significant local depopulation had begun by 1260, cutting population size by some 50 percent (see also Varien, this vol.).

The two major population declines in this series align, in a surprisingly clear way, with major declines in both of the low-frequency indices, although the decline of the smaller PI population is in conjunction with sharper declines in the pollen-based indices. (This is comparable to an effect noted by Berry and Benson in their chapter, where low population levels are less responsive to the same magnitude of drought than are later, higher populations in the same areas.) The PII population build-up appears slightly after the low-frequency indices indicate greatly improved conditions for farming. However, both the AD 800s PI population influx and the sharp peak in the PIII population in the early to mid-1200s coincide with deteriorating low-frequency conditions. I suggest that both of these peaks represent populations leaving less-favorable areas for the refugium of the central Mesa Verde. By that same logic, the Basketmaker III, early PI, and PII growth and immigration into the CMV would be viewed as responses to opportunities—leaving good areas for a better one. If the late PI and PIII immigrations are correctly viewed as responses to necessity—and note that they are both followed by partial or complete emigrations—then it is particularly remarkable that the PIII peak also overlaps with a period of very poor local high-frequency production conditions in the early 1200s. This provides information as to how truly bad production conditions must have been in the source areas (probably to the west and northwest) for these populations, particularly since the destination area was already densely populated.

This leads to the very tentative conclusion (really, just a hypothesis at this stage) that both the late PI and the late PIII immigrations into our area—visible in the population peaks in both periods—were caused by populations that turned out to be passing through the CMV and pausing there on their way south, out of the northern San Juan entirely. Even though these populations stayed in the CMV for only one or two generations at most, their presence would have exacerbated per-capita resource-supply problems caused by poor climate conditions in both cases.

My second tentative conclusion follows from the high population levels in the 1200s noted above, in conjunction with the maize-production conditions discussed in the previous section. Maize production is likely to have been low enough in the VEP during some portions of the 1200s to have caused severe stress and possibly widespread famine.

Other Critical Resources in the VEP

One advantage of our agent-based models (Kohler et al. 2007) is that they provide us with estimates of the per-household costs for obtaining enough maize, meat protein, water, and fuels through time, given the parameter estimates used and the human populations generated in the context of those parameter estimates (see also Johnson 2005; Johnson et al. 2005). Here, I report some preliminary results from a recent sweep of 7 parameters with 2 values each, resulting in 128 runs, using version 2.72 of the simulation. The populations of households averaged across these runs peaked at 2,672 in AD 988, which is considerably below our middle estimate of the population peak in the archaeological sequence (3,234 momentary households in the 1225–1260 period). For this reason, the landscape "histories" in the models may underestimate the degree of resource depression actually experienced.

Depression of high-ranked game (overhunting) by dense populations in prehistory has been well documented in many areas (Grayson 2001), and we see this effect for deer in all our simulations. Figure 5.5 (heavy dark gray line) shows the decline in the total number of deer on the landscape, averaged across these runs. This is in accord with research by Muir and Driver (2002), who document a widespread empirical pattern throughout the northern San Juan region, after PI times, of decreasing proportions of artiodactyl remains in archaeological assemblages.

More surprising is the effect that populations also had on lower-ranked game, at least according to our simulations. In an analysis of

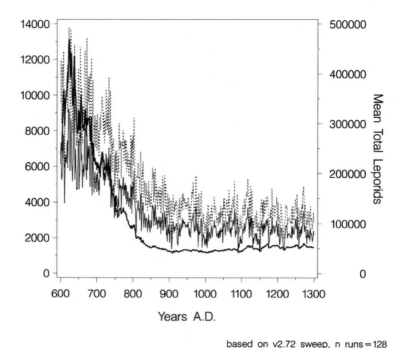

based on v2.72 sweep, n runs = 128

Figure 5.5. The dark solid line represents the annual average number of deer on the landscape, the medium-gray solid line graphs the number of hares, and the dotted line the number of rabbits, on the landscape (all three from the agent-based simulation). Reduction of lower-ranked game by the agents in the simulation might not be so marked if agents had access to domesticated turkey.

these same simulation results, Johnson (2008) noted a depression of hare (black-tailed jackrabbit) populations to approximately 30 percent of the number expected without human predation (see medium gray solid line in fig. 5.5). Results for rabbit (desert cottontails) are similar or more severe (see black dotted line in fig. 5.5). Averaged across all these runs, between 22 and 40 percent of the households were not meeting their modest protein goals (averaging 20 g/person/day from meat) in the last four hundred years of the simulation. Given this protein deficit, it is not surprising that analysis of faunal remains shows that the PII and PIII populations in our area raised and consumed turkey

(Driver 2002), even though they apparently had to feed turkeys corn. Our simulations do not include either wild or domestic turkey as a potential protein source, but since these same simulations point to protein as becoming limiting on this landscape, we plan to introduce wild turkey hunting, and raising domestic turkey, into future versions of the simulation.

Mean distance traveled by households to obtain water in these simulations increases from about 1.4 km early in the simulation to almost 3 km near the simulations' population peak; it then declined slowly through time. (For contemporary context, though, many women in rural India make round trips considerably longer than this, three times a day, to fetch enough water for their households [National Commission for Women 2005].) Mean distance traveled by households to obtain fuel wood increased from about 200 m early in the simulation to about 1 km by about halfway through the simulation and then remained relatively static. This last figure likely underestimates—perhaps greatly—distances traveled for fuel wood in the 1200s, since our agents are both less numerous and much less aggregated than were Pueblo households in the thirteenth-century VEP area. (Duff and colleagues, this volume, report little macrobotanical evidence for local woodland depletion surrounding PIII settlements, although forest reduction is suggested by their pollen data.) On the other hand, the simulation probably overestimates distances to water at this time, when settlement locations seem to have emphasized proximity to springs.

These data suggest to me a third tentative conclusion: despite the inherent richness of its deep soils, relatively high rainfall, and varied topography, by the 1200s the CMV landscape's ability to provide natural-resource services (especially wild game and fuel wood) to its dense farming populations was significantly reduced.

The Last Century in the CMV

Here, I combine all the data presented above with some results from other chapters in this volume, and with information from other regions, to suggest a synthetic model for the depopulation of the central Mesa Verde region.

From the late 1100s through about 1240, deteriorating low-frequency precipitation and temperature trends combined with very poor high-frequency production conditions to provoke massive population dislocations in the northern Southwest. People moved out of less-favorable areas to the west (see Glowacki, this vol.) into the central Mesa Verde region, the southern San Juan basin, and the northern Rio Grande. (For example, the kiva in Saltbush Pueblo in Bandelier National Monument was remodeled around AD 1200 to highlight a suite of San Juan characteristics, though Boyer and others [this vol.] attribute these to a southern rather than northern San Juan influence.) Populations in the CMV were by now extremely reliant on maize, both for their calories and, through the filter of turkey, for much of their protein, so poor maize production was doubly damaging.

The surge of population into the VEP study area between about 1220 and 1240, coupled with raiding from the Totah documented elsewhere (Kohler and Turner 2006) combined to produce a very defensive site posture and also considerable ritual intensification by AD 1240, especially in the eastern portions of the VEP area and on Mesa Verde, as noted by Glowacki (this vol.). The increased population exacerbated the highly unfavorable population/resource ratios that we have documented by comparing the actual population sizes achieved in our area with those emerging from the simulation (Kohler et al. 2008). The inefficient settlement poise on the landscape resulting from the defensive posture of community centers founded after about AD 1240 would only have made matters worse.

Although local high-frequency conditions and low-frequency temperature trends were somewhat more favorable by the mid-1200s, the period from 1240 to 1265 is one of several manifestations of the "Medieval megadrought" identified throughout the West by Herweijer and colleagues (2007), with the 1250s being especially unfavorable. These effects discouraged movement out of the CMV into other areas that were not as well watered.

The historically innovative response to the aggression that presumably accompanied famine—to concentrate population around water sources—was probably not conducive to public health and likely increased mortality rates. Fertility rates could also have been trending lower. Mace (2008) reviews the evolutionary logics for the lower fertility rates that affect later cities; these might also have operated, on smaller scales, in thirteenth-century aggregates.

Raiding among the coalitions of CMV communities that Kohler and Varien (in press) infer for the mid-1200s—or, possibly, harassment by mobile foragers—may have limited safe access to farm plots and hunting areas outside the villages. In any case, dispersed settlements more or less disappeared by the 1260–1280 period.

A final active emigration stream out of the CMV to the south was well established, at the latest, by the mid-1260s. By around 1270, more than half the population that had been there around 1240 was gone. Push factors would have been dominant in these departure decisions, though selective migration—the possibility of some attraction to social and religious developments in the northern Rio Grande—can't be excluded (see Lipe, this vol.).

Remaining populations faced sharply deteriorating high-frequency conditions after 1270. These people would have been motivated to leave by these poor conditions, by the sharply escalating violence documented at places like Castle Rock and Sand Canyon pueblos (Kuckelman, this vol.), and by problems of social effectiveness stemming from having lost significant numbers of their peers. Pull factors probably became increasingly important as the remnant populations sought to rejoin their kin in new and probably less strife-ridden locations to the south and southeast.

Discussion

One way to interpret this account is to conclude that climate change was chiefly responsible for the depopulation of the northern Southwest (and perhaps, therefore, for the dramatic and almost simultaneous transformation of societies and economies in the northern Rio Grande as well). After all, physical catastrophes have always brought on major evolutionary transitions and evolutionary innovation in living forms (Erwin 2006). In the specifically human record, the new Holocene climatic regime seems to have enabled the major subsistence and organizational transformations of the Neolithic (e.g., Richerson et al. 2001).

And yet, there is good reason not to overstate the degree of responsibility of climate change in the depopulation of the northern Southwest.

It is not clear that the climate of the 1200s was much worse than that of the 900s, and yet some populations hung on in the VEP area during the tenth century, although they radically altered their typical settlement locations and sizes to do so (Kohler 2007). Why did things turn out so differently in the last three decades of the 1200s from the way they were in the first three decades of the 900s? I think there are four reasons, all involving history to some extent: *demographic* history, *landscape* history, *social* and *institutional* history, and history of *conflict*.

In the Pueblo Southwest, populations grew rapidly from about AD 600 to 1200 as they underwent a Neolithic demographic transition (Kohler and Varien, in press; Kohler, Glaude et al. 2008). This demographic expansion was enabled by climatic amelioration, including both warmer and wetter conditions that allowed the spread of agriculture and increasingly dense populations into places like the Virgin Branch area, the Virgin River area, and Fremont areas. This expansion had only partly filled these new zones when the climatic downturn of the tenth century began. The relatively low population density meant that populations could rearrange themselves as necessary at this time with a minimum of conflict. Perhaps this was no longer possible by the last century of the northern Southwest's occupation.

And what of landscape history? Living things in general are enmeshed in two streams of vertical transmission: the genetic, which is of course broadly recognized, and the ecological, which is not so clearly acknowledged but which is at the core of the "niche construction" framework (Odling-Smee et al. 2003). The concept of niche construction recognizes that "organisms . . . interact with environments, take energy and resources from environments, make micro- and macrohabitat choices with respect to environments, construct artifacts, emit detritus and die in environments, and by doing all these things, modify at least some of the natural selection pressures present in their own, and in each other's [and their successors] local environments" (Odling-Smee et al. 2003:1). The dense human populations of the 1200s—more so than the much less numerous PI populations—altered the environment in many ways that we have already discussed. It is likely that there were other impacts that remain to be quantified—for example, on soil nitrogen and on topsoil resources. Presumably, Pueblo people also enriched their environments to some extent, for example through selection of maize varieties well suited to local conditions, turkey domestication, small-scale agricultural features that helped preserve surface water and sediment, and the much larger reservoirs that also conserved surface waters. On balance, though, it is highly probable that the sizes of the populations supported in the VEP area in the AD 1200s depressed per-capita availability of critical resources significantly, and that this was amplified by the effects of changing climates.

But of course, humans are not just like other organisms. To a greater extent than other organisms, humans are enmeshed in a third, cultural stream of inheritance that operates alongside of and interacts with the processes of genetic and ecological inheritance. For our purposes, this has two especially important consequences. The first is that through cultural and cognitive processes, humans overlay physical landscapes with a series of social rights of access (Adler 1996b) and systems of meanings that, when violated, threaten the operation of society.

The long-term processes of adaptation to the environment created by Pueblo farmers may have had some interesting social and institutional consequences relevant to understanding the thirteenth-century depopulation. Elsewhere, I have argued that lineages or subclans (represented archaeologically in the northern San Juan by linear, multihousehold roomblocks) represent increased salience for this level of social organization, at the expense of the household. This occurred by the mid-PI period at places like Grass Mesa Pueblo (Kohler and Reed, in press). Reed and I have proposed that this salience was due to the advantages of representing group membership unambiguously (as lineages do) for solving the coordination problem of forming large enough groups for the increasingly long-distance hunting of deer.

Whether or not that interpretation is right, the PI populations exhibited a degree of robustness not exhibited by the PIII populations, perhaps in part because of the evident modularity of organization. Here, I follow Jen (2005) in considering robustness to be a measure of feature persistence in systems under perturbation; the features in question might include aspects of the structure of the system or some measure of performance or function. Krakauer and Plotkin (2005) adopt this definition of robustness and use it to consider biological systems broadly. They point to a tension between transformation accompanied by the generation of diversity on the one hand, and the persistence of structural regularities on the other. They suggest that the proper aim of the study of robustness is to uncover the evolved mechanisms that promote the persistence of regularities.

According to Krakauer (2004), biological systems achieve robustness by employing specific principles; I list the eight most relevant of these in table 5.1. These seem to depend on what Krakauer (2004) calls "metaprinciples" of robustness on which the others depend in turn. These metaprinciples are the use of a multiplicity of self-contained units, discretely and sparsely connected, to ensure some autonomy of processing and "damage control"; and saturation effects to damp the consequences of nonlinearity in input. This chapter is not the place to rigorously translate these into terms useful for archaeologists, but in table 5.1, I make some trial analogies for these biological principles within southwestern societies.

With the possible exception (among the large PI VEP villages) of the McPhee cluster, whose society may have resisted decomposition and carried a germ of complexity all the way to Chaco Canyon (Wilshusen and Van Dyke 2006), the easy decomposability of PI villages along lineage or subclan lines probably contributed to the robustness of the PI populations, in the sense that some populations were able to persist in the VEP area following the collapse of the PI villages. Quite possibly these *societies* (and certainly the PI villages) were not generally very robust against social and environmental perturbations, but their easy decomposability allowed the persistence of *populations* nonetheless. Apparently, PII societies developed stronger institutions (such as sodalities) that tied lineages, subclans, or clans together, preventing this relatively easy social decomposition, but at some expense to degree of modularity and perhaps degree of distributed control. The PII communities do not cleave painlessly but are sufficiently interdependent that when one part fails, the totality fails. A possible result of the PII community reorganization is that small social and environmental perturbations would not cause the largest current social units to break into smaller segments—which would not be adaptive in the conditions of the intense social competition in which these societies existed—but these same changes may have resulted in decreased robustness against large perturbations. These tendencies seem to have been all the more true of PIII communities, especially after the mid-1200s intensification of communal ritual identified by Glowacki in her chapter in this volume.

Table 5.1. Principles for achieving robustness in biological systems and possible analogous mechanisms for achieving robustness in prehispanic northern San Juan–region societies

Principle	Definition/example	Possible mechanisms in prehispanic pueblo societies
Canalization	Mechanisms that suppress phenotypic variation during development (Waddington 1942)	Frequency-dependent-biased cultural transmission (conformist transmission) (Boyd and Richerson 1985:204–240)
Neutrality	Selective equivalence of different phenotypes (not an adaptive means of suppressing variability)	Unnoticed variability
Redundancy	E.g., in molecular biology, where removing or silencing a gene early in development results in no measurable difference in the phenotype—that gene is said to be redundant; error buffering	Many-to-one cultural transmission (Cavalli-Sforza and Feldman 1972)
Feedback control	Enables systems to operate efficiently over a range of inputs, as in immune effector responses	Social leveling mechanisms (e.g., accusations of witchcraft); exclusion
Modularity	E.g., minimizing pleiotropy (in which a single gene influences multiple traits) in genetic systems	Social organization emphasizing household, lineage, and clan results in highly modular settlements
Purging—antiredundancy	E.g., of infected cells through apoptosis, or programmed cell death; error removal	Banishment; killing of witches; household defection to other communities; residential mobility

(Continued)

Table 5.1. (*Continued*)

Principle	Definition/example	Possible mechanisms in prehispanic pueblo societies
Spatial compartmentalization	Can minimize interference among functionally unrelated reactions in separate compartments, and can minimize dependencies and propagation of errors	Dispersed settlements
Distributed processing	Differs from modularity and spatial compartmentalization in that a single function is emergent from the collective activities of the units	Decision-making authority and ritual processes distributed broadly (however, features such as sodalities that may contribute to persistence in the face of small perturbations may amplify responses to large perturbations)

Sources: Principles for achieving robustness in biological systems are after Krakauer 2004 and Krakauer and Plotkin 2005.

These changes proved advantageous for a while; PII- and PIII-style social organizations persisted at high population levels in the VEP area for about two centuries. But perhaps it is not coincidental that when these organizations failed, they failed catastrophically.

These social and institutional histories are thus connected with a final history: the history of conflict. As reviewed by Varien (this vol.), the CMV landscape witnessed cycles of conflict, with a first small wave peaking as the PI villages fell apart and their populations emigrated. This was followed by a larger wave of violence that marked, first, the resistance of local mid-PII populations to Chacoan expansion. This wave then crested in the mid-1100s as that system fell apart or was reorganized (Cole 2007; Kohler et al. 2009). Following a relatively calm early 1200s, violence was again rapidly accelerating just as the final depopulation was underway (Kuckelman, this vol.). As noted by Hill and colleagues (this vol.), conflict magnifies resource-acquisition (and social-coordination) problems in many ways. In the specific case of the VEP area, it may have rendered its eastern and least defensible but most productive portions completely uninhabitable. Kohler and others (2009) argue that escalating conflict usually results in eventual population loss, including emigration. In the end, the last to leave the VEP area were probably those with the greatest vested interests or sunk costs (Janssen et al. 2003), possibly including descendants of Chacoan elites (Kuckelman, Lightfoot, and Martin 2002:492) whose lineages presumably claimed the lands least susceptible to climatic downturns. These same individuals probably controlled many of the various nonresidential community-center structures reviewed by Glowacki (this vol.) in which community members invested so much of their energies.

Conclusions

In the northern Southwest from the mid-1100s until the mid-1200s, climate change that was very deleterious for farmers caused cascades of disruption and population movement. The movement was first into a few advantaged areas in the northern Southwest, including the central Mesa Verde region and the northern Rio Grande, and then later out of the northern Southwest entirely to destinations south and southeast. An unanswered question of great interest is whether resistance by already resident populations to streams of immigration into these favored areas resulted in social dynamics that intensified the identities of the earlier residents as a collective. If so, this reorganization may have helped them to either resist encroachment by the immigrant populations, or at least to continue to make a living on a more populous landscape.[2] But this reorganization also seems to have accelerated trends that had been visible for two centuries, resulting in a social structure that was highly tuned to intensely competitive social conditions, but which could not fall apart gracefully. Continued deleterious climate change in the context of growing population and an already depleted landscape exacerbated conflict, possibly in part between immigrant and resident populations. These processes eventually overwhelmed the ability of Pueblo communities to continue their livelihoods in the northern Southwest.

Although the depopulation of the northern Southwest was not the sort of instantaneous, one-off, "chance" event (like an earthquake or a tsunami) evoked by the image of "natural disaster," like many more obvious natural disasters (Torrence and Grattan 2002) it had significant, long-lasting effects on culture. It accelerated many trends already underway in the Greater Southwest: for those people of the northern San Juan who ended up in the northern Rio Grande, it brought on the true and final "pithouse-to-pueblo" transition, for which the late Pueblo I/early Pueblo II architectural changes had been only a preparation. It brought about the substantial weakening (at least in the eastern Southwest) of the household-and-lineage-based social organization that had channeled sociopolitical development for more than half a millennium. Pueblo II and III societies had tinkered with this organization but were unable to submerge it; that required a catastrophe. Finally, these events completed the long arc of the Chacoan system (Cameron and Duff 2008), launched—in one of the Southwest's most amazing ironies—in this same area four centuries earlier.

The emerging picture of a Southwest that is interconnected at a large scale—in which people, problems, or processes from one area readily cascade into other areas—reminds us of the difficulty of our subject but also presents explanatory possibilities unavailable to attempts to make sense of local prehistoric sequences using only local data. Learning how to appropriately apportion local processes and histories into regional processes and histories, and vice versa, remain important goals for a science of prehistory. "Life without a prime mover can be unnerving"—as Robb (2007:291) suggests in his synthesis of the Italian Neolithic—or it can generate fresh insights and new methods able to cope with complexity.

Acknowledgments

A first draft of this chapter, coauthored with C. David Johnson, was delivered at the seventy-second meeting of the Society for American Archaeology in the symposium "New Light on the Thirteenth-Century Depopulation of the Northern Southwest." In addition to the acknowledgments in the preface, I thank Johnson and the other members of the VEP extended research family for the background work that made this chapter possible, James Allison for his comments on this chapter during and after the seminar, and the two anonymous reviewers of the entire volume.

Notes

1. Spielmann and others (in press) argue that the ethnographic analogies on which such arguments are based are inappropriate because they are derived from societies lacking effective storage technologies. They suggest that storage technologies in southwestern societies would have been adequate to buffer against high-frequency variability in most cases.

2. Another possibility specifically for the VEP area is that these immigrants were welcomed to bolster the declining fortunes of a large "Northern Alliance" against depredations by an equally putative "Totah Alliance" to the south.

6

The End of Farming in the
"Northern Periphery" of the Southwest

James R. Allison

Prehispanic farmers belonging to the Virgin and Fremont traditions once occupied most of Utah and adjacent parts of Arizona and Nevada. Through much of the twentieth century, these areas were called the "Northern Periphery" of the Southwest, but in recent decades, both Fremont and Virgin have often been left out of syntheses of southwestern archaeology—even though they clearly had strong connections to the Southwest and represented, respectively, the northernmost and westernmost extensions of maize-based horticulture in western North America. This exclusion results from a combination of factors, the most important of which are geography and the territorial behavior of some archaeologists who chose to isolate Fremont archaeology from southwestern studies.

The goal of this chapter is to take a small step toward reversing that trend, to help (as Neil Judd once said) "the builders of the adobe dwellings [the Fremont] . . . [find] their rightful place in the story of our prehistoric Southwest" (Judd 1919:22). Specifically, I will discuss the end of farming in the Virgin and Fremont areas and consider what little evidence there is regarding how the depopulation of the Four Corners area may have affected or been affected by developments to the north and west. As reviewed by Varien in chapter 1, some archaeologists have claimed that the cascading effects of depopulations in more northern areas had a causal role in the thirteenth-century depopulation of the northern San Juan region (e.g., Davis 1964, 1965), although there has been little effort to document such effects.

I begin by briefly discussing some of the factors that have led the Northern Periphery to be left out of most syntheses of southwestern archaeology. The intellectual history I give does not directly relate to the abandonment of farming, but it is important to understanding the (mostly arbitrary) reasons why most previous discussions of the problem exclude these regions. I follow that discussion with one regarding the difficulties with chronology and important missing data ("known unknowns") that hinder inferences about demography and the timing of the end of farming in the Virgin and Fremont regions.

I then turn to what we do know. The radiocarbon records demonstrate that both Fremont and Virgin traditions ended close to AD 1300, and the latest sites in these areas suggest that the end of farming in the Virgin and Fremont regions was preceded by both aggregation and increased use of public architecture (presumably reflecting changes in social organization and/or ritual), although these changes occurred on a much smaller scale than did similar ones in the northern San Juan. Finally, I discuss the limited evidence for the ultimate fate of the Virgin and Fremont.

The Northern Periphery

Although hunter-gatherers occupied virtually the entire area at European contact, the area once called the Northern Periphery of the Southwest was occupied for more than one thousand years by prehispanic farmers identified by archaeologists as Fremont or Virgin Anasazi. This area straddles the Colorado Plateau and the eastern Great Basin and includes almost all of Utah, the northwest corner of Arizona, and portions of eastern Nevada (figs. 1.1, 6.1). Early archaeologists considered both the Fremont and Virgin regions as part of the Greater Southwest. For example, in 1915, Neil Judd conducted a reconnaissance in both regions and reported: "The outstanding result of this hurried survey was realization of the number and the relative importance of archaeological sites in the region traversed. Each exhibited, in greater or less degree, the effect of environment, but each had been occupied unquestionably by individuals we have come to regard as Puebloan" (Judd 1926:2).

Judd spent parts of the next five years working in the region, sandwiching his work "North of the Rio Colorado" between projects in better-known portions of the Southwest; in 1917, for instance, he spent the spring working on the restoration of Betatakin, then moved to Paragonah in southwestern Utah, where he excavated "some 40 odd houses and numerous associated structures" at the largest known Fremont settlement

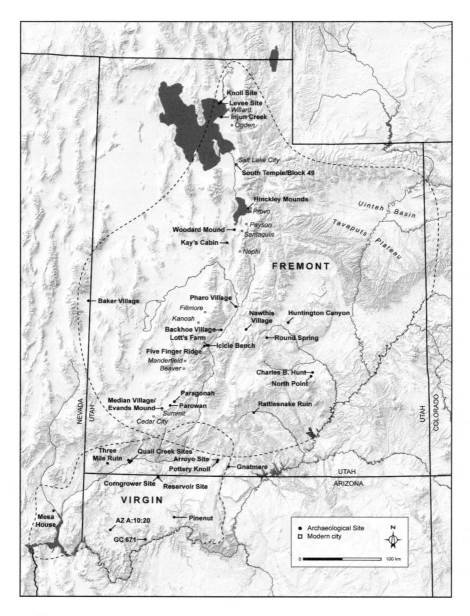

Figure 6.1. The approximate boundaries of the Fremont and Virgin regions, the locations of selected archaeological sites that date to the AD 1200s, and modern towns.

(Judd 1919:21). Between 1915 and 1920, he excavated other Fremont agricultural villages at Willard (north of Salt Lake City) and Beaver, as well as at several Virgin cliff dwellings near Kanab, and he documented numerous other sites "from the Grand Canyon . . . to the northern shore of the Great Salt Lake" (Judd 1926).

Starting at about the middle of the twentieth century, however, some Utah archaeologists began to dissent, arguing that the Fremont derived from indigenous Great Basin hunter-gatherer cultures to which "Anasazi traits were simply added" (Jennings and Norbeck 1955:8). In this view, which was most strongly expressed by Fowler and Jennings (1982), the Fremont were not peripheral to the Southwest, and were not really a southwestern culture at all—just a blip in the millennia-long hunter-gatherer prehistory of the eastern Great Basin. The Northern Periphery designation was seen as conferring "second-class status" on eastern Great Basin archaeology, and Kidder ([1924] 1962) was accused of "malign[ing] the Northern Periphery" simply by using the term (Fowler and Jennings 1982).

I agree with Fowler and Jennings (1982:111) that "whatever Fremont cultures are, they are more than simply country cousins of the Anasazi," and—despite the title of this chapter—I do not believe that going back to considering the Fremont and Virgin areas the "northern periphery" of the Southwest would be helpful. Still, it seems that the original rejection of the Northern Periphery concept had as much or more to do with defining and defending institutional turf than it did with the nature of the archaeological record (cf. Berry and Berry 2001).

Whatever Fowler and Jennings' motivation, the result of what they saw as "having freed the Fremont from the onus of peripherality" (1982:111) has been the theoretical and substantive isolation of Fremont studies and Fremont scholars from the southwestern research tradition. The Virgin region has also become isolated; as Lyneis says, by the 1970s, "knowledge of the region became constricted to those working within it" (1995:207). There have not been the same kinds of intentional efforts to separate it from the Southwest, but, due to its geographical remoteness from the large archaeology programs at the Arizona and New Mexico universities and the resulting small number of interested scholars, most southwestern archaeologists have little familiarity with Virgin region archaeology. Similar geographic factors helped ensure that the deliberate amputation of Fremont studies from southwestern archaeology succeeded.

Some Difficulties

Several other factors, in addition to the decoupling of Fremont and Virgin studies from the mainstream of southwestern research, make it difficult to answer some of the most important questions about the end of Fremont and Virgin farming. Most important is the lack of well-developed chronologies. Few Fremont or Virgin sites have tree-ring dates, so absolute chronology relies largely on radiocarbon dating, which makes the precise timing of events uncertain. Relative dating techniques are also poorly developed; Fremont ceramic chronology is essentially limited to the vague idea that corrugated ceramics date after about AD 1050 or so (Richens 2000), but even this does not help in northern Utah, where corrugated ceramics are never common. Painted ceramics are also less common in northern Utah than in the southern part of the Fremont region, and variation in painted Fremont ceramic designs has never been linked to chronology.

Ceramic chronology is better developed in the Virgin region, where a sequence of design changes roughly parallels ceramic change in the Kayenta region and allows sites to be assigned to general periods based on the Pecos Classification. Moderate quantities of better-dated red- and white-ware sherds imported from across the Colorado River confirm the general sequence. But at certain times, specifically during the Pueblo I and Pueblo III periods, the Virgin region was apparently relatively isolated from other Pueblo areas to the east, and ceramic change during these periods was slow.

Connections between the Virgin region and the rest of the Pueblo world strengthened at about AD 1050, the start of what most archaeologists working in the Virgin region call the late Pueblo II period. At this time, potters began to use Sosi- and Dogoszhi-style designs on white-ware ceramics and to make some corrugated gray-ware vessels, although they never stopped making plain gray-ware vessels. Also, San Juan Red Ware and Tsegi Orange Ware vessels appeared as trade items on late Pueblo II sites as far west as southern Nevada (Allison 2000, 2008; Lyneis 1992). By about AD 1150, however, connections to the east weakened considerably, and the pace of ceramic change slowed. Although some recognizably late white-ware designs occur, these late designs never replaced Sosi and Dogoszhi styles, which remained common through the end of the Virgin tradition.

I have argued that sites dating to the Pueblo III period (i.e., the late AD 1100s and 1200s) are characterized by high percentages of corrugated pottery (40 percent or more of sherd assemblages), the presence of at least some late white-ware designs, and (sometimes) the prevalence of crushed-sherd temper (Allison 2000, 2005). Because these measures are based on percentage representation within an analyzed sherd assemblage, distinguishing Pueblo III from late Pueblo II sites usually requires (at a minimum) sherd counts and can be difficult to do from ceramics alone, especially in the field. Many archaeologists working in the region therefore prefer to simply lump all sites with corrugated ceramics into the late Pueblo II period.

In both the Fremont and Virgin regions, then, it is difficult to recognize the latest sites without data from excavations. Further, even with excavations, dating usually relies on radiocarbon, and the imprecision of radiocarbon dating makes it difficult to know exactly which sites were among the last occupied. This situation contrasts with other parts of the Southwest, like the northern San Juan—especially in the central Mesa Verde region—where well-developed ceramic chronologies often allow archaeologists to recognize sites from the final phases of occupation based on surface evidence alone, and where numerous tree-ring dates allow extraordinarily precise dating of excavated contexts. Further, because of the difficulties in assigning even approximate dates to unexcavated sites, demographic studies in the Fremont and Virgin regions are severely limited.

Adding to the difficulties with chronology, many Fremont farming villages in the eastern Great Basin are located beneath modern towns and/or their associated agricultural fields. This pattern was noted by early Fremont archaeologists (e.g., Judd 1926; Malouf 1944), who remarked that both Fremont and early Mormon farming communities were "found along the base of the Wasatch Mountains where streams furnished water for the cultivation of foods" (Malouf 1944:319). The Mormon towns were established in precisely the best locations for irrigation-based agriculture, and the pattern suggests that horticulture at some of the largest and longest-lasting Fremont settlements similarly relied on water from these permanent streams, although there is no evidence for any sort of large-scale water diversion. This superpositioning makes it difficult to describe the extent of many of the largest sites, much less determine when they were occupied. The problem is exacerbated by the earthen nature of Fremont architecture; deteriorated adobe storage structures often formed mounds, but there was little in these mounds to impede plowing, even when it was done with nineteenth-century technology. Substantial remains are still present near and under some modern towns, but even in the early twentieth century, it was clear that much had been lost as the towns were built and fields leveled for farming (Judd 1926).

Talbot (2000a) summarizes historical and archaeological data for large Fremont village sites, most of which have been partially destroyed by historical and modern farming and settlement. He includes sites at or under (from south to north) Cedar City, Summit, Parowan, Paragonah, Beaver, Manderfield, Kanosh, Fillmore, Nephi, Santaquin, Payson, Provo, Salt Lake City, Ogden, and Willard, all of which lie along the route of Interstate 15 as it follows the Wasatch Front, and all of which are located where streams emerge from the mountains to the east (fig. 6.1). East of the Wasatch in the Sevier Valley, Backhoe Village covers more than 1 mi^2 beneath the town of Richfield (Talbot and Richens 1993). Eleven of the fifteen largest known Fremont sites are either largely destroyed or inaccessible because of historical or modern development, and this total excludes a number of suspected large sites (e.g., under Salt Lake City, Payson, and Cedar City) whose size cannot even be estimated.

Some excavation data are available for a number of these sites (e.g., Dodd 1982; Green 1961; Judd 1919, 1926; Madsen and Lindsay 1977; Maguire 1894; Marwitt 1970; Meighan et al. 1956; Seddon 2001; Sharrock and Marwitt 1967; Talbot et al. 2004), but the sites are all privately owned, and in Utah (unless human remains are present), there are no state laws or city ordinances that protect, or encourage scientific excavation of, privately owned sites threatened by development. Because of this, only the Block 49/South Temple site under Salt Lake City and Backhoe Village under Richfield have seen any excavation in the past thirty years, and these excavations were limited to small areas exposed by construction projects.

The Paragonah site provides some perspective on the scale of loss. Early historical accounts describe a site consisting of four hundred to five hundred mounds covering an area of about 2 mi^2 (Talbot 2000a:214). By the time Judd got there in 1915, he noted "between 40 and 50 [mounds] . . . yet the sage-covered fields in which they stood were even then being prepared for cultivation" (Judd 1926:36). By the time Judd returned in 1917, more of the mounds had been leveled, "leaving a bare half-dozen large elevations in the fields already under cultivation and several smaller mounds in the sage-covered area adjoining" (Judd 1919:1). The largest of these mounds, which Judd called "the Big Mound," was "a huge knoll, measuring approximately 225 feet in diameter and 10 feet high" (Judd 1919:3).

Judd's excavations in the Big Mound uncovered more than forty structures, including rectangular surface structures arranged around an open courtyard, as well as three large jacal surface structures that fit Talbot's (2000b:139) definition for "central structures" (Judd 1919, 1926:72; fig. 6.2). These central structures occur at a number of Fremont sites and are apparently a form of public architecture. Importantly, central structures at Baker Village and Five Finger Ridge (described below) appear to date to the AD 1200s, suggesting that the latest occupation at the Big Mound probably also dates to near the end of the Fremont sequence.

But by the time Meighan (1956) began work at Paragonah in 1954, the Big Mound had been destroyed. Meighan describes only thirty-two mounds remaining in the portion of the site that had never been plowed (Meighan 1956:3), and even the majority of those had been impacted by looting. Most of those mounds are still visible today, because they are on a small section of land owned by Southern Utah University that has been protected from development, but the vast majority of the settlement has been destroyed without professional excavation.

Paragonah was among the largest settlements in the Fremont region, but our knowledge of just how large it was is based mainly on nineteenth-century observations by nonarchaeologists, and there is no way to reliably determine how much of the site was occupied at any one time. Meighan estimates that "the site had a permanent population of between 100 and 400 persons" (1956:4), but this estimate relies on numerous assumptions that cannot be tested. There also is little evidence relevant

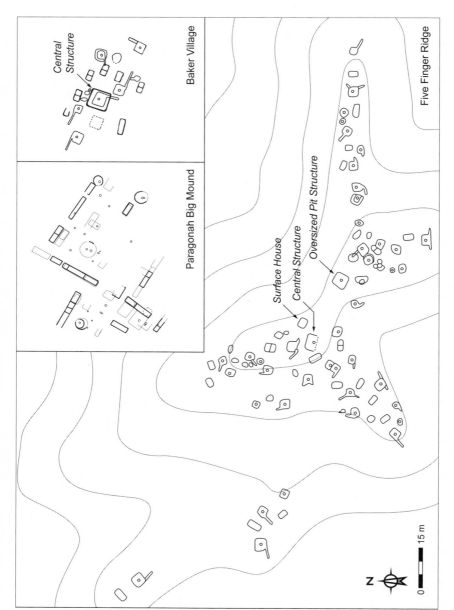

Figure 6.2. Plan maps of selected Fremont sites mentioned in the text.

to dating the abandonment of the site, and there is no way to reexamine the Big Mound, which likely contained structures representing the last periods of occupation. Similar data problems plague the interpretation of almost all the largest Fremont farming villages: we know they are big but cannot say how large they were at any particular time, when their occupation began, or when they were abandoned. At a minimum, this means there will be great uncertainty involved in any demographic reconstruction, and some of the gaps in our knowledge of large Fremont villages are unlikely to ever be filled.

Dating the End of Fremont and Virgin Farming

It is possible, however, to say something about how the Virgin and Fremont radiocarbon records compare, and to show that the end of farming corresponded closely with the depopulation of the northern San Juan region. In particular, the radiocarbon dates contradict some of the most common assertions about the timing of the end of the Virgin tradition. Traditionally, archaeologists have assumed that the Fremont tradition ended close to AD 1300 or 1350 (e.g., Berry and Berry 2001; Marwitt 1970:151; Talbot and Wilde 1989), while the end of the Virgin tradition has been placed at about AD 1150 or very shortly thereafter (e.g., Aikens 1966; Euler et al. 1979:1091; Gumerman and Dean 1989:121; Larson and Michaelsen 1990). Although many archaeologists working in the Virgin region now believe that many sites postdate 1150 (Allison 1996, 2005; Fairley 1989; Lyneis 1995, 1996), the dating of the latest sites remains controversial.

The radiocarbon records for the Virgin and Fremont regions do not support the idea that farming ended earlier in the Virgin region than in the Fremont, however. The histograms at the top of figure 6.3 are based on compilations of 409 Fremont radiocarbon dates and 162 radiocarbon dates from the Virgin region.[1] The ranges of radiocarbon dates associated with maize horticulture in the two regions are similar, although the histograms show some differences in the abundance of dates through time. Specifically, the number of Fremont dates peaks between 1000 and 950 radiocarbon years BP (probably corresponding to the early AD 1000s) and declines gradually until about 600 radiocarbon years BP (around AD 1300), with only a trickle of dates later than that. Berry and

Berry (2001; cf. Benson et al. 2007) also noted this pattern and argued that it indicated that Fremont populations peaked near AD 1000.

The Virgin dates show a more complex pattern, although this may largely be a result of the small sample of dates and dated contexts. A large number of dates cluster between about 1350 and 1150 BP (probably between AD 700 and 900), after which the number of dates drops before rising to peak again between 750 and 800 BP (corresponding roughly to the late AD 1100s or early 1200s). Again, only a few dates are more recent than 600 BP, suggesting that the Virgin tradition disappeared around AD 1300. It is not clear how closely (or whether) population trends followed the patterns reflected in the histograms, but clearly, the radiocarbon dates provide no support for the argument that the Virgin tradition ended around AD 1150, 150 years or more earlier than the Fremont.

More specifically, radiocarbon determinations of 800 BP or more recent imply that the dated events almost certainly occurred after AD 1200, and both the Virgin and Fremont radiocarbon records include a number of such dates. From the Virgin region, twenty-seven dates have radiocarbon ages of 800 BP or later; confidence intervals for the calibrated dates (fig. 6.3, bottom right) show that a few even appear to suggest true dates after AD 1300. The two latest of those dates, however, are uncorrected dates on maize; if they are approximately corrected by adding 250 radiocarbon years, they appear most likely to be from the late AD 1200s. Also, random effects attributable to counting error should mean that a few dates will always appear too late for the events they date (and a few too early). Overall, these dates strongly indicate that the Virgin tradition continued at least into the late AD 1200s.

A large number of Fremont dates similarly indicate late AD 1200s occupation (fig. 6.3, bottom left). In the Fremont region, there are fifty-nine determinations of 800 BP or later. Again, several appear likely to postdate AD 1300. It is more difficult in this case to dismiss the possibility of post–AD 1300 occupation than it is for the Virgin region; the Fremont occupation clearly continued until sometime near AD 1300, but the imprecise nature of radiocarbon dating leaves uncertainty about whether it continued slightly later than that.

Sites with these late dates are scattered thinly across both the Virgin and Fremont areas (fig. 6.1), although their distribution probably has more to do with where excavation has occurred than with the actual

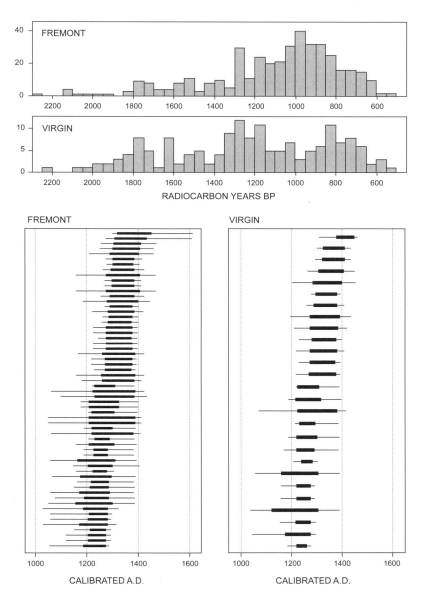

Figure 6.3. Radiocarbon dates from the Fremont and Virgin regions. At the top are histograms of the midpoints of the reported conventional radiocarbon ages. The graphs at the bottom show confidence intervals for the calibrated dates for radiocarbon determinations of 800 BP or later. The black boxes show 67 percent confidence intervals, while 95 percent intervals are shown by the lines.

distribution of AD 1200s occupations. A few Virgin sites that are dated only with ceramics are included on the map, and it is safe to assume that there are many other sites that were occupied in the 1200s that have not been dated.

So why have archaeologists traditionally assumed that the Virgin tradition ended around AD 1150 while the Fremont tradition continued until AD 1300? I think it is attributable to the lack of a well-developed ceramic chronology for the Fremont region; without recourse to ceramic chronology, Fremont archaeologists have relied almost exclusively on radiocarbon dates, while archaeologists in the Virgin region have given more attention to ceramics. Virgin ceramic styles roughly (but imperfectly) follow stylistic trends in the Kayenta region, and dates for Kayenta ceramic designs are assumed to apply more or less directly to their Virgin analogs. But this works better for some time periods than for others.

As noted above, ceramic assemblages from the latest Virgin sites can be recognized by their relatively high proportions of corrugated pottery (around 40 percent or more), by the presence of polychrome red wares, and by the presence of late white-ware designs reminiscent of the Flagstaff style. However, Sosi- and Dogoszhi-style white-ware designs are also common in ceramic assemblages from these sites, which makes them unlike AD 1200s assemblages from the Kayenta region. This has led some archaeologists to assume that the Virgin occupation ended before AD 1200, but the radiocarbon dates tell a different story.

Twelve radiocarbon dates are available from seven different sites where more than 40 percent of the ceramic assemblage is corrugated. I used the BCAL Bayesian radiocarbon calibration program (Buck et al. 1991; Christen 1994; Litton and Buck 1996) to calculate posterior probability densities for the beginning and end of the period represented by the eleven most recent of those dates, excluding one date from Three Mile Ruin as an obvious outlier (see below). This analysis[2] suggests that the Pueblo III period in the Virgin region (as defined above) most likely lasted around one hundred years, beginning at about AD 1200 and ending close to AD 1300 (fig. 6.4). The small number of dates, however, leaves uncertainty about the exact value of those parameters; a 67 percent confidence interval for the start of the Pueblo III period includes the years from AD 1156 to 1239, while the same interval for the end of Pueblo III is AD 1264–1328.

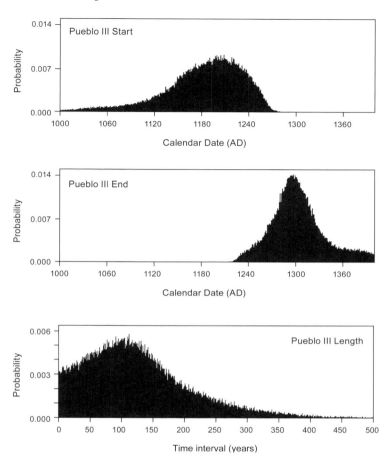

Figure 6.4. Posterior probability densities for the beginning (top), end (center), and length (bottom) of the Pueblo III period in the Virgin region, based on analysis of radiocarbon dates from sites with corrugated pottery frequencies above 40 percent. The analysis was done using the BCAL Bayesian radiocarbon calibration program (Buck et al. 1991; Christen 1994; Litton and Buck 1996).

The Virgin Region in the 1200s

During the final decades prior to the depopulation of the northern San Juan region, social and religious changes were reflected in increasingly aggregated villages, a settlement shift toward defensible locations, and new forms of ritual architecture. Some characteristics of the latest

Fremont and Virgin sites hint that similar, though much attenuated, changes may have occurred in those areas as well. The latest sites in the Virgin region show only a slight trend toward aggregation, although most are a bit larger than typical Virgin sites from earlier periods (Lyneis 1996). I focus on four sites here: Mesa House, Three Mile Ruin, the Corngrower Site, and AZ A:10:20 (fig. 6.1), all of which appear to be among the latest sites occupied in the western part of the Virgin region. That assessment relies almost entirely on ceramic dating for the first three of those sites. Because they are among the most thoroughly excavated late sites, they provide useful insights into site layouts and size.

Mesa House, located in the Moapa Valley of southeastern Nevada, was excavated in 1929 by Irwin Hayden (Hayden 1930). It has not been radiocarbon dated but it has a late ceramic assemblage, with about 69 percent of the ceramics corrugated. The core of the site comprises surface rooms surrounding a courtyard, including two large habitation rooms and about twenty-five smaller storage rooms (fig. 6.5, upper left). Another row of storage rooms extends from the southwest side of the main room block, ending in another large habitation room. Other habitation rooms are located around the margins of the site, without attached storage rooms. This suggests a modest degree of aggregation, with perhaps as many as ten households living at the site, and the differences in the ways storage rooms relate to habitation rooms suggest that some households may have controlled access to stored goods (Lyneis 1986).

Mesa House is located on a ridge top some 35 m above the valley floor. This location and the site layout led Hayden "to suppose a deliberate defensive arrangement as protection from raiding nomads" (1930:33). More recent archaeologists have also interpreted Mesa House as a defensive site and argued that it is evidence that the Virgin populations were pushed out of southeastern Nevada by the ancestors of the Southern Paiute (e.g., Ambler and Sutton 1989).

Not all late sites in the Virgin region appear defensive, however. Three Mile Ruin, for instance, has a broken circle of rooms surrounding a courtyard (fig. 6.5, middle left). It was partially excavated by the University of Utah in 1962 (Aikens 1965:47–62) and, like Mesa House, has a very late ceramic assemblage; slightly more than 70 percent of the ceramics are corrugated. The excavations uncovered three habitation rooms with a large number of smaller storage rooms attached. There

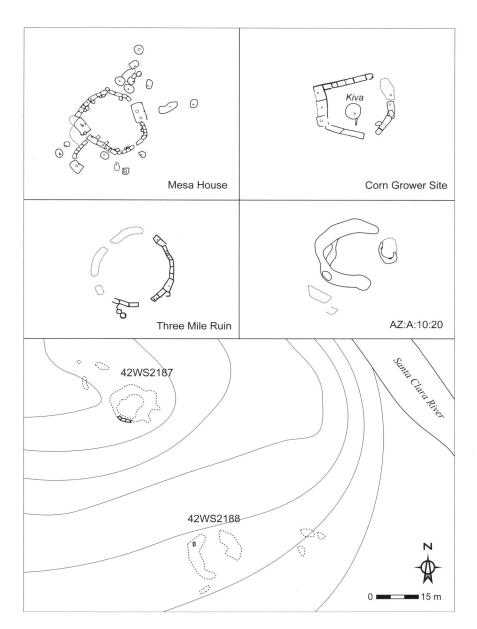

Mesa House

Corn Grower Site

Kiva

Three Mile Ruin

AZ:A:10:20

42WS2187

42WS2188

Santa Clara River

N

0 ▬▬ 15 m

Figure 6.5. Plan maps of selected Virgin sites mentioned in the text.

is no evidence at Three Mile Ruin for anything like the numerous habitation rooms lacking contiguous storage rooms that occur at Mesa House. A recently obtained radiocarbon date of 1020 ±40 BP comes from a poorly provenienced maize cob (the only one in the collections), which the excavators found while digging outside the wall of one of the habitation rooms. That date appears to be about two hundred years too old for the ceramic assemblage; it and a small number of Saint George Black-on-gray sherds suggest the possibility of a small earlier occupation.

In contrast to Mesa House, Three Mile Ruin is on a low terrace adjacent to the Santa Clara River floodplain. Also, while Three Mile Ruin is smaller than Mesa House, with probably at most only five or six habitation rooms, it appears to be part of a multisite settlement cluster including at least two other nearby sites, 42WS2187 and 42WS2188 (fig. 6.5, bottom), which also have very late ceramic assemblages (Allison 1990). At 42WS2187, a circular rubble mound encloses a courtyard, and the site looks like a smaller version of Three Mile Ruin, which is across the Santa Clara River, approximately 300 m to the northeast. The architecture at 42WS2188 also includes a roomblock in the form of a broken circle. Ceramics at 42WS2187 and 42WS2188 date both sites to the Pueblo III period (66 and 53 percent corrugated, respectively), although only small portions of the sites have been excavated, and neither of them is radiocarbon dated. Together, Three Mile Ruin, 42WS2187, and 42WS2188 appear to make up a multisite settlement that was about the same size as Mesa House—probably about 10 to 12 households total—although it is impossible to be certain with current data that the sites are absolutely contemporaneous.

The Corngrower Site is located just south of Short Creek, within the town of Colorado City, Arizona, and was the focus of several Southern Utah University field schools (Firor 1993; Frank and Thompson 1995; Walling and Thompson 1991, 1992, 1993, 1995). The superpositioning of numerous structures indicates a long occupation, but a total of fourteen surface rooms and a kiva appear to date to the latest occupation at the site (fig. 6.5, upper right). Hearths in four large rooms suggest that they were habitations. The rest of the surface rooms were probably used mainly for storage, although one small surface room also has a hearth.

The Corngrower site has not been radiocarbon dated, and much of the ceramic analysis has never been reported, but 67.5 percent of more than seven thousand potsherds recovered during site testing are corrugated (Walling and Thompson 1991), and the collections include a large number of Flagstaff-style white-ware sherds and polychrome red wares, confirming the late occupation.

It is not clear whether Corngrower was part of a larger, multisite community, but site density in the immediate vicinity is high, and the Reservoir Site, which has a late ceramic assemblage (81.8 percent corrugated; Allison and Colman 1998) and a radiocarbon date of 670 ± 90 BP, is only about a mile away.

As at other late Virgin sites, the rooms are arranged around an open courtyard or plaza area. At the Corngrower site, however, this courtyard space contains a masonry-lined pit structure that the excavators interpreted as a kiva. Although it lacks an identifiable sipapu, masonry-lined pit houses are uncommon in the region. Moreover, the structure has a well-constructed kiva-style vent shaft, and it has unusual floor features, including a square, slab-lined hearth and two pairs of clay-capped, sand-filled pits. Given the presence of several surface habitation rooms and the central location of the structure, it seems reasonable to consider this feature to be a kiva. Kivas are rare in the Virgin region (Lyneis 1996:21–22), however, and the presence of one at such a late site hints at changes in the use of ritual architecture in the period immediately preceding abandonment.

The fourth site, AZ A:10:20 (BLM), is located on the Shivwits Plateau about 90 km south of Three Mile Ruin. It is smaller and more isolated than the other sites described so far (fig. 6.5, middle right). The site is mostly unexcavated but includes a C-shaped rubble mound and several smaller structures. One large room, probably a habitation, is apparent in the main rubble mound, and it is likely that one or two other habitation rooms are also present. Like the other sites, it has a late ceramic assemblage (55 percent corrugated). Limited testing in 2006 yielded radiocarbon dates of 650 ± 50 and 750 ± 50 BP, suggesting occupation in the late 1200s. Full-coverage survey work near AZ A:10:20, which began in 2006, has not yet been completed, but the site does not appear to have been part of a larger cluster of contemporaneous sites.

Rather, it was probably a relatively isolated hamlet that was home to two or three families that lacked close neighbors.

The Fremont in the 1200s

Fremont sites dating to the 1200s look very different from Virgin sites, and some, especially those in the eastern Great Basin, show a much greater degree of aggregation. Some of the latest radiocarbon dates come from enormous settlements like the ones at Summit in the Parowan Valley, or Backhoe Village underneath the town of Richfield, but these sites have long occupational histories, and it is difficult to determine how large they were at any point in time. I will instead focus on two sites that appear to have been occupied primarily in the late 1200s: Baker Village and Five Finger Ridge.

Baker Village is located in far eastern Nevada, just west of the Utah/ Nevada state line (fig. 6.2, upper right). The excavated portion of the site includes seven pit structures; associated adobe surface storage structures; and a large adobe "central structure," with an area of approximately 50 m², that was built over an earlier pit structure (Wilde 1992; Wilde and Soper 1999). This central structure apparently served as some kind of public architecture; Hockett (1998) argues that the concentration of faunal remains within the Baker Village central structure indicates feasting.

Midpoints of radiocarbon dates from the site range from 980 to 690 BP; four of these dates are on maize, including the earliest and the most recent, while the rest of the dates are on charcoal and thus subject to old wood problems. The early maize date comes from a test pit, and its association with the excavated architecture is unclear (Wilde 1992:46). The other three maize dates (740 ± 70, 730 ± 100, and 690 ± 60 BP) come from an excavated pit house, a surface storage structure, and a midden, and these suggest occupation in the late AD 1200s (Wilde 1992:47). The charcoal dates suggest earlier occupation during the 1100s, but this is likely to be a product of dating old wood. It seems likely that at least four of the seven pit structures were all occupied at once, which would suggest a population of fifteen to twenty-five people in the excavated area.

Five Finger Ridge in central Utah is similar in many ways but was quite a bit larger (fig. 6.2). It was located on a knoll 40–50 m above the floodplain of Clear Creek, a small but permanent tributary of the Sevier River. The site was excavated by Brigham Young University in 1984 prior to its destruction during the building of Interstate Highway 70 (Talbot et al. 2000). The excavations found thirty-seven subrectangular pit structures, twenty-three circular or oval secondary pit structures, nineteen one- or two-room coursed-adobe surface storage structures, one surface habitation room, and one large central structure with jacal walls. In addition to the differences in shape, the subrectangular pit structures were distinguished from the secondary pit structures by their larger size, prepared floors, plastered walls, and substantial roofs. The secondary pit structures were expediently built, with use-compacted floors, unprepared walls, and probably brush superstructures.

Based on stratigraphic relationships and lack of superpositioning, as many as thirty-four of the thirty-seven subrectangular pit structures could have been contemporaneous, although Talbot (2000a:213) estimates only fifteen contemporaneous habitations. Sixty-two radiocarbon and nine tree-ring dates suggest an occupational span beginning in the eleventh century, with the major occupation in the 1200s, when the site appears to have been home to fifty to one hundred people. More specifically, the radiocarbon dates (all on charcoal) range from 1800 to 550 BP, although the earliest dates are clear outliers that are probably due to dating old wood.

While the latest Fremont sites clearly lasted until about AD 1300, occupation of some areas may have ended sooner. There are Fremont villages in the Uinta Basin in northeastern Utah, for example, including some large ones (e.g., Ambler 1966), but radiocarbon dates from the central Uinta Basin all predate AD 1000 (Spangler 2000a). In the rugged canyon country of the Tavaputs Plateau, south of the Uinta Basin, a complementary pattern occurs (Spangler 2000b). In this area, which includes well-publicized, archaeologically rich areas such as Nine-Mile Canyon and Range Creek, radiocarbon dates postdating AD 1000 are abundant, and they indicate use of the area through about AD 1300. Fremont sites on the Tavaputs Plateau are small and include numerous well-hidden and almost inaccessible granaries; small, apparently defensive habitations; and abundant rock art. This suggests that the Tavaputs Plateau was used from AD 1000 to 1300 by small, probably mobile, groups of people who were concerned with defense.

The eastern shore of the Great Salt Lake is another area where reliance on maize probably declined or ended earlier than AD 1300. Bone chemistry analysis on skeletal remains from fifty Fremont individuals recovered from the Great Salt Lake wetlands indicates that there was a large amount of variation in maize consumption, with variation patterned by both gender (males consumed more maize than females) and time (Coltrain and Leavitt 2002; Coltrain and Stafford 1999). Accelerator mass spectrometry radiocarbon dates were obtained for each individual, and those dating after about AD 1150 all had $\Delta^{13}C$ values suggesting little or no consumption of maize. Late dates from nearby pithouse villages (e.g., the Block 49 and South Temple sites under Salt Lake City [Talbot et al. 2004:155–158]) suggest, however, that maize horticulture continued later in some places around the Great Salt Lake.

After the Fremont and Virgin

Despite the apparent synchronicity, archaeologists have not seriously considered the possibility that the end of farming in the Virgin and Fremont regions may have been caused by regional-scale social disruptions caused by the depopulation of the northern San Juan and other parts of the northern Southwest. Instead, climate change and invading nomads have been popular explanations for the demise of both the Fremont and the Virgin (e.g., Ambler and Sutton 1989; Benson et al. 2007; Lindsay 1986). Paleoclimatic reconstructions show that in fact, the late–AD 1200s drought impacted the Fremont region (Benson et al. 2007), and both the Tavaputs Plateau sites and, more generally, aggregated sites such as Five Finger Ridge and Mesa House indicate a concern with defensive behavior (if not necessarily invading nomads) in parts of both the Fremont and Virgin regions. But it seems unlikely that any one factor accounts for the demise of farming.

Climatic variation likely played an important role, although given the geographical variability of the Fremont and Virgin regions and the variation in farming practices across the area, it is unlikely that drought alone caused the abandonment of farming. A precipitation reconstruction based on Tavaputs Plateau tree-ring data indicates that, as in the Central Mesa Verde, this area experienced generally dry conditions from about AD 1130 to 1300, with a pronounced multi-year drought beginning in the AD 1270s (Knight, Meko, and Baisan 2010). But this should not, by itself, have led to the complete abandonment of farming. For one thing, many Fremont sites were positioned along streams that would not have dried up in even the worst droughts. Given the generally arid Utah climate, it is unlikely that most Fremont were dry farming (although direct evidence of water-control features is rare), and even in drought years, the streams should have provided sufficient moisture to support farming, although drought may have reduced stream flows and agricultural productivity. Unusually late spring or early fall frosts in cold years may have been more challenging to farmers, especially to those living at higher elevations or in more northern latitudes. But it is not clear whether (or where) cold may have been a factor. High-frequency temperature reconstructions suggest considerable variability across western North America during the critical time period; tree-ring records from the Sierra Nevada suggest temperatures at or slightly above normal in the decades immediately before and after AD 1300 (Graumlich 1993; Scuderi 1993), but a similar record from east-central Idaho indicates a period of pronounced cooling that began in the late 1200s and lasted into the AD 1300s (Biondi et al. 1999). How well these reconstructions reflect the temperature fluctuations actually experienced by Fremont and Virgin farmers is unclear, although spatial correlation suggests that the Idaho record should be relevant to at least the most northern parts of the Fremont region (Biondi et al. 1999:1447).

Whatever the causes, the timing of the end of farming in (at least) the majority of the Fremont and Virgin areas coincided closely with both the late-1200s Great Drought (Douglass 1929) and the depopulation of the northern San Juan region. It is possible that Fremont or Virgin immigrants contributed to the social and demographic changes that occurred in the northern San Juan in the late thirteenth century, but what happened to Fremont and Virgin people is unclear; there has been a tendency in the Fremont literature for those who emphasize southwestern connections to assume that most Fremont probably migrated out to the south and east, while those authors who see continuity with the Archaic period and downplay southwestern influences generally think it more likely that the Fremont simply gave up farming and reverted to hunter-gatherer lifestyles. But there is little evidence to support either position.

It *is* clear that, as in the rest of the northern Southwest, the end of farming involved substantial depopulation. After about AD 1300, the areas previously occupied by the Fremont and Virgin were home to people with clear links to the historical Southern Paiute and Ute. With only a few exceptions, these people were highly mobile hunter-gatherers who lived in relatively small groups. It is difficult to estimate regional populations either before or after 1300, but populations were much smaller after 1300.

Exceptions to the highly mobile hunter-gatherer pattern include what has sometimes been called the Promontory culture in northern Utah, as well as ancestral Paiute horticulturalists in southwest Utah and the Moapa Valley of Nevada. "Promontory" sites are hunter-gatherer camps concentrated in the wetlands along the shores of the Great Salt Lake and Utah Lake (Allison 2002; Allison et al. 2000; Janetski and Smith 2007; Simms and Heath 1990). They are often large, with dense accumulations of trash, including large amounts of pottery, and they appear to represent multiseasonal residential bases from which people exploited marsh resources. Some archaeologists have argued that similarities in ceramics (among other things) reflect continuity between the Fremont and these late prehispanic hunter-gatherers (e.g., Dean 1992; Simms et al. 1997). Radiocarbon dates, however, suggest that they date to the AD 1400s and 1500s, and they probably do not immediately postdate the Fremont.

Southern Paiute horticulture also *might*, but probably does not, indicate continuity with earlier Puebloan farmers. When the first Europeans arrived, ancestral Paiutes were farming along permanent streams in the Moapa Valley and in southwest Utah (Allison et al. 2008). But again, the chronology suggests a break; most ancestral Paiute sites in the region, and especially those with evidence of farming, appear to date after AD 1500. One date of 670 ±50 BP from a site in southwest Utah that had maize in association with Southern Paiute Utility Ware (Walling et al. 1986) might indicate that Paiute farmers were in the area sometime close to AD 1300, which would strengthen arguments for continuity or contact with the Virgin. This, however, is suggested by only the one date, which is on charcoal and may be old wood.

Mitochondrial DNA studies may also be relevant to the question of continuity between Fremont and later populations, although the evidence is limited and far from conclusive. The frequencies of five mitochondrial

DNA haplotypes extracted from a subset of the skeletal remains found in the Great Salt Lake wetlands suggest that the Great Salt Lake Fremont were genetically more similar to archaeological and modern Native American populations from the Southwest than to Great Basin populations (O'Rourke et al. 1999; Parr 1998; Parr et al. 1996) (fig. 6.6). The patterns in figure 6.6 are striking, but these results should be interpreted cautiously. Sample sizes are small from many of the sampled populations, including the Paiute/Shoshone sample ($n = 9$) that most plausibly represents the post-Fremont occupants of northern Utah. Without data from a larger sample of modern Native Americans from the eastern Great Basin and data from a broader range of archaeological Fremont, Ancestral Pueblo, and Archaic populations, it is impossible to know what these patterns mean, although they do seem to imply a discontinuity between Fremont and subsequent populations.

The evidence for continuity between the Fremont and Virgin and subsequent populations is thus weak, but evidence for migration is no better. The occurrence of Bull Creek points at Pueblo III sites in southwest Colorado, including one at Castle Rock Pueblo (Crow Canyon Archaeological Center 2003; Kuckelman, this vol.), might be the best indication. Bull Creek points are one of several distinct regional styles of projectile points in the Fremont region (Holmer and Weder 1980). They are most common in the area around Glen Canyon and the Escalante River drainage, on both Fremont and Ancestral Pueblo sites. Interestingly, Bull Creek points (and, farther west, Parowan Basal-notched points) crosscut what are relatively sharp Fremont-Kayenta and Fremont-Virgin boundaries in the distributions of other kinds of material culture.

The few Bull Creek points that have been found in southwestern Colorado probably indicate some kind of contact with people to the west, but it is difficult to judge whether that contact involved migration, conflict, or trade. Other typical Fremont and Virgin artifact types are apparently absent in the northern San Juan region and the other areas to the south and east that would have presumably been the destinations for out-migrating Fremont and Virgin people. If migration was an important factor in the end of farming in the Fremont and Virgin regions, the migration seems to have been archaeologically invisible, unless people from these areas contributed to the AD 1200s population increases in some portions of the northern San Juan.

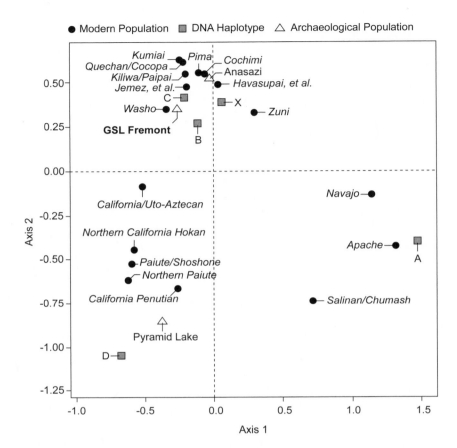

Figure 6.6. First two axes of a correspondence analysis of the frequencies of five mitochondrial DNA haplotypes in archaeological and modern Native American populations from western North America. Note that the Great Salt Lake Fremont population plots in a cluster that includes mostly southwestern and Baja California populations. Populations in this cluster tend to have relatively high frequencies of haplotypes B, C, and X, while the archaeological (Pyramid Lake) and modern Numic (Paiute/Shoshone and Northern Paiute) populations are distinguished from the Great Salt Lake Fremont primarily by high frequencies of haplotype D. The correspondence analysis is based on data reported by Lorenz and Smith (1996:311), O'Rourke et al. (1999:99), and Parr (1998:6).

Conclusion

I started this chapter with the stated goal of helping the prehispanic occupants of what was once called the Northern Periphery "[find] their rightful place in the story of our prehistoric Southwest" (Judd 1919:22)—or at least the part of the story that deals with the depopulation of the northern Southwest. This is not an easy thing to do, because the area involved is so large and chronological and demographic studies so underdeveloped. But farmers in both the Virgin and Fremont regions disappeared from the archaeological record close to the time at which people migrated out of the northern San Juan region. Previously popular assertions that the Virgin region was abandoned as early as AD 1150 are contradicted by radiocarbon dates from a number of sites, and occupation appears to have lasted into the late 1200s.

In the century prior to AD 1300, people in these regions generally appear to have lived in small settlements that may have included as many as about one hundred people but were usually half that size or less. There is not enough data for a good estimate of regional populations, but there must have been at least a few thousand people in each of the Fremont and Virgin regions in the AD 1200s. Evidence for either continuity with later populations or migration out of these regions is slim. The other possibility is a major, *in situ* population crash, but there is no direct evidence for that either, although populations were clearly smaller after the end of farming. It is, of course, conceivable—perhaps even likely—that population decline, migration, and continuity with later populations (which probably included Numic immigrants) all occurred in some combination.

Given the similarity in timing, it is unlikely that the end of farming in the Northern Periphery was unrelated to the depopulation of the larger region. As other chapters in this volume document, the last decades of occupation in the northern San Juan region were marked by social changes, including aggregation and increased use of ritual architecture. There are hints that similar processes occurred in the Virgin area and (especially) the Fremont area, although aggregation in those less densely populated areas was on a smaller scale, and the functions of Fremont central structures, which are the best candidates for ritual architecture, are not well understood.

It would be easy to speculate about the nature of the connections between the end of farming in the Fremont and Virgin regions on the one hand, and events in the northern San Juan area on the other. But it will take more and better data and more extensive efforts to synthesize the data before we can really test various possibilities. Efforts to better document and date the largest Fremont sites are especially needed; many have been obscured by modern development, but some portions of most sites remain, and study of museum collections and historical documents can supplement what will probably be limited archaeological work. Other potentially productive directions for research include further investigation of the dating and function of Fremont central structures and attempts to better document the scale and distribution of the latest communities in the Virgin region.

Much remains to be learned about the end of farming in the Northern Periphery, but it coincided closely with the migrations of Ancestral Puebloans from the northern San Juan region. The similarity in timing indicates that events in the Northern Periphery were connected to broader trends, and we won't really understand the depopulation of the northern Southwest until we can say with some certainty what happened to the Virgin and Fremont.

Acknowledgments

I am indebted to Scott Ure for drafting the figures in this chapter and to several people who commented on earlier drafts of the text. In particular, comments from Joel Janetski, Tim Kohler, Margaret Lyneis, Susan Ryan, Richard Talbot, Mark Varien, Aaron M. Wright, and two anonymous reviewers helped me to catch mistakes, refine my ideas, and improve my writing. Any problems that remain despite their help are, of course, my own responsibility.

Notes

1. My compilations, although undoubtedly incomplete, are an attempt to assemble all the radiocarbon dates associated with maize horticulture in the two areas. Included are dates from habitation sites as well as dates from other types of sites that were unquestionably associated with maize. In compiling the dates, I began with earlier compilations (Allison 2005; Berry and Berry 2001), which I supplemented with unpublished dates in my possession as well as a few published dates omitted in the earlier compilations.

2. My analysis used uninformative prior probabilities for all parameters. Including the Three Mile Ruin date makes the Pueblo III period appear slightly longer and start earlier. With the Three Mile Ruin date included, the posterior distribution for the start of the Pueblo III period peaks at about AD 1150, but there is little change to the posterior distribution for the end of the period.

7

The Impact of Long-Term Residential Occupation of Community Centers on Local Plant and Animal Resources

Andrew I. Duff, Karen R. Adams, and Susan C. Ryan

This chapter presents archaeobotanical and faunal data from Ancestral Pueblo contexts in the Sand Canyon Pueblo locality (see Lipe 1992:2–3, fig. 1.3) of the central Mesa Verde region to provide a long-term perspective on the use of economic plants and animals in the decades and centuries leading up to the region's depopulation. The Crow Canyon Archaeological Center (CCAC) conducted multiyear testing programs at Sand Canyon Pueblo (Bradley 1992, 1993; Kuckelman, ed., 2007, this vol.; Ortman and Bradley 2002) and Goodman Point Pueblo (Coffey and Kuckelman 2006; Kuckelman and Coffey 2007), sites that each include more than four hundred rooms and ninety or more kivas. These community centers were constructed and occupied in the last half of the thirteenth century and were among the last sites occupied in the region. The CCAC has also conducted multiyear testing programs at contemporaneous and earlier habitations near each of these late centers (Duff and Ryan 2006; Varien and Kuckelman 1999), work conducted as part of a larger research project known as the Sand Canyon Archaeological Project (Lipe 1992; Varien and Wilshusen 2002).

Here, we use data from these latter projects to examine changes in subsistence and the local environment resulting from centuries of landscape use and human alteration. These data provide a historical ecological context for these communities that helps us understand how the last decades of occupation may have differed from earlier periods, complementing the picture of the terminal occupations of Sand Canyon Pueblo (Kuckelman, ed., 2007, this vol.) and other regional sites.

Our interpretations will be based on (1) species and age information from tree-ring samples; (2) identification of plants used for fuel, structure-closing material, and food from flotation and macrofossil samples; (3) identification of plant pollen; and (4) identification of faunal remains. These data document the periods leading up to and during the initiation of the final regional depopulation, and they suggest that overall, pressure on food and nonfood resources increased over time in the Sand Canyon locality. Yet these impacts were relatively subtle and seem unlikely to have precipitated or required depopulation.

The Sand Canyon Locality

The data used here derive from residential settlements on the McElmo Dome (Ortman and Varien 2007; figs. 1.1, 1.2) examined by CCAC beginning in 1983 and continuing to the present. We emphasize data from excavations at Shields Pueblo (Duff and Ryan 1999, 2000, 2001; Ward 1997), supplemented by information from the Sand Canyon Archaeological Project Site Testing Program, hereafter referred to as the STP (Varien 1999a; Varien, ed., 1999). The Shields Pueblo project and the STP were designed to complement information derived from other CCAC research into late-thirteenth-century village occupations, including those at Sand Canyon (Kuckelman, ed., 2007), Castle Rock (Kuckelman, ed., 2000), Woods Canyon (Churchill 2002), and Yellow Jacket (Kuckelman, ed., 2003) pueblos, as well as other sites located throughout the region (Duff 2006a; Lipe and Ortman 2000; Ortman et al. 2000).

Shields Pueblo is a mesa-top village situated on an upland near the head of Goodman Canyon. The site consists of eighteen roomblocks scattered by mechanized plowing over a 35 ac (14 ha) area (fig. 7.1). Immediately south of Shields Pueblo is the Goodman Point Unit of Hovenweep National Monument, an archaeological preserve encompassing Goodman Point Pueblo—a late Pueblo III canyon-head village—and dozens of unit pueblos associated with the occupation of Shields and Goodman Point pueblos (Adler 1990, 1992; Adler and Varien 1994; Ortman and Varien 2007: fig. 11). From 1997 to 2000, the CCAC examined the development and depopulation of Shields Pueblo, testing more than fifty structures and numerous disturbed and undisturbed midden contexts, revealing a long but discontinuous occupation that began about AD 725. Occupation was sporadic between AD 725 and 1060, but it appears to have been continuous from AD 1060 until sometime after AD 1260.

A focal building at Shields Pueblo is interpreted as a Chaco-period great house, and a road (Hayes 1981:63) connects the great house at

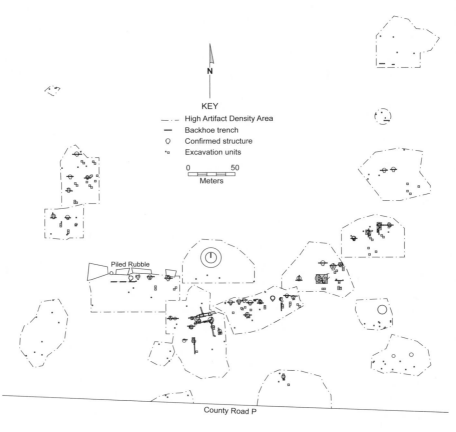

Figure 7.1. Plan of Shields Pueblo, showing areas of excavation and exposed structures. (Courtesy Crow Canyon Archaeological Center)

Shields to one at Casa Negra, the Chaco-period center in the neighboring Sand Canyon community (Adler and Varien 1994). Shields Pueblo appears to have been focal within the larger Goodman Point community from the Chaco era until the construction of neighboring Goodman Point Pueblo at or after AD 1250 (Coffey and Kuckelman 2006), when it eclipsed Shields. The latest tree-ring date for Shields Pueblo is AD 1258v, and several kivas at Shields have dates in the AD 1240s and 1250s (Crow Canyon Archaeological Center 2008; Duff 2006b, 2006c; Duff and Ryan 2001: table 1). Assuming that these structures were used for one or two decades after construction (see Varien 1999a), Shields Pueblo was occupied into the period of final regional depopulation,

AD 1260–1280, but it seems unlikely to have been occupied during the last days of Goodman Point and Sand Canyon pueblos (see Kuckelman, this vol.). Though some Shields Pueblo residents appear to have migrated from the region by the mid–AD 1200s and others may have moved to Goodman Point Pueblo when it was founded, the village and area around it continued to be actively used by remaining residents—probably including those at Goodman Point Pueblo—until regional depopulation. Given the disturbed nature of the site's surface, excavations emphasized testing of pit structures and other features that preserved deposits untouched by mechanized plowing. Most of the faunal and archaeobotanical data we use here come from these undisturbed contexts.

The STP conducted excavations at thirteen sites in the vicinity of Sand Canyon Pueblo (fig. 7.2) (Varien 2002; Varien, ed., 1999; Varien and Kuckelman 1999:fig. 1.7), of which eleven are interpreted to have been year-round habitations in use between 1180 and 1280. Five of these eleven also had earlier components (Varien 1999a:91, table 5.1). Two additional sites feature a tower and kiva. These are thought to have been either atypical residences or, more likely, special-activity locations occupied after AD 1225 (Varien 1999a:97–98, table 5.1). Ten of the STP sites were located on mesa-top or talus-slope contexts within a mile (1.6 km) of Sand Canyon Pueblo, while three were located within the sandstone-dominated lower Sand Canyon, roughly 4 mi (6.4 km) down-canyon from Sand Canyon Pueblo (Varien, ed., 1999). Midden, pit structure, and architectural contexts were tested at each site (Varien and Kuckelman 1999), providing the archaeobotanical and faunal data used here to broaden the spatial and temporal view provided by Shields Pueblo.

Data Sources

Botanical and faunal remains were systematically recovered from various contexts during the STP and Shields Pueblo projects to detect and interpret ancient patterns of food use, to assess what activities took place in structures, and to examine environmental change and how human impacts to the environment may have altered the composition of the surrounding plant and animal communities over time. Archaeo-botanical and faunal samples were primarily collected from structures and midden deposits. Pollen samples were collected from structural

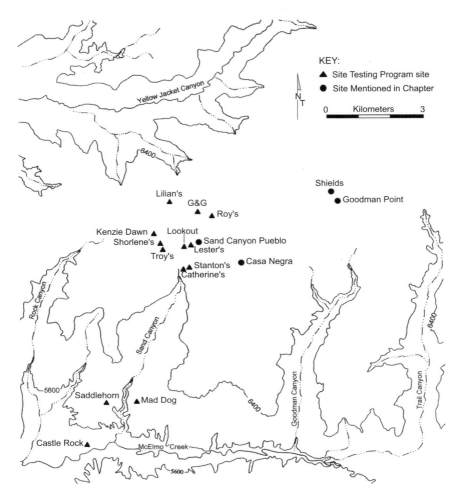

Figure 7.2. Shields Pueblo and the Sand Canyon locality (after Lipe 1992: fig. 1.3). (Courtesy Crow Canyon Archaeological Center)

contexts, with the addition of modern samples to characterize contemporary vegetation communities. Data used here come from the STP report (Varien, ed., 1999), the report for Shields Pueblo (in draft form, July 2008), and the CCAC online research database (Crow Canyon Archaeological Center 2008). The online database contains some data from Shields and the STP sites, as well as several other sites examined by Crow Canyon over the last twenty-five years.

Dating

Cultural deposits, structures, and features investigated at Shields Pueblo were assigned to Village Ecodynamics Project (VEP) modeling periods (Kohler, this vol.; Kohler, Johnson et al. 2007: table 4.2; Ortman, Varien, and Gripp 2007: table 3) when warranted, or to aggregates of these periods (Duff 2006b). In several cases at Shields Pueblo, these represent combinations of modeling periods aggregated to equate to commonly used Pecos-period subdivisions, such as early Pueblo III (AD 1140–1225). Site Testing Program sites were excavated prior to the development of the VEP and Ortman and colleagues' (2007) method for estimating the number of resident households at sites in each VEP modeling period. When possible, we use the VEP dating for the STP sites. In a few cases, however, we use the periods assigned at the time this project was reported. Table 7.1 provides the Shields Pueblo and STP household counts by modeling period as represented in the VEP database in July 2008 (Tim Kohler, personal communication, 2008).

Dendrochronological Wood Samples

These data consist of larger charred construction and possible fuelwood samples submitted for analysis to the Laboratory of Tree-Ring Research at the University of Arizona. Lab personnel provided species designations for all analyzed material, whether or not they could date the sample. Datable samples include both an innermost date, which can signal the initial year of tree growth, and a terminal date, which may represent the last year the tree was alive or may predate this event (Dean 1978a). Due to its better preservation, wood used in roof construction comes almost exclusively from samples collected from burned pit-structure roof strata, though other contexts are occasionally represented.

Archaeobotanical Samples

At Shields Pueblo, 165 systematically collected flotation samples from primary and secondary refuse were analyzed (Adams 2004: table 1). The samples analyzed from Shields Pueblo were chosen from a larger pool of field-collected samples, with the goal of maximizing spatial and temporal coverage within the site (Adams 2004). To these we add 162 systematically collected and analyzed flotation samples from 11 STP sites

Table 7.1. Number of households assigned to each VEP period for Shields Pueblo and the STP sites

Site number	Site name	725–800	1060–1100	1100–1140	1140–1180	1180–1225	1225–1260	1260–1280
5MT3807	Shields	18	28	41	33	45	39	
5MT181	Mad Dog							1
5MT262	Saddlehorn						1	
5MT1825	Castle Rock							14
5MT3918	Shorlene's						2	3
5MT3930	Roy's					1		
5MT3936	Lillian's						1	
5MT3951	Troy's							1
5MT3967	Catherine's					2	2	
5MT5152	Kenzie Dawn					1	2	
5MT10246	Lester's						1	2
5MT10459	Lookout						1	2
5MT10508	Stanton's						1	
5MT11338	G & G		1	1	1	1	1	

(Adams 1999), excluding the two special-function sites, Troy's Tower and Mad Dog Tower. Primary refuse was mostly ash collected from hearths, firepits, and ashpits. Secondary refuse was collected from midden deposits located either south of residential architecture or from within abandoned structures that were later filled with secondary refuse. Flotation samples from these contexts contain small seeds and other reproductive parts suggestive of past subsistence practices. They also contain small fragments of charred wood indicative of routinely burned fuels and wood types sought for other daily needs.

Macrofossil samples collected during excavation also provide important information on past plant use. At times, such sampling has recovered plant remains not normally found in flotation samples, which may provide information on contexts not sampled by flotation analysis. Excavators collected 935 macrofossil samples from Shields Pueblo, including larger plant remains such as wood, corn, beans, and other plants. These samples are especially valuable for documenting corn that was stored or where it was intentionally placed in a number of burned structures. Macrofossil samples were collected from roof fill, middens, thermal features, ashpits, and other contexts. Although our interpretations focus on the systematically collected flotation-sample datasets, the combination of flotation samples and larger macrofossils make Shields Pueblo one of the best-sampled sites for archaeobotanical remains in the region.

Pollen Samples

Forty-four pollen samples from Shields Pueblo were analyzed by Jones and reported by Adams (2006: tables 4–9), and thirty-two samples from STP contexts were analyzed and reported by Gish (1999: tables 17.1 and 17.4–17.12). Two hundred pollen grains were counted for all Shields samples (Adams 2006), while one hundred or two hundred grains were counted in STP samples (Gish 1999). All pollen data were considered as the relative percentage of each plant taxon within each pollen sample. Pollen-sample results discussed here are samples collected from pit-structure floors, naturally deposited sediments directly above the collapsed roofs, and samples from beneath and above "shrine" features constructed in the late thirteenth century atop collapsed kiva roofs at Shields Pueblo.

Twenty-seven pollen samples from Shields were collected from pit-structure or kiva floors. These samples were uniformly from sealed contexts, such as beneath a stone slab resting directly on the floor surface. Stone slabs were deposited on floors prior to intentional roof dismantling or burning, sealing the floor pollen that had been deposited when the structure was in use. Eleven samples from STP kiva floors are included, five of which derive from similarly sealed floor contexts. Six other STP samples are "floor scrapes" taken relatively close to the hearth, designed to capture likely economic pollen related to food preparation (Gish 1999). We believe that pollen recovered from such contexts contains mostly human-introduced pollen and limited amounts of naturally deposited pollen.

Five structure-fill pollen samples were collected from naturally deposited sediment in the strata immediately above roof-fall deposits in abandoned kivas and pit structures dating to AD 725–800 and AD 1140–1225 at Shields Pueblo. After either wood from kiva roofs was removed for use elsewhere or, more commonly, roofs were burned, the remaining roofing materials collapsed onto the pit-structure floor, creating a deep depression. These depressions initially accumulated sediment rapidly through high-energy water deposition (Kilby 1997). Over time, as the depressions filled in, deposition slowed and wind became the primary depositional agent (Kilby 1997; Varien 1999a). We assume that the sampled strata contain natural wind- and water-deposited sediment and pollen grains deposited within the first few years of structure abandonment. The initial fill sequence is assumed to have been dominated by summer monsoon rainstorms that produced rapid deposition/infill from immediately (2–3 m) surrounding sediment; rapid filling traps the pollen grains in reasonably well-dated contexts. Compared to the sealed kiva floor samples, we assume the cultural component of kiva roof-fill pollen samples to be reduced relative to natural deposition, and we expect these samples to reflect the composition of plant communities in the surrounding landscape. If pollen in fill was deposited primarily by natural processes and pollen from kiva floors primarily by cultural processes, then the analyses of these contexts allow us to make inferences regarding the changing nature of the surrounding vegetation over time, and whether use of specific economic plants increased or decreased over time.

Five additional pollen samples from the final depopulation (AD 1260–1280) and post-abandonment (AD 1280+) periods at Shields Pueblo were collected from three unusual masonry constructions interpreted as shrines, and from natural deposits 15 and 25 cm above one of these features. These features (described in greater detail below) consist of masonry circles constructed within the accumulating fill of intentionally burned kivas originally constructed in the AD 1240s and 1250s (Duff and Ryan 1999, 2000). Pollen samples were taken from under the lowermost course of stones in three of these features, and these samples were therefore almost certainly deposited within the AD 1260–1280 period, probably towards the end of that period. Two pollen samples were taken from natural strata 15 and 25 cm above one of these features (but below the plow zone), and these are used to proxy the post-depopulation environment.

Faunal Remains

Faunal data from Shields Pueblo and the STP sites are used to evaluate changes in the use of economically important animals over time. All Shields Pueblo faunal remains were analyzed by Rawlings (2006; Rawlings and Driver 2006). Driver and colleagues (1999) analyzed faunal remains from the STP sites. We present information about only the economic taxa of artiodactyls, lagomorphs, and a combined grouping of turkeys and large birds, though the original reports document a much wider range of animals. The proportions of these three major categories by period are examined, as are common indices that gauge the relative importance of these taxa.

Woodland Impacts

Harvesting wood and shrubs for construction and as fuel was a persistent activity during the prehispanic occupation, with the potential to impact the pinyon-juniper woodland communities surrounding community centers. Juniper was the primary and preferred construction material, dominating the combined analyzed samples from both Shields Pueblo and the STP sites (table 7.2). Though the sample size becomes much smaller when we restrict it to cutting or near-cutting dated samples (see Varien 1999b), juniper dominates the assemblage of structural wood in this dataset as well (table 7.3). Pinyon trees were sought less frequently, likely because their strength as construction timbers is inferior to that of juniper wood. Trees not common to the immediate area, such as Douglas

Table 7.2. Species represented in analyzed tree-ring samples

Species[a]	Shields Pueblo		STP sites	
	Count	Percent	Count	Percent
Douglas fir	20	0.7	7	0.8
Juniper	2,550	93.0	740	86.8
Pinyon	141	5.1	95	11.1
Ponderosa pine	10	0.4	2	0.2
Nonconiferous	5	0.2	1	0.1
Oak	2	0.1	0	0.0
Spruce/fir	1	0.0	2	0.2
Willow/Cottonwood	12	0.4	6	0.7
Total	2,741	99.9	853	99.9

[a] Some entries from sites in the CCAC online database lack a species designation. All complete data were used. Sites used for this analysis include Shields Pueblo, Castle Rock, G & G, Kenzie Dawn, Lester's, Lillian's, Lookout House, Mad Dog Tower, Roy's, Saddlehorn Hamlet, Shorlene's (Basketmaker component excluded), Stanton's, and Troy's Tower.

fir, ponderosa pine, and spruce/fir—all requiring travel to distant locations such as Ute Mountain, the Mesa Verde, or the canyons of the Dolores River—occur infrequently, as do oak and willow/cottonwood (table 7.2). Although use of higher-elevation timbers is emerging as one distinctive feature of Chaco-era structures, especially great houses (e.g., Varien et al. 2007:287), the three dated examples of these species in our sample post-date Chaco's influence (Shields Pueblo, ponderosa pine, 1196v; Saddlehorn Hamlet, spruce/fir, 1210vv and 1231vv).

The dated roofing timber record presents no clear case for a change in wood preference or availability through time (table 7.3). Similarly, there is little patterning evident in the average ages of trees harvested during different periods (table 7.3). Here, we have calculated the average age and standard deviation of all trees for which an interior and cutting or near-cutting date were reported, which is dominated by specimens lacking an absolute growth initiation date (evidenced by a "pith" ring). Thus, the averages reported should systematically underestimate the true age of the trees used for construction.

Notable jumps in the mean timber age at Shields Pueblo follow periods when the site appears not to have been occupied or after a period

Table 7.3. Ages of harvested structural timbers with cutting or near-cutting tree-ring dates in the Goodman Point/Sand Canyon Pueblo localities by VEP periods

Period (years AD)[a]	Shields Pueblo[b]				STP sites[b]			
	Mean age	S.D.	Count	Percent juniper	Mean age	S.D.	Count	Percent juniper
725–799	76	27	9	56				
1020–1059					204	25	2	100
1060–1099	187	73	3	100	104	28	5	100
1100–1139	104	63	11	100				
1140–1179	103	33	3	100				
1180–1224	123	85	18	94	166	71	14	100
1225–1259	106	57	31	100	108	38	18	100
1260–1280					108	62	8	82

[a] Village modeling periods after Ortman et al. 2007: table 3.

[b] Some sites or particular entries in the CCAC online database report only the latest tree-ring date, not the inner date for the specimen, or lack species information. Cutting and near-cutting dates were those with Tree-Ring Laboratory symbols "r," "b," or "v" (see Varien 1999c). All complete data were used. Sites with appropriate data used for this analysis include: Shields Pueblo, Castle Rock, G & G, Kenzie Dawn, Lester's, Lookout House, and Saddlehorn Hamlet.

of diminished occupation (see table 7.1), a pattern also evidenced in the STP sites data (table 7.3). This seems to indicate that people preferred to build with older trees when they were available, so that age of trees decreases with deforestation. Even so, it seems clear that suitable and relatively mature trees continued to be available within an acceptable distance (which may be larger for construction timbers than for fuel-wood) into the late 1200s, when Goodman Point and Sand Canyon pueblos were being constructed. In fact, the average age of all post–AD 1260 dated timbers from Sand Canyon Pueblo, which includes beams with noncutting end dates ("vv"), is 108 years ($n = 66$), virtually identical to the mean age of timbers used in previous periods.

Roof-closing materials within flotation samples and pollen within fill above roofs from Shields Pueblo do, however, reveal shifts in the composition of the surrounding landscape through time. Sagebrush and rabbitbrush were the most common closing materials used in kiva roof construction in all periods. Use of sagebrush was relatively consistent over time, while rabbitbrush use declined in the later periods (Adams 2004: table 14). Significantly, willow/cottonwood (combined, since macrofossils of these tree types are indistinguishable), a tree restricted to mesic habitats, was not used in roof construction until early Pueblo III times (AD 1140–1225), possibly indicating a shift in the local environment or construction material preference at this time. Use of willow/cottonwood as a closing material more than doubled to a presence in nearly 4 percent of all samples in the late Pueblo III period (AD 1225–1280), perhaps replacing rabbitbrush. Willow pollen occurs on nearly all kiva floors and structure fill at Shields Pueblo in all periods, but it increased over time in natural pollen rains (see below). Willow pollen is either not present or not reported for the STP sites (Gish 1999). The presence of willow, which is sensitive to drought and would have been affected by drier than average conditions, indicates that damp places were still present in the local environment, possibly growing around the springs and seeps associated with many of the Pueblo III community centers.

The flotation record indicates that common fuels used at Shields Pueblo throughout its occupation include juniper, pine, sagebrush, and maize cobs (Adams 2004). The presence of all these fuel resources within thermal features and middens declined from early Pueblo I to late Pueblo III at Shields (table 7.4). During this multicentury time

Table 7.4. Ubiquity and diversity of charred plant taxa within thermal feature/ashpit flotation samples by period from Shields Pueblo (Adams 2004) and STP sites (Adams 1999)

Periods	Shields Pueblo					STP sites	
	725–800	1020–1060	1060–1140	1140–1225	1225–1260	Pre-1250	Post-1250
Number of flotation samples	8	9	25	35	35	15	19
Plant and part(s)	Ubiquity (percent)						
Juniper (non-food parts)	100	100	72	71.4	71.4	73.3	89.5
Pine (non-food parts)	87.5	66.7	60	62.9	42.9	66.6	73.7
Sagebrush (non-food parts)	100	44.4	64	22.9	31.4	73.3	26.3
Maize (all parts)	100	100	76	48.6	42.9	46.6	52.6
Willow/cottonwood wood	0	0	24	20	22.9	6.6	15.8
Cheno-am seeds	37.5	66.7	84	40	28.6	40	15.8
Category of Use	Taxon diversity (number of separate plant taxa)[a]						
Subsistence resources	6	3	14	9	10	15	9
Fuels/other non-food resources	5	6	9	12	11	11	14

Sources: Shields Pueblo: Adams 2004; STP sites: Adams 1999

[a] Each taxon was counted only once, regardless of the variety of parts (i.e., juniper wood, twigs, scale leaves) identified within samples of each subperiod. In addition, note that maize cobs are useful as fuel once kernels have been removed.

Table 7.5. Mean percentage of pollen in structure fills, Shields Pueblo

Pollen type	Years AD			
	725–800 (*n* = 2)	1140–1225 (*n* = 3)	1260–1280 (*n* = 3)	Post-1280 (*n* = 2)
Pine	7.4	5.3	5.2	4.6
Juniper	18.9	20.0	14.0	10.4
Cheno-am	24.4	21.5	32.4	43.1
Sagebrush	31.1	28.8	24.0	20.3
Willow	1.3	1.6	3.5	6.5
Maize	0.2	0.1	0.5	0.2

span, the ubiquity of charred juniper wood, pine, and maize cobs/cupules declined notably, while willow again appears to have been used, in part to compensate for the decline in other materials. This curious pattern could have been caused by increased specialization in the species used for fires—that is, a trend toward building fires with one or two species instead of several. However, STP site data (Adams 1999: table 16.19) fail to support this pattern (table 7.4). Site Testing Program site fuels—which are more difficult to interpret, since location is not held constant—show increases in the ubiquity of juniper, pine, and maize in post–AD 1250 contexts. Increased ubiquity of willow/cottonwood mirrors the increase noted at Shields Pueblo, and it may in part reflect closed-array effects from a decline in sagebrush ubiquity in both records. Willow/cottonwood charcoal occurs at nine of the STP sites (Adams 1999) and was used for both fuel and construction.

Despite the relatively subtle impacts attested to in the timber, fuel, and closing material data, pollen does reveal a changing woodland in the area surrounding Shields Pueblo. Mean pollen-percentage data from structure fills at Shields Pueblo reveal a consistent decline in juniper, pinyon, and sagebrush pollen over time (table 7.5). Notably, sagebrush and rabbitbrush are the two shrubs first to occupy fallow fields today, and the pollen record does not indicate increasing sagebrush pollen at any time during Shields's occupation. Together, these data suggest a general reduction of both pinyon-juniper woodland and sagebrush parkland immediately surrounding Shields Pueblo over time, a signal we interpret as indicating agricultural intensification, with fallow periods short enough to deter regrowth of sage.

Foods

The most frequently recovered domesticated food from Shields Pueblo and the STP sites is maize. Maize is consistently recovered in all periods, including charred maize cob/cupule fragments indicative of secondary use as a fuel/tinder source. Beans and squash are presumed to have made up some percentage of dietary needs of residents; however, they rarely preserve well in archaeological sites, in part because of preparation methods and preservation issues. Ethnographically, beans are typically boiled rather than parched, and soft squash flesh simply doesn't preserve as well as many other plant foods. Beans were recovered, however, from five of the thirteen STP sites (Adams 1999), and both beans and squash were recovered from Shields Pueblo (Adams 2004: table 3).

Although reliance on maize appears to have been significant through-out the occupation, maize plant parts decline in thermal features from a high of 100 percent in the AD 775–800 and 1020–1060 periods to a low of 43 percent by AD 1225–1260 (table 7.4), possibly suggesting a decline in maize availability as both a food and a fuel. Paradoxically, however, the highest numbers of maize macrofossils (kernels, portions of ears, cobs) were recovered from six intentionally burned kivas con-structed and utilized during the late Pueblo III period (AD 1225–1280). The maize in these structures appears to have been used to fuel the fires, ensuring a more complete burning of the roof, while there was also likely to have been a ritual element to its use in closing these kivas. The presence of maize pollen on kiva floors is also highest (at 1.8 percent) during late Pueblo III, in comparison to earlier subperiods (0.3–0.6 percent). At Shields Pueblo, the ubiquity of maize in thermal features (table 7.4) generally declined during periods of climatically induced decreases in potential maize production, such as the prolonged drought from AD 1130 to 1180 (Van West and Dean 2000:23; Wright, this vol.) or the unfavorable times between AD 1200 and 1240 (Kohler, this vol.). The fact that these independently produced lines of evidence reinforce each other suggests that maize's ubiquity record is at least somewhat sensitive to its dietary availability.

An additional line of evidence regarding maize use just prior to depopulation comes from late-constructed stone features or shrines at Shields. Eight circular, dry-laid masonry structures built atop collapsed kivas were exposed during the excavations at Shields (Duff and Ryan 1999, 2000, 2001; Ryan 2000). These stone circles were constructed after the underlying kivas had burned, their roofs had collapsed, and the depressions created by their collapse had accumulated less than 0.5 m of sediment. The stone circles were then constructed atop uneven surfaces that appear not to have been leveled or otherwise prepared. Constructions ranged from two to three courses to a maximum of thirteen courses, and they are roughly 3 m in diameter. In all cases, the underlying kivas were tested and produced datable timbers. Only one of these late stone circles was built atop a kiva that had its beams removed for use elsewhere; all others appear to have had their complete roofs burned in place, and their floors often contained numerous still-usable artifacts, including reconstructable vessels. Pollen samples were collected from beneath the basal courses of three such features that overlay structures with latest dates of 1245v, 1255vv, and 1258v.

We interpret these stone circles to have been ritual features of some sort, likely shrines, an interpretation also suggested by members of the CCAC's Native American Advisory Group (Ryan 2000). The construction of these dry-laid stone circles was among the last acts for which we have archaeological evidence from Shields Pueblo, and we could not identify any functional purpose or use for them (e.g., there were no floor features or indications of roofing). The pollen samples clearly post-date the construction and use of the underlying kivas, and assuming that the kivas were used for a decade or more, the pollen samples are interpreted to date to the 1270s. Maize pollen was recovered from two of the three samples collected (each less than two percent), indicating that maize was still being grown during this period. In fact, maize pollen is present in Shields structure fills in roughly equal and quite low percentages throughout the site's occupation (table 7.5). One of the samples yielded a maize anther, or a cluster of five or more pollen grains, which indicates human rather than wind transport of the pollen. The maize anther suggests that the maize was either a ritual offering or that maize was grown within this structure. Knowing that maize pollen is a common offering at shrines and is used in other ritual contexts, we favor the interpretation that this maize was deposited as a ritual offering.

The most frequently used wild foods represented in pollen and flotation samples from the late Pueblo III period are members of the Chenopodiaceae and Amaranthaceae families (referred to hereafter as Cheno-ams). In pollen analysis, the Cheno-am designation includes goosefoot (*Chenopodium*) and all members of the pigweed family (Amaranthaceae); in flotation analysis, the Cheno-am designation is assigned to seeds that could represent either goosefoot (*Chenopodium*) or pigweed (*Amaranthus*) (table 7.4). These weedy annuals thrive in disturbed locations such as would be found on middens, along pathways, and in active and recently fallowed agricultural fields. In addition to Cheno-ams, a wide range of wild weedy and perennial plants provided foods for Shields Pueblo occupants. The diversity of these additional subsistence resources generally increased through time, reaching a peak between AD 1060 and 1140, then declined (table 7.4). Many of the key trend lines in plant use bend or flex during the AD 1060–1140 period, suggesting general shifts in resource use following this time.

Faunal remains suggest some changes in animal procurement over time (table 7.6). At Shields Pueblo, artiodactyls were relatively more prevalent in earlier periods, presumably before sustained local occupations reduced their availability. This is especially evident in the AD 1020–1060 period, when the artiodactyl index (artiodactyl/[artiodactyl + lagomorph]) spikes. Artiodactlys are relatively rare in STP sites. If they were ever more abundant in the Sand Canyon locality, this likely pre-dates sites sampled to date.

Although the proportion of lagomorphs varies, the lagomorph index (*Sylvilagus*/[*Sylvilagus* + *Lepus*]) remains essentially constant and quite high. This indicates that the smaller-bodied cottontails probably found in or near agricultural or fallow fields were the primary lagomorph target. Again, the exception comes with the slight decline in the AD 1020–1060 period at Shields Pueblo, when the larger-bodied jackrabbits were taken relatively more frequently, an occurrence perhaps again associated with the recolonization of the area by residents after an occupational hiatus and the lack of established cleared field areas.

The shift from ritual use of turkey in earlier times to its central production and use as a food source during the Pueblo II period and especially

Table 7.6. NISP, row percentages, and indices for selected taxa by period, Shields Pueblo and select STP sites

Period (years AD)	Artiodactyl	Lagomorph	Turkey/large bird
Shields Pueblo[a]			
725–800	10 (5.2%) 0.06	147 (76.6%) 0.90	35 (18.2%) 0.19
1020–1060	36 (8.8%) 0.20	144 (35.3%) 0.76	228 (55.9%) 0.61
1060–1140	301 (6.9%) 0.07	3514 (80.9%) 0.82	529 (12.2%) 0.13
1140–1260	68 (1.8%) 0.03	2108 (57.0%) 0.85	1521 (41.1%) 0.42
1260–1280	20 (2.5%) 0.03	521 (65.1%) 0.89	259 (32.4%) 0.33
STP sites			
1180–1260[b]	27 (1.4%) 0.03	822 (43.4%) 0.89	1045 (55.2%) 0.56
1260–1280[c]	20 (2.6%) 0.05	407 (52.0%) 0.87	355 (45.4%) 0.47

[a] *Source*: Rawlings and Driver 2006: table 15.
[b] Sites: Roy's, Saddlehorn Hamlet, Lillian's, Stanton's, Catherine's, and Kenzie Dawn. *Source*: Driver et al. 1999: table 18.1.
[c] Sites: Castle Rock Pueblo, Troy's, and Mad Dog Tower. *Source*: Driver et al. 1999: table 18.1.

the Pueblo III period (Munro 1994) is evident in the Shields data. Turkey indices ([turkey + large bird]/ [turkey + large bird + lagomorph]) increase over time. Rawlings (2006:183) notes that if turkey burials are removed from the Shields data, the high turkey index at AD 1020–1060 (table 7.5) declines to 0.21, which makes the increased use of turkey after AD 1140 more evident. Site Testing Program site faunal data derive primarily from periods after 1140. Turkeys were probably closely tended, likely by female household residents (Rawlings 2006), and isotopic analysis of turkey bone from Shields indicates that they were fed corn (Rawlings 2006).

The faunal data reveal some changes after AD 1260 relative to earlier periods, including slight increases in artiodactyls and a more notable decrease in turkey relative to the immediately preceding period. Despite these changes, these data suggest that sufficient gathered and husbanded animal resources were available to residents as the region was being depopulated, a situation that contrasts starkly with the final season(s) of occupation evidenced in the Sand Canyon Pueblo data presented by Kuckelman (this vol.).

Human Impacts and Depopulation

Archaeologists in the Mesa Verde region have long assumed that human activities on local landscapes over many centuries impacted plant and animal communities, and that these impacts in turn affected the subsequent choices of humans, especially toward the end of sustained occupation. We generally have not had sound empirical datasets to evaluate the degree to which these changes affected decisions to leave the region, but we are beginning to accumulate this type of essential information. Data presented here mark another contribution to this growing literature (see also Adams and Bowyer 2002; Kohler and Matthews 1988; Stiger 1979; Varien et al. 2007).

During the long occupation of Shields Pueblo, most of the shifts in the archaeological plant and faunal record appear to have been anthropogenic in origin, with the possible exception of maize ubiquity. During the last three centuries of regional occupation, the pollen record from kiva fills documents declines in juniper, pinyon pine, and sagebrush in the area surrounding Shields Pueblo. Continued human impact likely fostered these unidirectional trends. Climate-induced environmental change might be expected to generate fluctuations in pollen production that correlate with wetter or drier, or colder or warmer, periods. Yet such fluctuations are not apparent in the Shields Pueblo pollen record. The spike of Cheno-am pollen in the AD 1260–1280 period suggests extremely high populations of these plants on the landscape, as would be consistent with large quantities of disturbed land. The occupation of Goodman Point Pueblo by nearly all the community's residents may have stimulated even more localized land clearing for fields and/or shorter fallow periods in the immediate vicinity of Shields Pueblo, and this signal may be reflected in the pollen data.

The fact that willow/cottonwood wood and willow pollen increase during the later portion of Shields' occupation, and that willow is present in many of the STP sites, suggests that damp habitats were still available in the locality and were being increasingly relied upon for wood. This is consistent with VEP modeling of spring flows, which suggests relatively steady spring production despite annual variability in rainfall (Kohler et al. 2007:71). The trees were likely associated with springs and seeps at the canyon heads later enclosed by Goodman Point and Sand Canyon pueblos (Lipe and Ortman 2000) or Goodman Lake, adjacent to Goodman Point Pueblo. There is, however, a rival interpretation for the late increases in willow/cottonwood fuel wood and closing materials and willow pollen. Kohler and Matthews (1988) noted increases in cottonwood through time in the Pueblo I village fuel wood record in the nearby Dolores Archaeological Project area, attributing it to the joint effects of decreased availability of more-preferred species, as well as to the increased representation expected of more quickly growing species relative to more slowly growing species, under woodland depletion.

Prior to the final regional depopulation around AD 1280, the overall plant record at Shields Pueblo suggests that occupants had affected areas of the surrounding pinyon-juniper woodland by their harvest of pinyon and juniper wood for construction elements and fuel, as well as by clearing woodland and sagebrush parkland areas for agricultural fields. They relied heavily on maize, beans, squash, and annual weedy plants for subsistence, in addition to a range of annual and perennial wild plants. The use of juniper, pine, and leftover maize parts for fuel had declined, and people were instead using a more diverse suite of woody fuels than they had in earlier times. This suggests that preferred wood species in the area had been impacted, most likely due to increased use related to a larger residential population, something also noted for the Dolores area following an earlier cycle of population consolidation and long-term residential occupation (Kohler and Matthews 1988).

Even though the woodland in these localities had been altered, juniper and pinyon wood remained the most common materials for construction and fuel throughout the occupation of Shields Pueblo, including the period just prior to the final depopulation. In addition, the flotation records of both Shields Pueblo and the STP sites preserved small juniper and pinyon parts (twigs, scale leaves, needles, bark scales, and cone scales), supporting the inference that living or recently dead trees were still growing within a reasonable distance of these pueblos, and that occupants were not forced to utilize debarked roof timbers as their final fuels (Adams 1999, 2004). The pressures of more than two centuries of use do not appear to have diminished the harvesting of live mature trees of preferred species for construction; timbers harvested at the end of the region's occupation were similar in age and in species to those harvested earlier. In fact, the average age of structural timbers reported here does not differ dramatically from the regional picture generated using only wood with pith and cutting dates (Varien et al. 2007:287, fig. 5G), despite the acknowledged "undercount" of true ages embedded in our dataset. It is possible that residents may have had to venture farther or expend more energy to procure these beams, a proposition we cannot gauge, given present evidence. A potential indication of timber pressure is the consistent use of recycled beams at Sand Canyon Pueblo (Bradley 1992, 1993), also highlighted by Adams and Bowyer (2002:140), but we should also note that beam recycling occurred throughout the region's occupation.

Increasing use of Cheno-am seeds through time suggests increasing presence of active and possibly fallow agricultural fields, one signal of agricultural intensification, which would have made Cheno-ams more abundant and more likely to have been harvested in greater quantities. The plant evidence generally implies that by the final decades of occupation, people had opened the pinyon/juniper woodland, altered the relative proportions of some of its major taxa, and increased the amount of disturbed habitats favored by weedy plants. Taking all of this into consideration, it appears that the residents of Shields Pueblo exploited their local fuel and construction timber resources enough to change the locally available plant community, but not to the extent that would have required fundamental alterations to subsistence strategies. Adams and Bowyer (2002) come to much the same conclusion for the Sand Canyon Pueblo locality, working primarily with data from the STP sites.

Faunal data similarly track subtle changes, but the most dramatic shifts predate regional depopulation by a century or more. Artiodactyls were never very common, but their numbers appear to have been suppressed by persistent predation well before AD 1200. Residents of the Sand Canyon locality came to rely on tended turkeys for much of their meat, a shift well underway by AD 1180. Rabbits were a constant food source in proportions that suggest a consistent landscape, or at least consistent predation strategies by hunters on the modified landscape, as people preferentially hunted cottontails that would have preferred open, disturbed habitats like their agricultural fields.

Conclusions

Human impact on the environment and the drier than average, colder than average, and increasingly unpredictable conditions that character-ized the late AD 1200s (Kohler, this vol.; Wright, this vol.) were cer-tainly a partial catalyst for the emigration from the central Mesa Verde region. Annual fluctuations and the consistent recurrence of stressful periods were a part of every Mesa Verde–region resident's life experi-ence, and group memory would hold information about similar periods in the more distant past.

Behavioral responses to these conditions ultimately led to decisions to leave the region. It appears that the residents of Shields Pueblo left the village in an orderly and planned fashion, ritually closing kivas and their usable contents in what would have been emotionally charged confla-grations, and, within a season of these fires, constructing shrines above the collapsed roofs of these kivas. Economic plant and animal remains collected from contexts dating to the final decades of occupation suggest that maize was still being successfully grown, that many of the same wild plants were being utilized, and that the same animals were available and regularly taken. Willow indicates both that water for water-seeking trees remained—the springs essential throughout the region's occupation continued to produce water, as they still do—and also, possibly, that more slowly growing species were becoming relatively less abundant on the landscape. Anthropogenic alteration of the Sand Canyon locality is documented in the data presented here, yet these same data do not evi-dence major disruptions that would have necessitated emigration.

The social climate of the later AD 1200s, perhaps especially in distant regions, was clearly relevant and apparently even attractive to regional residents (Cameron and Duff 2008; Cordell et al. 2007; Lek-son and Cameron 1995). As households opted to reconfigure themselves within the larger region (Glowacki 2006, this vol.) or chose to depart altogether in the late twelfth and early thirteenth centuries (Duff and Wilshusen 2000; Kohler, this vol.; Varien, this vol.), these actions would have both social and practical impacts on remaining residents. Younger families—often yet to hold important social positions within their communities—tend to be on the leading edge of immigration trends (Duff 1998), and their labor departs with them when they immigrate. These actions impact both the biological and social viability of remaining communities.

The communities that remained in the Mesa Verde region during the late thirteenth century were increasingly isolated when viewed in terms of connections to the remainder of the occupied Southwest. Though the community centers that remained were still large in size, their loss of relatives to migration also created the connections that later could have been drawn on to facilitate the transition to new destinations, chiefly in the northern Rio Grande (Ortman, this vol.; Lipe, this vol.). Increasing violence characterized many late–AD 1200s sites, often in their final use (e.g., Kuckelman, this vol.; Kuckelman, Lightfoot, and Martin 2000, 2002). Even though the physical landscape may have remained viable, the changed social landscape was no longer sustainable.

Despite detectable alteration to local resources, we believe—as do most other contributors to this volume—that answers to the age-old question "Why was the Mesa Verde region depopulated?" will increasingly feature what we can reconstruct about social processes and actions, especially now that we are able to provide empirical data that seem to suggest that we need to look beyond immediate aspects of the environment and economy.

Acknowledgments

We thank the Amerind seminar participants, and especially the volume editors, for their constructive comments, all of which have improved our discussion. Additionally, we thank Susan J. Smith and John Jones for comments on and discussion of the Shields Pueblo pollen data. Research at Shields Pueblo was supported by the Crow Canyon Archaeological Center and by grants from the Colorado Historical Society and the National Geographic Society (#6016-97, #6292-98, #6559-99, and #6860-00); all support is gratefully acknowledged.

8

Catalysts of the Thirteenth-Century Depopulation of Sand Canyon Pueblo and the Central Mesa Verde Region

Kristin A. Kuckelman

The identity of the factors causing all the Pueblo farmers in the northern San Juan area to leave by the late AD 1200s looms as perhaps the most intriguing and intensely pondered archaeological issue in the northern Southwest. For more than a century, a variety of possible environmental and social causes have been proposed, including drought, cooler temperatures, altered rainfall patterns, environmental degradation, resource depletion, population pressures, religious upheaval, social disruption, violence, and other possible factors (e.g., Ahlstrom, Van West, and Dean 1995; Benson, Peterson, and Stein 2007; Cameron 1995; Cameron and Duff 2008; Cordell 1997:365–397; Cordell et al. 2007; Dean et al. 2000; Dean and Van West 2002; Glowacki 2006; Kohler 2000; Kohler et al. 2008; Kuckelman 2002; Kuckelman, Lightfoot, and Martin 2002; Larson et al. 1996; Lipe 1995; Lipe and Varien 1999b:339–343; Newberry 1876:89; Nordenskiöld [1893] 1979:170; Petersen 1994; Petersen and Matthews 1987; Salzer 2000b; Van West and Dean 2000; Varien et al. 1996; Varien et al. 2007). The past fifteen years have witnessed both a burgeoning of research on "push" factors that might have compelled residents to emigrate from the region and also proposals for "pull" factors that might have drawn Pueblo farmers to new areas.

Several obstacles have hampered efforts to pinpoint the specific catalysts that stimulated decisions to emigrate. The best data available still lack the resolution requisite for researchers to accurately assess the timing, rate, and size of population movements from the region and indeed to even specify when the regional depopulation began. Understanding this timing is crucial for evaluating which of the myriad possible environmental and social factors might have stimulated decisions to emigrate. In addition, compelling evidence of how changing environmental conditions in the late 1200s did, in fact, impact farmers has

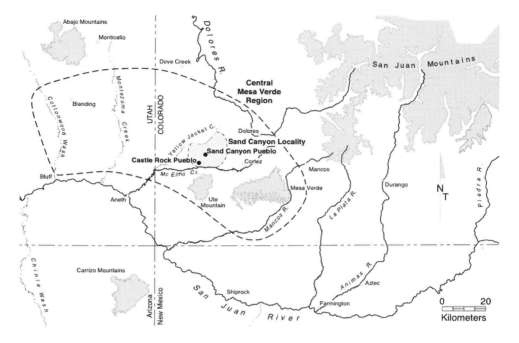

Figure 8.1. The central Mesa Verde region, showing locations of Sand Canyon Pueblo and Castle Rock Pueblo. Goodman Point Pueblo is 4.5 km northeast of Sand Canyon Pueblo. (Courtesy Crow Canyon Archaeological Center)

proven elusive, as has direct evidence of social strife that one might reasonably expect to have contributed to the complete depopulation of any geographic region. In this chapter, I present evidence from recent excavations at Sand Canyon Pueblo and other terminal-Pueblo III sites (fig. 8.1), confirming that both environmentally induced subsistence stress and lethal conflict immediately preceded, and thus were almost certainly factors in, the depopulation of the Mesa Verde region.

Evidence from Sand Canyon Pueblo

The Crow Canyon Archaeological Center conducted excavations at Sand Canyon Pueblo from 1984 through 1993 (fig. 8.2), investigating about 5 percent of the site. These excavations generated a substantial body of data that offers insights into the regional depopulation as well as the demise of Sand Canyon Pueblo itself (Kuckelman, ed., 2007;

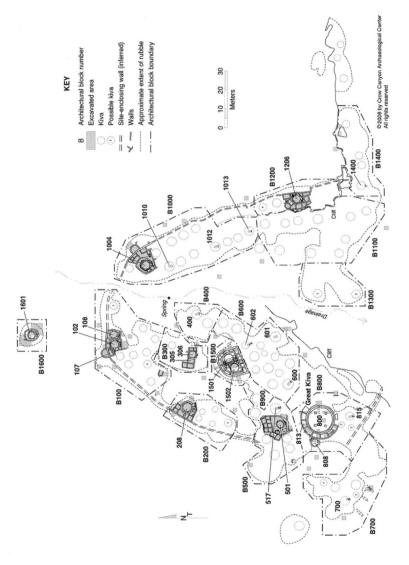

B   Architectural block number

Excavated area

Kiva

Possible kiva

Site-enclosing wall (inferred)

Walls

Approximate extent of rubble

Architectural block boundary

0   10   20   30
Meters

©2008 by Crow Canyon Archaeological Center
All rights reserved

Figure 8.2. Plan map of Sand Canyon Pueblo. (Courtesy Crow Canyon Archaeological Center)

Kuckelman 2009). This village (or community center) was occupied from approximately AD 1250 to 1280, when the region was experiencing its final years of residence by Pueblo people.

Here, I review evidence that residents of Sand Canyon Pueblo experienced considerable subsistence stress near the time of regional depopulation. I do this by comparing animal and plant remains recovered from middens with those from abandonment contexts such as structure floors, thermal features, and collapsed roofing debris. The former reflect subsistence practices during most of the occupation of the village, whereas the latter provide evidence for subsistence strategies at the end of the occupation, which approximately coincided with the onset of the Great Drought in about AD 1276. In addition, I review osteological and taphonomic analyses of human remains that provide evidence of both nonlethal violence in the mid–AD 1200s and a large-scale, devastating attack that ended the occupation of the village. I focus primarily on the depopulation of Sand Canyon Pueblo and offer what appears to be, from all available data, the most likely scenario for the village's demise during the regional depopulation.

Sand Canyon Pueblo, constructed around the head of a small canyon that drains into upper Sand Canyon, was among the largest villages in the Mesa Verde region. Numerous other masonry villages built in the mid–AD 1200s in the region were constructed in similar settings. Founded about AD 1250, the pueblo grew rapidly during the 1260s and was occupied until sometime after the latest tree-ring date, AD 1277vv. The pueblo housed some 400 to 600 residents and contained approximately 90 kivas, 420 rooms, numerous towers, a D-shaped bi-wall building, a great kiva, and other structures and features (fig. 8.3). Characteristics of the pueblo that can be interpreted as defensive include a massive masonry enclosing wall that contains angled sighting apertures but few access openings; towers accessible only from inside the pueblo, abutting the outside face of the enclosing wall; and the spring-encompassing layout of the pueblo.

To obtain the highest-possible temporal resolution from this corpus of excavation data, I considered structure stratigraphy, condition of roofing debris (burned vs. unburned), evidence of structure dismantling, the location of collapsed roofing material in relation to structure floors, and characteristics of artifact assemblages found in abandonment contexts.

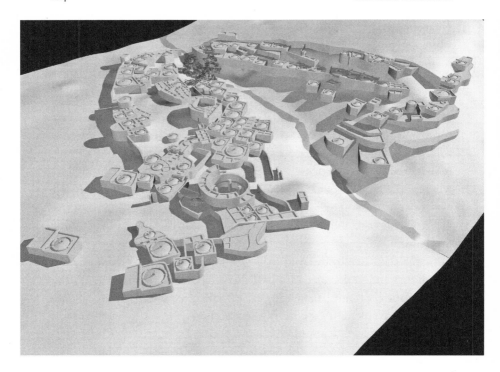

Figure 8.3. Reconstruction of Sand Canyon Pueblo. (Computer model by Architect Dennis R. Holloway, courtesy Crow Canyon Archaeological Center)

Detailed descriptions and interpretations of abandonment and postabandonment events for each of the 111 excavated or tested structures at this site are contained in *The Sand Canyon Pueblo Database* (Crow Canyon Archaeological Center 2004), and a discussion of roof burning within the village is also available (Kuckelman 2002:238–240). Because kivas were the primary residential structures, I used abandonment characteristics of each of the twenty-four tested or excavated kivas as an indicator of the abandonment mode of each associated suite of residential structures (hereafter referred to as kiva suites) in the village (Kuckelman 2009).

The results, extrapolated to include the entire village, suggest that, of the estimated ninety kiva suites in the village, as few as twenty-one (23 percent) or as many as sixty-six (73 percent) were probably uninhabited before the major attack that precipitated the abandonment of the pueblo. This range of estimates results from the small sample size. The village was occupied for such a brief span of time (twenty-five to thirty years) that most suites were undoubtedly still in use when emigration from the pueblo commenced; however, three of the twenty-four kivas that were tested had been partly dismantled, suggesting that at least a few suites were abandoned before emigration, when materials were still being salvaged for new construction.

Even though many kiva suites might have been uninhabited before the village was attacked, multiple lines of evidence suggest that village-wide depopulation occurred relatively rapidly and that those kiva suites that had fallen out of use before the village was attacked might have stood empty for only a few months, and probably not longer than a few years, before the attack.

Another facet of this study was to look for evidence of the causes of village depopulation, so I searched for evidence of dietary stress in the food remains. To detect possible changes in subsistence practices that might have occurred near the end of occupation and that thus might illuminate deteriorating conditions contributing to the regional depopulation, I compared the composition of animal and plant assemblages from midden deposits with those from abandonment contexts.

The "abandonment context" category includes primary refuse (refuse left where it was created) and defacto refuse (usable items left on use surfaces). In general, most assemblages that I categorized as being from abandonment contexts were found either on floors, in collapsed roofing debris, or in thermal features such as hearths; in addition, they were found in contexts in which there was no evidence of subsequent cultural activity. I chose these assemblages as being indicative of the latest actions, behaviors, and conditions in the village.

Faunal Data

The faunal assemblage from Sand Canyon Pueblo contains a total of 10,848 identified bones (number of identified specimens, NISP). Domesticated turkey (*Meleagris gallopavo*), cottontail rabbit (*Sylvilagus* sp.), and artiodactyl (mostly *Odocoileus hemionus*, or mule deer) are the key taxa in this assemblage (table 8.1). A comparison of the percentage of turkey bones (food refuse) from secondary refuse to that from abandonment contexts reveals a marked drop in turkey consumption near the end of village occupation. In contrast, the percentages of bones representing

Table 8.1. Percentages of bones of key taxa among identified specimens, Sand Canyon Pueblo

Taxa	Secondary refuse ($n = 3{,}968$)	Abandonment contexts ($n = 2{,}674$)	Entire assemblage of identified bones (NISP) ($n = 10{,}848$)
Turkey[a]	55	14	31
Cottontail[b]	14	27	22
Artiodactyl[c]	1	13	6

[a] Turkey (*Meleagris gallopavo*) and "large bird"
[b] *Sylvilagus* sp.
[c] Deer (*Odocoileus* sp. and *Odocoileus hemionus*), pronghorn antelope (*Antilocapra americana*), medium artiodactyl, Artiodactyla, and bighorn sheep (*Ovis canadensis*)

wild animals such as deer are greater in abandonment contexts than in secondary refuse, indicating that residents procured and consumed a negligible amount of deer meat during nearly the entire span of village occupation. The incidence of cottontail bones is also greater in abandonment contexts. The greater proportion of bones from wild animals in abandonment contexts indicates an increase in the consumption of the meat of these animals near the time of village depopulation.

To further examine these subsistence shifts, I calculated various indices for this nonhuman bone assemblage. The turkey index evaluates the intensity of turkey production (Driver 2002:147). It is calculated by dividing the NISP of turkey bones by that of rabbit and hare (lagomorph) bones. The results (table 8.2) indicate a dramatic drop in the intensity of turkey production and a coincident shift in faunal exploitation by the residents near the end of village occupation.

The lagomorph index, calculated by dividing the NISP of cottontail bones by that of all lagomorph bones combined, is designed to evaluate the amount of human impact on an environment (Driver 2002:146; Szuter and Bayham 1989:92). Values for this index from the Sand Canyon Pueblo assemblage are comparable to those for other assemblages from similar sites in the region (Driver 2002: fig. 7.7). The lagomorph indices for secondary refuse vs. abandonment contexts (table 8.2) at Sand Canyon Pueblo are also similar, which suggests that at least some aspects of the local environment remained relatively stable during the brief occupation of the village.

Table 8.2. Comparison of nonhuman bone indices, Sand Canyon Pueblo vs. Castle Rock Pueblo

	Sand Canyon Pueblo		Castle Rock Pueblo	
Index	SR	AC	SR	AC
Turkey[a]	2.95	0.45	1.07	0.59
Lagomorph[b]	0.75	0.84	0.83	0.87
Artiodactyl[c]	0.06	0.30	0.03	0.06

Note: SR = Secondary refuse; AC = Abandonment context.
[a] Turkey index is the NISP of turkey divided by the NISP of lagomorphs (Spielmann and Angstadt-Leto 1996:90). For this assemblage, lagomorphs comprise the sum of bones identified as *Sylvilagus* sp., *Lepus* sp., and Lagomorpha. "Turkey" as used here sums *Meleagris gallopavo* plus unidentified large bird remains.
[b] The Lagomorph Index is the frequency of cottontail (*Sylvilagus* sp.) bones in the total lagomorph assemblage (Driver 2002:146; Szuter and Bayham 1989:83); that is, the number of *Sylvilagus* bones divided by the sum of all lagomorph bones. In this assemblage, lagomorphs consist of cottontail, jackrabbit (*Lepus* sp.), and all lagomorph bones that could not be identified to species.
[c] The Artiodactyl Index is the frequency of artiodactyl bones in the total of artiodactyl bones plus lagomorph bones (Driver 2002:147; Spielmann and Angstadt-Leto 1996:84; Szuter and Bayham 1989:83). In this assemblage, lagomorph bones consist of cottontail (*Sylvilagus* sp.) and jackrabbit (*Lepus* sp.), as well as lagomorph bones not identified to species, and artiodactyla bones consist of deer (*Odocoileus hemionus* and *Odocoileus* sp.), pronghorn (*Antilocapra americana*), bighorn sheep (*Ovis canadensis*), and all "medium artiodactyla" bones not identified to species.

The artiodactyl index, used to assess the availability of large game (Driver 2002:147; Spielmann and Angstadt-Leto 1996:83; Szuter and Bayham 1989), is calculated by dividing the NISP of artiodactyl bones by the combined NISPs of artiodactyls and lagomorphs. The very low index for secondary refuse at Sand Canyon (table 8.2) indicates a minimal availability of large game during most of the occupation, while the much higher index for abandonment contexts reflects greater availability of this wild resource just before occupation ended.

Muir (2007: par. 53) found that, given the size and the taxonomic richness of the Sand Canyon Pueblo faunal assemblage, the number of taxa represented in midden subassemblages was much lower than expected. These subassemblages also display a lower-than-expected evenness value, reflecting the dominance of the remains of only a few taxa (Muir 2007: par. 53). Muir's findings thus provide corroboration that the Sand Canyon villagers exploited an unusually sparse number of animal taxa for animal protein during most of the occupation of the village and a much wider variety of taxa near the end of village occupation.

The faunal data in general, then, indicate that the residents of Sand Canyon Pueblo relied heavily on turkey for animal protein during most of the occupation of the village. Near the time of depopulation, however, their use of turkey declined, and they procured and consumed the meat of an unusually wide variety of game, including pronghorn antelope, bighorn sheep, mule deer, and bobcat—species that these villagers had seldom previously procured.

Archaeobotanical Data

Archaeobotanical data from this site also reveal significant shifts in subsistence near the end of occupation. Remains of domesticates—gourd, butternut squash, and beans, for example—were found almost exclusively in middens. The predominant domesticate consumed by residents was maize, as indicated both by the carbon isotope levels in human remains at the site (Katzenberg 1995, 1999) and by the ubiquity of maize kernels in middens (Adams, Kuckelman, and Bowyer 2007). However, a low incidence of maize kernels in hearth fills suggests that maize was not being widely prepared or consumed just before occupation ended. Maize kernels were identified in 50 percent of the flotation samples collected from the earliest contexts at Sand Canyon Pueblo, but in only 8 percent of samples from the latest contexts.

In addition, a much wider variety of wild plant foods was represented in hearths that were last used at the end of village occupation. Of twenty-four total taxa represented in well-dated samples, only thirteen were found in midden samples, whereas twenty were found in those from abandonment contexts. These results indicate that residents exploited a wider variety of wild plant foods just before village occupation ended. The increased consumption of wild plants diverged from the established, largely agricultural subsistence strategy practiced by Pueblo people during the final centuries of the occupation of the Mesa Verde region and suggests that this subsistence shift was prompted by food stress (Adams, Kuckelman, and Bowyer 2007).

Human-Remains Data

Numerous aspects of the human remains at Sand Canyon Pueblo also lend insights into the depopulation of the village and the region. Osteological data attest to the generally healthy condition of the residents of this village, with the exception of a possibly elevated incidence of infectious disease (Kuckelman and Martin 2007). The overall health of the residents confirms that the maize-and-turkey subsistence strategy practiced during most of the village's occupation was effective and successful, although villagers could have suffered acute nutritional stress near the end of village occupation, even to the point of starvation, without visible skeletal effect.

Antemortem fractures on the crania of at least four individuals from Sand Canyon Pueblo reflect the occurrence of nonlethal violence in the central Mesa Verde region during the mid-thirteenth century (Kuckelman, Lightfoot, and Martin 2002: table 3; Kuckelman and Martin 2007: table 12; Lambert 1999: table 6.1). Lethal skull fractures detected on the remains of at least seven individuals at Sand Canyon Pueblo (Kuckelman and Martin 2007: table 12) offer indisputable evidence that violent death also occurred during this time period. Human remains exhibiting this type of injury, as well as other types of perimortem trauma, did not receive formal burials and were found exclusively in abandonment contexts, constituting compelling evidence of warfare associated with village depopulation. The timing of the attack, sometime after the latest tree-ring date for the village (AD 1277vv), also associates this warfare temporally with complete regional depopulation.

In addition to these seven individuals with perimortem cranial trauma, the remains of at least sixteen individuals at Sand Canyon Pueblo who did not exhibit direct evidence of violent death were deposited in abandonment contexts with no evidence of formal interment (Kuckelman 2009: table 7). Their remains were found in abandonment contexts in virtually every architectural block in the village. These people thus probably also died at the end of village occupation and might have been killed in the attack, but in a manner that left no skeletal impress. These remains included those of men, women, and children ranging from one year in age to their early fifties (Kuckelman 2009: table 6). The data indicate that some villagers were killed on rooftops, and their remains were either left where they fell or were thrown into a nearby structure. Some were trapped and killed in kivas. One middle-aged male was apparently struck down in a face-to-face attack, but most individuals with lethal head trauma were struck from behind, perhaps while fleeing.

The remains of several individuals of both sexes and various ages found in architectural blocks 100 and 1000 exhibit congenital and developmental anomalies (Kuckelman and Martin 2007: table 15); consanguineous groups thus died in their respective residential suites. It is therefore extremely likely that these individuals were residents of Sand Canyon Pueblo rather than members of the attacking party. Some victims, such as subadults, older adults, the ill, and possibly some with mental disability, would have offered little resistance to attackers. Robust adult males in their prime might have survived the attack or been absent from the village when the attackers chose to strike.

The human remains from Sand Canyon Pueblo thus reveal that the villagers were subjected to some violence in the mid–AD 1200s. As the region was undergoing final depopulation about AD 1280, a lethal and catastrophic attack ended the occupation of the village.

A Sand Canyon Pueblo Synthesis

These findings regarding the process and circumstances of the depopu-lation of Sand Canyon Pueblo, as well as additional data presented in greater detail elsewhere (Crow Canyon Archaeological Center 2004; Kuckelman, ed., 2007; Kuckelman 2009), suggest the following sequence of events. The village, founded about AD 1250, was constructed rapidly around a canyon-head spring and within a massive enclosing wall. The presence of antemortem skull fractures on the remains of several indi-viduals from Sand Canyon (Kuckelman, Lightfoot, and Martin 2002: table 3; Kuckelman and Martin 2007: table 12) indicate that residents of the pueblo were victims of nonlethal violence sometime during the occupation of the village.

The subsistence base of the residents was heavily weighted towards domesticates, primarily maize and turkey. Cottontail rabbits were the wild animals most often consumed. Because skeletal remains of the vil-lagers reflect generally good health, during most of the span of village occupation, this subsistence strategy was clearly successful. However, data suggest that, late in the occupation of this pueblo, residents consumed much less maize and many fewer turkeys. Turkey flocks would have consumed prodigious quantities of maize and water, and the reduction in their numbers could have resulted from a failure of maize crops. One-fourth to three-fourths of the residents departed before the events that resulted in the complete depopulation of the settlement, but many villagers remained in spite of adverse conditions. Secondary refuse began to accumulate in public architecture such as the great kiva, and Block 1500 (the D-shaped bi-wall block) was converted to domestic use. Near the end of village occupation, perhaps because of dwindling population or difficult times, these structures were apparently no longer used for rituals and ceremonies.

The remaining residents turned to a predominantly hunting-and-gathering subsistence strategy, probably to compensate for dwindling domesticated food resources. They exploited a greater variety of wild animals and plants, particularly just before final depopulation, and perhaps profited from a small degree of rebound in wild animal populations as initial regional depopulation eased predation pressures. In the months before Sand Canyon Pueblo suffered its attack, the residents acquired more artiodactyl meat and also hunted a more diverse range of game, including animals seldom procured previously and that might have necessitated long-distance hunting expeditions. Ownership of the village and the spring was probably maintained by those residents not directly participating in these strenuous and potentially perilous forays.

Sometime after AD 1277, a devastating attack resulted in the deaths of many of the villagers and brought the occupation of the pueblo to an abrupt end (Kuckelman 2007a, 2009; Kuckelman, ed., 2007; Kuckelman, Lightfoot, and Martin 2002; Kuckelman and Martin 2007). The remains of some victims were subjected to trophy-taking or other forms of dismemberment. Not all indicators of anthropophagy (Turner and Turner 1999)—the consumption of human flesh—were present on these remains; however, the disarticulated and fragmented condition of specific remains, as well as the commingling of fragmented human bone with nonhuman bone in food refuse, compels one to consider anthropophagy as a possibility, especially within this context of subsistence stress.

Rather than being killed by attackers, some individuals who died at the end of village occupation might have starved or succumbed to illness resulting from a nutritionally weakened condition. However, no evidence of chronic malnutrition was detected on any remains from the site, and one might reasonably assume that the remains of individuals who died under such circumstances during the occupation of the village would have been interred in a considerate manner rather than being deposited in abandonment contexts.

The data suggest that the lapse of time between the departure of the first wave of emigrants to leave the village and the onslaught of the attackers was relatively brief, perhaps several months to a few years. After the attack, many kiva roofs were intentionally burned. This action might have been a ritual "closing" (see Kuckelman 2003; Lightfoot 1993:298; Wilshusen 1986) by those who survived the attack or by friends or relatives from a nearby village.

The Sand Canyon data thus suggest that a failure of the maize-and-turkey subsistence base in the AD 1270s resulted in a shift to a predominantly hunting-and-gathering strategy. The movement across the landscape necessitated by this survival tactic was no doubt adversely impacted by violence, both threatened and realized, and a major warfare event sealed the fate of the village at the same time the region was in the throes of complete depopulation.

The Depopulation of Castle Rock Pueblo

Can any aspect of the depopulation of Sand Canyon Pueblo be detected at other terminal Pueblo III sites in the region? In several ways, the data from Sand Canyon Pueblo are uniquely suited to illuminate conditions associated with the thirteenth-century depopulation of the northern Southwest. The large, single-component assemblages from this site were deposited during the final decades of regional occupation. The latest tree-ring dates from Sand Canyon Pueblo so nearly coincide with regional depopulation that one can reasonably assume that residents who abandoned their homes in this village did so in order to migrate from the region. For these reasons, I consider it very likely that any stimuli for the depopulation of this village were also germane to the regional depopulation. Moreover, this site was among the three largest in the Village Ecodynamics Project study area for the AD 1260–1280 period (Kohler and Varien 2009), so its fate is of obvious importance to the region.

Few other excavations of late Pueblo III settlements in the Mesa Verde region meet the requirements for this type of case study. These requirements include systematic sampling, modern analytic techniques, and assemblages sufficiently large for reliable comparisons of occupational vs. abandonment-context subsistence data. Perhaps most important, the occupation must be firmly dated by dendrochronology to the final years of regional occupation, which ensures that the associated assemblages include the remains of the meals consumed and reflect the events occurring just prior to regional depopulation around AD 1280.

Castle Rock Pueblo is one of few other sites approaching these requirements, although because its assemblages are much smaller than Sand Canyon's, the resulting conclusions are more tentative. The medium-sized village of Castle Rock was constructed around and on top of a prominent butte (fig. 8.4) approximately 7.5 km southwest of Sand Canyon Pueblo. Partly excavated by Crow Canyon archaeologists between 1990 and 1994, this village was founded in about AD 1256 and was home to an estimated 75 to 150 residents (Kuckelman, ed., 2000; Kuckelman, Lightfoot, and Martin 2002). The latest tree-ring date for the site, 1274vv, suggests that residents who left the village did so to migrate from the region. Many aspects of the depopulation of this pueblo have been discussed at length elsewhere (Kuckelman 2000; Kuckelman, Lightfoot, and Martin 2002), although the following evidence of subsistence stress near the end of village occupation has not been presented previously.

The nonhuman bone assemblage for Castle Rock Pueblo is much smaller than that for Sand Canyon (cf. tables 8.1 and 8.3); however, characteristics of the two assemblages suggest that residents of these villages employed similar subsistence strategies. The same key taxa are represented, confirming that turkey and cottontail were the primary sources of animal protein for the residents of both villages. A comparison of the percentages of turkey bones in secondary refuse and the entire assemblage of identified bones from the two sites may indicate that the residents of Castle Rock were more dependent on cottontails and less dependent on turkey during most of that occupation. The Castle Rock data in table 8.3—like those from Sand Canyon—indicate a marked drop in the consumption of turkey near the end of occupation.

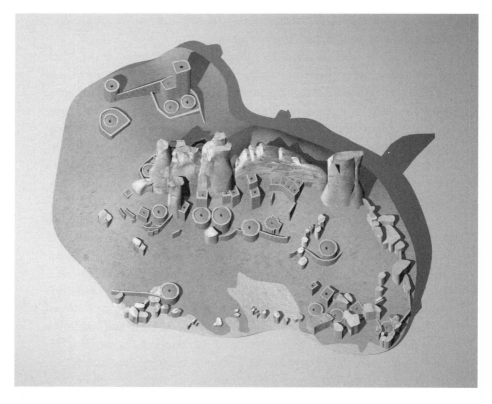

Figure 8.4. Reconstruction of Castle Rock Pueblo. (Computer model by Architect Dennis R. Holloway, courtesy Crow Canyon Archaeological Center)

A comparison of various nonhuman bone indices (table 8.2) illuminates similarities and differences between the assemblages from the two villages. The turkey index for the Castle Rock assemblage is much higher for secondary refuse than for abandonment contexts; thus, the intensity of turkey production dropped in both villages near the end of their occupations. The lower index for secondary refuse from Castle Rock Pueblo suggests that its residents were less dependent on turkey production than were those of Sand Canyon Pueblo during most of the occupation of these villages. The lagomorph indices for both secondary refuse and abandonment contexts are similar for the two settlements, indicating that some aspects of the landscape remained relatively stable during these occupations. Of the people occupying the two villages,

Table 8.3. Percentages of bones of key taxa among identified specimens, Castle Rock Pueblo

Taxa	Secondary refuse ($n = 1,177$)	Abandonment contexts ($n = 638$)	Entire assemblage of identified bones (NISP) ($n = 2,508$)
Turkey[a]	39	19	28
Cottontail[b]	30	28	34
Artiodactyl[c]	2	1	2

[a] Turkey (*Meleagris gallopavo*) and "large bird" combined
[b] *Sylvilagus* sp.
[c] Deer (*Odocoileus* sp. and *Odocoileus hemionus*), pronghorn antelope (*Antilocapra americana*), medium artiodactyl, Artiodactyla, and bighorn sheep (*Ovis canadensis*)

Castle Rock residents appear to have had less access to large game near the end of occupation, as indicated by the relative artiodactyl indices. Perhaps the much smaller population at Castle Rock lacked the resources necessary to field long-distance hunting parties.

Analyses of the human remains from Castle Rock Pueblo reveal further similarities between the two villages. The residents of Castle Rock also enjoyed general good health from their largely maize-and-turkey subsistence strategy, although antemortem cranial fractures observed on the skulls of a minimum of four residents of Castle Rock Pueblo (Kuckelman, Lightfoot, and Martin 2002: table 3) corroborate evidence of the ongoing, nonlethal violence found on Sand Canyon remains.

Evidence of violent death is even more unequivocal among the human remains from Castle Rock than among those from Sand Canyon Pueblo. Perimortem cranial fractures indicate that a minimum of four Castle Rock individuals suffered fatal blows to the skull, and abundant additional perimortem fractures attest to the deaths of many of the forty-one men, women, and children whose remains were found in abandonment contexts at the site (Kuckelman, Lightfoot, and Martin 2002). In addition to cranial fractures, the teeth of two individuals had been broken off by blows to the mouth, and one individual had suffered a slicing wound to a tibia. There is also compelling evidence that anthropophagy occurred after the attack (Kuckelman, Lightfoot, and Martin 2002); additional perimortem wounds were undoubtedly masked by the abundant fracturing and other bone modification associated with anthropophagy. The data thus indicate that a fatal attack ended the occupation of the village. The timing of these events at Castle Rock, sometime after the latest tree-ring date for the village (AD 1274vv), associates this warfare temporally with the Great Drought, the attack on Sand Canyon Pueblo, and the complete depopulation of the region.

Depopulation in a Regional Context

When Sand Canyon and Castle Rock pueblos were founded, other residents of the region were also establishing or joining aggregated settlements (Varien 1999a; Varien et al. 1996), many of which enclosed water sources and incorporated defensive features (Lipe and Ortman 2000; Lipe and Varien 1999b), suggesting that communities felt threatened (Kuckelman 2002; Kuckelman, Lightfoot, and Martin 2000; LeBlanc 1999; Lipe 2002:212). The presence of antemortem skull fractures on the remains of numerous individuals from Sand Canyon and other settlements (Cattanach 1980:415; Kuckelman, Lightfoot, and Martin 2002: table 3; Kuckelman and Martin 2007: table 12; Lambert 1999:141; Morris 1939:82) indicate that violence was not uncommon in the region in the mid–AD 1200s, and such wounds could have been inflicted during intervillage ambushes or raids. Although some of this healed cranial trauma could have resulted from domestic violence—which is typically directed toward women or children—or from intravillage abuse directed against specific adult females (e.g., Martin 1997), many of these wounds are likely to have been inflicted during warfare events.

The subsistence base of Pueblo farmers across the region appears to have been heavily weighted toward maize and turkey and was thus excessively dependent on the particular climatic and environmental conditions necessary for growing maize. The onset of a severe drought—the so-called Great Drought—by AD 1276 is clearly reflected in the tree-ring record (Douglass 1929; see also Wright, this vol.). This drought continued until 1299, and its effects have been documented in numerous environmental studies. In all likelihood, maize crops were either much diminished or destroyed by this and other adverse environmental conditions discussed in other chapters of this volume. Data from Sand Canyon and Castle Rock pueblos indicate that more cottontails and fewer turkeys were eaten; turkey flocks might have been reduced because they consumed abundant quantities of maize and water. Earlier periods of severe drought in the region, such as that from AD 1130 to 1180, also resulted in widespread migrations and serious strife (Berry and Benson, this vol.; Billman 2008; Billman et al. 2000; Kuckelman, Lightfoot, and Martin 2002).

The data presented here suggest a shift from farming toward a hunting-and-gathering lifestyle during the terminal portion of regional occupation. Under these conditions, communities would have competed for drought-diminished wild plant and animal resources across the landscape, and a downward spiral in the availability of consumable resources might well have been initiated. Perhaps the quantity of stored food available at the onset of the drought dictated when the decision to migrate became inescapable for each residence group.

Evidence of warfare from this period is abundant and continues to mount, and it is likely that subsistence stress and the increased reliance on hunting and gathering were related to the escalation of violence at this time. Direct evidence in the form of lethal skull fractures is indisputable and has been found on remains from Sand Canyon, Castle Rock, and elsewhere across the region (Cattanach 1980:415; Kuckelman, Lightfoot, and Martin 2002: table 3; Kuckelman and Martin 2007: table 12; Lambert 1999:141; Morris 1939:82). The cranial-depression fractures alluded to here are so similar to each other in size and shape that they were probably inflicted by a common type of weapon—probably a sharp-bitted stone axe (Cattanach 1980:415; Kuckelman 2002:241; LeBlanc 1999:113; Woodbury 1954:42) hafted onto a wooden handle. Stone axes are abundant at sites dating from this period. Trophy-taking accompanied warfare events at several settlements, including Sand Canyon Pueblo (Kuckelman 2009; Kuckelman, Lightfoot, and Martin 2002; Lambert 1999:141), and compelling evidence of warfare-associated anthropophagy has also been documented (Kuckelman, Lightfoot, and Martin 2002).

Indirect evidence of warfare includes aggregated population; defensible village locations with associated springs; defensive architecture; rock-art images depicting conflict; traditional oral accounts of violence; and human remains that were deposited in abandonment contexts, weathered, disarticulated, or damaged by carnivores (Kuckelman 2002). Ongoing excavations at Goodman Point Pueblo, a terminal Pueblo III, canyon-rim village located approximately 4.75 km east-northeast of Sand Canyon

Pueblo (fig. 8.1), have also revealed probable violence-related conditions on human remains in abandonment contexts.

Determining the identity of the attackers is an issue that will be difficult to resolve. Although the presence, in abandonment contexts, of a few projectile points that might have originated outside the region leaves open the possibility of non-Pueblo attackers from the west (Kuckelman, Lightfoot, and Martin 2002:505–506; Till and Ortman 2007), this evidence is far from conclusive. Because there are few data suggesting non-Pueblo incursions, one must conclude that, in all likelihood, the attackers were residents of Pueblo settlements within the Mesa Verde region (Bradley 2002; Kuckelman 2002:245–246, 2006:134, 2009; Kuckelman et al. 2007: par. 201; Lightfoot and Kuckelman 2001:64; Lipe 1995:161–162; Lipe and Varien 1999b:341). That is, to date, there is no convincing evidence that non-Pueblo warriors destroyed villages in the central Mesa Verde region during final regional depopulation.

Thus, aggregated and fortified settlements across the region prospered with their protected water sources and maize-and-turkey subsistence strategies until drought, and no doubt other social and environmental stresses, sent the system into a downward spiral of resource competition, hunger, strife, and warfare. Because the drought was widespread, because Pueblo people throughout the region shared a maize-dependent subsistence strategy, and because evidence of warfare in the late AD 1200s is not restricted to Sand Canyon Pueblo, it is likely that the conditions and events leading to the demise of Sand Canyon, Castle Rock, and possibly Goodman Point pueblos are representative of those in settlements across the region and were thus significant catalysts of the depopulation of the entire region.

Conclusions

The data from Sand Canyon and Castle Rock pueblos constitute the most compelling direct empirical evidence to date of subsistence stress and violence as catalysts in the final depopulation of the Mesa Verde region in the late thirteenth century. A dramatic shift from farming to hunting and gathering just before the depopulation of these two community centers, especially when paired with independent evidence of the onset of the Great Drought in AD 1276, suggests that the residents of the region experienced considerable subsistence stress and contrived to outlast deleterious environmental conditions. Ultimately, however, either the largely hunting-and-gathering strategy failed as well, or pervasive violence and an associated hostile regional atmosphere overshadowed and curtailed this attempt to outlast the drought. Emigration was thus stimulated at least in part by the failure of the established subsistence base to support a large population in the face of an abrupt climatic downturn.

Research efforts are bringing the complicated mosaic of the depopulation of the northern San Juan into ever sharper focus. The results thus far suggest that the stimuli that "pushed" residents to emigrate were more compelling than those that "pulled" people to new areas of settlement—although some types of catalysts will necessarily leave clearer evidence than others—and the complete picture was undoubtedly a complex interweaving of both types of factors.

9

The Social and Cultural Contexts of the Central Mesa Verde Region during the Thirteenth-Century Migrations

Donna M. Glowacki

Between AD 1220 and 1290, the northern San Juan region went from being one of the most densely populated areas of the prehispanic Southwest to being entirely depopulated. Explanations for this widespread departure emphasize drought, resource depletion, and ensuing violence as prime stimuli underlying the depopulation (Cordell 2000; Haas and Creamer 1993; Kohler et al. 2008; Kuckelman 2002:250; LeBlanc 1999; Lipe 1995:159–162; Varien, Van West, and Patterson 2000). Yet we also know these factors do not adequately account for how this large and densely populated area became uninhabited by the end of the 1200s, as they would not have forced everyone to leave the region. Violence, drought, and resource depletion have a variable effect on populations because they are structured by local conditions and mediated by social institutions and individual actions (e.g., Field 2004; Shimada et al. 1991:263). In addition, drought and resource depletion were not uniformly felt across the northern San Juan region (Ryan, Adams, and Duff 2007; Van West 1994; Van West and Dean 2000; Varien et al. 2007), which suggests that at least parts of this region could have sustained population. Despite this opportunity, the northern San Juan was completely depopulated by the end of the thirteenth century.

Environmental fluctuations and their impact on agricultural productivity, in particular, have played a central role in explaining the depopulation of the northern San Juan (Cordell et al. 2007; Kohler et al. 2008; Kohler and Van West 1996; Varien et al. 1996:104–105, 2000). Complete regional depopulation is not a predestined outcome of drought and poor agricultural yield, however. For example, during the severe drought of the mid-1100s, people living in the highly aggregated pueblos of the Classic Mimbres in southwestern New Mexico chose to move into small, dispersed hamlets to mitigate drought conditions by maximizing land use instead of leaving the region (Hegmon, Nelson, and Ruth 1998; Nelson 2000). Various strategies are and have been used for coping with drought and other climatic shifts, including food storage, agricultural intensification, diversification, exchange, short-distance movements, and reorganization (Braun and Plog 1982; Cashdan 1990; Colson 1980; Halstead and O'Shea 1989; Minnis 1996; Rautman 1993). The responses that a given population selects depend on the magnitude of the situation balanced with a desire to be able to reverse the response if conditions improve (Halstead and O'Shea 1989:4; Minnis 1996:71). Thus, I assume that a widespread, long-distance population movement is a last resort, and its selection implies that all other options have been exhausted.

In the northern San Juan region, various strategies were used to cope with climatic downturns. Although some people likely left the region during the severe drought in the mid-1100s, one of the outcomes of this difficult time was also increased population aggregation (Glowacki 2006; Varien et al. 2007: fig. 5D) rather than widespread population dispersal, as occurred in the Mimbres region. For example, the population of large villages established prior to the mid-1100s, such as the Lowry complex, Yellow Jacket Pueblo, and the Goodman Point complex, increased (VEP I database v5.3), and new aggregated villages such as Woods Canyon Pueblo and Yucca House were constructed (Churchill, ed., 2002; Glowacki 2001:44; Ortman et al. 2000:127–130). By the end of the 1200s, however, emigration from the region was the predominant strategy for coping with the prevailing conditions, including drought and poor agricultural yield. Given that other options and strategies were available to mitigate the poor climatic and agricultural conditions and that there seem to have been areas that remained agriculturally viable, why not stay? What were the other contributing factors that led to the decision to leave the northern San Juan?

The response to poor environmental and climatic conditions, the permanence of the response, and the scale of any resulting migration depends on both the natural and social landscape (Minnis 1996:60). Our working models accounting for the natural landscape and paleoclimate are based on a wealth of data (e.g., Kohler, this vol., and Wright, this vol.), but more emphasis needs to be directed toward delineating the social landscape—the economic, political, and religious organizations and interaction networks defining social relationships—if we are truly to understand what transpired. It is through these social mechanisms and institutions that poor environmental conditions were successfully mitigated or not. While it has long been recognized that social factors played a role in the depopulation of the northern San Juan (Cordell et al. 2007; Davis 1965; Lipe 1995; Van West and Dean 2000:38–39; Varien 1999a:216; Varien et al. 1996:103–105, 2000), to paraphrase a statement by Bill Lipe during our seminar, getting at cultural and social explanations is "tough stuff," and, consequently, there is much we do not understand about how social factors contributed to the circumstances prompting the migrations.

The social landscape fostering the depopulation was created by complex interactions among numerous social and ecological variables that operated on multiple spatial and social scales and were structured by history and situational responses to changing demands. To gain an understanding of such a complex landscape requires a detailed and comprehensive assessment of the key factors structuring the social circumstances preceding and during large-scale processes such as regional depopulation (Demarest 2004:240; Drèze and Sens 1989; Geertz 2005; Oliver-Smith 1996; Yoffee 1988). Because of advances in the discipline of anthropology during recent decades, we can now conduct these types of large-scale analyses. The recent availability of large amounts of digital site data from institutions such as the Colorado Office of Archaeology and Historic Preservation (OAHP) allows for the examination of settlement patterns at a regional and pan-Southwest scale (e.g., Hill et al. 2004). As a consequence, we can now more readily bring social factors, especially the nature and timing of organizational changes, to the forefront of explanations for the depopulation of the northern San Juan through systematic regional analyses of key variables. Through such efforts, we can study the social and cultural contexts preceding and during the migrations and identify specifically what it is socially about the regional depopulation that requires further explanation and study. Moreover, these types of analyses allow us to consider large-scale historical developments and link them directly with corresponding environmental and climatic conditions for an integrated understanding of the circumstances prompting regional depopulation.

One of the keys to understanding the depopulation of the northern San Juan is a careful analysis of social and cultural intraregional variation.

It is important to account for intraregional variation in order to unpack the circumstances preceding the migrations because: (1) regional depopulation was far from uniform, as migrations started much earlier in some areas than others; and (2) the circumstances leading up to the depopulation differed across the region. For people living in the western portion of the region, there was intraregional population movement prior to the departure from the northern San Juan, while dramatic population growth took place in the eastern portion. Consequently, important social differences developed between the eastern and western portions of the northern San Juan that underlie variation in the circumstances prompting emigration. Intraregional population movement and consolidation in the eastern portion of the central Mesa Verde, in particular, created a social setting conducive to change and ultimately caused instability that led to vulnerability to the subsequent impacts of drought and violence (see also Davis 1964, 1965). The ideas presented in this chapter draw on an intraregional comparative analysis of population distribution, settlement organization, and occupation histories across the northern San Juan region from AD 1150 to 1300 (Glowacki 2006). I originally examined the entire region, but here I focus on the central Mesa Verde region, which was the most densely settled portion of the northern San Juan (Lipe 1995:143; Varien 2000:6–7), to discuss how the dynamics of this densely settled core differed from those of the rest of the region (fig. 9.1).

Analyzing Intraregional Variation to Describe Social Contexts

In our explanations for the thirteenth-century migrations, we often conflate intraregional circumstances and assume more uniformity than was invariably present. Nonetheless, there was great variation in environmental setting, climate, and settlement organization across the northern San Juan region that translated into differing options available to inhabitants depending on where they lived. For example, Mesa Verde Proper—the physiographic feature including Mesa Verde National Park—is considered part of the central Mesa Verde based on the shared settlement pattern of large, aggregated, canyon-oriented pueblos and similar demographic trends (Lipe 1995, 2006; Varien 2000; Varien et al. 1996). However, the difference in elevation—with Mesa Verde Proper being roughly 460 m

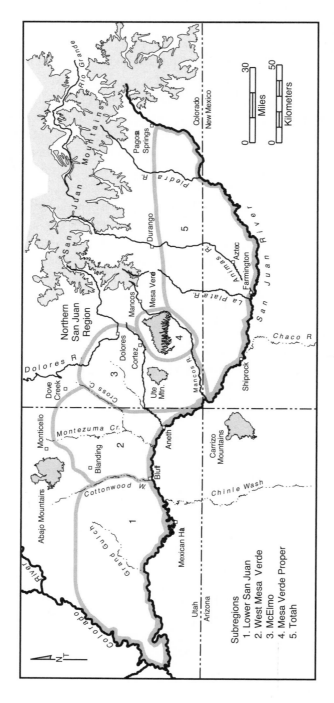

Figure 9.1. The northern San Juan region, with major physiographic features and subregions identified. The subregions of central Mesa Verde are Mesa Verde Proper, McElmo, and West Mesa Verde. (Courtesy Donna M. Glowacki)

(1,500 ft) higher than surrounding areas—provided increased rainfall in Mesa Verde Proper, and its southern aspect afforded a longer growing season. Thus, different circumstances and options were available to people living on Mesa Verde Proper than in other parts of the region—not the least of which would have been agricultural productivity that was probably better than that in adjacent areas to the northwest, particularly during the cool and/or dry conditions challenging the thirteenth-century inhabitants (Adams and Petersen 1999:32). These advantages likely led to different opportunities, interaction networks, experiences, and responses to the circumstances of the 1200s.

This situation was reversed for the western portion of not only the central Mesa Verde but also the northern San Juan region as a whole, because southeastern Utah is lower and drier, receiving 15–30 cm less precipitation than the eastern portion of the region (Wright, this vol., table 4.1), and farming was (and is) difficult. People living in the far western and eastern peripheries of the northern San Juan experienced different environmental and climatic conditions, and they had ready access to adjacent regions. These environmental and social circumstances structured exchange networks, subsistence, and settlement patterns in ways that were different than what is seen elsewhere in the region (see also Allison, this vol.; Dean, this vol.; Glowacki 2006). We need to account for the influences these differences had on options available to inhabitants in order to better describe the circumstances prompting migration.

In my previous analysis, I used subregions as analytical units to compare settlement, demography, occupation, and architecture to assess the extent to which differing social and environmental settings shaped social organization and interactions throughout the northern San Juan region (Glowacki 2006). Five subregions—Totah, Mesa Verde Proper, McElmo, West Mesa Verde, and Lower San Juan (fig. 9.1)—were examined using data derived from a regional database of more than 3,720 Pueblo III period sites. This analytical approach allowed the independent examination of areas traditionally lumped together to evaluate the degree of uniformity within the region. Here, I focus on the three subregions that comprise the central Mesa Verde region: Mesa Verde Proper, McElmo, and West Mesa Verde. I examine two variables—the occupation history and the distribution of community centers and public architecture—to examine variation in the social and settlement histories among these subregions that surely structured the circumstances of depopulation.

The occupation history of each subregion from AD 1150 to 1300 was determined by aggregating the momentary room counts of community centers (large sites), which has proven to be a useful method for evaluating population trends both across the Southwest (Hill et al. 2004) and in the northern San Juan (Lipe 1995; Varien et al. 2007; Wilshusen 2002). Building on previous research, community centers in the northern San Juan Pueblo III habitation site database were identified as any site with one or more of the following criteria: (1) fifty or more rooms and kivas, (2) more than nine estimated households, and (3) public architecture (Adler and Varien 1994; Lipe 2006; Lipe and Varien 1999a; Varien et al. 1996, 2007; Varien 1999a:141–143). Evaluating subregional occupation histories based on community centers provides a reasonable gauge of demographic trends and a consistent site sample.[1] The distinctive size and complex histories of these sites imply that they became important locations on the landscape, structuring not only settlement organization but also social, economic, and political interactions within each center as well as among nearby smaller settlements and other contemporaneous community centers.

Room-count data were available for 122 of the 170 community centers in the three subregions of the central Mesa Verde region. The raw room count for each site was adjusted to produce a momentary room count, which is the number of rooms at a site likely to be in use at any given time during its occupation span. The momentary room count was calculated for each site using the duration of occupation and an average site use-life of forty years (Varien 1999a:107–111; Varien et al. 2007). Momentary room counts for each site were distributed across their respective occupation span and were then aggregated by subregion and displayed by twenty-year intervals to construct an occupation-history profile for each subregion (table 9.1; fig. 9.2). These profiles allow for the ready comparison of occupation trends, such as when population peaked and when the rate of emigration increased, across subregions. They indicate significant variation in the history of occupation within the central Mesa Verde region (fig. 9.2). These differences in occupation are further explored vis-à-vis the distributions of community centers and of public architecture among the central Mesa Verde subregions.

Table 9.1. Average size of community centers in the central Mesa Verde subregions, AD 1140–1300

Years AD	Mesa Verde Proper			McElmo			West Mesa Verde			Central Mesa Verde		
	Momentary room count	Number of sites	Average size (rmct)	Momentary room count	Number of sites	Average size (rmct)	Momentary room count	Number of sites	Average size (rmct)	Momentary room count	Number of sites	Average size (rmct)
1140–1160	238	15	16	985	28	35	419	22	19	1642	65	25
1160–1180	238	15	16	1409	37	38	419	22	19	2066	74	28
1180–1200	238	15	16	1409	37	38	1111	31	36	2758	83	33
1200–1220	473	18	26	2596	53	49	989	25	40	4058	96	42
1220–1240	1072	24	45	2526	51	50	948	23	41	4546	98	46
1240–1260	1016	21	48	3240	54	60	452	15	30	4708	90	52
1260–1280	302	11	27	2799	46	61	452	15	30	3553	72	49
1280–1300	72	8	9	132	7	19	369	12	31	573	27	21
Total sites	27			60			35			159		

Note: This table is based on only those centers with room counts, not the total number of centers found in each subregion. Shading indicates peak occupation.
Source: Extracted from Glowacki 2006: table 3.4.

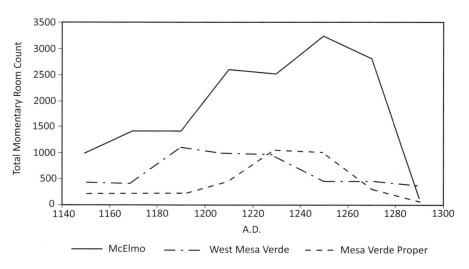

Figure 9.2. Occupation histories of the Central Mesa Verde subregions.

Eastern Consolidation and Western Differentiation (AD 1200–1240)

Social and cultural differences between the eastern and western portions of the northern San Juan have a long history (Matson 1991; Potter and Chuipka 2007:425–426). Although the nature and location of the boundary varied through time, eastern and western differences became pronounced in the central Mesa Verde region in the mid-1200s. Comparable numbers of people were living in the McElmo and West Mesa Verde community centers at the start of the 1200s, but this changed by the 1240s, when people began to emigrate from West Mesa Verde centers in increasing numbers (table 9.1, fig. 9.2). Although some people likely left the region altogether (Ahlstrom, Van West, and Dean 1995; Duff and Wilshusen 2000), the co-occurrence of population decline in one area and growth in another suggests that at least some of these people were immigrating to the centers in the McElmo subregion from West Mesa Verde (fig. 9.2). Recent analysis of population within the McElmo subregion supports this inference and indicates there was population growth in the study area after AD 1225 that likely involved at least some immigration (Varien et al. 2007: fig. 5b). This settlement synchrony—population decline in one area correlating with growth in another (Peregrine 2006)—contributed to the consolidation of a majority of the regional population into the McElmo and Mesa Verde Proper subregions, significantly reshaping the regional social landscape and affecting social organization and interaction.

The eastward migrations in the mid-1200s underscore important differences in the settlement histories and practices between the eastern and western portions of the central Mesa Verde. Not only are there key differences in population levels and settlement patterns, but also in public architecture, associated ritual practices, and interaction networks. For one, the site density of the McElmo and Mesa Verde Proper subregions (0.33 sites per km²) was nearly twice that of West Mesa Verde (0.19 sites per km²; see Glowacki 2006: table 3.1). The lower population levels and more dispersed settlement pattern in West Mesa Verde would have impacted resource needs and interaction differently than in the McElmo and Mesa Verde Proper subregions. There were also eastern and western differences in the nature of community centers. Community centers were larger and more densely concentrated in the McElmo subregion than anywhere else (table 9.1; Glowacki 2006). In contrast, on average, community centers in West Mesa Verde were more dispersed and smaller than in the McElmo subregion. This trend extended into the more western lower San Juan subregion, with community centers decreasing in size and becoming increasingly dispersed. There is also temporal patterning showing when community centers reached their maximum extent. Community centers were largest in West Mesa Verde from AD 1180 to 1240, whereas community centers were largest in Mesa Verde Proper from AD 1220 to 1260 and in McElmo from AD 1240 to 1280 (table 9.1). These temporal trends suggest there were differences in the nature of aggregation and the role of community centers in the western portion of the central Mesa Verde pre- and post-1240.

Using the total number of sites for each subregion as a proxy for population size, the proportion of community centers among the total sites can be used to gauge the extent to which large sites dominated the social and cultural landscape. This proportion was the same in both the West Mesa Verde and McElmo subregions (0.06) and only slightly lower in Mesa Verde Proper (0.04; see Glowacki 2006: table 3.3). These proportions suggest that there was some level of organizational similarity regardless of the differences in size and community-center density.

That there were organizational differences between eastern and western community centers is perhaps more apparent in the notable variation in architecture and pottery. Architectural features characterizing the 1200s occupation of the central Mesa Verde, such as towers, enclosing walls, multi-walled structures, and plazas, were more frequent in the McElmo and Mesa Verde Proper subregions than in West Mesa Verde. Of these features, the distribution of the multi-walled structures, which will be discussed further below, suggests a marked difference in cultural practices; there are no multi-walled structures west of Aneth, Utah, which is at the subregional boundary between the McElmo and West Mesa Verde subregions. These structures are thought to be an important locus of ritually based authority (Glowacki 2006; Lekson 1999; Lipe and Ortman 2000; Reed 1958; Vivian 1959), and the near absence of them in the western portion of the central Mesa Verde and the northern San Juan indicates a fundamental difference in religious organization (Glowacki 2009).

Turning to differences in pottery production and use, highly visible exterior designs—frequently present on bowls from community centers in the eastern subregions—are nearly absent on western bowls (Robinson 2005:70–75, fig. 5.7). This shift in pottery-design placement, both in the northern San Juan and elsewhere, has been linked to increasing participation in communal activities (Bowser 2002; Mills 1999, 2007; Ortman 2000a, 2002; Robinson 2005; Spielmann 2004). The lack of exterior bowl designs in the west indicates that this type of symbolic display was less important in western social and ritual practices. In addition, recent instrumental neutron activation analysis indicates that pottery circulation networks for Mesa Verde Black-on-white bowls and Mesa Verde Corrugated jars varied (Glowacki 2006:112–128, figs. 5.1 and 5.3). For example, there is no evidence that the Mesa Verde Black-on-white bowls produced in the lower San Juan—the western extreme of the northern San Juan—were imported by people living in the McElmo subregion, but vessels produced using resources available in the McElmo area were found in the lower San Juan. Mesa Verde Corrugated jars also appear to have been circulated in relatively circumscribed eastern and western networks (Glowacki 2006:123–125). The differences between the two areas in settlement, nondomestic architecture, and pottery point to growing social and cultural separation within the central Mesa Verde by the early to mid-1200s. Those living to the west not only had different organization and interaction networks but also were not participating in the intensified ceremonial practices developing in the eastern subregions (Glowacki 2009).

Climatic hardships may have induced people to emigrate from West Mesa Verde centers in search of reliable water sources and productive farmland. There was a prolonged period of cool temperatures and short-term droughts in the early 1200s that likely reduced agricultural productivity (Kohler, this vol.; Kohler et al. 2008; Van West and Dean 2000; Wright, this vol.). These conditions would have made the drier climate of West Mesa Verde a challenging landscape for farming, and they perhaps encouraged people to move into the more agriculturally viable McElmo subregion (Wright, this vol.). Yet we also know people did not have to leave in the early-to-mid 1200s because the tree-ring record shows occupation continued in West Mesa Verde into the 1260s (table 9.1; Lipe 1995). There seems to be more to this intraregional population movement than solely environmental pressures to seek better farmland because at least some people chose to stay in West Mesa Verde.

Many community centers established during the AD 1220–1240 interval were built in relatively poor agricultural areas, suggesting that other factors may have also motivated people to move to the McElmo subregion (Varien 1999a; Varien et al. 2007: fig. 5). These seemingly marginal areas in the McElmo subregion may have been better relative to their previous locations or perhaps people were trying to secure reliable water sources as many of the centers established in the mid-1200s were located on canyon edges near or on springs (Lipe 1995:153; Varien 1999a:149). Yet, there were also social and organizational changes in the McElmo subregion during the mid to late 1200s that may have also proved attractive to people living in the environmentally challenging West Mesa Verde subregion (Glowacki 2006).

In the east, the 1200s were a period of social intensification and religious revitalization that transformed Ancestral Pueblo culture in the central Mesa Verde region (Glowacki 2009). The consolidation of population in McElmo and Mesa Verde Proper was associated with population growth, increased aggregation, innovation in the spatial organization of villages, and a renewed emphasis on key forms of public architecture.

As a consequence, one of the many considerations in deciding to migrate east was that there were important religious and political implications associated with either remaining in the western portion of the region or joining those in the east (see also Ware 2008).

It seems that people living in the West Mesa Verde subregion were between two historically and culturally different areas. People living farther west in the Lower San Juan, Kayenta, and Fremont areas were removed from happenings in the eastern portion of the Northern San Juan. These areas, for example, had virtually no Chacoan influences and had a much more dispersed settlement pattern and a different pottery tradition (Allison, this vol.; Dean 1996b, this vol.). Since those who remained in West Mesa Verde were not as involved in the intensified ceremonialism happening in the east, they may have become more affiliated with people living farther west. The population decline in the west and subsequent differences between the eastern and western portions of the central Mesa Verde imply that people in West Mesa Verde were actively choosing to either (1) join the social developments and religious traditions in the east (and incidentally perhaps improve their production as farmers in so doing), (2) maintain their lifestyles in the west, or (3) leave the region altogether.

Examining social contexts at a subregional scale inherently draws attention to how the circumstances and timing of long-distance, large-scale emigration differed across the region. The divergent histories of the eastern and western subregions show that emigration was not simultaneous, but rather cascaded across the northern San Juan (see also Davis 1964, 1965). More specifically, it seems the western depopulation process began earlier than in the east, given the numbers of people leaving the large, aggregated villages of West Mesa Verde by the 1240s. The marked differences between eastern and western areas during the mid-1200s structured migration routes from the region, as evidenced by the archaeological record and Pueblo oral histories (see also Cordell et al. 2007). For example, the Hopi are most frequently associated with the Ancestral Pueblo people from Kayenta and southeastern Utah (Gilpin et al. 2002:93). These connections suggest that Ancestral Pueblo people living in the western portion of the northern San Juan region tended to migrate to the Hopi areas, passing through northern Arizona at places such as Mummy Cave in Canyon de Chelley (Scott Travis, 2008, personal communication). Ancestral Pueblo people in the eastern areas had stronger connections to the Keresan and Tewa pueblos in northern New Mexico (Cordell et al. 2007; Gilpin et al. 2002; Lipe and Lekson 2001; Ortman, this vol.; Roney 1995). The specifics of how the migrations unfolded were much more complex than discussed here, and the tendencies described above were not mutually exclusive, but rather reflect what seems to be a broad trend, as the eastern and western distinctions within the northern San Juan region broadly correspond with the historical trajectories of the eastern and western pueblos of today. I am not suggesting that the mid-1200s was when the eastern and western pueblo organizations were established. There is a long history of transformation, syncretism, and innovation involved in the formation of the modern pueblos and significant change occurred during the post-1300 era (Ware and Blinman 2000) and in reaction to subsequent Spanish contact and the Pueblo Revolt (Suina 2002). However, I am suggesting that there were deep historical connections within central Mesa Verde that contributed to the processes underlying the development of the modern Pueblos.

Societal Change and Classic Mesa Verde: The Implications of Eastern Consolidation

By AD 1240, the northern San Juan region was one of the most densely occupied areas of the Southwest (Hill et al. 2004, this vol.), and most of these people were living in the eastern portion of the central Mesa Verde (Glowacki 2006). Population continued to increase and aggregate into community centers in the McElmo subregion until widespread emigration began in the mid-1200s (Glowacki 2006; Varien et al. 2007; Wilshusen 2002). Peak population levels were also reached on Mesa Verde Proper and were associated with increased aggregation into cliff dwellings such as Balcony House, Cliff Palace, and Spruce Tree House (Brisbin et al. 2008; Fiero 1999:32–33; Lipe 1995: table 1; Nordby 2001). By the mid-1200s, settlement intensification and change in the McElmo and Mesa Verde Proper subregions had become critical to northern San Juan regional dynamics.

Population growth and consolidation into these subregions promoted a social environment conducive to change. It was during the AD 1220–1260 period that Mesa Verde Black-on-white pottery designs became most elaborate, and there were sweeping organizational changes in village layout. By the 1220s, at least sixteen new centers were established in the McElmo subregion (table 9.1), and they differed from those built during the previous period. Large villages were no longer constructed in the conventional linear, front-oriented layout (e.g., Yellow Jacket), but were more inwardly focused and had a bilateral layout (as at Sand Canyon and Yucca House; Glowacki 2001, 2006; Lipe 2006; Lipe and Ortman 2000; Ortman and Bradley 2002). These changes in settlement layout suggest that people were experimenting with novel social organizations that may have involved transitioning from a household-based organization to one that was more communal and potentially less kin-based than the previous organization (Bernardini 1996; Ware and Blinman 2000). Mesa Verdean hallmarks—such as towers, multi-walled structures, enclosing walls, and pottery forms typifying the Mesa Verde series, such as mugs and kiva jars (Breternitz, Rohn, and Morris 1974; Lipe and Lekson 2001)—also became increasingly common at McElmo and Mesa Verde Proper community centers (Glowacki 2006: table 3.5; Lipe and Ortman 2000).

The intensification of ceremonialism and modifications to ritual practice were, likely, outcomes of the consolidation of people in the McElmo and Mesa Verde Proper subregions and experimentation with village organization in the mid-1200s (Glowacki 2009). This is reflected in changes in architecture that involved concurrent innovations in both communal and exclusionary structures, and presumably their associated ritual practices. Changes in architecture and pottery in the mid- to late 1200s indicate that communal rituals and gatherings became an increasingly important component of ceremonialism in eastern Mesa Verde. Although there were antecedents for plazas in Chaco Canyon, the increased use of plazas at community centers in the mid- to late 1200s allowed for more inclusive gatherings, perhaps accommodating the increasing number of people living in centers, including western migrants. This change in ritual practice did not exclude great kivas, which continued to be constructed at late sites. Increasing inclusivity must have been important, however, because some great kivas, such as the one at Sand Canyon Pueblo, had their roofs removed in the late 1200s (Churchill, Kuckelman, and Varien 1998; Lipe 1989; Lipe and Ortman 2000:112). Coincident with the change in communal space,

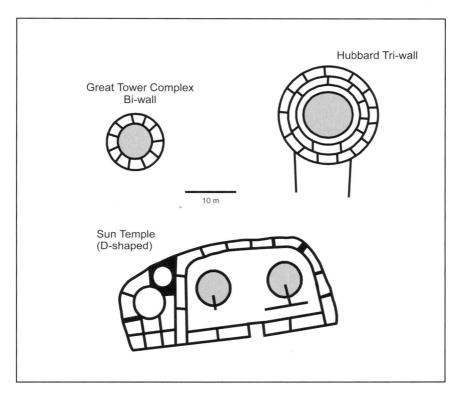

Figure 9.3. Plan views of examples of multi-walled structures in the central Mesa Verde.

Mesa Verde Black-on-white bowls were widely circulated among people in the McElmo, Mesa Verde Proper, and Totah subregions (Glowacki 2006). The frequency of exterior designs and bowl sizes also increased (Hegmon 1991; Mills 1999; Ortman 2000a, 2002; Robinson 2005).

Another organizational change was marked by the proliferation of multi-walled structures in the mid-1200s, which are thought to be exclusionary ritual architecture (Lekson 1999; Lipe and Ortman 2000:111; Reed 1958; Vivian 1959). Multi-walled structures are either circular or D-shaped, with a courtyard for one or two kivas that was surrounded by a single or double row of rooms conforming to the shape (fig. 9.3). These structures were probably accessed by specific groups or households within community centers and may have been associated with the proliferation of ritual sodalities (Glowacki 2009). Although tri-wall structures have antecedents in Aztec and Chaco (Lekson 1983, 1999; Vivian 1959), multi-walled structures were most common in the McElmo and Mesa Verde Proper subregions, and they did not become key features at large villages until after AD 1225 (Churchill, Kuckelman, and Varien 1998). Moreover, the bi-wall and D-shaped forms seem to have been new forms associated with the developments in the McElmo and Mesa Verde Proper subregions.

The distribution of multi-walled structures indicates some degree of organizational similarity among the McElmo, Mesa Verde Proper, and Totah subregions (Glowacki 2006; Lekson 1999), but there are important distributional differences as well. The general pattern in the area encompassed by the Totah, Mesa Verde Proper, and McElmo sub-regions is that tri-walls were more eastern, bi-walls more central, and D-shaped structures more western in their distribution (Glowacki 2006: fig. 3.10). This distinctive geographic distribution indicates possible differences in the ways in which similar processes of differentiation and exclusion were put into practice in these three subregions. For example, D-shaped structures are not found in Chaco or at Aztec (Glowacki 2006; Lipe 2006). The distribution of multi-walled structures also suggests experimentation with this architectural form, and presumably with the practices and status affiliated with use of these structures. This latter point is further illustrated by the recent excavations of several multi-walled structures at Goodman Point Pueblo, including a D-shape and two bi-wall variants (i.e., including additional rooms and/or kivas; Kuckelman, Coffey, and Copeland 2009).

The 1220s marked the beginning of a period of considerable population growth and consolidation in the McElmo subregion, and yet there was substantial emigration by the 1260s. During that intervening forty-year interval, there were dramatic social changes, as evidenced by increasing aggregation and the establishment of new community centers with distinctive layouts and public architecture, often in canyon-rim settings. These changes occurred as *in situ* population grew and western immigrants moved into the McElmo and Mesa Verde Proper sub-regions. These transformative social processes happened in a relatively short amount of time and undoubtedly produced an intense period of interactions that may have caused social tension and instability. Not only is there evidence of violent conflict in the 1200s (Kohler and Turner

2006; Kohler et al. 2008; Kramer 2002), but increasing emigration from McElmo and Mesa Verde Proper is archaeologically evident prior to AD 1260. These migrations preceded the onset of the so-called Great Drought and the intense violence in the late 1270s and early 1280s (e.g., at Castle Rock and Sand Canyon Pueblos; Kuckelman et al. 2003). Social factors, like political and religious organization and interaction networks, structure people's ability to cope with changing demands such as increasing population and varying agricultural productivity (Drèze and Sen 1989:46–47; Oliver-Smith 1996:316; Van West 1994). The fact that notable emigration occurred before AD 1260 suggests that the mid- to late-1200s migrations from the northern San Juan region were also brought about by social problems—perhaps some kind of disruption of social networks and ceremonialism—and the drought and intensified violence that began nearly two decades later more precisely explain why the depopulation became complete.

A number of factors—such as rapid population growth, intensified aggregation, changes in religious practices, the accommodation of immigrants, evident violence, low agricultural productivity, and competition for resources—operating at a variety of scales made the 1200s a challenging time and may have led to widespread instability. Of these, the impact of religious change, although recognized (Lekson 1999:160–161; Lipe 1995:163; Ware and Blinman 2000:400–401), has received less attention, in part because it is difficult to study via material culture. Yet I believe it may have been critical in creating social conditions conducive to regional depopulation. Religion is the foundation of Pueblo culture, and it structures gender roles, social behaviors, marriage partners, planting and harvesting schedules, and politics, among other things (Ortiz 1969; Parsons 1939). Through rituals and associated activities, religion can integrate communities by fostering cooperation (e.g., Adams 1991), but it can also be a source of conflict, even among groups in the same community or within the same religion (e.g., Whiteley 1988, 2008).

The rapid changes and increasing population in McElmo and Mesa Verde Proper brought about innovations in ritual and settlement organization that diverged from traditional practices. The changes in settlement layout, an increasing emphasis on plazas, and the use of multi-walled structures, particularly D-shaped structures, were all notable modifications that evolved from what Lipe (2006:263–268) has termed the

"San Juan Pattern," which was rooted in the deep history of the San Juan Basin Pueblo people. Although perhaps intended to help mitigate the turbulent circumstances, these changes may have actually contributed to social tensions. In addition to these architectural changes, for example, we also see evidence of the revival of traditional Chaco practices in the resurgence in great-house occupation and modification in the 1200s (Bradley 1996; Cameron 2005; Lipe 2006:303; Lipe and Varien 1999b). The simultaneous changes in architectural spaces associated with ritual and the retention or reclamation of architectural signatures of Chaco suggest divergent ideas and organization. Thus, it seems to me that oppositions inherent in maintaining continuity while accommodating progressive change may have created a social environment conducive to the development of factions and internal conflicts.

There is history to the development of factions and conflict in Pueblo religion (Parsons 1939; Plog and Solometo 1997; Whiteley 1988; Whitley 2008). As suggested, given the quickly shifting social landscape of the mid-1200s, factionalism was likely an integral component of the circumstances prompting the Mesa Verde migrations. This would have been particularly true if there was dissatisfaction with the effectiveness of new religious practices and a perception of their failure in ameliorating the poor climatic conditions and low agricultural productivity (Glowacki 2009; Wright, this vol.).

Likely at the heart of these religious and organizational changes was the changing relationship between Chaco and the northern San Juan region. There is a long and interrelated history among the people of the central Mesa Verde, Aztec, and Chaco Canyon involving social interaction, migration and resettlement, conflict, and the exchange of goods and ideas (Cameron 2005; Lipe 2006; Wilshusen and Van Dyke 2006). Wilshusen and Van Dyke (2006), for example, have recently suggested that north-to-south population movements in the 800s and early 900s contributed to the development and florescence of Chaco. The long and interrelated histories of these areas created deeply rooted connections that influenced social interactions, political relationships, and religious practices, and this strong link was not weakened until the late-1200s depopulation (see also Cameron 2005:246).

This disconnection is materially evident because the late-1200s migrations involved discarding most of the cultural signatures associated with the McElmo and Mesa Verde Proper subregions (see Lipe, this vol.) and, by default, material connections with Chaco and Aztec. Moreover, many of the migrants from the McElmo and Mesa Verde Proper subregions are believed to have ended up in the Rio Grande, where there was substantial Late Developmental and Early Coalition occupation coincident with Chaco (Boyer et al., this vol.), but little Chacoan influence (Fowles 2004a). That the depopulation was widespread and long lasting, and that practices at southern destinations were readily adopted, suggests that the decision to migrate also implied forsaking the material connections to previous ideologies and practices, if not the deeply embedded Chacoan history and associated beliefs. Thus, although other factors also contributed to disrupting social patterns in the mid-1200s, religious changes and a move away from material connections associated with Chacoan ideological practices may have been particularly significant.

The Process of Depopulation

Emigration is an important strategy for coping with deteriorating social and environmental conditions (Tainter 1988:199). The depopulation of the northern San Juan region by the end of the 1200s was an extended and historical process that was likely influenced by the social responses of the 1100s. The depopulation began with a major emigration from West Mesa Verde that coincided with a simultaneous population increase and consolidation in the east. The early- to mid-1200s emigrations from West Mesa Verde were likely shaped by individual and household circumstances and may have depended on factors like poor crop yields and the attractiveness of growing community centers in the McElmo subregion. These intraregional population movements are critical for understanding the overall depopulation process because they provide important context for the social circumstances prompting the second, and final, emigration that followed shortly thereafter.

In contrast, population was more concentrated in the McElmo and Mesa Verde Proper subregions, which contained among the best farmland in the region. In large part, it was the intensified dynamics in the McElmo and Mesa Verde Proper subregions during the mid- to late 1200s that ultimately generated the second period of large-scale emigration ending in the complete depopulation of the region. In light of this, emigration from the eastern subregions may have been driven by shared circumstances that were widespread and quickly perceived as serious concerns because people rapidly left McElmo and Mesa Verde Proper at roughly the same time (fig. 9.2; Lipe 1995:152; Varien et al. 1996:103; Varien et al. 2007; Wilshusen 2002:119–120). The relatively rapid emigration from these subregions suggests that people were leaving in substantial numbers, possibly including some large-sized groups in addition to small, kin-based groups and individuals.

As the above summary highlights, there is temporal and situational variation within large-scale processes like regional depopulation. Moreover, the loss of population itself can contribute to the disintegration of an established social order as it becomes more difficult to maintain organizations and institutions (Hill et al. 2004; Tainter 1988). Consequently, the circumstances initially fostering large-scale emigration change as noticeable numbers of people emigrate and social coherence can no longer be maintained. It is the nature of these new circumstances that affects whether an entire population leaves an area or a greatly reduced population remains behind to reorganize and continue.

Thus, in the case of the late 1200s northern San Juan depopulation, what initiated the depopulation process is not the same as what caused it to be complete. Once people started leaving McElmo and Mesa Verde Proper, the circumstances initially fostering large-scale emigration from the region would have been altered. As we know, conditions steadily worsened after AD 1260, due not only to the loss of population but also to the severe drought conditions of the late 1270s (Van West and Dean 2000) and escalating violence (Kuckelman et al. 2003; LeBlanc 1999). These conditions came on the heels of challenging climate throughout the 1200s (Kohler, this vol.; Varien et al. 2007) and may have also reminded people about how terrible conditions were during the AD 1130–1180 drought. This association would have contributed to the dynamics prompting the rapid and complete depopulation of the northern San Juan region at the end of the 1200s (Glowacki 2009). The association may also have caused migration from the region to become ideologically linked to the eventual rejection of material connections to Chacoan ideology and the social and religious developments in the central Mesa Verde region, and as a consequence, complete regional depopulation may have become inevitable. As we move forward in our efforts to understand the depopulation, we need to carefully consider not only the geographic variation in scale but also the temporal variation. For in this case, the "pushes" that prompted the initial migrations differed from those at the end of the occupation, which were also likely accompanied by "pulls" from those recently settled in the south.

Acknowledgments

Various stages of this work were supported by the Florence C. and Robert H. Lister Fellowship, the Joe Ben Wheat Scholarship, a National Science Foundation (NSF) Dissertation Improvement grant (BCS-012487) and the NSF Biocomplexity grant (BCS-0119981) funding the Village Ecodynamics Project I, and several grants from the Anthropology Department at Arizona State University. I owe a great debt to many who shared data, ideas, and time, and I am grateful for their support. I'd also like to thank Tim Kohler, Mark Varien, and Aaron M. Wright for inviting me to participate in both the Society of American Archaeology session and the Amerind seminar and John Ware and the Amerind staff for providing a wonderful and productive setting. Finally, thanks to all the seminar participants for the stimulating conversations that helped refine my ideas and spark new ones.

Note

1. Using only large sites to assess population trends for a subregion, of course, does not account for the total population because people were also living in smaller pueblos during this time (e.g., Mahoney, Adler, and Kendrick 2000). Nonetheless, it is reasonable to assume that a majority of the large sites within the region have been recorded (i.e., it is likely that relatively fewer large sites than small sites within the region have been overlooked). In the McElmo subregion, an estimated 70 percent of the population was living in large sites rather than small sites by the mid-1200s (Varien et al. 2007; Wilshusen 2002:118). Thus, a majority of the population is accounted for when analyzing the data from large sites. However, because these population trends were solely based on data from large sites, population increases can be due to local processes of aggregation (i.e., within the subregion and/or the immediate locality), immigration from other subregions, or both.

10

Evidence of a Mesa Verde Homeland for the Tewa Pueblos

Scott G. Ortman

One of the most enduring and compelling questions of southwestern archaeology is what happened to the many thousands of people who lived in the Mesa Verde region in the AD 1200s. By the middle decades of that century, Ancestral Pueblo people had lived in the region for more than six hundred years, the Montezuma Valley itself was home to approximately twenty thousand people (Varien et al. 2007), and many thousands more lived on Mesa Verde Proper and in southeastern Utah (Glowacki 2006). Yet by AD 1285, the entire region was empty (see Varien, this vol.).

Current research suggests that final depopulation of the region was preceded by several decades of population decline (Duff and Wilshusen 2000; Varien et al. 2007) and that a portion of the late–AD 1200s population perished during the final depopulation of several villages (Kuckelman, this vol.; Kuckelman 2002; Kuckelman, Lightfoot, and Martin 2002; Lightfoot and Kuckelman 2001). It is unlikely, however, that the entire Pueblo population died in place or reverted to hunting and gathering, so a sizeable portion of the AD 1200s Mesa Verde–region population must have relocated to other areas of the Southwest, where the archaeological record indicates coeval population increase. By this measure, a likely destination for at least some Mesa Verde migrants was the northern Rio Grande region of New Mexico. This region was inhabited long before the Mesa Verde collapse (Dickson 1979; Kohler and Root 2004a; Lakatos 2007; McNutt 1969; Marshall and Walt 2007; Orcutt 1999; Wiseman 1995), but in-migration is a plausible explanation for the dramatic increase in the number and size of new settlements established there between AD 1200 and 1325 (Anschuetz 2005; Crown, Orcutt, and Kohler 1996; Fowles 2004a; Hill, this vol.; Snead, Creamer, and Van Zandt 2004).[1] Many thousands of people appear to have moved into the northern Rio Grande region during the same period that many thousands of people were also leaving the Mesa Verde region.

In this chapter, I summarize a range of studies I have pursued as part of my doctoral dissertation research (Ortman 2009) to further investigate this hypothesis. This research brings together multiple lines of evidence to suggest that the homeland of at least one Rio Grande ethnic group, namely, the Tewa-speaking pueblos, was in fact in the Mesa Verde region. The basic hypothesis of this chapter is not new, but it is by no means universally accepted. Indeed, despite more than a century of research, there is still no consensus on how the historic pueblos of the Rio Grande relate to earlier archaeological cultures of the San Juan drainage (Boyer et al., this vol.; Cameron 1995; Collins 1975; Cordell 1995; Davis 1965; Dutton 1964; Ford, Schroeder, and Peckham 1972; Lakatos 2007; Lekson et al. 2002; McNutt 1969; Mera 1935; Reed 1949; Steen 1977; Wendorf and Reed 1955).

I focus here on evidence related to the ancestry and language of the Tewa people because genes and language bind more tightly to people and are less subject to social manipulation than material culture. Thus, evidence related to these aspects of human inheritance should provide more reliable indicators of population movement than the material-culture indicators that have been the focus of previous argument. Lipe considers the archaeological dimension of the problem in his contribution to this volume. For a fuller treatment of the analyses presented here, and for my analysis of the archaeology of Tewa origins, readers should consult Ortman (2009).

The Tewa Pueblos

There are seven contemporary pueblos in which Tewa is the dominant language spoken today. Six of these (Ohkay'owinge, Nambe, Pojoaque, Santa Clara, San Ildefonso, and Tesuque) are located in the northern Rio Grande region of New Mexico, and the seventh (Tewa Village) is located on Hopi First Mesa, in Arizona. Based on evidence from place names, oral tradition, historic Spanish documents, and archaeology (Anschuetz 2005; Harrington 1916; Marshall and Walt 2007; Mera 1935; Schroeder 1979), it is clear that Tewa-speaking peoples once occupied a larger portion of the northern Rio Grande region. In the north, ancestral Tewa sites occur throughout the area bounded by the Santa Fe divide on the south, the Jemez Mountains on the west, the Sangre de Cristo Mountains on the east, and the lower Rio Chama drainage in the north. This area is known to archaeologists as the Tewa basin (Anschuetz 2005). To the south, ancestral Tewa sites also extend across the Santa Fe divide and into the Galisteo basin southeast of Santa Fe.[2]

The seventh Tewa-speaking community, on Hopi First Mesa, formed as a result of a migration from the Rio Grande in 1696, a few years after the reconquest of New Mexico.[3] The history of the Hopi-Tewa is interesting in its own right, but for the purposes of this chapter, the critical point is that all lines of evidence suggest that mutually intelligible dialects of Tewa were spoken throughout the Tewa and Galisteo basins at the time of Spanish contact.[4] This, in turn, suggests that the ancestral form of Tewa, from which all known dialects derive, was spoken in a single speech community at some point in the not-too-distant past. The evidence and arguments reviewed in this chapter suggest that this speech community was located in the Mesa Verde region, and that a large portion of its people migrated to the northern Rio Grande over the course of the thirteenth century.

The Sources of the Tewa Population

The only aspect of migration that is true in all cases is that it involves the movement of people from one place to another. And whereas individuals can change their material practices, learn a new language, or change their place of residence, they cannot alter their genes. Thus, genetic data should provide a reliable means of inferring population movement, if in fact any has occurred. The most direct source of such data is ancient DNA, but due to repatriation and reburial of certain collections, difficulties in obtaining ancient DNA, and the thorough regional sampling needed to address the problem, it may be some time before we are able to address the sources of the Rio Grande Tewa population using such evidence. In the meantime, a practical alternative is to use skeletal morphology as a proxy for genetic data. A number of recent studies have confirmed that phenotypic traits, and especially metric traits, do preserve a signal of regional genetic structure and mating networks (Carson 2006; Cheverud 1988; Konigsberg and Ousley 1995; Relethford

2004; Relethford and Lees 1982; Sparks and Jantz 2002), and the great advantage of phenotypic traits for population genetic analysis is that such data have been collected from skeletal remains with archaeological context for more than a century.

Numerous studies of biological variation have been conducted in the Southwest (e.g., Akins 1986; El-Najjar 1981, 1986; Mackey 1977, 1980; Schillaci 2003; Schillaci and Stojanowski 2005). Several of these have emphasized the biological unity of Pueblo groups over their diversity (Corruccini 1972; El-Najjar 1978; Schillaci, Ozolins, and Windes 2001), but inadequate sample sizes and gaps in regional coverage have limited the interpretability of these results. To improve on these studies, I compiled a large database of craniometric data from published sources, archival documents, and personal files (Ortman 2007, 2009). Multi-observer datasets have their problems, but they are not as intractable for craniometric data as they often are for archaeological datasets. Measurements of skeletal morphology are based on well-defined and unambiguous landmarks, and it is usually possible to distinguish related measurements taken from different landmarks. Also, measurements taken by different analysts using the same landmarks are usually highly correlated. For example, in the dataset I compiled, the correlation between measurements taken by two different analysts for the same specimens is greater than .99 (see Ortman 2009: ch. 5). It therefore appears that, with proper care, it is feasible to compile and analyze multi-observer craniometric datasets.

The dataset I compiled contains data for 12 craniofacial measurements that are unaffected by cradleboarding, collected from remains of approximately 1,200 adults of known sex. These remains were recovered from more than 120 archaeological sites arrayed across the San Juan drainage and Rio Grande region that date before and after the Mesa Verde depopulation. I grouped these samples according to the archaeological district in which each site occurs, following the definitions of Adler and Johnson (1996) for the pre–AD 1275 period, and of Adams and Duff (2004) for the post–AD 1275 period.

To analyze these data, I followed procedures developed by Relethford that estimate the genetic relationship or R matrix directly from osteometric data. These methods use a model of metric traits as polygenic traits governed by equal and additive effects of several genes (see Relethford and Lees 1982). This approach is the current standard in biodistance studies (Konigsberg and Buikstra 1995; Relethford 2003; Relethford and Blangero 1990; Relethford, Crawford, and Blangero 1997; Scherer 2007; Schillaci 2003; Schillaci and Stojanowski 2005; Steadman 1998, 2001; Stojanowski 2005). The advantage of *R*-matrix analysis is that it enables one to estimate three distinct parameters that are useful for investigating regional population structure: the genetic distances between samples, a measure of regional genetic variability known as Wright's F_{ST}, and relative estimates of gene flow for each sample. To maximize the number of variables and cases in the analysis, I pre-treated the data in two ways. First, I included all individuals for which at least four of the twelve measurements are available and estimated missing data using maximum-likelihood methods based on the EM Algorithm (Allison 2001). Second, I controlled for sexual dimorphism by standardizing the raw data in R-mode within sex, then pooling the standardized data for analysis.

Table 10.1 presents a portion of the minimum genetic distance matrix derived from the *R* matrix of the craniometric dataset. Specifically, this table presents distances between samples from regional populations dating before and after AD 1275 in the northern Southwest. The patterns of biological affinity reflected in this table are complex, but one consistent pattern is that post–AD 1275 populations of the northern Rio Grande region, including those from the Santa Fe, Pajarito, Chama, Cochiti, Tano, Pecos, and Salinas districts, appear more closely related to earlier populations of the Four Corners region than they are to earlier populations of the northern Rio Grande, including the Valdez, Kwahe'e, and Galisteo populations.

Figure 10.1 presents a principal-coordinates analysis of the *R* matrix of the craniometric dataset, which provides an overall summary of relationships among the sampled populations. Many details of this figure are interesting, but I will focus here on clusters of samples that appear to represent biological lineages. First, there is a clearly defined cluster of populations in the central area of the chart that includes samples dating after AD 1275 from the Pecos, Chama, Pajarito, Tano, and Salinas districts, and samples dating prior to AD 1275 from the Mesa Verde, McElmo, and southeast Utah districts. Second, the Chaco, Cibola, El Morro, and Cochiti samples form a second, more loosely related

Table 10.1. Minimum genetic distances among regional populations

District	Taos	Chama	Jemez	Pajarito	Santa Fe	Pecos	Tano	Cochiti	Albuquerque	Puerco	El Morro	Salinas
Southeast Utah	.1088	.0432	.0195	.0271	.0611	.0553	.0552	.1857	.1212	.2309	.0819	.0476
McElmo	.0424	.0627	.0431	.0263	.0287	.1182	.0292	.2424	.0487	.1531	.0663	.0980
Mesa Verde	.0949	.0901	.0176	.0316	.0991	.1476	.0318	.2195	.1044	.2417	.0445	.0839
Totah	.0521	.1661	.1763	.0918	.0424	.2250	.1113	.5069	.0881	.0979	.2082	.2168
Piedra	.1693	.0885	.0982	.1290	.1607	.0706	.1139	.2300	.1810	.3362	.2952	.1244
Chaco	.1737	.1185	.0718	.0581	.1586	.2213	.1092	.2288	.2330	.3160	.0249	.0954
Cibola	.1472	.0315	.0319	.0258	.0956	.1333	.0597	.1730	.1730	.2261	.0151	.0807
Valdez	.1063	.2123	.2527	.2260	.1733	.1987	.1861	.4282	.3845	.2365	.1127	.1435
Kwahe'e	.2692	.2851	.1342	.1621	.2626	.2749	.1847	.4300	.2580	.5328	.3540	.2334
Galisteo	.4167	.6759	.7235	.5970	.3553	.5482	.5670	.9319	.5598	.3228	.8344	.6402

Note: Column heads represent regional samples from sites dating after AD 1275, and row heads represent regional samples from sites dating prior to AD 1275. Data are standardized minimum genetic distances derived from the R matrix of the craniometric data set.

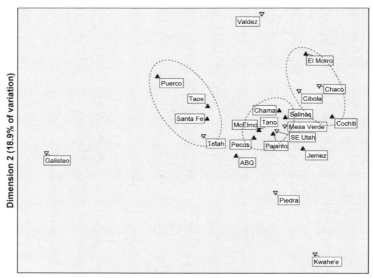

Figure 10.1. Principal coordinates analysis of the *R* matrix of the craniometric data set. The first two eigenvectors have been scaled by the square roots of their eigenvalues. Up-facing solid triangles indicate post–AD 1275 populations, and down-facing open triangles indicate pre–AD 1275 populations. Suggested lineages are circled.

lineage. Third, samples from the Puerco, Taos, Santa Fe, and Totah districts appear to form a third, loosely related lineage.

These results indicate that Late Coalition– and Classic-period populations of several ancestral Tewa districts (Pajarito, Tano, and Chama) descended primarily from earlier Mesa Verde–region populations (southeast Utah, McElmo, and Mesa Verde), and not from early Rio Grande populations (Galisteo, Kwahe'e, and Valdez).[5] They also suggest that ancestors of Eastern Keres communities lived primarily south of the San Juan river, not in the Mesa Verde region or in the Totah. Finally, the grouping of the Santa Fe sample with samples from either end of the Rio Grande region, despite the close affinity of the former with Mesa Verde region samples, suggests that the post–AD 1275 Santa Fe district population resulted from the mixing of indigenous Rio Grande populations with immigrant Mesa Verde populations.[6]

Table 10.2 presents an analysis of gene flow, following the model developed by Relethford and Blangero (1990). The most important parameter for interpreting the results is the residual variance. When this value is significantly less than zero, it indicates that the population in question experienced less than average gene flow, and when it is significantly greater than zero, it indicates that the population experienced greater than average gene flow, relative to the overall pattern of genetic variation among the samples in the analysis. The results of this analysis emphasize two points. First, post–AD 1275 samples from districts occupied by Tewa speakers in historic times (Pajarito, Tano, and Chama) did not experience greater than average gene flow relative to other regional populations, including earlier Rio Grande populations. This suggests that the ancestral Tewa populations of these areas did not result from significant admixture of previously distinct populations. Second, although sample sizes are small, pre–AD 1275 populations of the Tewa basin (Kwahe'e), Galisteo basin (Galisteo), and Taos Valley (Valdez) appear to have been experiencing significant gene flow due to in-migration from one or more genetically distinct populations. Third, this same pattern is also apparent in the post–AD 1275 sample from the Santa Fe district, which was home to a significant Developmental-period population (Dickson 1979; McNutt 1969; Scheick 2007; Stubbs and Stallings 1953). These patterns suggest that, over the course of the thirteenth century, in-migrating Mesa Verde people either swamped or displaced existing populations of the Pajarito, Chama, and Tano districts, but they intermarried with existing populations in the Santa Fe district.

In sum, these analyses of metric traits suggest that ancestral Tewa genes derive primarily from the Mesa Verde region, but that early Rio Grande populations also contributed, in proportion to their numbers, to the resultant ancestral Tewa population.

The History of the Tewa Speech Community

Even if there was a large influx of people to the northern Rio Grande from the Mesa Verde region in the thirteenth century, it would not necessarily mean that these migrants brought the Tewa language with them. Retention of a language by immigrants depends on many factors,

Table 10.2. Relethford-Blangero analysis of craniometric data set

District (major sites)	N	Distance from regional centroid	Pheno-typic variance (V_p)	Expected variance (V_e)	Residual variance (V_r)	S.E. (V_p)	P ($V_r \approx 0$)
Period 1							
Cibola (Kin Tiel, Village GK, Whitewater)	33	.0221	0.657	0.929	−0.271	.0175	.0000
Piedra (Navajo Reservoir District)	13	.1157	0.610	0.840	−0.230	.0466	.0004
Southeast Utah (Grand Gulch, Alkali Ridge)	33	.0162	0.738	0.934	−0.196	.0207	.0000
Totah (Salmon, Aztec, Tommy site)	57	.0936	0.898	0.861	0.037	.0211	.1079
Mesa Verde (Wetherill Mesa)	56	.0172	1.001	0.933	0.068	.0266	.0265
McElmo (Lowry, Sand Canyon, Ute Mtn)	58	.0048	1.034	0.945	0.089	.0228	.0024
Valdez (Taos Valley Valdez Phase sites)	8	.1690	1.011	0.789	0.222	.0618	.0042
Galisteo (LA3333)	6	.5914	0.848	0.388	0.460	.0879	.0003
Kwahe'e (Tewa Basin Kwahe'e Phase sites)	11	.1820	1.362	0.777	0.585	.1160	.0004
Chaco (Pueblo Bonito, small sites)	65	.0627	1.700	0.890	0.810	.0801	.0000
Period 2							
Jemez (Kwasteyukwa, Amoxiumqua, Guisiwa)	42	.0198	0.655	0.931	−0.276	.0296	.0000
Taos (Pot Creek, Picuris)	17	.0596	0.686	0.893	−0.207	.0212	.0000
El Morro (Heshotuła, Pueblo de los Muertos)	29	.0503	0.728	0.902	−0.174	.0147	.0000
Pecos (B/W-Glaze A)	89	.0868	0.699	0.867	−0.168	.0239	.0000

Salinas (Gran Quivira)	65	.0685	0.832	0.885	−0.052	.0244	.0567
Pajarito (Puye, Otowi, Tsankawi)	81	.0063	0.918	0.944	−0.026	.0295	.3973
Tano (Las Madres, San Cristobal)	55	.0228	0.934	0.928	0.006	.0140	.6766
Chama (Sapawe, Te'ewi)	30	.0297	0.951	0.921	0.030	.0188	.1384
Puerco (Pottery Mound)	27	.1627	0.910	0.795	0.115	.0370	.0100
Santa Fe (Pindi, Arroyo Hondo)	27	.0389	1.218	0.913	0.305	.0352	.0000
Cochiti (LA70, LA6455)	29	.1917	1.082	0.768	0.314	.0492	.0001
Albuquerque (Tijeras, Paako)	28	.0752	1.266	0.878	0.388	.0575	.0000

Notes: Period 1 < AD 1275, Period 2 > AD 1275. Standard errors are estimated by jackknifing across variables. Significance is estimated from the Student's T distribution (2-tailed, $N-1$ degrees of freedom) of the residual variance over its standard error. Regional populations are presented in ascending order of residual variance within each time period.

including the pace and duration of migration, the social scale of migrating groups, and social conditions in the source and destination areas (see Ortman and Cameron, in press). One can imagine several scenarios in which Mesa Verde immigrants would have shifted their language from that of their homeland to that of the destination area. To determine whether the Tewa language was adopted by Mesa Verde immigrants or was brought with them, I have broken down the problem into several smaller and more tractable questions and attempted to answer each one using various lines of evidence.

How Long Has Tewa Been a Distinct Language?

The Tewa language could not have been brought to the northern Rio Grande from the Mesa Verde region if it was not yet a distinct language in the thirteenth century. So, a basic question one needs to answer is: How long has the Tewa language been distinct from other languages of the Kiowa-Tanoan family to which it belongs? Kiowa-Tanoan languages for which there is at least minimal documentation include Northern Tiwa, Southern Tiwa, Tewa, Towa, Piro, and Kiowa. Kiowa is spoken by a community of the southern plains today; the others were spoken in various pueblos of the Rio Grande region at the time of Spanish contact, and all but Piro are still spoken today (Harrington 1909). The traditional view of historical relationships among these languages is that Kiowa is the most divergent dialect and thus separated earliest from the rest, followed by Towa, then Tewa, and then, finally, Northern and Southern Tiwa (Davis 1959; Hale and Harris 1979; Harrington 1909; Trager 1967). In recent years, however, the reality of Kiowa-Tanoan subgroupings has been questioned (Hale and Harris 1979; Kroskrity 1993:55–60; Watkins 1984), so I decided to take a fresh look at Kiowa-Tanoan subgroups using currently accepted methods.

When linguists say that languages are in the same family, what they mean is that it is possible to reconstruct aspects of the language that was ancestral to all the extant dialects of that family. Hale (1967) accomplished this for the Kiowa-Tanoan languages. He reconstructed the phonology (system of phonemes, or meaningful sound contrasts) in the language ancestral to Kiowa, Towa, Tewa, and Tiwa, as well as a system of morphophonemic alternations (predictable changes in pronunciation in certain phonetic environments) that must have characterized the protolanguage. He also identified the sound changes from the protolanguage in each of the descendant dialects.

The most secure method linguists have found for identifying subgroups within a language family is to identify innovations from the protolanguage that are shared in certain descendant dialects but not in others (see Ross 1997). Because language change is conservative, the probability that the same set of changes would occur independently in two distinct languages is low, the implication being that these changes occurred only once, before the dialects that share these innovations diverged from a common ancestor. The logic is essentially the same as that used in creating biological phylogenies on the basis of shared genetic mutations ("derived" characters).

Hale did not consider the implications of his reconstruction for Kiowa-Tanoan subgrouping, but it can be used to illustrate groups of shared innovations that define the traditional subgroups of Kiowa-Tanoan. For example, the changes that distinguish Tanoan from Kiowa are (1) KT *b > T mV̨, bV; and (2) KT *d > T nV̨, dV. What these symbols indicate is that, sometime after the dialect ancestral to Kiowa became isolated from the dialect ancestral to all other Tanoan languages, initial /b/ and /d/ sounds in Tanoan words changed to /m/ or /n/ sounds when the initial /b/ or /d/ was followed by a nasalized vowel. By the same logic, the shared innovations that define Tiwa-Tewa as a subgroup of Tanoan that excludes Towa are (1) T *tsʰ > TT s, (2) T *ʐ > TT ž, and (3) T *gʷ > TT w. And finally, the innovations that define proto-Tiwa as a subgroup of Tiwa-Tewa that excludes Tewa are (1) TT *ʐ > PTi ts, (2) TT *kʷʰ > PTi xʷ, and (3) TT *s > PTi ł. Thus, patterns of shared phonetic innovations support the traditional view of subgroupings in these languages.[7]

This detour into Kiowa-Tanoan phonology is relevant because establishing the branching pattern of the Kiowa-Tanoan family tree is a step in estimating when Tewa became a distinct language. Based on the analysis above, it is possible to infer that Tewa became a distinct language sometime prior to the diversification of proto-Tiwa into Northern and Southern Tiwa. How might one estimate when this latter event occurred? One method used in historical linguistics to address such questions is the "words and things" approach (Campbell 1998:339–368; Fowler 1983; Hill 2001; Kirch and Green 2001: ch. 4; Mallory 1989:143–185).

The principle behind the method is that, when one can reconstruct a word for a cultural item in a protolanguage, we can also assume that the item itself was known to the speakers of that language. If one can also date the initial appearance of that item using archaeological evidence, one can argue the date of diversification of the protolanguage was some-time after the introduction of that item.[8]

I used this method in combination with sound correspondences worked out by Hale (1967), Davis (1989), and Trager (1942), and extant lexicons for Kiowa-Tanoan languages, to reconstruct a number of proto-Tiwa words for cultural items that appeared relatively late in south-western prehistory, but prior to the era of Spanish colonization.[9] The reconstructed forms are: *łowo (viga, "wood-pole"), *nąkʰų́ (adobe, "earth-rock"), *cial (gourd rattle), *cud- (shirt), *p'okú- (tortilla, "water-corn"), *t'okʰę (cotton), *pisólo (blanket), *cɨlmūyu (turquoise), and *todi (macaw). A cognate form is known for each of these terms in both the Taos dialect of Northern Tiwa and the Isleta dialect of Southern Tiwa. Although words for most of these items exist in other Kiowa-Tanoan languages as well, they are not cognate with the Tiwa forms.[10]

All of the items referred to by these terms appear to have been known in the proto-Tiwa speech community before it split into north-ern and southern branches. Archaeological evidence suggests that this split could not have taken place prior to AD 1200, because this is when the most recent items on this list (tailored shirts and griddle stones on which tortillas were cooked) first appeared in the archaeological record (Jeançon 1929:17; Osborne 2004:37–43; Smiley et al. 1953:38). The remaining items all appeared for the first time between AD 980 and 1100, suggesting that the Tiwa-Tewa split occurred prior to this period. For example, turquoise ornaments and macaws first became widespread with the rise of the Chacoan Regional System after AD 980 (Harbottle and Weigand 1992; Hargrave 1970:54), and roofs supported by vigas resting on load-bearing walls also first occur in the architecture of this period (Lekson 1984; McKenna and Truell 1986; Varien 1999c). Also, the earliest documented use of puddled adobe for wall construction occurs in mid–AD 1000s sites in the Rio Grande (McNutt 1969) and in early AD 1100s sites of the Bis sa'ni community on Escavada Wash, near Chaco Canyon (Marshall 1982:178–185, 348–349). Finally, the cul-tivation and weaving of cotton fabrics, including blankets, only became widespread in the northern Southwest after AD 1000 (Ortman 2000b), and gourd rattles are not clearly present in Ancestral Pueblo contexts dating prior to AD 1050 (Ortman 2009: ch. 7).

The Tiwa-Tewa split could have occurred more recently than the period suggested by these data because languages are always in the process of replacing vocabulary. Thus, the absence of a Tewa cognate for a reconstructible proto-Tiwa term does not necessarily mean that the Tiwa-Tewa speech community lacked such a term or knowledge of the associated cultural item. It could be that the Tewa language had a cognate that has been lost since it diverged from proto-Tiwa. However, because seven proto-Tiwa items first appeared within a relatively narrow time frame, one can construct a statistical test to assess the likelihood of Tewa divergence prior to the AD 980–1100 period. The null hypothesis in this case is that the Tiwa-Tewa speech community had not yet split by this period, and that vocabulary replacement is responsible for the absence of cognates for these seven proto-Tiwa terms in Tewa. The question being asked is thus: What is the probability of all seven terms being replaced, given that a certain percentage of cultural vocabulary is still shared between Tiwa and Tewa? Previous lexicostatistical work (Davis 1959) suggests that approximately 57 percent of *basic* vocabulary is still shared between Tiwa and Tewa. In addition, Tiwa and Tewa cognates are available for 70 percent (63 of 90 forms) of the cultural vocabulary I was able to reconstruct in my own study (Ortman 2009: appendix C). Because the binomial probability of the null hypothesis (total vocabulary replacement) is $<.01$ so long as the actual shared cultural vocabulary is at least 48 percent, it would appear reasonable to conclude that Tewa had indeed become a separate language by the AD 980–1100 period. This means there was a distinct Tewa language being spoken somewhere prior to the depopulation of the Mesa Verde region.

Did Tiwa and Tewa Diversify within the Rio Grande Region?

If the Tewa language diversified from proto-Tiwa within the Rio Grande region, it would suggest that thirteenth-century migrants from the Mesa Verde region adopted the Tewa language upon arrival in the Rio Grande region, and it would argue against the idea that Mesa Verde people spoke Tewa prior to the migration. There is some basis for this view.

One of the principles commonly used in linguistics to help define the homeland of a language family is called the "center of maximum diversity" principle (Sapir 1916; also see Bellwood 2005:227–229). The basic idea of this principle is that the homeland of a language family is often in the area where the greatest diversity of descendant dialects is spoken. According to this principle, and based on the fact that all Kiowa-Tanoan languages but Kiowa and Hopi-Tewa are spoken in the Rio Grande region today, it is reasonable to hypothesize that the Kiowa-Tanoan homeland was within the Rio Grande region. This would in turn support the hypothesis that Tewa diverged from Tiwa within this region.

However, three lines of evidence argue against this hypothesis, suggesting instead that the Tewa-Tiwa split occurred outside the Rio Grande region. The first comes from the modern-day distribution of the Tiwa and Tewa speech communities. If the Tiwa and Tewa languages had diversified within the Rio Grande, we would expect the Northern and Southern Tiwa speech communities to have ended up adjacent to each other, with Tewa at one end or the other, but this is not the case. Northern and Southern Tiwa, the most similar Kiowa-Tanoan dialects, are in fact spoken at opposite ends of the Pueblo area in the Rio Grande region, with Tewa, Towa, and Keres in between. It is more parsimonious to explain this distribution as the result of in-migrating groups, including Tewa speakers, splitting what was once a continuous Tiwa language distribution into a northern and southern group.

The second line of evidence comes from cultural vocabulary reconstructed for Kiowa-Tanoan. Hill's (2008a, b) recent work provides suggestive evidence that Kiowa-Tanoan was spoken by Eastern Basketmaker groups, and my own reconstructions of Kiowa-Tanoan cultural vocabulary support this view (see Ortman 2009: ch. 7). Maize macrofossils dating to the Basketmaker II period (ca. 1000 BC to AD 500) have been found in the Rio Grande region (Vierra and Ford 2006), but Basketmaker II sites are far more common in the San Juan region to the west (see Charles and Cole 2006; McNutt 1969). This suggests that the focal area of Kiowa-Tanoan settlement was also west of the Rio Grande region, thus leaving open the possibility that the more recent Tewa-Tiwa split involved the breakup of a social network that was either completely outside the Rio Grande region or encompassed both the San Juan and Rio Grande regions.

The third line of evidence against the *in situ* diversification model comes from a study of place names. From a careful study of Harrington's (1916) encyclopedic compendium and his personal papers, as well as those of Trager, I have identified seventeen topographical features for which toponyms have been recorded phonetically in both the Tewa and Taos (Northern Tiwa) languages. If Tiwa and Tewa diversified within the Rio Grande region, one might expect a certain number of these paired toponyms to date from the period prior to the Tiwa-Tewa split, and thus to be cognate. Table 10.3 lists these seventeen paired toponyms and their English glosses, and it interprets the nature of the relationship between each pair.

There are only three pairs among these seventeen feature names that are possibly cognate, and none are clearly so.[11] However, note that the first pair refers to Sleeping Ute Mountain, a prominent landform in the Mesa Verde region and not in the Rio Grande region. These two forms are not cognate, but because Tiwa has likely been spoken in the Rio Grande region from the time it became distinct from Tewa, it would seem more likely that the Taos form is a loan translation from Tewa. There are two pairs in table 10.3 for which it is clear the Taos form is older than the Tewa form, because the Tewa form incorporates the Tewa term for the Taos people. In addition, there are two pairs for which it is clear that the Tiwa form is the older toponym that was subsequently loaned into Tewa, because the two forms are phonetically similar but the Taos form has a transparent morphological analysis, whereas the Tewa form does not (see Campbell and Kaufman 1976; Shaul and Hill 1998). One of these terms, for Sierra Blanca Lake, refers to a lake that figures prominently in Tewa origin narratives. The fact that the name of this place is a loan from Tiwa suggests that Tewa speakers learned of it from Tiwa speakers who preceded them in occupying the Rio Grande. This will prove important in the analysis of oral tradition later in this chapter.

Finally, there are four sets that are clearly noncognate loan translations for which the direction of translation is unclear, and there are four sets for which the Tewa and Taos forms are clearly unrelated and were coined independently. So overall, there is no definite evidence that Tewa and Tiwa speakers have inherited a common stock of place names in the Rio Grande region from the period of time before their languages

Table 10.3. Paired Tewa and Taos place names

Landform (JPH pp.)	Tewa form	Tewa gloss	Taos form	Taos gloss	Interpretation
Ute Mountain (565)	Phaa p'in	Yucca mountain	Pʰuot'ęp'ianenemą[1]	Basket mountain	Calque from Tewa
Tres Piedras (173)	K'úwăk'uu	Mountain sheep rocks	K'uwaqiuną	mountain sheep rocks	Cognate, loan or calque
Tusas Mountains (172)	Kíp'in	Prairie dog mountain	Kitʰɨp'ianena	Prairie-dog-dwelling mountain	Calque from Taos or cognate
Ojo Caliente (159)	P'osíp'oe	Moss-greenness-water	P'oⁿuop'ó'ona	Water-hot creek	Unrelated
Sierra Blanca Lake (567)	Sip'opʰe	[Unexplained]	Tsip'ophúntha[2]	Eye water black at covering?, -high?	Tiwa loan
Taos Peak (177)	Máxwolop'in	[Unexplained]-mountain	Móxʷoluna		Taos loan
Taos Mountain (175)	Thawíp'in	Taos [dwell-gap] mountains	Poxʷlap'ianenemą[1]	Lake mountain	Taos priority
Taos Creek (178)	Thawíp'oe	Taos [dwell-gap] creek	'Iatopʰayp'ó'ona	Red willow water	Taos priority
Santa Fe (460)	'Ogap'oegeh	Shell-water-at	Hulp'ó'ona	Shell river	Calque
Orejas Mountain (177)	De'oyep'in	Coyote ears mountain	Tuxʷat'oⁿiotʰuntʰo[1]	Fox ear place	Calque
Sierra Blanca (564)	P'ints'ç'ii	Mountain-white	P'ianp'otʰɨbo[1]	Mountain-white-place	Calque

Tierra Amarilla (111)	Nãnts'eyiwe	Earth-yellow-at	Nąmts'úlito[1]	Earth-yellow-place	Cognate or calque
Jicarilla Peak (339)	T'úmp'in	Basket mountain	P'uot'iẹp'ientha[2]	Basket-mountain-at	Calque
Sandia Peak (44)	Oekuup'in	Turtle mountain	Kep'ianenemą[2]	[?]-mountain	Unrelated
Abiquiu Mountain (130)	Ábeshup'in?äy	Abiquiu [chokecherry-end] mountain-little	P'ianp'omúluna[2]	Mountain water jar	Unrelated
Abiquiu (135)	Pʰésúbú:?u	Stick-end-town	Kultʰɨtta[2]	[?]	Unrelated
Red River (174)	P'ip'oge?imp'oe	Red water creek	Tisiup'ó'ona	[?]-river	Unrelated

Note: All Tewa data are from Harrington (1916), with page number in parentheses. Taos data are from this same source unless otherwise noted: (1) George L. Trager Papers, U.C. Irvine, box 40; (2) J. P. Harrington Papers, Microfilm Edition, reel 49, frame 0195-019.

became distinct. In contrast, there are a number of toponyms suggesting that Tiwa has been spoken in the Rio Grande region for a longer period of time than has Tewa. This, in turn, argues against the hypothesis that the Tiwa-Tewa split occurred within the Rio Grande region.

How Long Has Tewa Been Spoken in the Northern Rio Grande?

If one could amass evidence that Tewa was spoken in the Rio Grande region prior to AD 1200, it would weaken the argument that Mesa Verde migrants brought the Tewa language with them. It is possible to address this question through the study of place names for archaeological sites in the Rio Grande. Starting once again from Harrington's (1916) compilation, augmented by Ellis (1964), I have correlated archaeological sites with Tewa names with New Mexico state site numbers, and I have used dating information in recent compilations of northern Rio Grande archaeological sites (Anschuetz 2005; Crown, Orcutt, and Kohler 1996; Fowles 2004a, b; Marshall and Walt 2007; Scheick 2007; Snead 1995; Snead, Creamer, and Van Zandt 2004; Trierweiler 1990) and in the New Mexico Archaeological Records Management Section files to estimate the occupation spans of these sites. I have also compiled a list of Taos names for archaeological sites by working through the personal papers of Harrington and Trager.

Nearly all Tewa ruin names have a clear morphological analysis, and I have found no examples of paired ruin names that are cognate in Tewa and Northern Tiwa. It is therefore highly likely that all Tewa names for ancient settlements were coined by Tewa speakers. It also appears that Tewa names were established for these sites when they were occupied.[12] This, in turn, means that the Tewa language must have been spoken in the Rio Grande region prior to the abandonment dates of the oldest archaeological sites for which names in the Tewa language are remembered.

Table 10.4 presents a list of names, site numbers, glosses, and occupation dates for the longest-abandoned settlements for which names are remembered in the Tewa or Taos languages. This list is drawn from a larger list of sixty-four such sites for which these data are available. The other sites in this list were abandoned more recently than the sites listed here. Several points are worthy of discussion. First, there are eight sites with remembered names in the Tewa language that were constructed

Table 10.4. Early villages with Tewa (or Taos) names

Form	Site Number	Gloss	Ceramic Dates (AD)
1) Tsipiwiʔówînkeji	LA21422	Flaking-stone issuing gap pueblo ruin	1250–1325
2) Navahuʔówînkeji	LA21427	Cultivable field arroyo pueblo ruin	1250–1325
3) Pʰinikʰwiʔówînkeji	LA180	Dwarf cornmeal gap pueblo ruin	1250–1325
4) P'ibidiʔówînkeyi	LA264	Little red mound pueblo ruin	1250–1350
5) K'aatayʔówînkeyi	LA245	Cottonwood grove pueblo ruin	1250–1350
6) Tekʰeʔówînkeyi	LA271	Cottonwood bud pueblo ruin	1200–1350
7) Kaap'oeʔówînkeyi	LA300	Leaf water pueblo ruin	1250–1350
8) Shųp'ódéʔówînkeyi	LA918	Cicada head pueblo ruin	1275–1350
9) Nakeʔmuu	LA12655	Land point village	1250–1325
10) P'ôkutựo (Taos)	LA12741	Water-dry-at (El Pueblito Site)	1050–1190
11) T'oytựĮna (Taos)	LA260	People-house (Pot Creek Pueblo)	1260–1320
12) Phaa p'in-	5MT5006	Yucca mountain village ruin	1240–1280

Sources: 1) Harrington 1916:236; Trierweiler 1990:50; 2) Harrington 1916:244; Trierweiler 1990:50; 3) Harrington 1916:245; Hewett 1906:16; 4) Harrington 1916:380; Ortman 2009; 5) Harrington 1916:380; Ellis 1964; 6) Harrington 1916:336; 7) Harrington 1916:150; 8) Harrington 1916:150; 9) Hewett 1906:25-26; Vierra et al. 2003; 10) George L. Trager Papers, U.C. Irvine, Box 40; Fowles 2004b:230; 11) George L. Trager Papers, U.C. Irvine; Crown (1991); 12) Jeançon (1925:39); Glowacki 2001.

and abandoned during the Late Coalition period, AD 1275–1350, the period that brackets the final depopulation of the Mesa Verde region.

Second, table 10.4 includes an ancestral Northern Tiwa site (LA12741, the El Pueblito Site) abandoned at the end of the Late Developmental period, approximately AD 1190. This is the longest-abandoned village-sized site in the northern Rio Grande for which I have identified a name in the Tewa or Taos language. Sites abandoned at the end of the Developmental period in the Tewa basin, such as the Pojoaque Grant site (LA835), do not appear to have Tewa names. The fact that no Late Developmental aggregates have Tewa names but at least one such site has a Taos name generally supports the conclusions of the paired top-onym analysis, namely, that Tiwa has been spoken in the northern Rio Grande for a longer period of time than has Tewa.

Third, the only site with a Tewa name abandoned earlier than the end of the Coalition period is actually a site in the Mesa Verde region. The name of this site is known from an oral tradition surrounding it, recorded by Jean Jeançon, an archaeologist who worked closely with Tewa people in the early twentieth century:

> In the early days of his contact with the Tewas of Santa Clara, the writer was told stories of the coming of these people from a great village in southwestern Colorado in the dim past. The accounts were so graphic and exact that he copied a map made by his informant of the village, which must have been in ruins at that time, and located in a part of the country in which the man had never been, and only knew from tradi-tions, and a few years later visited a ruin which in situation and sur-rounding corresponded with the description given him, and was able to identify the place as the one from which the Tewa claimed that they came. While the ruin is a great mound at present, there is enough of [an] outline left to positively identify it with the map and as a result of information given by the writer and from other sources, the name of the ruin was changed from the one by which it had been known to that by which it is known to the Tewa. The site here referred to was for-merly known as the Aztec Springs ruins, but is now known as the Yucca House, which is the name that the Tewa call it. (Jeançon 1925:39)

The archaeological site of Yucca House (5MT5006), around which this tradition centers, is a large Ancestral Pueblo village on the east flank of Sleeping Ute Mountain. The site was first described by Jackson (1876:377–378), first mapped by Holmes (1878: plate XL), and later mapped and described by Fewkes (1919:26–27). The site contains a McElmo-style great house that may have been constructed during the Chacoan era, AD 1060–1140 (Marshall et al. 1979:313; Powers, Gillespie, and Lekson 1983:174–177), but a recent review of pottery, tree-ring dates, and architectural details (Glowacki 2001) indicates that the surrounding village dates from the Late Pueblo III period (AD 1240–1280) and represents a "canyon-rim pueblo"

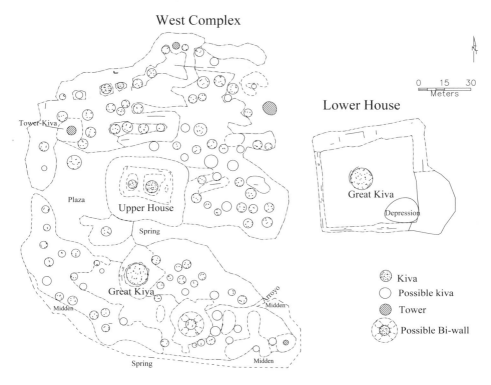

Figure 10.2. Yucca House (5MT5006), an Ancestral Tewa village that combines a bowl-shaped, canyon-rim pueblo characteristic of the late Pueblo III Mesa Verde region and a rectilinear plaza pueblo characteristic of the Late Coalition–period Rio Grande. (Courtesy Crow Canyon Archaeological Center)

analogous to Sand Canyon Pueblo (Lipe and Ortman 2000; Ortman and Bradley 2002). Yucca House was thus one of the last villages occupied by Ancestral Pueblo people in the Mesa Verde region, and its inhabitants were likely involved in the final depopulation of this region. Even though we don't know what Jeançon's informant's map looked like, Yucca House (fig. 10.2) has several distinctive features, including a great house and a large rectangular enclosure with a kiva in the plaza that may represent an early expression of the plaza-oriented village plan that became the standard form throughout the Pueblo world by the early AD 1300s. These features distinguish Yucca House from other large sites in the area, and they would have been identifiable even from a rough-sketch map.

In light of the tradition surrounding Yucca House recorded by Jeançon, it is significant to add that Harrington independently recorded place
names for related topographical features in the vicinity of Yucca House.
He recorded the name Phaa p'in ("Yucca Mountain") for "a mountain
somewhere near the Montezuma Valley in southwestern Colorado" that
"gives Montezuma Valley its Tewa name" (Harrington 1916:565). Neither
Harrington nor his informant knew precisely where this mountain was,
but it is clear that this term applies to Sleeping Ute Mountain because
this feature is labeled using a calque of the Tewa name (Sierra del Datil,
"Mountain of Yucca Bananas") in the 1778 Pacheco Map of the
Dominguez-Escalante Expedition (Warner 1995:144–145). Harrington also
recorded a Tewa name for the Montezuma Valley (*Phaa p'innae'ahkongeh*,
"Plain of the Yucca Mountain"), along with statements to the effect that
ancestors of the Tewa lived in this area in the past: "This is a large valley in southwestern Colorado. It is said that in ancient times when the
Tewa were journeying south from Sip'op^he the K'osa, a mythic person
who founded the K'osa society of the Tewa, first appeared to the people
while they were sojourning in this valley" (Harrington 1916:564).

Thus, the tradition surrounding Yucca House recorded by Jeançon,
and the additional place names and traditions recorded by Harrington,
provide substantive evidence that Tewa-speaking people once inhabited
the Mesa Verde region. Namely, these traditions surround an ancestral village and link to an archaeological site and environs that exhibit
evidence of occupation during the late 1200s, and thus were plausibly
occupied by people who emigrated to the Rio Grande region.

In summary, this analysis of native names for archaeological sites
suggests that the Tewa language has definitely been spoken in the northern Rio Grande from the Late Coalition period onward. There is no
evidence to suggest whether or not Tewa was spoken in the northern
Rio Grande during the Developmental period, but there is positive evidence that Tiwa was spoken in this region at that time. Finally, there is
positive evidence that Tewa was spoken in the Mesa Verde region in the
thirteenth century.

Was Tewa Spoken in the Mesa Verde Region?

Thus far, I have discussed evidence that Tewa has been a distinct language from some time prior to the middle AD 1000s, that it was spoken

in the northern Rio Grande region from at least the middle decades of the AD 1200s, and that it may have been spoken in the Mesa Verde region prior to that time. Is there additional archaeoliguistic evidence that might buttress this final claim? I believe there is, and that this evidence lies in material expressions of conceptual metaphors embedded in the Tewa language.

Conceptual metaphors are cognitive models that use the imagery of a concrete source domain to conceptualize and reason about an abstract target domain (Fauconnier 1997; Fauconnier and Turner 1994; Gibbs 1994; Kovecses 2002; Lakoff 1987, 1993; Lakoff and Johnson 1980, 1999). In previous work, I have suggested that such metaphors can be deciphered from patterns in material culture, using methods derived from cognitive linguistic research (Ortman 2000b, 2008a; Ortman and Bradley 2002; also see David, Sterner, and Gavua 1988; Hays-Gilpin 2008; Potter 2002, 2004; Preston Blier 1987; Sekaquaptewa and Washburn 2004; Tilley 1999; Whitley 2008). I have also argued that the conceptual metaphors of past speech communities can be reconstructed linguistically, through attention to: (1) *polysemy*, the multiple senses of words; (2) *etymology*, the ways in which new words are formed; and (3) semantic change identified through the comparative method (Ortman 2003, 2008c, 2009: ch. 9; Sweetser 1990:23–48). When a metaphor is embedded in the origins, subsequent history, or related senses of a word, it implies that the concept was conventional among *past* speakers of the language, at the time the word was coined or when the new sense was attached to it. It should therefore be possible to identify the past location of a speech community by linking systems of conceptual metaphors enshrined in language to the archaeological expressions of these systems in a plausible previous homeland.

In previous work, I have reconstructed several *material metaphors* that were expressed in Mesa Verde–region material culture during the final decades of Ancestral Pueblo occupation. Each of these metaphors utilized the imagery of containers, actual pots and baskets, as the source domain (fig. 10.3). Reconstructions of these metaphors have been presented in Ortman (2000b, 2006, 2008a, 2008b, 2009) and in Ortman and Bradley (2002), and readers interested in the details should consult these sources. Table 10.5 lists the deciphered metaphors, along with specific expressions of these concepts in Mesa Verde–region material

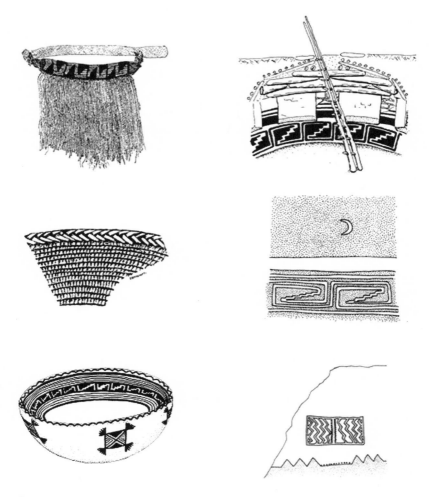

Figure 10.3. Container imagery in Mesa Verde–region material culture. Upper left, plain-weave skirt; middle left, coiled basket; lower left, painted bowl with band design and blanket motif on exterior; upper right, cutaway of kiva with pottery-band mural and cribbed roof; middle right, kiva mural combining pottery-band design below and sky imagery above; lower right, horizon scene with blanket image in the sky. (Courtesy Crow Canyon Archaeological Center.)

Table 10.5. Expressions of container metaphors in Mesa Verde material culture

---

Pottery vessels are textiles
    Pottery bowls are coiled baskets
    Pottery bowls are plaited baskets
    Cooking pots are coiled baskets

Buildings are containers
    Granaries are seed jars
    Kiva walls are pottery bowls
    Kiva roofs are coiled baskets

The community is a pottery vessel
    Villages are pottery bowls
    Plazas are pottery bowls

The world consists of containers
    The sky is woven
    The earth is a pottery bowl
    The emergence place is a water-filled vessel

---

culture. In the following paragraphs, I summarize the conclusions of these studies.

Twelfth- and thirteenth-century pottery of the Mesa Verde region was decorated in a thoroughly geometric style, with designs in black paint on a white-slipped surface. Many researchers have noted parallels between the painted designs on this pottery and the woven objects recovered from contemporaneous cliff dwellings. I have studied these correlations and found abundant evidence that this stylistic unity derived from a conceptualization of painted pottery vessels as woven objects (Ortman 2000b), especially coiled and plaited basketry. I've also found that cooking pots were manufactured using techniques analogous to coiled and twined basketry and imitated the surface textures of baskets (Ortman 2006).

Mesa Verde people also conceptualized buildings as containers for people, in the same way that actual pots and baskets contained food (Ortman 2008a). For example, the central component of residential architecture was a small subterranean kiva, and one of the primary ways the walls of such structures were decorated was with a mural painted in a style identical to the banded designs on pottery bowls. In addition, there are a number of granaries that were decorated as pottery seed jars, and the cribbed roofs of most kivas mirror the appearance and construction of an overturned, coiled basket. Also, the architecture of thirteenth-century, canyon-rim villages and plazas, and the communal activities that took place in these spaces, suggest that villages and plazas in the AD 1200s were imagined as communal pottery serving bowls (Ortman 2006, 2009: ch. 9; Ortman and Bradley 2002; also see fig. 10.2).

Finally, Mesa Verde people appear to have conceptualized the world as consisting of containers (Ortman 2008a). A second common theme of architectural mural decoration consists of dado patterns in which the lower portion is red, the upper portion is tan to white, and there are sets of projecting triangles and dots running along the boundary between the two colors. These compositions appear to be abstractions of the horizon with projecting landforms, and this landscape imagery is combined with container imagery in several compositions (fig. 10.3). This, in turn, suggests that Mesa Verde people imagined the world as consisting of an earthen pottery bowl below and a woven, vegetal basket above. In addition, pottery vessels were used to represent the emergence place itself. Many kivas in Ancestral Pueblo sites have a small, round hole in the floor north of the hearth. This feature is called the sipapu, after the Hopi term, and represents the emergence place for many pueblo groups today. During the AD 1200s, sipapus in Mesa Verde–region kivas were often created using an olla neck or mug with the bottom broken out (Cattanach 1980:51; Morris 1991:674; Ortman and Bradley 2002; Rohn 1971:74). This suggests that the emergence place was imagined as a pottery vessel containing water.

It is important to emphasize that the conclusions presented above are supported in every case by a range of patterns in material culture that are consistent with generalizations concerning the ways humans express conceptual metaphors in everyday behavior. A metaphor hypothesis accounts for these diverse patterns readily and parsimoniously. Another point to emphasize is that the material metaphors I have reconstructed for Mesa Verde culture are not isolated and unrelated, but rather form a coherent conceptual system. And although expressions of certain concepts do occur across broader areas of the Southwest, the container imagery discussed here forms a coherent complex only in the Mesa Verde region (see, for example, Ortman 2008a). These facts support

the claim that these metaphoric expressions reflect the cognitive uncon-
scious of the people who inhabited the Mesa Verde region during the
twelfth and thirteenth centuries. In other words, it is reasonable to view
the conceptual metaphors behind these material expressions as ideas
that had become deeply ingrained through the enculturation process,
and that were materialized in a number of mutually reinforcing ways in
ritual and in daily life. One would therefore expect these concepts to
have influenced the language of Mesa Verde people as well.

With knowledge of these material metaphors in hand, I have examined major sources of Kiowa-Tanoan lexical data to determine whether
these same concepts are enshrined in the etymologies and meanings of
relevant words in specific languages. Analyses of these data (Ortman
2003, 2008b, 2008c, 2009: ch. 10) suggest that nearly all the metaphorical expressions identified in the Mesa Verde archaeological complex
have reflexes in the Tewa language, whereas other Kiowa-Tanoan languages contain little to no evidence of these metaphors. One example
of a Tewa word whose etymology reflects a Mesa Verde metaphor is
natʔú ("pottery"), which is a compound of nan ("earth, clay") and tʔú
("baskets"). Another example is the word for a pitched roof, tʔúpʰáʔdiʔ,
the etymology of which—tʔún ("[coiled] basket") + pʰe ("stick, timber") + di ("of")—expresses the metaphor ROOFS ARE BASKETS. These
data suggest that at one time, people who spoke Tewa made pots and
roofs that expressed basket imagery. Weaving imagery does not appear
to have actively structured Rio Grande black-on-white pottery decoration (Ortman 2009: ch. 13), but it clearly did structure Mesa Verde
pottery traditions (Ortman 2000). Likewise, kiva roofs in Rio Grande
sites do not have a basket shape, but the cribbed roofs of most Mesa
Verde kivas do look like overturned, coiled baskets (Ortman 2008a).
Thus, it is difficult to imagine how natʔú or tʔúpʰáʔdiʔ could have come
to exist in the Tewa language if it had never been spoken in the Mesa
Verde region.

In other cases, it is the multiple senses of Tewa words that express
Mesa Verde metaphors. One example is provided by the multiple senses
of p'okwin. The core sense of this word is clearly "lake" because this is
its primary meaning in Tewa; the word incorporates the Tewa term for
water (p'o), and it is cognate with Tiwa terms for "lake" (p'axwiane in
Northern Tiwa, p'ahwi:re in Southern Tiwa). Yet the Tewa term is also

applied to a kiva, to a ceremonial bowl, or to a ruin. These extended senses form what Lakoff (1987) calls a conceptual chain. In Tewa belief, the original people emerged from a lake, and as mentioned previously, the kiva is one representation of this emergence place (cf. p'okwi-kʰoyi ["lake + roof hatch of a kiva"]). Also, the primary object of ceremonial leaders whose activities take place inside the kiva is a ceremonial bowl (p'okwingéh ["lake-place"] or p'okwisä̌ʔä̌wéh ["lake-bowl"]) that is filled with water and used to represent p'okwin during ceremonies. In addition, the souls of these leaders are believed to become ancestral cloud beings (ókʰùwà, cf. okʰúwá ["cloud"]) after death, and to dwell under the surface of lakes. A ruin, then, is the dwelling place of ancestors who have become clouds, and thus ruins are also p'okwin. These multiple senses of p'okwin link lakes with the emergence place, kivas, and pottery bowls and clearly reflect several metaphorical expressions involving containers and kivas in Mesa Verde material culture. Several of these concepts are expressed in Tewa basin archaeology, but in all cases they appear earlier in Mesa Verde archaeology.

Finally, an example of semantic change within Kiowa-Tanoan that implies the development of a Mesa Verde metaphor in the Tewa language is found in the history of Tanoan *búlu ("pottery bowl"). At some point after Tewa became distinct from Tiwa, reflexes of this form began to be applied to bowl-shaped topographical features (bú:ʔú ["large dell"], be:ʔe ["small dell"]), plazas (búpíngéh [bú:ʔú + pín ("heart, middle") + géh ("place")]), and villages (bú:ʔú ["village"])[13]. This semantic change implies that, at one point in the history of the Tewa speech community, Tewa-speaking people constructed bowl-shaped villages in bowl-shaped settings. There are no ancestral Tewa villages in the Rio Grande region that fit this description, but such villages were typical of the Late Pueblo III period in the Mesa Verde region, as noted earlier. So if Tewa had never been spoken in the Mesa Verde region, one would have to ask how the Tewa language came to apply a word for bowl-shaped things to villages.

These and a variety of additional data (see Ortman 2009: ch. 10) lead to the following conclusions: (1) evidence for all the conceptual relationships expressed by Mesa Verde container metaphors is embedded in the Tewa language, (2) northern Rio Grande material culture does not express many of the conceptual relationships that are fossilized in words of the Tewa language and expressed directly in Mesa Verde region material culture, and (3) the Mesa Verde metaphors that are fossilized in the Tewa language are not embedded in other Kiowa-Tanoan languages. These findings strongly suggest that the Tewa speech community was located in the Mesa Verde region during the AD 1200s and that this speech community shifted its location from there to the northern Rio Grande over the course of the thirteenth century.

Social Memory of Mesa Verde Occupancy by Tewa Speakers

The final line of evidence I examine in this chapter is Tewa oral tradition. Ethnographers have published several statements regarding the prior homeland of the Tewa Pueblos, and these accounts regularly mention the Mesa Verde region as a prior homeland. Jeançon recorded an explicit statement by Aniceto Swaso, a Tewa from Santa Clara Pueblo:

> We were a long time coming down to this country; sometimes we stop long time in one place, but all the time it was still too cold for us to stay, so we come on. After while some people get to what you call Mesa Verde, in Colorado. . . . Then they began to get restless again and some go west on the San Juan River, some of them come by way of the Jicarilla Apache country, some come the other way by way of Cañon Largo, Gallinas, and the Chama. (Jeançon 1923:75–76)

Alfonso Ortiz, a Tewa anthropologist, also recorded statements to the effect that the Tewa people lived in southwestern Colorado prior to moving to the Rio Grande valley:

> Many Tewa elders show a very detailed knowledge of the region north and northwest of San Juan into what is now southwestern Colorado. This is true even if they have never been there themselves . . . such detailed knowledge does lend credence to the Tewa's migration traditions and claims that they once occupied an area considerably to the north and northwest of where they are now. (Ortiz 1969:148–149)

In the early twentieth century, certain Tewa people also remembered the name of an ancient homeland located far to the northwest of the present-day Tewa basin. Harrington reported that "the old cacique of Nambé seemed to know a vague place in the north named Tewayóge 'great Tewa place' (*Tewa* name of the tribe; *yo* augmentative; *ge* 'down at, over at')" (1916:572). Ellis confirmed and amplified Harrington's statement in a report on the past use of territory for agriculture by Nambé Pueblo:

> The Tewas on the east side of the Rio Grande referred to their territory as Teguayo, 'Place of the Tewas,' even as they also referred to their earlier home in the northwest on the San Juan, apparently either in Mesa Verde or a little farther east in the Upper San Juan around Aztec and the basin of the Navajo Reservoir. As 'Teguayo' was also used to designate a mythical ancestral place of origin, the term puzzled the Spaniards, but causes little difficulty if one realizes that the Pueblos (like ourselves) often duplicate some old names in new areas. (Ellis 1974:2)

References to Tewayó, a mythic land northwest of Santa Fe, occur in Spanish documents dating as far back as the Pueblo Revolt period. For example, Tewayó is plotted northwest of colonial New Mexico in a map dating to the AD 1680s (see Bloom 1934). However, the Spanish became confused regarding the location and significance of this place, and this confusion has led many recent scholars to discount the idea that Tewayó referred to an ancient homeland (e.g., Hodge 1912:712; Sanchez 2006; Tyler 1952). Untangling the historical and scholarly confusion surrounding Tewayó is beyond the scope of this chapter (but see Ortman 2009: ch. 8). Here, it is sufficient to note that its significance and location were finally cleared up by Fray Silvestre Vélez de Escalante in a letter he wrote to Fray Morfi, his superior, a few years after the Dominguez-Escalante Expedition of 1776:

> Before finishing this letter I desire to indicate what is my opinion, at least, upon the Tehuayo and upon the Gran Quivira, whose imaginary greatness has given much to think over from the beginning of the last century to the present. The Tehuayo, according to the diary of Oñate and other ancient narratives, should be considered at the most two hundred leagues to the northwest from Santa Fe; and it is nothing but

the land by way of which the Tihuas, Tehuas, and the other Indians transmigrated to this kingdom; which is clearly shown by the ruins of the pueblos which I have seen in it, whose form was the same that they afterwards gave to theirs in New Mexico; and the fragments of clay and pottery which I also saw in the said country are much like that which the said Tehuas make today. To which is added the prevailing tradition with them, which proves the same; and that I have gone on foot more than three hundred leagues in the said direction up to 41 degrees and 19 minutes latitude and have found no information whatever among the Indians who today are occupying that country of others who live in pueblos. (Twitchell 1914:278–279)

Escalante focused on the Pueblo Indian traditions of which he had first-hand knowledge and attempted to link these traditions to his direct experiences in the lands northwest of Santa Fe. Those experiences included visits to Ancestral Pueblo ruins on the rim of the Dolores River valley in the Mesa Verde region (Warner 1995). Escalante thus determined, through archaeological and ethnographic observations, that the most likely location of Tewayó, the ancient homeland of the Tewa people, was in fact in the Mesa Verde region. In so doing, he brought Spanish understanding of Tewayó in line with Tewa oral traditions that were remembered by at least a few individuals well into the twentieth century.

Before concluding this section, it is important to address one aspect of Tewa oral tradition that could be construed as evidence that these pueblos originated in the Rio Grande region and not in the Mesa Verde region. The Tewa origin narrative has been recorded independently by several researchers, including Alfonso Ortiz (1969:13–14), Elsie Clews Parsons (1994:9–15), and Jean Jeançon (n.d.). In all cases, this narrative refers to the primordial place of emergence as Sip'op^{h}e, which lies beneath a brackish lake called ʔOkhangep'okwinge or "Sandy Place Lake." Harrington (1916:567) associated these names with Sierra Blanca Lake in the San Luis Valley of Colorado. The question these data raise is: Why do Tewas consistently talk about their place of emergence as a lake near the headwaters of the Rio Grande if in fact they lived to the northwest, in the Mesa Verde region, before migrating to the northern Rio Grande region?

There are a few reasons why I think Tewa origin narratives do not undermine the hypothesis suggested by other lines of evidence. First, following the earlier discussion of p'okwin, the notion that Tewa people emerged from a lake does not necessarily mean that they emerged from a specific lake. Naranjo relates an interview she had with an elder Tewa man regarding this issue in the following passage:

> *P'oquin* is a high-context word [that] simply means 'lake' [in English]. But in Tewa that's not the case. *P'oquin* is a metaphor that means many things. [For example,] the *p'oquin* is a kiva too, so it's a sacred place. Where there is a *kha-je*, there is a *p'oquin*, or sacred place. Therefore, those places that are *p'oquin* [include] not only the kiva but where you collect Douglas Fir for ceremonial dances; where you bring the Douglas fir to is a prayer shrine, a *p'oquin*. If we came from *P'oquingeh*, it does not mean that we came from a body of water, literally, although that's the way anthropologists and archaeologists have interpreted it. That's the only way they can interpret it if they don't know Tewa [and] they don't understand the many contexts and meanings of *p'oquin*. (Naranjo 2006:53–54)

This passage suggests that ʔOkhąngep'okwinge, in the San Luis Valley, may simply represent the prototypical "lake" in Tewa worldview, based on its characteristics and geographical relationship to the historic Tewa territory, rather than being the actual place where Tewa ethnogenesis occurred.

Tewa worldview provides a solid basis for thinking of Sandy Place Lake in this way. Ortiz explains:

> All peoples try to bring their definitions of group space somehow into line with their cosmologies, but the Pueblos are unusually precise about it. This precision has many, almost inexhaustible, implications because the Pueblos attempt to reproduce this mode of classifying space on a progressively smaller scale. Since all space is sacred and sacred space is inexhaustible, these models of the cosmos can be reproduced endlessly around them. . . . All the Pueblos also have a well-elaborated conception and symbolization of the middle or center of the cosmos, represented by a sipapu, an earth-navel, or the entire village. Usually there are many centers because sacred space can be recreated again and again without ever exhausting its reality. . . . The elaboration of the notion

of the center has the further implication that the dominant spatial orientation, as well as that of motion, is centripetal or inward. . . . Thus a Pueblo priest, when setting out a dry painting, will first carefully set out the boundaries and then work his way *inward* toward the center. (Ortiz 1972:142–143)

This centripetal orientation reinforces Naranjo's explanation that Tewa people conceive of the world as having layers of lakes, which are located at the far edges of the world, on the tops of their cardinal mountains, at springs closer to home, and within the kivas in their villages. Notice also that, due to this centripetal orientation, events that happened longest ago happened farthest away. Finally, the characteristic Tewa ritual circuit, which is followed in recounting emergence narratives, kiva ceremonies, and plaza dances, always begins in the north (Kurath 1969; Laski 1959; Ortiz 1969). What all this means is that the prototypical emergence place must be a lake located in the far north, beyond the edge of the current Tewa world. Sandy Place Lake fits these criteria perfectly.

Second, as Ellis hinted in her discussion of Tewayó, Pueblo people tend to map pre-existing cosmographical ideas onto whatever environment they find themselves in. In other words, as one moves through the world, the system of lakes that place that person in the center moves as well. A documented example of this process is that the primary cardinal mountain and associated lake of each Tewa pueblo varies in accordance with its geographical location (see Ortiz 1969; Ortman 2008b). This leaves open the possibility that Tewa cosmographical ideas developed elsewhere and were translated to the northern Rio Grande landscape as ancestral Tewas settled into it. This process appears to be reflected in the transfer of directional shrine systems and cardinal mountains from the Mesa Verde region to the Tewa basin (Ortman 2008b), and it is also suggested by the analysis of paired Tewa-Taos place names discussed earlier in this chapter. Specifically, the Tewa name for the actual emergence place, Sip'op[h]e, is unanalyzable in Tewa, and it appears to be a loan from the proto-Tiwa toponym *tsip'aphún- ("eye-water-black").[14] This toponym loan from Tiwa suggests that Tewa speakers learned of Sierra Blanca Lake from Tiwa speakers, who maintained similar cosmographical beliefs as they settled the northern Rio Grande landscape.

Conclusions

In this chapter, I have amassed a range of evidence suggesting that the Tewa language, and most ancestral Tewa genes, originated in the Mesa Verde region. A summary of this evidence is as follows:

- Metric traits collected from human skeletal remains suggest that Late Coalition– and Classic-period populations of the Tewa and Galisteo basins descended primarily from earlier Mesa Verde region populations.
- Metric traits also suggest that pre–AD 1275 populations of the Rio Grande experienced significant in-migration, and that after AD 1275, immigrants from the Mesa Verde region intermarried with indigenous populations of the Santa Fe district but swamped or displaced existing populations of the Pajarito Plateau, Chama drainage, and Galisteo basin.
- Reconstructed cultural vocabulary suggests that the Tewa language was distinct from other Kiowa-Tanoan languages prior to the AD 980–1100 period.
- Analysis of paired Tewa and Taos place names suggests that Tewa diverged from Tiwa outside the northern Rio Grande region.
- Analysis of Tewa and Taos names for archaeological sites in the northern Rio Grande indicates that Tiwa can be documented in this region from the Late Developmental period, but Tewa can only be documented from the Late Coalition period.
- At least one named ancestral village in southwestern Colorado and events that occurred there were remembered in the early twentieth century, and this site can be identified by matching up archaeological surface remains with the description of the site in the oral tradition.
- Additional toponyms and associated traditions for the environs surrounding this ancestral village have also been recorded independently, despite the fact that neither the informant nor the investigator had been to these places themselves.
- The Tewa language enshrines a number of material metaphors that are not fossilized in other Kiowa-Tanoan languages and are expressed by Mesa Verde material culture, but that in many cases are not expressed by northern Rio Grande material culture.

- Ethnographers have recorded several statements by Tewa people indicating their belief that their former homeland was in southwestern Colorado.
- In the early twentieth century, certain people in Tewa-speaking communities knew the location and Tewa name of this previous homeland.
- Knowledge of the location and name of this homeland was even more widespread among Tewa people in the seventeenth century, and it is reflected in Spanish documents of the period.

Taken together, these data make a strong case that a form of speech directly ancestral to all Tewa dialects was spoken in the Mesa Verde region in the thirteenth century, and that this language was brought to the Rio Grande as a result of large-scale population movement from the Mesa Verde region during that century. There are certainly alternative explanations one might develop for certain of these lines of evidence, but I think the fact that there are so many logically independent lines of evidence leading to the same conclusion offers a significant challenge to models of Tewa origins that do not involve substantial in-migration from the Mesa Verde region.

These findings do not necessarily indicate that the entire population of the Mesa Verde region moved to the northern Rio Grande during the thirteenth century. Indeed, it seems far more likely that the Mesa Verde–region population dispersed broadly, and that groups of immigrants joined existing communities across the Pueblo world. What these data do suggest, however, is that the many thousands of people who migrated to the Tewa and Galisteo basins in the thirteenth century colonized a frontier landscape in such a way that the language, gene pool, and historical identity of the immigrants was preserved.

The evidence discussed here also does not indicate that Tewa was the only Pueblo language ever spoken in the Mesa Verde region. Indeed, by the time Tewa emerged as a distinct language, Ancestral Pueblo people had already been living in the Mesa Verde region for several centuries. Recent syntheses of Mesa Verde–region archaeology indicate that the Ancestral Pueblo occupation of this region occurred in two roughly three-hundred-year cycles of population growth and decline (Varien et al. 2007), and there is nothing in the data presented here to rule out

the possibility that the dominant language of the early cycle was different from that of the late cycle. However, these data do suggest that a
form of Tewa speech ancestral to all extant dialects was the dominant
language throughout the Mesa Verde region during the second cycle of
Ancestral Pueblo occupation.

Finally, the many lines of evidence suggestive of a Mesa Verde homeland for the Tewa pueblos do not suggest that contemporary Tewa culture and society bear a straightforward relationship to the earlier culture
and society of the Mesa Verde region. As Lipe and Boyer and others
note in their contributions to this volume (chapters 11 and 12), there are
surprisingly few characteristics of Late Coalition– and Classic-period
material culture that necessarily derive from Mesa Verde material traditions. Indeed, the degree of material discontinuity between Mesa Verde
and northern Rio Grande material culture is striking, given the wide
range of evidence suggesting that Mesa Verde immigrants formed the
majority of the ancestral Tewa population. The problem deserves much
more attention than can be devoted to it here. For now, I will simply
state that it appears difficult to account for the disjunctions between
Mesa Verde and Rio Grande material culture without positing a significant social movement, perhaps akin to the Pueblo Revolt of 1680,
which would have encouraged Mesa Verde migrants to discard many
homeland traditions in favor of traditions developed by earlier peoples
of the Rio Grande and by earlier immigrants. I believe that there are
more material continuities than some would propose, but regardless, it
may not be a stretch to suggest that a widespread, contagious, and perhaps militant desire for significant social change was part of the social
dynamic that led to the final depopulation of the Mesa Verde region.
Glowacki (this vol.) makes a similar suggestion, as do Cameron and
Duff (2008).

Acknowledgments

Portions of this research have been supported by the National Science Foundation (NSF DDIG-0753828), Arizona State University, the American Council of
Learned Societies, the Andrew W. Mellon Foundation, and the Robert and Florence Lister Fellowship from Crow Canyon Archaeological Center. I would like to
thank Bill Lipe for introducing me to the literature on Tewayó and for biblio-
graphic research in this area. I would also like to thank Betsy Brandt and Laurel
Watkins for their help with the linguistic analyses, and Christopher Stojanowski

and Jane Buikstra for their help with the biodistance analyses. Michelle Hegmon and Keith Kintigh helped me to formulate a coherent way of investigating this massive and complex problem. Eric Blinman, Bill Lipe, Tessie Naranjo, Steve LeBlanc, Laurel Watkins, and two anonymous reviewers provided many helpful comments on earlier versions of this chapter. Finally, I would like to thank the staff and administration of Crow Canyon Archaeological Center for supporting my doctoral studies in a number of ways.

Notes

1. However, Boyer and others (this vol.) and Maxwell (1994) suggest that robust intrinsic growth could account for these changes. For an extended discussion of previous studies of population in the northern Rio Grande, see Ortman (2009: ch. 3).

2. The people of these Galisteo-basin villages were labeled Tʰanut'owa, or "down-country people," by their northern brethren. Throughout this paper, unless otherwise noted, Tewa terms are presented using the orthography developed by Esther Martinez for the San Juan dialect (Martinez 1982).

3. Most previous writers considered these immigrants to have derived from Southern Tewa villages (Dozier 1954; Kroskrity 1993; Parsons 1994), but it is also possible that these immigrants were of Northern Tewa origin (Marshall and Walt 2007:40–47; Yava 1978). All accounts are in agreement that the Hopi-Tewa immigrants came primarily from the northern village of Ts'ä̱wadi, located on the lower Rio Santa Cruz, across the Rio Grande to the east of Santa Clara Pueblo. It is also clear that inhabitants of several Tano villages moved north and joined their northern kinsmen during the Pueblo Revolt, and that many people from San Cristobal in particular ended up at Ts'ä̱wadi by the early 1690s (Marshall and Walt 2007). However, it is unclear whether Ts'ä̱wadi was an established village when the Southern Tewas settled there, and Hopi-Tewas remember their homeland village by its Northern Tewa name rather than the Southern Tewa names Yam P'ham-ba or San Cristobal, both of which were transferred to Ts'ä̱wadi when the Southern Tewas moved there (Harrington 1916:486).

4. For example, Harrington (1916:483–485) collected a short vocabulary from a Pueblo Galisteo descendant in 1908 that showed that the southern and northern dialects were mutually intelligible as recently as AD 1794, when the last inhabitants of Pueblo Galisteo moved to Santo Domingo Pueblo. Kroskrity (1993:55–60, 71–77) also compared the phonology and basic vocabularies of the present-day Hopi-Tewa and Ohkay'owinge dialects and found them to be very similar, suggesting that they were even more so in 1696. Finally, Speirs (1966:30–36) highlighted several phonological differences between the dialect of Santa Clara Pueblo and that of the other five northern Tewa Pueblos, but found none that interfered with mutual intelligibility.

5. Note that post–AD 1275 regional samples from other portions of the northern Rio Grande, including Pecos, Jemez, Salinas, and Albuquerque, also exhibit

significant affinity with at least one Mesa Verde region sample. This suggests that people from the Mesa Verde region may have migrated to destinations throughout the northern Rio Grande region, in addition to areas occupied by Tewa-speaking people in historic times.

6. In an earlier work (Ortman 2009: ch. 5), I demonstrate that these patterns in biological affinity are not due to missing data estimation or to sampling error, and I also show that, according to the theory of neutral genetic variation, ancestral Tewa populations could not have descended directly from earlier local populations.

7. The situation is somewhat more complicated than is presented here, but these details do not affect the overall conclusion. See Ortman (2009: ch. 6) for an extended analysis of Kiowa-Tanoan phonology.

8. I have pursued this method in lieu of glottochronology because most linguists no longer believe the latter is useful for dating language splits.

9. The list of sources consulted for Kiowa-Tanoan lexical data include Elizabeth Brandt (personal communication, 2006), Frantz and Gardner (1995); Hale (1962); J. P. Harrington (1916, 1928); C. T. Harrington (1920); Henderson and Harrington (1914); Martinez (1982); Robbins, Harrington, and Freire-Marreco (1916); Trager (1946); Laurel Watkins (personal communication, 2008); and Yumitani (1998). In another work (Ortman 2009: ch. 7), I discuss ninety forms that are reconstructed to form various subgroups of Kiowa-Tanoan and analyze their dates of first appearance in the archaeological record. The discussion here is abstracted from this larger analysis.

10. Several of these words ("viga," "adobe," "tortilla") were created from existing words. The terms for "cotton" and "blanket" are probably loans from Uto-Aztecan—e.g., the Tohono O'odham *tokih* ("raw or absorbent cotton, cotton string, any material made of cotton" [Saxton et al. 1983]) and the Hopi *pösaala* ("blanket, rug, wrap, especially a man's" [Hill 1998:441])—and the term for "turquoise" is probably from Keres (the proto-Keres *šúwimu* means "turquoise" [Miller and Davis 1963:326]). I have not been able to identify a source for "macaw," "moccasin," or "shirt."

11. When working with place names, it is difficult to distinguish true cognates from calques or loan translations because toponyms are often compounds, and to the extent that these compounds have transparent morphological analyses, they can be translated into other languages. When this occurs between closely related languages, like Tewa and Taos, the resultant translation will combine morphemes that are themselves cognate. In addition, toponyms can be simplified during the translation process or through the loss of morphemes over time, thus diluting evidence of cognacy.

12. Tewa names for sites that are ruins today typically end in 'ówînkeyi ('ówîn ["village"] + keyi ["ruin"]) to distinguish them from 'ówînge or occupied villages (e.g., Oke'ówînge for San Juan Pueblo; Thawi'ówînge for Taos Pueblo). However, there is evidence that 'ówînkeyi were originally 'ówînge. For example, the site known today as Yûnge'ówînkeyi was occupied and recorded as Yûnge'ówînge in

sixteenth-century sources (Harrington 1916:227). Also, the ancestral Keres site of Tyuonyi (occupied ca. 1350–1550) is known in Tewa as Puqwige'ówînkeyi, "pueblo ruin where the pottery bases were wiped thin" (Harrington 1916:411; Kohler, Herr, and Root 2004:239). Tewa oral tradition indicates that this name derives from the practices of its ancient inhabitants (Harrington 1916:411; Kohler, Herr, and Root 2004:239), which in turn suggests that the name originated when the site was occupied. These and other examples suggest that 'ówînkeyi are sites that were named by Tewa speakers during their period of occupancy.

13. The various Tewa reflexes of proto-Tanoan *búlu are related via sound symbolism. In a large number of paradigms for Tewa forms, the front vowels /e/ and /a/ indicate smaller scale, whereas the back vowels /o/ and /u/ indicate larger scale (Harrington 1910:16). As examples, compare ʔi pije, "to this place," with hae pije, "to yonder place," and ʔo pije, "to that remote place"; compare heʔe, "small groove, arroyito," with huʔu, "large groove, arroyo"; compare pʰigi, "small and flat," with pʰagi, "large and flat"; and compare be:gi, "small and round," with bu:gi, "large and round." The Tewa forms be:, "pottery bowl, vessel, fruit"; be:ʔe, "small dell"; and bú:ʔú, "large dell, village, plaza," also follow this pattern, with smaller entities indicated by a front vowel and larger entities by a back vowel.

14. If the Tewa form were cognate, the original sound would be a /ts/ instead of /s/. It is also important to note that this place is viewed as the emergence place among Southern Tiwa speakers (Harrington 1920) in addition to Tewas.

11

Lost in Transit

The Central Mesa Verde Archaeological Complex

William D. Lipe

In the mid– to late AD 1200s, a distinctive archaeological complex flourished in the central Mesa Verde area (CMV) of southwestern Colorado and southeastern Utah.[1] Including specific types of material culture, architecture, and community spatial patterning, this complex was a regular part of the cultural production and environment of thousands of people, yet most elements disappeared from the southwestern archaeological record along with the complete depopulation of the area by about 1280. Was this because most members of the CMV population died or failed to reproduce biologically, so that the cultural complex perished along with the people who had produced it? Or did most of the people responsible for this complex migrate to other parts of the Southwest but adopt or develop different cultural traits in their new homes? Several lines of evidence support the second hypothesis and indicate that a substantial number of CMV emigrants eventually resettled in the northern Rio Grande area (NRG). This chapter examines the CMV archaeological complex of the 1200s and compares it with the archaeological complex(es) present in the NRG just prior to, during, and immediately following the presumed migration(s). I will conclude by describing some possible scenarios that might account for what appears to have been rapid cultural change among the late thirteenth-century Mesa Verde migrants.

The CMV archaeological complex of the late 1200s occurred in at least sixty communities centered on villages of fifty to more than seven hundred rooms (Lipe 2002). This was the most populous part of the larger Mesa Verde culture area. Most but not all elements of the CMV cultural complex occurred in the other Mesa Verdean subareas during the 1200s (i.e., eastern, far western, and Totah). Some elements of this complex also occurred in the southern part of the San Juan drainage basin at this time, but I wish to focus on the CMV.

If, in fact, a large number of people migrated from the CMV to the NRG in the late AD 1200s, they did not reconstitute in their new home the distinctive cultural complex they had practiced right up to the time they left their homeland. If individual traits from this complex appear in the NRG, they do so extremely rarely (e.g., Amsden 1931:48). Most traits of the CMV complex also occur only rarely if at all in other parts of the Southwest, including areas that might also have received immigrants from the Mesa Verde region.[2]

Possible culture-change scenarios must take into account how quickly CMV migrants resettled in the NRG, what the role of intervening populations might have been, whether migration flows had been established before the large movements in the late 1200s, and how the Mesa Verde emigrants negotiated sociocultural positions with respect to people already residing in the NRG. Some of these scenarios will be briefly explored later in this chapter.

The relative archaeological invisibility of CMV migrants is especially puzzling in light of evidence that some of the migrants from the neighboring Kayenta culture area preserved several distinctive cultural traits, even in settlements as far south as southern Arizona (Clark 2001; Haury 1958; Hill et al., this vol.; Lindsay 1987; Lindsay and Dean 1983; Lyons, Hill, and Clark 2008; Rouse 1958; Stone 2003; Stone and Lipe, in press; Woodson 1999).

That the CMV had a large population in the generations prior to its final abandonment is demonstrated by recent analyses of demographic data. An 1800 km[2] study area (less than a third of the CMV area) had an estimated average momentary population of more than nineteen thousand people in the AD 1225–1260 period and more than ten thousand between 1260 and 1280 (Varien et al. 2007). Population decline began in about 1260 and accelerated in the late 1270s; construction activity ended in about 1280 (Lipe 1995; Varien et al. 1996; Varien et al. 2007).

Some have argued that migrations out of the CMV area started well before 1260 (Cordell et al. 2007; Duff and Wilshusen 2000). This is possible, but if it is true, it evidently did not result in local population decline. Glowacki (2006, 2007) suggests that the southeastern Utah population began to drop by the early 1200s, but that some or most of this population moved into the Colorado portion of the CMV, helping create a population boom there in the mid-1200s (also see Lipe 2002).

Lines of evidence linking the archaeological culture of the Mesa Verde region to the Pueblo people of the NRG include oral traditions (Ellis 1967; Ortiz 1969); Tewa place names for several locations in southwestern Colorado (Harrington 1916); Tewa traditional knowledge of specific sites in the Mesa Verde area (Jeançon 1925); conceptual metaphors expressed in Mesa Verde material culture and architecture on the one hand, and Tewa language, on the other (Ortman 2000b, 2003, 2008b); much greater similarities between Mesa Verde and NRG skeletal populations after AD 1250 (Ortman 2007); and substantial increases in NRG population beginning at about 1250 (Cordell 1995; Crown, Orcutt, and Kohler 1996). Ortman (this vol.) reviews evidence indicating links between CMV emigrants and NRG Tewa groups.

This evidence does not exclude the probability that some Mesa Verde migrants joined with non-Tewa communities in the Rio Grande area, several of which have oral traditions of Mesa Verde connections. Boyer and colleagues (this vol.) offer alternatives to Ortman's proposed CMV-Tewa linkage. Glowacki (2006) also suggests that there were migrations of Mesa Verdean people from southeastern Utah to Hopi, where there are traditions linking some ancestral groups to the Mesa Verde region.[3] Lekson and others (2002) propose that migrants from somewhere in the greater Mesa Verde region established or joined several villages in southwestern New Mexico, where pottery made in the general McElmo Black-on-white design tradition is relatively common. However, the suite of distinctive CMV traits discussed here is not present at sites in any of these areas.

Central Mesa Verde and Northern Rio Grande Archaeological Complexes

As noted, the archaeological complex common in the CMV area up to the time of depopulation included a number of traits or elements that do not subsequently occur (or that occur only rarely) in the NRG. The elements "lost in transit" include the following: canyon-rim villages, commonly with a bilateral layout; "Prudden unit" household complexes; towers; D-shaped and circular bi-walls; south-facing household kivas with a southern recess, a bench, pilasters, and cribbed roof;

pecked-block "McElmo-style" masonry; classic Mesa Verde Black-on-white pottery design; kiva jars; Mesa Verde–style mugs; the Mesa Verde Corrugated jar form; and artiodactyl humerus scrapers. There also are traits that are present both in the CMV and the NRG, as well as traits that are not present in the CMV complex but that appear for the first time in the NRG during and shortly after the presumed migrations of the AD 1200s. This evidence is reviewed below.

Settlement Patterns

During the late AD 1000s and 1100s, most CMV inhabitants lived in communities of dispersed residences located close to arable upland soils. Community centers were marked by a great kiva and/or a somewhat greater density of houses. In the period AD 1080–1130, Chacoan-style great houses were often built in locations central to dispersed communities (Varien 1999a, 2002). In the mid–AD 1200s, settlements increasingly shifted to canyon heads or rims, almost always near a good spring. Where natural shelters were available, cliff dwellings were often built. Aggregation increased substantially, and by the late 1200s, the majority of the CMV population lived in canyon-oriented villages of fifty to seven hundred rooms (Lipe 2002; Lipe and Ortman 2000; Varien et al. 2007).

In the NRG, settlements were typically small and dispersed during the early 1200s, though a few larger aggregates occurred (Boyer and Lakatos 2008; Boyer et al., this vol.; Crown, Orcutt, and Kohler 1996). Aggregation increased rapidly between AD 1250 and 1300, and by the early 1300s, very large pueblos (of several hundred to several thousand rooms) appeared in some portions of the NRG (Creamer 1993; Crown, Orcutt, and Kohler 1996; Snead 2008b). On the Pajarito Plateau, however, average habitation site size increased only from about sixteen rooms in AD 1250–1290 to seventy-one rooms in the late 1300s (Kohler, Herr, and Root 2004:294). Although some NRG settlements are in or near canyons and/or in defensible locations, the strong preference for canyon settings seen in the CMV is lacking.

Habitation Units

For centuries, CMV habitations displayed the "Prudden Unit" pattern,[4] in which the typical household-level habitation unit has a small block of conjoined surface living and storage rooms "fronted" by a small subterranean kiva that functioned primarily as a domestic living and work space but with features indicative of ritual use as well (Lekson 1988; Lipe 1989; Lipe and Ortman 2000; Lipe and Varien 1999a:283–284). Also associated is a midden area. These units often occur as single-household homesteads, but with settlement aggregation, they join together to form multihousehold roomblocks or clusters. In relatively level upland settings, the kiva and midden are south or southeast of the surface rooms. In the large, canyon-oriented villages, this spatial structure may be modified to accommodate the topography, with the habitation unit "facing" downslope to the drainage (although a north–south orientation is preserved in the kiva itself). In the habitation units incorporated into these late aggregates, the ratio of rooms to kivas remains low (e.g., three to ten rooms per kiva).

In the NRG, habitation sites of the early 1200s typically housed one to a few households and occurred in dispersed community clusters (Boyer and Lakatos 2008; Boyer et al., this vol.), although there were a few larger aggregates (Crown, Orcutt, and Kohler 1996). On the Pajarito Plateau (Kohler and Root 2004a; Root 1992; Schmidt 2006; Vierra et al. 2002; Worman 1967), habitation sites are relatively small, with ten to twenty surface rooms and often one or two kivas or kiva-like structures. These small habitations are similar to the Prudden units of the CMV, but they typically "face" east rather than south and are not as predictable in layout (especially in terms of the presence and relative positioning of a kiva). Kiva architecture resembles that of earlier pit structures (Lakatos 2007) and is generally more variable and less formal and elaborated than is the case for CMV kivas.

By the late 1200s, "plaza-oriented pueblos" appeared in the NRG, becoming common in the early 1300s (e.g., Creamer 1993; Powers and Orcutt 1999:559; Snead 2008b). In these settlements, household-level habitation units are hard to recognize from surface evidence because kivas are typically few in number and are found in the plaza. In excavated sites, household habitations can be recognized from patterns of access among rooms.

Community Patterns

In the early 1200s, dispersed community patterns are broadly similar in the CMV and NRG, although public architecture and settlement clustering indicative of a community center are rare in the latter area. In the CMV, relatively large aggregates consisting of multiple linear roomblocks appear in the late 1100s through the mid-1200s (Lipe 1999a; Lipe and Ortman 2000).

By the late 1200s, CMV canyon-oriented aggregates typically display a distinctive layout (Lipe and Ortman 2000). Roomblocks consist of multiple habitation units, each with its own kiva. A natural drainage channel usually divides the village into two parts; in some of the larger cliff dwellings, walls and rows of structures that restrict access between two parts of the site serve this purpose (Nordby 2001; Rohn 1965). The bilateral division is seldom symmetric; there are typically more habitation units and/or "public architecture" structures on one of the sides. Also typical is an informal plaza, formed by leaving a space free of construction. A D-shaped or circular bi-wall structure is almost always present, and occasionally a great kiva. The bi-walls have peripheral rooms probably used for storage, as well as one or two interior open spaces in which a kiva was sometimes built. A masonry wall often partially or completely encloses the village. Towers are built into habitation units and/or stand just below the canyon rim. In some villages, there are room-dominated blocks possibly used for suprahousehold-level storage (Lipe 2002; Lipe and Ortman 2000).

The CMV's late canyon-oriented villages are "front-oriented" (Reed 1956) in that they face a particular direction. On the other hand, the individual habitation units usually face downslope toward a drainage and hence are oriented inward toward the center of the site; in this sense, the village can be perceived from within as like a bowl tipped up on one side (Ortman and Bradley 2002).

The plaza-oriented pattern that appears in the NRG in the very late 1200s is significantly different. An early example is Burnt Mesa Pueblo on the Pajarito Plateau (Kohler and Root 2004b; Kohler and Root, eds., 1992); its main construction episode probably began in the 1270s or 1280s (Kohler and Root 2004b:211), although Powers and Orcutt (1999:559–561) argue that it may have begun somewhat later. Two-storied in part, it had an estimated sixty-five rooms arranged in a rectangle that completely encloses a central plaza, where the site's single kiva is located.

Pot Creek Pueblo, in the Taos area, grew into a large, multi-storied aggregate in the 1270s, with some expansion in the very early 1300s

(Crown 1991). Its several roomblocks are oriented toward plazas but do not fully enclose them. There are several kivas in the plazas, including one of great-kiva size (Crown 1991). The layout is less formal than that seen at many of the other NRG plaza pueblos, but it clearly was not modeled after the CMV villages of the 1270s.

By the early 1300s, numerous NRG villages exceeded one thousand rooms—for example, Arroyo Hondo covered 6 ac and included twenty-four one- and two-story roomblocks arranged to enclose or partially enclose thirteen rectangular plazas (Creamer 1993:1). More than one thousand rooms were built between about AD 1315 and 1330, during the site's first occupation phase (Creamer 1993:2–4). The room-to-kiva ratio varies among NRG plaza-oriented villages, but there are consistently far more rooms per kiva among them than in the earlier small NRG habitations or in the large late-CMV villages (Lipe 1989). In other words, the "social scale" of kiva use was much greater in the NRG plaza villages (Lipe 1989). The plaza sites are not "front oriented," and they lack the towers, bi-walls, and site-enclosing walls characteristic of the CMV aggregates.

Anyon and LeBlanc (1980) propose that a plaza-oriented village layout first appears in the Mimbres area between AD 1000 and 1150. Adams (1991:102–103) argues that villages having plazas enclosed by roomblocks first appeared in the southern Mogollon area in the early 1200s. A few plaza-oriented pueblos dating to the early to mid-1200s are also found in the upper Little Colorado River drainage, including at Broken K Pueblo (Hill 1970) near Snowflake, Arizona, and perhaps several sites near Zuni (Adams 1991:102–103). After about AD 1275, the plaza-oriented pattern spread through the Western and Eastern Pueblo areas, including the Rio Grande (Adams 1991:84–85, 102–103). Thus, this type of village plan was new to all the NRG inhabitants at the end of the 1200s, whether they were new immigrants or descendants of long-time residents.

Structure Types and Architectural Details

The CMV and NRG share a number of generic characteristics of Pueblo-style architecture. The task here is to examine detailed similarities and differences that might indicate the presence or absence of cultural connections, or perhaps alternatively, the effects of rapid cultural change.

The D-shaped and circular bi-walls—buildings that must have played a central role in the ceremonial and political organization of the late CMV villages (Lipe 2002)—do not appear in the NRG. Great kivas occur in both the CMV and NRG in the late 1200s, although those in the latter area tend to be smaller and considerably less formal and elaborate. Towers, though common in the CMV, appear rarely if at all in the NRG before, during, or after the late 1200s. The CMV towers probably had multiple functions, including surveillance (Johnson 2003), advertising a village's defensive potential (Tainter and Tainter 1991), and actual defense in time of attack. They probably also had ritual and/or ideological functions.[5] The CMV site-enclosing walls were probably defensive (Kenzle 1997) and may also have regulated access to the village. These features are rare or nonexistent in the NRG. It is not clear whether the nonhousehold storeroom complexes observed in some CMV sites (Lipe and Ortman 2000) have a parallel in NRG villages.

Some of these CMV structure types can be traced back to the early 1200s (bi-walls) or 1100s (towers) (Lipe and Ortman 2000; Lipe and Varien 1999b), while great kivas were present in the area by the Basketmaker III period (McLellan 1969). Site-enclosing walls, storeroom complexes, and the building of towers on canyon rims and detached boulders appear confined to the late canyon-oriented villages. The earlier towers are generally part of a household habitation unit, where they are frequently linked by a tunnel to a kiva.

A similarity between the NRG and the CMV in the AD 1200s is that both areas have round kivas, in contrast with most other parts of the Pueblo Southwest at this time. On the other hand, NRG and CMV kivas differ in detail (Wendorf and Reed 1955), although there is a small amount of overlap when an attribute-by-attribute comparison is done (Smith 1998). Differences in kiva architecture between the two areas appear rooted in regional traditions established well before the 1200s (Lakatos 2003, 2007; Lipe 1989; Wendorf and Reed 1955).

Central Mesa Verde kivas of the late 1200s are typically circular in plan and masonry lined, with a southern recess, a bench, and six pilasters on the bench to support the lower timbers of a cribbed roof. There is typically a circular-plan hearth, a deflector, and a ventilator tunnel that passes under the southern recess. A sipapu frequently occurs in the floor north of the hearth. The sipapu, hearth, deflector, and ventilator tunnel comprise a north–south or northwest–southeast axis for the structure. In open settings not constrained by topography or the crowding together of buildings, the kiva is typically located south or southeast of the surface roomblock. Even when it is not, as in some of the late canyon-oriented aggregates, the kiva's north–south orientation is usually maintained (e.g., as at Cannonball Ruins [Lipe 1999b; Morley 1908]).

The NRG kivas of the 1200s are also typically circular in plan, with some exceptions (Boyer and Lakatos 2008). They lack a bench, pilasters, and a recess; their flat roofs were supported by four interior posts. A sipapu is frequently present. There is a distinctive hearth-ash pit-deflector complex that appears in Rio Grande pit structures well before AD 1200 (Lakatos 2003, 2007) but is lacking in the CMV. Kivas of the NRG have a ventilator tunnel and are usually, though not always, oriented to the east (Root 1992; Smith 1998).

In the late 1200s, the CMV "household" kivas continued to be mainly domestic, with evidence for ritual use as well (Lekson 1988; Lipe 1989; Lipe and Ortman 2000), while the NRG plaza kivas appear to be primarily for ritual activities. The CMV pattern thus placed the highly symbolic and ritually important kiva at the center of household-level activities, while by the late 1200s, NRG plaza kivas appear to have been used by social groups with membership drawn from across the village (Lipe 1989).

Another architectural contrast between the CMV and NRG is the widespread use in the former area of pecked-block "McElmo style" masonry (Lipe and Varien 1999b:318–319) and the absence of this technique in the latter area. McElmo-style masonry was generally used in CMV kivas on walls below the bench and on the inward-facing surfaces of pilasters. It was also common on the exterior surfaces of towers and on some surface-room exterior walls. This masonry treatment thus appears focused on public and/or ritually important wall surfaces. In the NRG, much construction relied on adobe or soft stone, but even where sufficiently hard sandstone was used, McElmo-style masonry was absent.

Ortman (2008b) has recently pointed out similarities between directional shrines associated with the Castle Rock community in the CMV and similar shrines surrounding Tewa villages. Ortiz (n.d.) also suggests that the Mesa Verde "keyhole-shaped" kiva form (resulting from the southern recess) may have survived in the layout of certain Tewa shrines. These are generally located at some distance south or southeast of the village and have keyhole-shaped openings oriented toward the village.

The lack of NRG functional equivalents for some of the common CMV structure types suggests that during and after the presumed migrations, the NRG aggregated communities were organized rather differently than were the CMV villages on the eve of regional depopulation. In particular, the lack of "public architecture" and of clearly demarcated household habitation units in the NRG plaza pueblos makes a striking contrast with the late CMV villages.

Artifact Types

As noted, several artifact types or styles common in the CMV are absent or very nearly so in the NRG. These include the classic Mesa Verde Black-on-white design style, kiva jars, mugs, the vessel form characteristic of the Mesa Verde Corrugated pottery type, and artiodactyl humerus scrapers.

The general similarity between CMV and NRG Black-on-white pottery of the AD 1200s has long been recognized (Cordell 1995; Cordell et al. 2007). A shift from mineral to organic paint took place about AD 1100 in the CMV, and nearly one hundred years later in the NRG. In the 1200s, NRG Black-on-white pottery had several similarities to the CMV type McElmo Black-on-white. In the CMV, the frequency of McElmo declined during the 1200s, while the related but more elaborate Mesa Verde Black-on-white style increased. This style was at its highest frequency at the time of the final CMV depopulation. Yet the Mesa Verde Black-on-white style very rarely appears on NRG ceramics. Santa Fe Black-on-white, the predominant NRG pottery type throughout the 1200s, shows only a general relationship with the Pueblo III Mesa Verde design tradition (Wilson 2008). Galisteo Black-on-white, which appears in the NRG at about 1300, resembles McElmo Black-on-white in design style, although its crackled slip, color, and sherd temper are similar to those attributes of Mesa Verde Black-on-white.

The kiva jar is a globular ceramic vessel with a flanged orifice and close-fitting lid, commonly decorated in Mesa Verde Black-on-white style. The form was named by Kidder, who remarked that "the name kiva-jar is applied to these vessels because the great majority of them have been found in ceremonial rooms"[6] and that the kiva-jar form "seems to occur only in Mesa Verde sites or in sites obviously related to the Mesa Verde culture" (Kidder [1924] 1962:202).

Mesa Verde–style mugs (with the maximum diameter typically greatest at the base) are another typical CMV artifact of the 1200s (Oppelt 1989; Putsavage 2008). They are present in most or all CMV habitation units, yet are rare to nonexistent in sites of the NRG. Bradley (1996) suggests that CMV mugs may reference earlier Chacoan pitchers, as part of a revitalization movement incorporating memories of Chaco. He proposes that Mesa Verde mugs were used primarily in ritual contexts (Bradley 1996:248). In a recent study, Putsavage (2008) used use-wear evidence, depositional context, spatial distributions, and vessel form to conclude that most mugs showed evidence of regular use as drinking vessels, probably in domestic contexts, but that their high frequency in burials might indicate ritual importance as well.

A general similarity between the CMV and NRG in the 1200s is in the use of corrugated gray "utility" vessels. However, Mesa Verde Corrugated has a distinctive "egg-shaped" vessel form, and a strongly everted rim (Breternitz, Rohn, and Morris 1974; Wilson and Blinman 1995). The NRG corrugated vessels of the 1200s have more or less globular bodies and lack the distinctive shape and rim form of Mesa Verde Corrugated. In addition, after about AD 1250, "smeared corrugated" becomes common in NRG ceramic assemblages, a treatment absent or very rare in the CMV.

One final distinctive CMV artifact type that was "lost in transit" is the artiodactl humerus scraper (see Rohn 1971:220 for good photographs). The humerus condyle serves as the grip, and the shaft is cut diagonally to produce a beveled edge presumably used for scraping; most examples show evidence of wear and/or resharpening by grinding. This artifact type occurs widely across both the southern and the northern San Juan regions, but it is virtually absent in the NRG. Kidder illustrates a fragmentary example from Pecos and remarks, "There should here be noted the complete absence from Pecos, save for a single somewhat doubtful specimen, of the end-scraper made from the humerus of the deer. That bone can be, and by certain peoples of the San Juan commonly was, fashioned into a very serviceable tool" (Kidder 1932:235).

Several other artifact types present in the NRG during the AD 1200s are generally similar to those in the CMV, including a slab or flat metate, two-handed manos, full-grooved stone axes, and small side-notched arrow points (McNutt 1969:108). These artifacts occurred widely in the Pueblo Southwest at this time, so learning whether their presence in the NRG could be attributed to an introduction from the CMV would require more detailed chronological and morphological comparisons than can be attempted here.

McNutt (1969:108) notes that the keeping of turkeys appears in the NRG in "the Santa Fe period," presumably the AD 1200s. This is contemporaneous with a substantial intensification of turkey husbandry in the CMV in the mid-1200s (Muir and Driver 2002). On the Pajarito Plateau, the frequencies of turkey remains are low until the late 1200s, when they rise dramatically (Kohler, Powers, and Orcutt 2004:298). This might result from CMV migrations or from an independent response to population growth and depletion of local wild fauna.

Overall, the cultural differences between the CMV and NRG indicate that any migrants from the CMV in the late 1200s must have adopted social and cultural practices already well established in the area and/or those that were newly present (e.g., living in large plaza-oriented villages). This was a time of substantial demographic and sociocultural change for all the residents of the NRG, whether they were indigenous or migrants.

Migration and Culture-Change Scenarios

If we are not to disregard the evidence indicating a substantial migration from the CMV to the NRG in the late 1200s (e.g., Ortman, this vol.), how do we explain the relative archaeological invisibility of the presumed migrants? What circumstances could have resulted in the rapid cultural change that is implied? Several possibilities come to mind: (1) pre-existing relationships shaped the cultural changes that accompanied the final migrations in the late 1200s, with populations located between the CMV and NRG perhaps having a role in the outcome; and (2) modes of community organization and ideology practiced or being developed in the NRG served as "pull" factors for CMV migrants, with sociocultural change being one of the drivers of migration.

CMV-NRG Relationships in the 1200s

Migration is typically a process that takes place over a period of time, rather than as a discrete event (e.g., Duff 1998). Migrants are often motivated both by "push" factors in their home environment and "pull" factors in the migration target area (Anthony 1990; Cameron 1995). Duff and Wilshusen generalize about the process as follows:

> our conception of the Northern San Juan "abandonment" as a sudden and catastrophic event is probably wrong. Cross-cultural data indicate that population movements rarely happen suddenly. It is much more likely that the Northern San Juan migrations were part of a larger social process that took decades, if not centuries. Choosing to emigrate is usually a thoroughly considered decision. People generally have detailed knowledge about the places to which they choose to relocate, and they usually move to places where they have existing relationships. (Duff and Wilshusen 2000:169)

In general, throughout the 1200s, the CMV and NRG had a number of cultural similarities, implying some level of continuing contact and cultural interchange. For example, Cordell (1995; Cordell et al. 2007) argues that CMV and NRG pottery design traditions resemble one another more than either resembles any other tradition from the northern Southwest. Although evidence of interregional trade is sparse in the CMV area in the middle and late 1200s (Lipe 2002, 2006), obsidian that has been recovered and identified is predominantly from the Jemez Plateau (Arakawa 2006). Cordell and colleagues (2007) and Roney (1995, 1996) argue that social networks linking the CMV and NRG populations had been established by the early to mid-1200s.

Some have suggested that the rapid population increase in portions of the NRG (such as the Pajarito Plateau) in the early 1200s might represent a "first wave" of immigration from the Mesa Verde area (Roney 1995:176, citing Collins 1975). Such immigrants could have provided hosting and acculturation models for relatives who migrated later (Duff and Wilshusen 2000). The shift from mineral to organic paint and the appearance of the Santa Fe Black-on-white style suggest that ties with the CMV area became stronger at this time. Wilson (2008), however, sees Santa Fe Black-on-white as largely a local development, with perhaps some influence from groups making McElmo Black-on-white in the Puerco drainage.

The dispersed settlement patterns and relatively low room-to-kiva ratios present on the Pajarito Plateau during its population increase in the early 1200s resemble CMV patterns. My impression, however, is that a detailed comparison of the full cultural inventories of the NRG and CMV in the early 1200s would reveal nearly as many differences as are present in the late 1200s. Furthermore, evidence cited by Ortman (this vol.) indicates that a strong Mesa Verde biological signal does not appear in the NRG until after 1250. In addition, the large population that remained in the CMV as late as the 1270s would have constituted a large migrant group, regardless of whether or not there had been previous migrations.

Even without assuming substantial migration into the NRG prior to 1250, the general cultural similarities that had been established by that time imply some kind of regular communication and the possibility that kinship networks linked residents of the two areas. During the Pueblo III period, the communities located along the eastern edge of the San Juan (geologic) basin were positioned to link the Totah portion of the Mesa Verde area with the northern and central Rio Grande (Cordell 1995; Duff and Wilshusen 2000; Roney 1995, 1996). In the 1200s, these communities probably received immigrants from the southern (Chacoan) part of the San Juan region (Bice and Sundt 1972; Moore and Blinman 2008). There is also some indication of immigrants from the northern San Juan (Mesa Verde) area, possibly in the early 1200s, and more clearly in the late 1200s (Davis and Winkler 1959; Duff and Wilshusen 2000; Pippin 1987; Roney 1995, 1996). These eastern San Juan Basin communities may well have provided communication and perhaps kinship links between CMV and NRG populations.

If CMV migrants settled in these areas just west of the NRG, they or their descendants could have moved into the NRG upon abandoning their settlements in the very late 1200s or early 1300s. Prior to such a move, there would have been opportunities for acculturation of Mesa Verde migrants to both local and NRG patterns. This would certainly be true for those entering the area in the early 1200s, and even for migrants resulting from the final depopulation of the CMV and Totah areas.

At Guadalupe Ruin in the middle Puerco River valley, located west-northwest of Albuquerque, new construction was undertaken starting in the AD 1260s (Pippin 1987). Although the site had earlier occupations and most assemblages are somewhat chronologically mixed, the late-1200s occupation clearly displayed several elements of the CMV archaeological complex—bowls and mugs decorated in the Mesa Verde Black-on-white style, south-oriented kivas with a bench and pilasters, artiodactyl humerus scrapers, and heavy reliance on turkeys. The pottery assemblage also includes Santa Fe Black-on-white and other indicators of connections to the NRG. The latest tree-ring date at Guadalupe is 1279+vv (Pippin 1987:100), indicating that the actual cutting date is some unknown number of years later. Pippin (1987:114) provides evidence that the site was abandoned by AD 1300. Guadalupe may well have housed a group from the Totah or CMV area that "paused" for a generation just west of the NRG before moving into the latter area or some other part of the Rio Grande region.

These data indicate that a Mesa Verde "site unit intrusion" (Rouse 1958) may have occurred on the western periphery of the NRG in the late 1200s. The fact that no similar site-unit intrusions appear in the NRG proper suggests either that CMV groups did not migrate directly into the NRG in the late 1200s or that they became rapidly acculturated to NRG society.

Even if the pattern evident at Guadalupe was duplicated throughout the middle Puerco and other localities lying just west of the NRG, the number of sites dating to the late 1200s in those areas does not seem large enough to account for more than a small fraction of the CMV and Totah populations at the time the final emigration flow took place, between about 1260 and 1280. Roney's (1995, 1996) review of the survey data indicates that most of the AD 1200s communities in this area are known. Clearly, more research on the chronology, population sizes, and cultural connections of these communities would be worthwhile.

Push and Pull Factors and Rapid Sociocultural Change

The late AD 1200s were a time of significant environmental, demographic, social, and cultural change throughout the Pueblo world (Adler, ed., 1996; Hill et al. 2004). Wright (2008, this vol.) has provided evidence of environmental "push" factors that are likely to have contributed to depopulation of the CMV in the late 1200s (also see Ahlstrom, Van West, and Dean 1995; Dean and Van West 2002). With regard to possible environmental "pull" factors, Cordell and others (2007) have recently summarized evidence that precipitation patterns in the NRG and CMV were frequently different, so that droughts usually did not occur concurrently in both areas (though the complementarity appears weak in the late 1200s). Over the long run, however, this complementarity might have promoted some types of interdependence between the populations of the two areas. Furthermore, Dean (1996a) presents evidence that starting in the middle 1200s, the CMV probably experienced unpredictable disruptions in the timing and strength of winter and summer storms; the NRG, on the other hand, continued to have a predictable summer-dominant rainfall pattern (Cordell et al. 2007).

Were there sociocultural "pull" factors as well? Certainly, CMV populations must have been aware of the rapidly growing Pueblo communities in the NRG (and elsewhere) in the AD 1200s. Furthermore, it would have been apparent that these evidently successful communities had developed or were developing modes of community social organization different from those practiced in the CMV.

The CMV depopulation marked the end of the "San Juan pattern" (Cameron and Duff 2008; Lipe 2006) that had emphasized household and lineage autonomy (as well as north–south directional symbolism and particular ways of using architecture to represent emergence beliefs and community social organization). For several hundred years, CMV households had moved flexibly within and between larger settlements and among agricultural locations (Varien 1999a). Each nuclear or extended family household had its own kiva and hence its own sacred symbols representing the cosmological beliefs underlying the "ultimate sacred propositions" (Rappaport 1971) that held society together (Lipe 1989).

Over time in the CMV, the "San Juan pattern" led repeatedly to formation of multihousehold roomblocks of varying sizes, implying that families tended to grow in place and form corporate residential groups. In an area of high spatial variance in agricultural productivity and family fertility, some such groups would have become larger and more prosperous than others. The potential was there for a few localized kin groups to accumulate considerable social power. In the southern San Juan region, a similar process may have led to the formation of social and political elites at Chaco Canyon (Sebastian 1992).

This general pattern of household and lineage autonomy continued through the 1200s, when CMV communities became increasingly aggregated and appear to have developed peer-polity competition (Lipe 2002) accompanied by sporadic warfare (Kuckelman, this vol.). Some communities probably became socially and politically dominant over at least a few others. There may also have been competition for religious and political power within larger communities in the late 1200s (Lipe 2002), although evidently this did not result in a single primate center for the region or even in very great intra- or intercommunity power differentials (but see Lekson 1999 for an alternative view).

Although the San Juan pattern of relative household and lineage autonomy continued as long as the CMV was occupied, it seems clear that after about AD 1240, the increasingly aggregated CMV villages were also experimenting with new or at least newly visible forms of sociopolitical or socioreligious leadership and organization. This is suggested by substantially increased investment in nondomestic architecture (e.g., bi-wall structures, tower complexes, village or precinct enclosing walls, suprahousehold storage complexes). The bilateral division of villages into two parts also appears (although something like this was present earlier at some of the major Chacoan great houses).

These developments are most pronounced in the largest sites in the most densely settled parts of the northern San Juan drainage—the Totah and CMV regions. In the sparsely settled Far Western area, the old pattern of dispersed small settlements persists, with little investment in new or newly reworked forms of nonresidential architecture. In these areas, the classic Mesa Verde Black-on-white design style is also less common, and both mugs and kiva jars are rare. Even within the CMV, briefly occupied habitation sites in marginal agricultural areas tend to have architecture that is significantly less formal, standardized, and elaborated. Lipe and Varien (1999a:266–270) provide examples from the 1100s of this effect. Much earlier, in the late AD 800s, CMV groups near Dolores had radically simplified their architectural and community patterns just prior to local depopulation (Lipe et al. 1988:1235–1246).

Returning to the CMV archaeological complex of the late 1200s: a number of the complex's most distinctive elements may have symbolized and helped maintain the way in which social relationships and ritual activities were organized (Hegmon 1989) in the large villages of that time. Architectural and artifactual symbolism would have helped represent these patterns as being rooted in history (Cameron and Duff 2008; Lipe 2006). However, the assumptions upon which the social order of the late CMV communities rested may have been increasingly threatened by the stresses of warfare, drought, and other environmental changes.

If CMV emigrants adopted different patterns of community organization and ideology upon settling in the NRG, it would have been dissonant to maintain material and symbolic forms so strongly associated with the social order of the CMV villages. As noted, NRG settlements of the early 1200s, at least on the Pajarito Plateau, are rather similar to those of the CMV. Subsequent aggregation in the two areas, however, resulted in very different community patterns. The plaza-oriented village layout that appears in the NRG in the late 1200s lacks ostentatious public architecture of the sort seen in the late CMV villages. Furthermore, NRG households no longer have their own kiva, and their boundaries are submerged within the larger residential roomblocks surrounding the plaza. Village inhabitants looked inward to the plaza or plazas; the kiva or kivas were there, and not spatially associated with any particular habitation unit or roomblock. The implication is that a kiva did not "belong" to a specific residential group (Lipe 1989). More likely, kivas drew membership from multiple households and kin groups, as in the historical and present-day Pueblos. Thus, although there were formal continuities through time in NRG pit structure and kiva architecture (Lakatos 2007), there would have been dramatic changes in how kivas were used as they shifted from a household- or hamlet- to a village-level social scale. This kind of shift did not take place in the large CMV villages of the middle and late 1200s.

As compared with the last villages of the CMV, the architecture and layout of the NRG villages of the late 1200s and early 1300s imply a greater social investment in the organization and operation of the community, as well as lesser autonomy for households or multihousehold residential groups. There must have been differences in social power among individuals and kin groups within these pueblos, but the architecture and living arrangements seem designed to keep these differences from being overtly visible. Overall, the architecture and spatial patterning of the NRG plaza-oriented villages seem compatible with general principles and patterns of historical and present-day Pueblo social organization. These patterns include strong religious sodalities that cross-cut kin and residential groups, as well as a substantial investment in leveling mechanisms that reduce the overt display of social differences and power. These social and ideological changes in the NRG area (Ruscavage-Barz and Bagwell 2006) were part of those taking place throughout the Pueblo world at the end of the thirteenth century, ushering in what Brew (1943:242) long ago called "the Golden Age of the Pueblos."

Forms of community organization being practiced and developed in the NRG (and elsewhere in the Pueblo Southwest) may have been attractive to the increasingly stressed communities of the CMV (Cameron and Duff 2008; Lipe 1995). Given the centrality of religion to Pueblo sociopolitical organization, this "pull" may have been viewed as an opportunity to revitalize religious ideology and practice (Wallace 1956; also see Bradley 1996). Many of the CMV cultural traits noted above may have been associated with the old patterns of community organization, social relationships, and ideology that were being given up. Although it is difficult to understand how artiodactyl humerus scrapers or a particular form of corrugated vessel would have been tied to such changes, perhaps they were in some way contextually or conceptually related to ritual or social practices.

A Hypothetical Scenario for Late 1200s Migration and Culture Change

Several speculations follow, some of which may serve as hypotheses to orient future research:

- Before AD 1260, the CMV and NRG became linked by networks of information exchange and possibly kinship. Settlements in the Totah area, eastern San Juan Basin, and Rio Puerco drainage served as intermediaries for the flow of information and perhaps of people.
- In the early and middle 1200s, some Mesa Verde migrants formed or joined communities just west of the NRG.
- In the late 1200s, these relationships provided prospective migrants with information about social and environmental conditions in the NRG.

- Existing relationships also enabled CMV migrants to find role models and social connections (fictive kin or clan membership) needed when they settled in the NRG.
- Not only NRG agricultural opportunities, but aspects of existing and newly emerging religious practice and community organization were attractive to migrants who had lost confidence in their own social, religious, and subsistence patterns.
- Many cultural patterns given up by late-1200s CMV emigrants were linked to social and religious practices they were rejecting in favor of existing or new ones in the NRG; CMV migrants may have played a role in developing some of these new patterns.
- Late-1200s emigration from the CMV was accompanied by increased mortality and low fertility that reduced the number of migrants.
- The completeness of the CMV depopulation was due not only to the emigration of numerous people, but to the fairly rapid demise of those left behind (see Kuckelman 2007b, this vol.).
- Central Mesa Verde migrants entered the NRG in small groups and did not present themselves as socially or militarily dominant.
- Existing NRG communities had social institutions capable of integrating newcomers (much as in historical and present-day Pueblos).
- The rapid growth of population and large villages in the NRG after about 1250 may well have involved active recruitment of both local and distant groups and individuals by emerging leaders competing for followers (Lightfoot 1984).
- Increased warfare in the greater Rio Grande area in the late 1200s may also have led to recruitment of migrants by some NRG communities to strengthen their defensive and offensive capacities.[7]

Concluding Comments

This discussion has dealt with the archaeologically visible elements of CMV and NRG cultures, primarily during the AD 1200s. The lack of a clear archaeological signal identifying CMV migrants does not exclude the possibility that they retained other cultural traits distinguishing them from long-term NRG residents. For example, the Tewa language continues to be used (along with Hopi [and English]) in the community of Hano, more than four hundred years after its establishment by migrants from the Rio Grande area (Dozier 1954). However, it seems unlikely that the Rio Grande ancestry of this group would be archaeologically detectable today. Whether the earliest Tewa occupation at Hopi would have been archaeologically visible is a question that to my knowledge has not been researched.

Clark (2001) argues that even when migrants do not adopt a social strategy of visibly displaying ethnicity, their origins may be recorded in low-visibility technological attributes of material culture (also see Carr [1995] and much earlier, Colton [1939:20–21; Colton and Hargrave 1937]). Recently, Nauman (2007) has shown that at the Cox Ranch site cluster in New Mexico, technological variables such as coil size and indentation spacing distinguish groups representing two different "learning communities" that can be associated with different geographic origins. Studies of this sort might reveal whether elements of CMV technological styles were retained at thirteenth-century NRG sites.

Lyons and colleagues (2008) recently concluded that Kayenta migrants to the Tonto basin areas of Arizona may have suppressed visible displays of their distinctive ethnic identity in the context of large existing populations and competition for arable land. A similar situation may have obtained in portions of the NRG, where large numbers of migrants were augmenting rapidly growing indigenous populations. It is also significant that CMV types of outlying shrines appear to have been introduced to the NRG (Ortiz n.d.; Ortman 2008b), while the more visible types of artifacts and structures that would identify CMV migrants were not.

If, in fact, the thirteenth-century migrations from the CMV to the NRG were accompanied by rapid cultural change, this implies a strong predominance of horizontal as opposed to vertical patterns of cultural transmission, as well as the operation of frequency-dependent and/or indirect biases (Boyd and Richerson 1985). These processes would have led CMV migrants to copy existing or attractive new behaviors encountered in the NRG. Earlier, reference was made to the respective visibility and invisibility of Kayenta and Mesa Verde migrants. If Kayenta social organization emphasized strong unilineal principles, as in the historical Western Pueblos (Dozier 1970), this would seem to favor emphasis on vertical transmission. On the other hand, if the historical Rio Grande (and especially Tewa) emphasis on bilateral kinship and flexible membership in various associations (Dozier 1970; Fox 1967) was part of both the CMV and the NRG patterns, this might have permitted rapid horizontal transmission.

Lowell (2007) proposes that warfare-related gender imbalances may have resulted in the selective reproduction of material culture among migrants to the Grasshopper area in Arizona. It is likely that CMV migrants were affected by warfare, but it is difficult to attribute the resultant large-scale culture changes to gender imbalances. The CMV traits that were lost seem likely to include some probably associated with male roles as well as some associated with female roles. Further examination of gender effects seems warranted, but it is beyond the scope of this chapter.

In conclusion, what are the implications of the thirteenth-century Mesa Verde migrations for a more general understanding of how migrants "stand out or blend in" (Stone and Lipe, in press) when they arrive in new homes? Below are some general expectations (Lipe 2007a, 2007b) that can perhaps be examined in future studies. The outcomes (i.e., blending in or standing out) likely depend on the effects of several conditions acting additively or synergistically.

Proposition 1: Migrants should "stand out" (i.e., preserve distinctive visible cultural patterns) to the extent that they

- move to unoccupied areas or areas with very low competition for land and other resources;
- are farmers displacing foragers;
- move as whole communities or large social segments/enclaves;
- don't share a basic way of life and beliefs with host populations;
- numerically overwhelm host populations;
- are significantly unequal in social status or power vis-à-vis host populations (e.g., conquerors versus conquered);
- use visible ethnicity as a social strategy.

Proposition 2: Migrants should "blend in" with a host culture to the extent that they

- share a basic way of life and beliefs;
- are attracted to a host's ideology;
- follow earlier migrants as part of long-term migration flows;
- are viewed by hosts as social equals;

- don't use visible ethnicity as a social strategy;
- fit into a host culture's practices for integrating newcomers (e.g., shared clan or religious society affiliations); and
- must compete for land and other resources with existing populations.

Notes

1. As discussed here, the central Mesa Verde region extends from approximately the Mesa Verde Proper in southwestern Colorado to Cottonwood Creek in southeastern Utah (see Varien and Wilshusen 2002: fig. 1.1).

2. Exploring the total time-space distribution of the traits comprising the CMV complex is beyond the scope of this chapter (but see Putsavage 2008 regarding mugs).

3. Pueblo IV–period Hopi yellow-ware sherds occur relatively frequently in the far western part of the Mesa Verde area in Utah (Lipe 1970:137–138). Although none represent habitations, they may record visits to shrines and/or trips to acquire resources.

4. The pattern is named for T. M. Prudden, who first recognized it (Prudden 1903).

5. In the CMV, towers appear in the early 1100s and are often connected to household-level kivas by a tunnel, a building practice that continued into the 1200s, when towers also became more common and varied in form and location. These late towers frequently occur apart from household contexts and on canyon rims or isolated boulders (Lipe and Varien 1999b:319–320). Isolated towers and some other nonhousehold structures were often built over bedrock cracks that permit entry from below (Thompson et al. 1997; William Lipe, personal observation), perhaps to represent the pervasive Pueblo cosmology of emergence from an underworld.

6. Kidder's hypothesis about the association of kiva jars with kivas has not been confirmed or disconfirmed by systematic studies based on more recent excavation data. My impression is that many types of CMV artifacts are strongly associated with kivas because of the centrality of these structures to the everyday life of households.

7. Lipe and Varien (1999a:266–270) provide examples from the 1100s of this effect. Much earlier, in the late AD 800s, CMV groups near Dolores had radically simplified their architectural and community patterns just prior to local depopulation (Lipe et al. 1988:1235–1246).

8. Schaafsma (2000) discusses the proliferation and elaboration of war imagery in the NRG but sees this as beginning about 1325. However, the large-scale aggregation that began in the late 1200s may well have been promoted by defensive concerns (LeBlanc 1999).

12

Remodeling Immigration

A Northern Rio Grande Perspective on Depopulation, Migration, and Donation-Side Models

Jeffrey L. Boyer, James L. Moore, Steven A. Lakatos, Nancy J. Akins, C. Dean Wilson, and Eric Blinman

The depopulation of large parts of the northern Southwest by Pueblo people is an iconic event in the intellectual development of southwestern archaeology. The Pecos Classification (Kidder [1924] 1962) codified a complementary relationship between the central "Anasazi" area (the northern San Juan/Mesa Verde and southern San Juan/Chaco regions) and the eastern Pueblo area (the northern Rio Grande region). In the Pecos framework, the Pueblo III period ended with depopulation of the San Juan regions, while the Pueblo IV period began as large villages formed in other areas of the northern Southwest, including the northern Rio Grande. This sequential framework still contributes to archaeological interpretations that couple temporal and cultural continuity between the San Juan regions and the post–AD 1300 northern Rio Grande. Those interpretations usually invoke migrations of people from the former to the latter and imply that historical northern Rio Grande Pueblos are descendant from San Juan populations.

Depopulation of the San Juan regions by AD 1300 is beyond dispute, and chapters in this volume provide detailed descriptions of the circumstances, with emphasis on the northern San Juan. As archaeologists working in the northern Rio Grande, however, we are not confident about assumptions and models that present those circumstances as formative events for the cultures of the northern Rio Grande. Numerous attempts have been made to reconcile the timing, visibility, and impacts of proposed movement(s) of people from the San Juan regions into the northern Rio Grande (e.g., Ahlstrom, Van West, and Dean 1995; Cordell 1995; Cordell et al. 2007; Dean, Doelle, and Orcutt 1994; Dutton 1964; Ford, Schroeder, and Peckham 1972; McNutt 1969; Mera 1935, 1939; Moore 2008; Peckham 1984; Reed 1949; Wendorf 1954; Wendorf and

Reed 1955; Wilson 2008). Most, however, are largely based on viewpoints from the donating sides rather than from the presumptive receiving side of such movements.

Like Cordell (1995), we recognize a variety of problems with reconstructions of twelfth- and thirteenth-century population movements into the northern Rio Grande. We also see several areas of research that must be addressed to understand population movement into the northern Rio Grande. For example, if population movement as a significant event or process is a matter of scale (Cordell 1995), then data relevant to identifying and describing immigration into the northern Rio Grande must be collected at regional and interregional scales. There must be comparable evidence, chronological *and* material, from the donating *and* receiving regions (Haury 1958). Further, interregional aspects of population movement cannot be addressed synchronically, since the dynamics at AD 1250–1300 in the San Juan and northern Rio Grande regions are only relevant within their respective social-cultural-economic trajectories. Consequently, migration from one region to another must be addressed through comparisons of diachronic trajectories. In other words, if a single site or assemblage is inadequate to identify significant population movement (Cordell 1995:206–207), then it follows that a specific point in time is equally inadequate because the significance of the archaeological record at that point is predicated on the specific trajectories that led to it.

In this chapter, we assert a perspective of indigenous, long-term cultural development in the northern Rio Grande. This perspective demands that northern Rio Grande people be viewed as active participants in their own culture-historical trajectories and in their interactions with peoples in other regions. Northern Rio Grande Pueblo people were neither so few in number nor so intraregionally disengaged that the dynamics of their cultural developments were determined by events and processes occurring in other regions.

The northern Rio Grande was not a nearly empty landscape available for use or colonization by people from other regions. From about the middle of the first millennium AD, the region was home to a growing, expanding indigenous population that developed its own suite of traditions comprising a cultural trajectory superficially similar to but actually quite distinct from those of the San Juan regions.

This perspective is certainly not new—witness Peckham (1984); Peckham's position in Ford, Schroeder, and Peckham (1972); Stubbs (1954); Wendorf (1954); and Wendorf and Reed (1955), for instance—but its substance and implications have been ignored in models of interregional Pueblo interaction and movement that emphasize donation-side perspectives, particularly from the northern San Juan. Nonetheless, the northern Rio Grande record is far from silent regarding interregional interactions, including San Juan immigration.

People of the Northern Rio Grande

Previous population reconstructions for the northern Rio Grande suggest inconsequential Developmental-period (ca. AD 600–1200) populations before a dramatic increase began in the 1300s (Crown, Orcutt, and Kohler 1996; Dean, Doelle, and Orcutt 1994; see also Cordell 1995). Resulting graphs of population increase are compelling visual suggestions of an in-migration that is usually linked to the twelfth-century decline of the southern San Juan Chaco system and the thirteenth-century depopulation of the northern San Juan region. Although pre–AD 1100 northern Rio Grande settlement is well documented (e.g., Boyer 1994, 1997; Frisbie 1967; Lakatos 2006; Lakatos and Post, in press; Schmader 1994), these data have not been adequately synthesized in prevailing northern Rio Grande population reconstructions. In large part, this is because published syntheses have focused on post–AD 1100 occupations of subregions that were unoccupied by Pueblo people before that time. Consequently, assessing northern Rio Grande population trends in relation to postulated immigrations has been impossible because the pre–AD 1100 population could not be considered.

As Dean, Doelle, and Orcutt (1994) point out, prehistoric population estimates ordinarily combine site and room function with chronology, resulting in figures that reflect general trends rather than precise demographic fluctuations (though see chapter 3 of this volume for a different approach). Establishing population estimates is particularly challenging when using data from surface inventories generated over many years using varied approaches (see Ortman, Varien, and Gripp 2007). In the northern Rio Grande, where chronometric data are limited and pottery assemblages do not yet support high-precision dating (Wilson

2003), population trends are largely grounded in phase-based chronologies and settlement patterns (Crown, Orcutt, and Kohler 1996; Dean, Doelle, and Orcutt 1994).

Methods

To improve our understanding of Developmental-period population trends, a database of AD 600–1200 structural sites was compiled from the New Mexico Cultural Resource Information System and from previous research (Lakatos 2006; Lakatos and Post, in press). Site records were consulted for forty-nine U.S. Geological Survey 7.5 min quadrangles within the central corridor of the northern Rio Grande. The quadrangles were grouped into three subregions: Albuquerque to Cochiti (ABQ-COH, twenty-one quadrangles), La Bajada Mesa to Velarde (BAJ-VEL, seventeen quadrangles), and the Taos Valley (TSV, nine quadrangles). The subregions, shown in figure 12.1, approximate the locations of modern Pueblo linguistic groups (Keres [ABQ-COH], Tewa [BAJ-VEL], and northern Tiwa [TSV]) and also correspond to topographic and environmental variation that likely conditioned population settlement and movement. Subregions flanking the central portion of the study area that also had Developmental-period occupations, such as the lower Rio Jemez, the upper Rio Pecos, the Picuris area, and the eastern flanks of the Sangre de Cristos, were not included in this preliminary study. Other subregions that generally lack Developmental-period sites, such as the Pajarito Plateau, the Galisteo Basin, and the Rio Chama drainage, were also not included.

When possible, sites were assigned to hundred-year periods based on reported age, associated ceramic types, or chronometric dates. Because archaeologists working in the northern Rio Grande generally use period- and phase-based chronologies, most sites in the database have date assignments in excess of one hundred years. Those sites were reassigned to hundred-year intervals based on the proportional percentage of excavated structures dating to each hundred-year interval within each of the three geographic subregions (Lakatos 2007). Sites that lack clearly described temporal components or structural elements or are aceramic were not included in this reconstruction.

The three subregions were used to monitor the numbers and location of sites for each hundred-year interval. Estimated numbers of residential

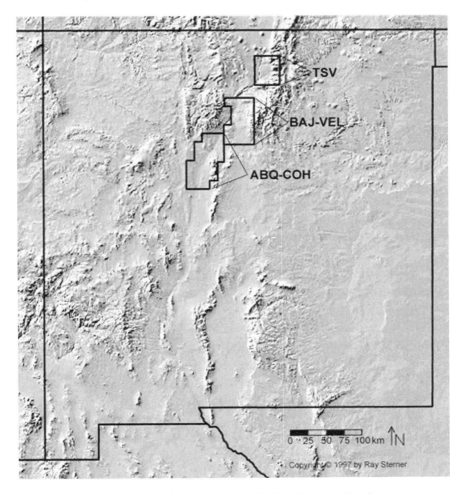

Figure 12.1. Overview of New Mexico and subregions used in the current study. Adapted from Sterner (1997). (Courtesy of Ray Sterner and North Star Science and Technology, LLC.)

structures for each interval were calculated by dividing the number of reported sites by the estimated percent of surveyed space in each sub-region, and by assuming two contemporaneous residences per site (Laka-tos 2007; Stuart and Gauthier 1981). This approach does not account for all sites occupied at a particular time within each subregion, for varia-tions in survey coverage, or for uneven reporting practices. As a prelimi-nary study, however, it does offer a baseline for estimating population during and after the Developmental period. It is a conservative estimate, for three reasons.

First, the quadrangles included in this study do not represent the entire spatial range of Developmental-period occupation. Including other sub-regions would increase the overall population estimates. Second, longevity of site occupation, as discussed below, is based on an assumption of relatively high settlement mobility. If residential sites had longer occupations, overall population estimates would be increased. Finally, this study focuses on structures arguably used to house single families, primarily pit structures. By the late twelfth century AD, settlements began to include substantial surface structures arguably used to house multiple families. Including such structures in a population reconstruction would require methods better suited to projecting numbers of families housed in multiroom structures. Because our purpose was to characterize Developmental-period demographics, we focused on single-family residential structures.

Population trends in this study are based on estimated numbers of households, defined as social units occupying the same residential structure (Wills 2001; Wilshusen 1988). Average prehistoric Pueblo household sizes ranged between five and eight people and remained stable over time and across space (Lightfoot 1994; see also Kosse 1989). Momentary household estimates were calculated following Duff and Wilshusen (2000:173) and assume a fifteen-year habitation-structure use life (fig. 12.2; Varien et al. 2007: fig. 4). Momentary populations for each subregion and hundred-year interval were calculated by multiplying the estimated number of households by six (Hill 1970; Lightfoot 1994; Varien et al. 2007). Total population for each hundred-year interval reflects the sum of subregional momentary population estimates.

Results

The early Developmental-period (ca. AD 600–900) population in the ABQ-COH subregion remained relatively low, fluctuating between about 100 and 160 households containing 590 to 980 people (table 12.1). We suspect, although we cannot demonstrate, that the AD 800–900 figure is artificially low, perhaps representing a lack of artifacts that can be securely used to date sites to that century. Between AD 900 and 1000, the ABQ-COH population increased to about 340 households,

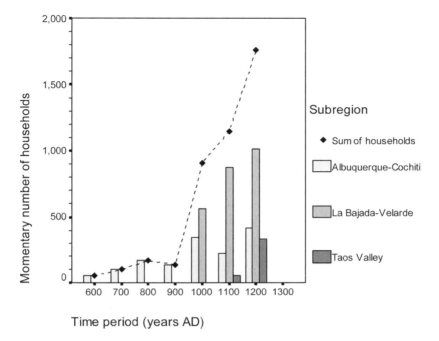

Figure 12.2. Momentary number of Developmental-period households, by subregion, AD 600–1200.

and the BAJ-VEL subregion, previously unoccupied by Pueblo people, was settled by 560 households, together totaling about 5,450 people. By AD 1100, the ABQ-COH population declined to fewer than 220 households, while the BAJ-VEL population increased to about 870 households and the TSV was settled by about 50 households. In all, an estimated 6,870 people inhabited the study area at AD 1100.

By AD 1200, the ABQ-COH population had increased to 418 households (2,508 people), but most of the approximately 10,600 people in the study area lived in the BAJ-VEL (1,014 households; 6,084 people) and the TSV (330 households; 1,980 people) subregions. These population figures, especially for the late Developmental period (ca. AD 900–1200), are substantially greater than previous estimates (fig. 12.3). The higher regional numbers and evidence of subregional population expansion result in a new and more dynamic view of regional population trends.

To estimate population at AD 1300, we used the hundred-year and two-hundred-year changes between AD 1100 and 1200 and between

Table 12.1. Population estimates for the Northern Rio Grande subregions, AD 600–1200

Time interval (years AD)	Momentary number of households	Momentary population[a]	r[b]	km² per household	Hamlets[c]		Villages[d]	
					Minimum	Maximum	Minimum	Maximum
Albuquerque-Cochiti (ABQ-COH)								
600–700	99	594	—	32.65	5	17	3	6
700–800	163	978	.0050	19.97	8	27	5	10
800–900	134	804	−.0020	24.20	7	22	4	8
900–1000	343	2058	.0094	9.48	17	57	10	21
1000–1100	219	1314	−.0045	14.80	11	37	7	13
1100–1200	418	2508	.0065	7.76	21	70	13	25
La Bajada–Velarde (BAJ-VEL)								
800–900	0	0	—	0	0	0	0	0
900–1000	534	3384	—	4.71	28	94	17	34
1000–1100	872	5232	.0044	3.05	44	145	26	52
1100–1200	1014	6084	.0015	2.62	51	169	30	61
Taos Valley (TSV)								
900–1000	0	0	—	0	0	0	0	0
1000–1100	54	324	—	26.76	3	9	2	3
1100–1200	330	1980	.0181	4.38	17	55	10	20

Total Northern Rio Grande

600–700	99	594		79.00	5	17	3	6
700–800	163	978	.0050	48.39	8	27	5	10
800–900	134	804	–.0020	58.67	7	22	4	8
900–1000	907	5442	.0191	8.68	45	151	27	54
1000–1100	1146	6876	.0023	6.87	57	191	34	69
1100–1200	1763	10578	.0043	4.46	88	294	53	106
1200–1300	2712[c]	16273[c]						
1200–1300	3506[f]	13526[f]						
1200–1300	2710[g]	16262[g]						
1200–1300	2452[h]	14714[h]						

[a] Momentary population = momentary number of households × 6.

[b] Coefficient of population growth (Odum 1971:181), calculated from mid-interval of the previous century to mid-interval of the present century.

[c] Hamlets: minimum = momentary number of households / 20 (Adler 1994); maximum = momentary number of households / 6 (Kintigh 1994).

[d] Villages: minimum = momentary population / 200; maximum = momentary population / 100 (Adler 1989).

[e] Projected, based on growth rate of previous century.

[f] Projected, based on growth rate of previous two centuries.

[g] Projected, based on growth rate (r) of previous century.

[h] Projected, based on growth rate (r) of two centuries.

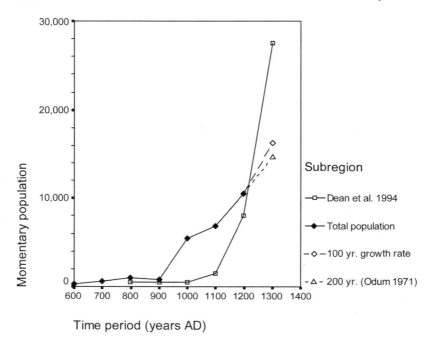

Figure 12.3. Momentary population estimates for the northern Rio Grande, AD 600–1300.

AD 1000 and 1200 (table 12.1) to project population growth between AD 1200 and 1300 (hundred-year rate = [end population − initial population] ÷ initial population; the two-hundred-year rate was calculated using an average of the two hundred-year rates for AD 1000–1100 and 1100–1200). We also compared the results to those obtained by extrapolating the instantaneous coefficient of population increase calculated for these same intervals, which assumes exponential growth (Odum 1971) into the 1200s. The results, presented in table 12.1, allow us to model the effects of intrinsic Developmental-period growth on population numbers in the Coalition and early Classic periods. Using these growth rates, the projected total northern Rio Grande population at AD 1300 was between 13,500 and 16,260 people (2,254 to 2,710 households; fig. 12.3).

These figures are lower than those presented by Dean, Doelle, and Orcutt (1994) by about 11,200 to 14,000 people (1,867 to 2,333 households). The discrepancies may be due to the different methods used, as well as the inclusion, in previous reconstructions, of a larger geographic area than was included in our reconstruction. Because we want to model intrinsic growth through the thirteenth century to the beginning of the fourteenth century using demonstrable trends in the Developmental period, our reconstruction does not include recorded Coalition- and early Classic-period sites, nor does it involve subregions where Pueblo sites were infrequent or not present before the thirteenth century.

While our estimates are based on a fifteen-year pit-structure use life during the Developmental period, evidence for surface architecture was more substantial after AD 1000, perhaps indicating increasingly longer site occupancy between about AD 1000 and 1200. Longer site occupations would increase the population estimates and significantly reduce the difference between Developmental- and projected Coalition-period estimates.

Population figures presented here suggest that most previous reconstructions significantly underestimated the Developmental-period population and perhaps overestimated the Coalition-period population. These factors decrease the population influx needed to explain Coalition-period and later population increase. Support for this position is found in Dickson (1975), who produced similar trends in population growth for the Developmental and Coalition periods. Maxwell also found that the "intrinsic growth rate in the lower Rio Chama Valley [during the Coalition and Classic period] is not unlike the growth rates estimated for other regions of the prehistoric pueblo world" (1994:17). His analysis showed that migration did not have a "striking effect" on regional population growth, supporting observations made by Wendorf and Reed (1955). As we noted earlier, our methods are intended to provide preliminary estimates for the Developmental period, and we believe that they accurately represent conservative population figures for that period and intrinsic population trends during the Developmental and Coalition periods.

Trends in available land per household for each time interval and subregion were calculated using population estimates and the areas of the included quadrangles in square kilometers. Before AD 900, individual ABQ-COH households had 20–32 km^2 of available land (table 12.1). However, by AD 1000, the amount of land per ABQ-COH household dropped to less than 10 km^2, while households in the newly occupied BAJ-VEL had about 5 km^2 each. The ABQ-COH population decline in the AD 1000s increased the amount of land per household in that subregion to more than 15 km², while the corresponding BAJ-VEL population increase reduced the amount of available land to 3 km²/household. Yet households expanding into the TSV had more than 26 km² available apiece. By AD 1100, the amount of land per household in the entire study area had decreased to slightly less than 7 km². During the twelfth century, available land steadily declined in each subregion, so that by AD 1200, ABQ-COH households had less than 8 km² each, and BAJ-VEL and TSV households had less than 3 and 5 km², respectively, reducing the study-area average to less than 4.5 km²/household.

Regional population grew throughout the Developmental period, punctuated by subregional decreases as the population periodically shifted farther north (table 12.1; fig. 12.2). Each northerly pulse resulted in a temporary increase in available land per household (table 12.1), allowing people to remain residentially mobile and perpetuating traditional socioeconomic practices, while mitigating scalar stress and potential conflicts over arable land (Adler 1989; Crown, Orcutt, and Kohler 1996). Sustained population growth began during the tenth century and resulted in a continual decline in the amount of land per household, which reached its lowest levels in the Developmental period by AD 1200. If characterizations of initial aggregation as a density-dependent process are correct (as Kohler, Powers, and Orcutt [2004] have argued for the Pajarito Plateau), then these trends set the northern Rio Grande population on a trajectory toward aggregation in the tenth century, well before depopulation of the southern San Juan and then the northern San Juan region. Finally, when those regions were abandoned at the end of the thirteenth century, the most sparsely populated subregion in the northern Rio Grande with the most available land per household was the area south of La Bajada Mesa, not the northerly subregions. Although there was room for immigrants within the northern Rio Grande, especially in the ABQ-COH area, the population estimates presented here support other studies (Dickson 1975; Maxwell 1994) that suggest there is little need for immigration to explain northern Rio Grande demographic trends. Further, since these are conservative figures, reasonable adjustments could be made that would increase the population-size estimates and make immigration even less likely to have been a factor in population growth.

Material Culture and Cultural Identity

Material indicators of cultural identity have been both invoked and rejected in prevailing interpretations of the San Juan migrations. In some instances, the obvious presence of material-culture markers is used to identify northern San Juan site-unit intrusions in the southernmost part of the southern San Juan region and central New Mexico (e.g., Davis 1964; Lekson et al. 2002). On the other hand, the absence of such markers in the northern Rio Grande is explained, in part, by the "cascade of events" (Kohler et al. 2008:153) that led to overt San Juan material-culture traits being abandoned or lost through assimilation (Cordell 1979:103; Cordell 1995; Lipe, this vol.; Roney 1995:179). The former position suggests that we know where northern San Juan migrants went because we can see their material remains: the presence of evidence is the evidence of presence. The latter position suggests that even without material remains, we still know where they went, so the important question is why they looked so different when they got there: the absence of evidence is the evidence of presence, but in unpredictably changed form.

Clark (2007b) suggests that, rather than examining showy aspects of material culture that might express ethnicity, evidence of group membership should be sought in more mundane aspects of life, such as those that represent enculturation through behavioral training. These are deeply embedded characteristics that carry canonical information (*sensu* Rappaport 1979) about who you are and to what group you belong. In a study of Pueblo movement into the Hohokam area, Clark (2001) defined data sets that help distinguish immigrants from the indigenous population, including "domestic spatial organization, foodways, and embedded technological styles reflected in the nondecorative production steps of ceramic vessels, textiles, walls, domestic installations, and other non-utilitarian items" (Clark 2001:18). Domestic spatial organization was the most useful indicator, because "it reflects culturally specific aspects of social organization . . . and cosmology" (Clark 2001:41). By looking at how people built their houses, how they made pottery and textiles, what they ate, and how they organized their villages and homes, a better picture of similarities and differences between populations can be drawn. In many ways, this is what Lipe (2006) has done in defining "the San Juan pattern."

Architecture

Shared knowledge regarding architectural form, function, and construction practices—as well as the significance of objects and their spatial relationship—develops in the context of a particular cultural setting. Built space provides order to the world and serves as a medium for disseminating important information about social behavior, cultural identity, and worldview. Using built space to communicate, manipulate, and maintain social behavior is a well-documented worldwide phenomenon (Adler 1993; Eliade 1987, 1991; Hendon 2000; Ortiz 1972; Rapoport 1969). If we assume that the nonrandom distribution of architectural patterns is the result of continuous cultural processes disseminated through descent or residence, then long-term patterning combined with limited spatial extent is considered a traditional, cultural, or ethnic practice (Allison 1999; Hill 1970). Given its important role in society, architecture is an ideal artifact for examining cultural interaction, influence, and continuity (Gilman 1987).

Although intraregional variation is present, changing suites of architecture, settlement patterns, and ceramic styles within a broad San Juan tradition characterize the roughly two-hundred-year periods of the Pecos Classification (Kidder [1924] 1962). Aided by increasingly refined dating and environmental studies, changes in San Juan material remains are well ordered and reflect coherent patterns of adaptation. Northern Rio Grande patterns, although equally well ordered and coherent, are quite different. For instance, synchronic comparisons of northern Rio Grande and San Juan pit structures show that northern Rio Grande structures were unlike contemporaneous San Juan structures (Lakatos 2009, 2006; Moore 2009). Further, diachronic trends are distinct within each region, demonstrating continuities in architecture indicative of different cultural traditions.

The complex cultural trajectories defining the Basketmaker III period through the Pueblo II period in the San Juan regions are only superficially similar to those of the Developmental period in the northern Rio Grande. By AD 600, the familiar triad of pithouse architecture, pottery, and agriculture appeared in the Albuquerque area. This triad manifested itself differently in the northern Rio Grande than in the San Juan regions, however. The near-absence of surface architecture; the absence of pit-structure antechambers and benches; the low frequencies of locally produced ceramics with high ratios of utility-to-decorated wares, each represented by a narrow range of vessel forms; and the low storage capacities reflecting relatively low levels of agricultural production define a distinct, incipient cultural trajectory in the northern Rio Grande (Lakatos and Post, in press).

In the late ninth and early tenth centuries, the northern Rio Grande population expanded north into the Santo Domingo basin, and then farther north above La Bajada Mesa and into the Tewa basin (Lakatos 2007, this chapter). As population increased and expanded, surface architecture became more common and pit-structure form and orientation became more formalized, while remaining distinct from San Juan patterns (Lipe 2006). The northern Rio Grande hearth-ash pit-ventilator complex was frequently enhanced using an adobe collar and an unshaped stone, often categorized as a deflector. By the late eleventh century, this core feature complex was incorporated into some surface rooms and sometimes included an ash grinding stone or anvil (e.g., Boyer, Moore, and Lakatos 2001; Creamer and Haas 2003; Green 1976; Loose 1974). In addition to perpetuating the core feature complex, northern Rio Grande pit structures were consistently oriented to the east and southeast (Lakatos 2006), contrasting with the southern orientation of San Juan pit structures. By the late twelfth century, as regional climatic events coincided with population movements, settlement expanded north to the Taos Valley (Boyer 1997), still expressing the same regional architectural patterns (Lakatos 2007).

In each of these circumstances, northern Rio Grande populations expanded into new areas and maintained intrinsic architectural patterns, including ritual facilities (Lakatos 2007). By the late thirteenth century, enhancements to the core feature complex included prominent deflectors, sometimes decorated, and loom or screen supports. Other common patterns include east-facing kivas and surface roomblocks, and kiva features—including ventilators and roof supports—in some surface rooms (cf. Adler and Dick 1999; Allen 1971; Bussey 1968; Carlson, Linse, and Kohler 1990; Jeançon 1929; Kidder 1958; Schmidt 2007; Stubbs and Stallings 1953; Vickery 1969; Wetherington 1968; Worman 1967). Expression of these core features continued through the early twentieth century in Tewa villages, as shown by the presence of east-oriented kivas with prominent hearth-ash pit-deflector complexes, which are sometimes incorporated into roomblocks (Arnon and Hill 1979:297; Edelman 1979:309; Edelman and Ortiz 1979; HABS/HAER 1934; Ortiz 1979:279; Speirs 1979:318; Stubbs 1950).

Two deviations from this long-term trajectory of northern Rio Grande continuity might reflect San Juan immigration or influence. First, pit structures in two Pajarito Plateau sites—Saltbush Pueblo and LA 12199 (Snow 1971; Zier 1982)—are reported to possess southern keyhole recesses and benches, which are iconic San Juan features. Although these features are evident in plan drawings, profiles show that the keyhole floors were well above pit-structure floors, at or near the elevations of nearby surface rooms. They also show that the benches were, in fact, narrow sills near the tops of pit-structure walls. If these architectural details indeed express San Juan cultural connections, they are rare, subtle, and not at all typical of such expressions in the San Juan regions. The two structures also contained ash pits, which are persistent northern Rio Grande features but are uncommon in San Juan structures after AD 1100. Interestingly, these same two sites also had higher frequencies of nonlocal white-ware types, such as Socorro Black-on-white (a middle Rio Grande type), and higher diversities in white-ware decoration motifs when compared to contemporaneous local sites of the same size (Kohler, VanBuskirk, and Ruscavage-Barz 2004). This supports the results of an earlier investigation in which Ruscavage-Barz (2002) found that paste differences in Santa Fe Black-on-white reflect household-level production, while design-element homogeneity suggests an inclusive social fabric with no evidence for ethnic or group differentiation.

The second deviation is that some Coalition- and Classic-period hamlets and villages have both south- and east-oriented pit structures (Adler 2007; Creamer 1993; Lange 1968; Smith 1998; Snow 1971, 1976; Zier 1982). Examples occur on the Pajarito Plateau and in the Rio Chama area, but most south-oriented structures appear in sites below La Bajada Mesa. The presence of south-oriented structures, standard at San Juan sites, persists in Keres village kivas today, and contrasts with the eastern orientations of northern Tiwa and Tewa kivas.

The significance of the prehistoric deviations from the dominant northern Rio Grande pattern is uncertain. They could represent accommodation of immigrants bearing San Juan concepts into larger indigenous communities. If so, the influence was inconsistently expressed and temporally short lived, with the strongest expression in areas where sites are considered antecedent to historical Keres communities.

The architectural history of the northern Rio Grande reflects little direct evidence for the incorporation of San Juan immigrants, either during the early tenth century (Duff and Wilshusen 2000) or during the later depopulation of the San Juan regions (Smith 1998). The exception, based on population trends and architectural manifestations, is within the region occupied by historical Keres villages in the Rio Jemez and Rio Grande valleys south of La Bajada Mesa.

Community Organization

The late twelfth and early thirteenth centuries in the northern Rio Grande are marked by colonization of nonriverine uplands that were previously only lightly occupied, such as the Pajarito Plateau and the Galisteo basin. Changes in settlement pattern toward more nucleated communities are easily visible and documented in these areas; consequently, community studies have concentrated on sites dating to the Coalition and Classic periods (e.g., Kohler, ed., 2004; Ruscavage-Barz 1999; Snead 2008a). Definitive research on Developmental-period community development is harder to find (Adler 1993; Boyer 1994, 1995, 2000, 2002), leading to an implied linkage of northern Rio Grande community formation with archaeological concepts of aggregation and the timing of large-scale San Juan immigration. Yet, considering the persistent cultural patterning and population growth evident in the northern Rio Grande, we argue that understanding the trajectory of community organization in the late Developmental period is an essential prerequisite to interpreting later patterns of settlement and land use.

In fact, community studies in nonriverine or upland areas like the Pajarito Plateau and Galisteo basin are really examining communities that appeared "suddenly" in those areas. These bursts of Pueblo colonization have traditionally been considered a hallmark of wholesale San Juan immigration into the northern Rio Grande. Rarely are these aggregated communities considered to be the result of indigenous population growth, expansion, and occupation of previously unoccupied—though not unused—areas, a pattern characteristic of the preceding Developmental period (Lakatos 2003). Focusing studies on these

Coalition-period colony sites exaggerates evidence for the appearance of aggregated communities and marginalizes evidence for *in situ* processes of aggregated community development that actually began in lowland, riverine settings during the late Developmental period (e.g., Creamer and Haas 2003:35–36).

Excavated late Developmental-period sites typically include one or two pit structures, sometimes associated with a small surface structure, and a shallow midden (Boyer 1994; Lakatos 2006; and references therein). These units do not have the organizational regularity of San Juan Prudden Units, considered to be the fundamental component of larger Pueblo III communities in those regions (Lipe 2006; Lipe and Ortman 2000). Instead, Developmental-period residential sites might well be described as unpredictable in layout, and habitations occur as single units or in loose clusters of units sometimes referred to as communities (Anschuetz, Acklen, and Hill 1997; Cordell 1979; Wendorf and Reed 1955).

An oft-cited example of a site in the northern Rio Grande thought to resemble early San Juan communities is LA 835 in the southern Tewa basin (e.g., Anschuetz, Acklen, and Hill 1997; Ellis 1975). This site contains more than twenty "house groups" consisting of ten- to twenty-room surface units with associated pit structures, and a large pit structure sometimes referred to as a "great kiva" (Stubbs 1954; Wiseman 1995). Ceramic and tree-ring dates reflect occupation between about AD 900 and 1150, with overlapping or sequential rather than contemporary house-group occupations and probably only a small population associated with the "great kiva" (Wiseman 1995). This does not disqualify LA 835 as a community, but it does reinforce the notion that Developmental-period communities were dispersed even in cases where a possible integrative structure is present.

Although it can be difficult to establish actual contemporaneity within groups of late Developmental-period sites, evidence points to the existence of community integration before population aggregation and the construction of substantial villages (Lakatos 2007). For instance, studies of excavated pit structures in the Taos Valley show that about 20 to 25 percent contained unusual features and were treated atypically during construction, use, and abandonment (Adler 1993; Boyer 1995, 2000). Subsequent unpublished investigations in the Taos Valley indicate that such structures could comprise as much as one-third of pit structures. The different forms and treatments were present during the entire 175-year length of the Developmental period in the Taos Valley (ca. AD 1050–1225), so the different forms and treatments are not temporal trends. Rather, Adler (1993) and Boyer (2000) suggest, these structures represent low-level integration (Adler's term) of small communities or subcommunity groups commonly referred to as hamlets.

Kosse's (1989), Kintigh's (1994), and Adler's (1994) research, following Johnson's (1979, 1982) model for social responses to scalar stress from population increase, suggest that hamlets typically contain six to twenty households. Using the preliminary population data (table 12.1), we can project the presence of eight to twenty-seven hamlets in the northern Rio Grande by AD 800, all located south of La Bajada Mesa. By AD 1000, the projected number of hamlets increased from 45 to 151, as the population expanded north to the Santa Fe River drainage and into the Tewa basin. Continued expansion pushed into the Taos Valley in the late eleventh century, and by AD 1200, the projected number of hamlets, now mostly north of La Bajada Mesa, was 88 to 294.

Based on population estimates and projected numbers of hamlets, we can suggest that northern Rio Grande households and hamlets were integrated into larger community groups. Adler's (1989:37) research suggests that villages whose residential and integrative structures are comparable in size to those of the Developmental period typically contain one hundred to two hundred people. Using these figures, we can project that the 88 to 294 hamlets in the northern Rio Grande by AD 1200 could have been further integrated into 53 to 106 village-level communities (table 12.1), reflecting 1.7 to 2.8 hamlets per village. Using that range, we can also project that pre–AD 800 hamlets were integrated into 4.7 to 9.5 (i.e., 5 to 10) villages, and AD 800–1000 hamlets into 26 to 54 villages. Combining conservative Developmental-period population numbers and archaeological models of structure and feature function with cross-cultural figures for community integration levels allows us to assert that numerous communities, integrated at different levels, existed throughout the northern Rio Grande well before the San Juan regions were depopulated. Since most northern Rio Grande communities were located north of La Bajada Mesa by AD 1200, they would have presented social and physical impediments to large-group immigration into the northern subregions like the Tewa basin.

Integration of dispersed households, hamlets, and villages can be difficult to recognize by residential proximity because of problems with establishing site and structure contemporaneity. It can, however, be identified through the presence of facilities that reflect multihousehold integrative mechanisms (Adler 1993; Boyer 1995, 2000, 2002; Lakatos 2007). For instance, while Adler (1993) contends that no specialized ritual facilities existed in the Taos Valley during the Developmental period, Boyer (2000) disagrees, pointing to several sites having unusually large pit structures with anomalous features and treatments, and one site with a facility described as a "dance floor" (Loose 1974). Boyer's position is that these facilities represent integration of community groups that included multiple hamlets.

Boyer (2002) also argues that integrative facilities associated with northern Rio Grande groups are not represented exclusively by pit structures with unique suites of features. Instead, such structures may indicate, but do not define, extramural areas that served as integrative spaces. These "plazas without walls" (Boyer 2002) are consistent with the traditional Pueblo focus on center or middle places and the notion that structural locations are selected by the presence of the center place rather than vice versa (Swentzell 1988). In this light, kivas or proto-kivas are potential, but not necessary, features of center places. The important integrative feature is the space itself, since architecture does not define the plaza space (Swentzell 1988:16). Archaeologically, we may see this situation as groups of residential and other sites that represent either contemporaneous or, more likely, overlapping occupation of an area around or near that space. Recent investigations at one such complex in the southern Tewa basin (LA 388, LA 390, LA 391, and LA 3119) identified residential pit structures and surface architecture set around an area used repeatedly for human burial and other activities (Akins, Lakatos, and Boyer 2003; Boyer 2001, 2002; Boyer, Akins, and Badner 2002). We suspect that the LA 835 complex, discussed earlier, involves a similar situation, and that many such complexes of residential and community-center features characterize the Developmental period. Focusing investigation on architectural features, a common practice in the past, has likely hampered our ability to identify integrative space.

As the indigenous population of the northern Rio Grande grew during the Developmental period, community integrative mechanisms were established well before aggregation began in the Coalition period. The inception of plazas (center places), part-time ritual structures (residences/proto-kivas), and specialized ritual structures (kivas) occurred while residence patterns remained dispersed and relatively mobile. Population growth and integration set the context within which people began to aggregate during the late Developmental and Coalition periods in order to balance population and landscape resources, effectively creating more available landscape space by coalescing people. Over time, communities took the form of surface roomblocks adjacent to or surrounding a plaza (e.g., Hibben 1937; Kohler and Root 2004a, 2004b; Stubbs and Stallings 1953; Wetherington 1968; among many others). This form is not unique if we recognize that plazas—center places—were present within dispersed Developmental-period communities. Even in late Coalition and Classic-period aggregated communities, plazas were still not exclusively defined by surrounding architecture; rather, architecture was placed near and around the selected plaza space (Swentzell 1988).

Through integration of place, and perhaps social and economic management, numerous Pueblo communities existed in the northern Rio Grande before AD 1200, and their form and organization contrasts with San Juan communities. While archaeologists (most recently Moore 2009; see also Lipe and Ortman 2000; Ortman et al. 2000; Windes 2007) have noted that San Juan communities are often arranged in a street-like pattern, this is not the case for Developmental communities in the northern Rio Grande, which seem to be arranged around central, open spaces. San Juan communities are also often focused on monumental public architecture, which is clearly missing in the northern Rio Grande. While the large pit structure at LA 835 is sometimes cited as an example of monumental architecture, it is the only known feature of its type in the northern Rio Grande during the Developmental period, it is poorly described, and one example does not make a pattern. This structure may simply represent a short-lived experiment with new forms of community integration. Similar, later experiments may be represented by the large kivas at Arroyo Hondo Pueblo (Creamer 1993); at Pot Creek Pueblo, where the experiment was probably unsuccessful (Crown 1991; Wetherington 1968); and at Picuris Pueblo (Adler and Dick 1999).

Assemblage Structure

Technological aspects of artifact assemblages can provide information on cultural identity (Clark 2001, 2007). In addition to how things
are made, the ways in which assemblages are structured—how new
items or styles are added to an existing repertoire and what happens to
older items and styles when new items or styles are added—may also be
indicative of cultural identity. Differences between the structures of San
Juan and northern Rio Grande pottery and projectile-point assemblages
may contribute to definitions of cultural identity.

Wilson (2003) points out important differences between San Juan and
northern Rio Grande ceramic traditions. These differences are reflected
in assemblage composition and the acceptance of innovation in technology and style. The differences are well defined in each region through
the twelfth century, and the unique qualities of the northern Rio Grande
tradition persist well into the Classic period. San Juan pottery assemblages are structured and sequential; pottery types succeed and mostly
replace one another, and pots were built in the same way at any one
time. In contrast, northern Rio Grande assemblages are cumulative,
with several styles and methods of vessel construction in use at any
given time. San Juan assemblages from the tenth through thirteenth
centuries generally contain 25 to 40 percent decorated wares and 60 to
75 percent utility wares. Contemporary northern Rio Grande collections contain only 5 to 6 percent decorated wares and 94 to 95 percent
utility wares, with the decorated proportion increasing only to about 10
percent through the Coalition period.

The adoption of organic paint for white wares occurred differently
in the two areas (Wilson 2003). This shift was gradual in the San Juan
regions, beginning in the late eleventh century, but it was more abrupt
in the northern Rio Grande, supplanting the use of mineral paint in
most areas about AD 1150–1200. While that shift in the northern Rio
Grande coincided with the initial occupation of new geographic areas
and potters' exposure to new material resources, concurrent changes in
decorative style are not apparent.

One type in particular, Galisteo Black-on-white, has been described
as a Mesa Verde Black-on-white analog that indicates immigration from
the northern San Juan (Cordell 1995; Roney 1995), despite contrary

indication from style and technology (Dutton 1964). Wilson's (2008) detailed study of pottery from Galisteo basin sites concluded that Galisteo Black-on-white is, in fact, an adaptation to locally available marine or geological clays rather than the riverine clays that were more commonly used in other parts of the northern Rio Grande. Consequently, its superficial resemblance to Mesa Verde Black-on-white is due to resource similarities rather than the cultural identity of the potters. In that context, the significance of similarities in decorative elements, such as rim ticking, cannot simply be ascribed to cultural identity, and Wilson (2008) contends that, stylistically, Galisteo Black-on-white is derived from Santa Fe Black-on-white. Other pottery types, such as Pindi and Rowe Black-on-white, have design styles similar to those of Santa Fe Black-on-white but differ in paste compositions. These types have simply been categorized as varieties of Santa Fe Black-on-white, with no reference to ethnic differences. There is, then, no clear reason to infer ethnic or cultural differences to the makers of Galisteo Black-on-white.

Moore's (in press) comparison of northern Rio Grande projectile-point assemblages with San Juan assemblages from Dolores (Phagan 1988), Salmon Ruin (Moore 1981), and Chaco Canyon (Lekson 1997) suggests differences equivalent to those observed in pottery: projectile-point styles in Developmental- and early Coalition-period assemblages were cumulative, while San Juan styles were essentially successional. That is, older styles in the northern Rio Grande were not abandoned, although they did decrease in use over time. In contrast, one or two styles generally dominate San Juan assemblages at any given time, with older styles occurring infrequently. This was particularly true at Salmon Ruin, where two types dominated during the early occupation. Although these types continued to be used into the later occupation, they were clearly being replaced by two other types (Moore 1981). Too few data are yet available to assess whether the cumulative northern Rio Grande pattern extends into the Classic period, but it does hold for the Coalition period in the Tewa basin (Moore 2009a).

The lack of any strong material-culture evidence for intrusive northern San Juan sites in the northern Rio Grande casts doubt on models that propose direct migration, especially since relatively clear evidence for thirteenth-century northern San Juan intrusions has been found along the Rio Puerco of the east, near Acoma, west of Mount Taylor, and in central New Mexico near Magdalena and Truth or Consequences (Davis 1964; Lekson et al. 2002; Roney 1995). The intrusive nature of these sites is suggested by the dominant presence of northern San Juan ceramic assemblages in areas where those types were not formerly produced. The absence of similar cases in the northern Rio Grande suggests that northern San Juan movement into that region either did not occur or took different forms from those seen elsewhere.

Assertions of pre-existing, long-distance ties that established social pathways between northern San Juan and northern Rio Grande peoples in advance of migration (e.g., Cordell et al. 2007) need to be corrected. They rest first on general, panregional similarities in ceramic design styles. However, framed, banded, and geometric styles were widely distributed in the northern Southwest, and their presence in the northern Rio Grande was a horizon-style derivation from earlier local styles or, at most, was influenced by interaction with the southern San Juan pottery traditions during the Developmental period (Wilson 2008). The assertions also rest on the misperception that Galisteo Black-on-white was an analog of Mesa Verde Black-on-white. As Wilson (2003) has shown, however, Galisteo Black-on-white is best viewed as a late variety or derivative of Santa Fe Black-on-white. Although there is abundant evidence of pottery exchange connecting northern Rio Grande communities with populations in the middle Rio Grande Valley, Mogollon, Cibola, and southern San Juan regions (Frisbie 1967; Wiseman and Olinger 1991), there is little evidence for direct social or economic ties with the northern San Juan. Similarly, materials like turquoise and obsidian that almost certainly originated in the northern Rio Grande are rare on thirteenth-century northern San Juan sites (Lipe 1995:158) and probably reached those sites through down-the-line exchange, perhaps with southern San Juan communities serving as middlemen. Proposed direct socioeconomic connections between the northern San Juan and the northern Rio Grande populations also tend to ignore the presence of people in intermediate areas. For instance, the Gallina region, whose occupants were arguably ancestral Towa (Ford, Schroeder, and Peckham 1972; Reiter 1938; Wiseman 2007; but see Kulischek 2006; Simpson 2008), is characterized by minimal evidence for socioeconomic interactions with adjacent regions: "The stagnation of Gallina ceramic traits may be attributed to the low level of outside contacts, an idea supported by the near absence of trade ceramics from neighboring regions in all but the southern Cuba district" (Simpson 2008:21; see also Cordell 1979:46).

Faunal and Human Indicators of Subsistence Practices

Subsistence practices in the northern Rio Grande differ from those in the San Juan, and these differences persist across the Developmental/Coalition threshold. For instance, although turkeys were domesticated early in all areas, they appear to have played a less significant role in the northern Rio Grande, where they were kept but probably not bred in the early Developmental-period (AD 600–900) sites at Peña Blanca. A large sample from early Developmental contexts yielded only 3.1 percent turkey bone and a single piece of egg shell, while turkey contributed 25.9 percent of a small Coalition-period sample that had no egg shell (Akins 2008a). Both bones and eggshell are rare in Pojoaque-area assemblages until late in the Developmental period, when the total is just more than 10 percent (Akins 2009). Even Coalition- and Classic-period Arroyo Hondo assemblages have relatively few turkey bones; only 8.6 percent of the overall minimum number of individuals (MNI) and 2.8 to 13.5 percent of the counts by time period were turkey (Lang and Harris 1984:154–176). Turkey makes up only 2.5 percent of late Coalition-period assemblages recovered from recent excavations at the Pueblo de Santa Fe (LA 1051), and only 3.6 percent of early Classic assemblages. These figures from sites compare to a range of 22.5 to 73.6 percent at Pueblo III sites in Montezuma Valley and Mesa Verde (Muir and Driver 2002:189), suggesting the northern Rio Grande— with a few exceptions, such as the late Coalition Burnt Mesa Pueblo Area 1 (Kohler and Root 2004b)—did not have the same level of turkey use as the northern San Juan into the Classic period.

While reliance on turkey was apparently minor, northern Rio Grande populations relied heavily on artiodactyls for animal protein, and more on wild resources in general (Akins 2009). Artiodactyl indices (a relative measure of artiodactyl to lagomorph counts) are consistently high in the northern Rio Grande. Late Developmental-period assemblages from the Pojoaque area have indices between 0.62 and 0.73; early Coalition-period LA 3333, in the eastern Galisteo basin, has an index of 0.86; and at Arroyo Hondo Pueblo, the index for the Coalition period is 0.59, while the peak for the Classic period is 0.57. At the Pueblo de Santa Fe, the late Coalition index is 0.61, while the early Classic index is 0.65. These figures compare with indices between 0.20 and 0.48 from sites near Dolores, Colorado, and between 0.10 and 0.42 from sites in Chaco Canyon (Akins 2008a).

Differences between the northern Rio Grande and northern San Juan should be expected, regardless of population affiliation, given adaptations to differing environmental conditions and the influences of human population density on resource mix. Greater individual mobility within northern Rio Grande human populations is indicated by consistently more robust femur development than is seen in San Juan populations (Akins 1995, 2008b, 2008c), which suggests considerable travel, presumably to acquire wild resources, and may reflect subsistence adaptation to northern Rio Grande environmental diversity. Additionally, differences in female upper-body development (the muscles and bones used in corn grinding) indicate that northern Rio Grande populations were less involved in corn processing, supporting the possibility that they were also less reliant on intensive agriculture. Maximum humerus midshaft diameters among females from the La Plata area of northwestern New Mexico are larger than those of males from the same area, as well as those of females and males in the northern Rio Grande, regardless of time period (Akins 2008b, 2008c). While remains of agricultural plants—particularly corn—are consistently found at Pueblo sites in the northern Rio Grande, data from faunal assemblages and human skeletal remains suggest that the indigenous population was less reliant on agricultural production than were earlier and contemporaneous people in the San Juan regions.

Assessing Human Biometric Data

Immigration of significant numbers of people to the northern Rio Grande should be reflected by genetic differences in human skeletal remains, assuming populations in the donating and receiving regions remained sufficiently isolated from each other until immigration began. Cranial measurements have long been used to investigate relationships between Pueblo groups (e.g., Akins 1986; Corruccini 1972; Mackey 1977; Schillaci, Ozolins, and Windes 2001). In this volume, Ortman provides a cranial biometric argument that people from the central Mesa Verde region were the genetic progenitors of the Tewa. In addition to genetic relatedness, Ortman argues, the Tewa population—which he believes to be derived from the northern San Juan—shows little significant mixture with other contemporary populations, while an earlier Tewa basin population and a Galisteo basin population show evidence of significant in-migration and genetic mixture.

Our review of the biometric data, however, suggests several potential problems with interpretations that link central Mesa Verde and historical Tewa populations. Our major concern is for the reliability, sensitivity, and appropriateness of the biometric data for this purpose. The data were generated by a number of people, from early researchers (e.g., Ernest A. Hooton, Alex Hrdlicka, and Erik K. Reed) to current researchers (e.g., Nancy J. Akins, Maria O. Smith, and Michael A. Schillaci). Analysts often view cranial landmarks differently, and even the same analyst using the same calipers will not always record the same measurement twice. Consequently, comparability and variability problems are inherent, and individual analyst procedures can create both false clustering and false differentiation of clusters. Grouping data from multiple sites and analysts to create larger data sets may be necessary for the regional scale of this endeavor, but the grouping process does not necessarily compensate for inherent comparability problems. We have more specific reservations about the use of estimates to compensate for missing data and the standardization of raw data to control for sexual dimorphism. None of these issues necessarily invalidates the results of the biometric analyses, but without explicit consideration of the variability of each population characterization, we are hesitant to embrace the conclusions of this analysis.

Small sample sizes almost always characterize Southwest craniometric studies. This is particularly true in the northern Rio Grande, where clayey soils often result in poor bone preservation. Crania that are complete enough for biometric studies often comprise a small portion of those recovered from specific contexts and, therefore, may or may not be representative of the population as a whole. For example, of the ninety-nine adults excavated from late Coalition–early Classic period Pindi and Arroyo Hondo Pueblos, only twenty-seven (27 percent) could be used in Ortman's study. The Galisteo basin sample (LA 3333) of six came from an early Coalition population of thirty-five adults

(17 percent) found in a frontier cultural setting in which associated material culture suggests the possibility of a heterogeneous community. Only three of eleven adults from LA 391 (27 percent), a late Developmental site that is most likely ancestral Tewa, could contribute to the Tewa basin sample. Small sample sizes coupled with variation in the number of complete crania in each sample raise the possibility of clustering effects in which a population may be inaccurately characterized because of an aberrant sample from a single component. This problem can be compounded by failing to account for temporal variation within and between samples.

Differences in the amount of missing data between samples may also influence the outcome of the biometric analyses. In Ortman's data set, one-third of the potential measurements are missing. Some populations have large numbers of individuals with valid measurements (less than 10 percent missing), while other data sets have up to 38 percent missing data. Ortman's derivation of substitute values through multivariate analyses within the combined sample is explicit and defensible, but the effects of value substitution on perceptions of similarity and difference are unknown. For the variables used in the R matrix principal-coordinates analysis (Ortman, this vol., fig. 10.1), substitute data characterize 10 percent or less of the northern Pajarito population, the two Galisteo basin populations, and the two Taos Valley populations. On the other hand, substitute data comprise 30 to 38 percent of the values for the southeastern Utah, McElmo, Mesa Verde, Navajo Reservoir (upper San Juan), Cibola, Chama, Cochiti, Albuquerque, and El Morro populations (the data discussed here were provided by Scott Ortman, personal communication, 2008). The impacts of the substitution procedure are unknown without demonstration that data sets with no missing values are statistically identical to data sets with substitute values. In any case, we expect that any effect will be differentially expressed, especially where large samples coincide with large frequencies of missing values and small samples coincide with few missing values.

Even if our misgivings about the data quality and multivariate procedures can be dispelled, we explicitly question the final interpretation that central Mesa Verde people genetically overwhelmed or displaced pre-existing populations of the Tewa and Galisteo basins. While we expect that genetic similarity and continuity would result in biometric similarity, biometric similarity alone need not reflect genetic relatedness and must be assessed in light of other evidence. Biometric analyses of this sort actually measure statistical closeness of populations—however they are defined—rather than genetic relatedness per se. Therefore, the way in which populations are defined for analytical purposes becomes a critical point, since it creates the bridging argument for correlating statistical closeness with genetic relatedness. For instance, table 10.1 in this volume suggests that the Mesa Verde sample is closer to Jemez than to the northern Pajarito or Galisteo groups, and that the northern Pajarito and Chama populations are closest to Cibola (Zuni). Strong or exclusive relationships between these particular populations are improbable in a cultural-historical sense, despite the proposed biometric similarity. Given the scarcity of supporting archaeological data and ethnohistorical information, we likewise suspect that the proposed biometric similarity between Mesa Verde and Tewa-basin populations has no underlying genetic basis. While we are somewhat surprised that the Taos Valley, Tewa basin, and Galisteo basin populations all look distinct in the biometric analyses, we note that these populations are represented by the smallest sample sizes and have unusually low numbers of missing data values. These circumstances may also be influencing the perception of similarity and dissimilarity.

In keeping with other data presented in this chapter, our perspective emphasizes *in situ* development, with selected and restricted genetic admixture from multiple outside populations (principally southern San Juan, middle Rio Grande, Plains, and perhaps some northern San Juan). We point out, as well, that we are not the first to suggest in situ development of the Tewa Pueblos based on biometric evidence. Schillaci and others' biometric analysis concluded, "The Mesa Verde sample . . . appeared as an outlier in all of our analyses and there is no direct evidence of a site unit intrusion into the Rio Grande area by San Juan/Four Corners groups" (2001:143). Despite Ortman's reliance on much of Schillaci's data, the substantial differences in analytical results and conclusions probably reflect differences in how the data were grouped and analyzed, as well as the much larger scope of Ortman's study. The data and analytic issues must be resolved before we can comfortably accept biometric arguments for direct genetic connections between northern San Juan and Tewa populations.

Pathways to the Northern Rio Grande

Although we have argued for a strong, indigenous Pueblo cultural trajectory and a lack of evidence favoring conventional models of substantial, direct northern San Juan migration into the northern Rio Grande, we believe that immigration did occur as corporate groups or communities moved in from the southern San Juan. Following the disruption of southern San Juan communities in the late twelfth century, these groups—arguably ancestral Keres—moved through the Rio Puerco and Rio Jemez valleys onto the southern Pajarito Plateau and into the Santo Domingo basin in the thirteenth century. Support for this model includes evidence for continuous contact between inhabitants of the southern San Juan and northern Rio Grande, as well as an archaeological record of site-unit intrusions, adaptations, and assimilation in the middle Rio Puerco and Rio Jemez valleys (Moore 2008; Roney 1995), and by the distribution of historical northern Rio Grande language and culture groups.

Moore (2008) presents a model suggesting that southern San Juan migration to the northern Rio Grande was punctuated rather than direct, using communities along the southeast edge of the San Juan basin as springboards. Socioeconomic ties, evidenced by movement of pottery and turquoise, existed between the southern San Juan and northern Rio Grande regions from the early Developmental to the Coalition period and may have established familiarity that prepared the way for later population movement. It is worth noting that these ties stopped short of the embrace of Chacoan architectural (religious) styles by Rio Grande populations.

Ceramic assemblages from the Rio Puerco Valley along the southeast edge of the southern San Juan show considerable influence from the northern Rio Grande after the mid-twelfth century. The result was ceramic styles that were technologically southern San Juan but stylistically northern Rio Grande (Bice 1994; Bice, Davis, and Sundt 1998; Hurst 2003). People moved east from the Rio Puerco into the Rio Jemez drainage by the late twelfth century, and they eventually spread to the lower Rio Jemez Valley and onto the southern Pajarito Plateau. Three southern Pajarito sites—Casa del Rito (LA 3852; Kohler and Root 2004a), Saltbush Pueblo (LA 4997; Snow 1971), and LA 12199 (Zier 1982)—exhibit characteristics indicative of this movement. As noted earlier, northern Rio Grande and nonlocal pottery types (interestingly, mostly from the middle Rio Grande rather than the southern San Juan) are present and exhibit a wider range of design styles than those at indigenous sites (Kohler, Van-Buskirk, and Ruscavage-Barz 2004), while village layouts and kiva forms appear to exhibit some southern San Juan characteristics.

The role of northern San Juan immigrants in this model is unclear. The late thirteenth-century period of northern San Juan depopulation (Varien et al. 2007) postdates the initiation of southern San Juan movement into the Rio Jemez Valley, so northern San Juan immigrants would have moved into or through southern San Juan communities—a scenario that would have promoted assimilation rather than site-unit intrusion. Probable northern San Juan site-unit intrusions in the Rio Puerco Valley, such as that at Guadalupe Ruin (Pippin 1987), are often defensive in location and form, with evidence suggesting conflict with Gallina populations and with Rio Puerco-Jemez southern San Juan communities. Some northern San Juan communities clearly moved to the south as corporate groups, bypassing the northern Rio Grande altogether (Davis 1964; Lekson et al. 2002; Roney 1995). Other northern San Juan communities may have become fragmented into family groups. If these groups eventually entered the northern Rio Grande, they did so by assimilating into southern San Juan or northern Rio Grande communities and have not been identified archaeologically.

Sharp contrasts between Moore's model and conventional models for thirteenth-century population movements lie in their differing implications for the linguistic history of Puebloan peoples. Ortman (2007, this vol.) explicitly links northern San Juan populations with the Tewa speech community. Moore's model accommodates the likelihood that both northern and southern San Juan populations were ancestral Keres speakers. If northern San Juan migrants were part of the Keres speech community (as is assumed for the southern San Juan peoples), it would have facilitated their thirteenth-century integration into already established and acculturated Keres communities in the Rio Puerco and Rio Jemez drainages, on the southern Pajarito Plateau, and in the Santo Domingo basin. Northern San Juan migrants who overshot access through the Rio Jemez corridor would have found themselves in a culturally and linguistically distinct landscape, resulting in a high degree of visibility for as long as they persisted as distinct communities (e.g., Lekson et al. 2002). Such northern San Juan migrant communities would have become analogous in visibility and cultural status to the Kayenta migrant communities in southern Arizona (Lyons 2003). To date, none have been found in the northern Rio Grande.

What Next? Directions for Further Research

The perspective on indigenous development in the northern Rio Grande presented in this chapter is an effort to shift the focus of research on immigration into the northern Rio Grande from the donating to the presumed receiving side. The need for that shift is great, since existing migration models do not involve accurate characterizations of northern Rio Grande archaeological and ethnohistorical records. We are not proposing a specific receiving-side model (e.g., Cordell 1995) with which to view immigration to the northern Rio Grande (although see Moore 2008). Instead, we are confident that additional work will validate the perspective presented in this chapter, and will allow researchers to develop and assess a variety of models for northern Rio Grande cultural development, the deep origins of the distinct ethnic identities of Tanoan and Keres peoples, and patterns of interaction between the people who held and still hold those deeply distinct identities.

Anthony (1990:895) states that archaeological examinations of migration are often unproductive because of inappropriate assumptions and inadequately defined concepts regarding the conditions under which migrations occur. We assert this to be the case in most models alleging substantial, direct movement from the northern San Juan into the northern Rio Grande. We are particularly concerned that those models do not give significant consideration to the archaeological records of regions between the northern San Juan and the northern Rio Grande, which is necessary to identify the directions of migratory movement, the sizes and natures of migrating groups, and the potential formal variety of migratory movement—short- versus long-distance movement, leap-frogging, migration streams, short-term return migration, etc. (Anthony 1990). Equally as important, they do not consider existing conditions in the northern Rio Grande that would have been impacted by significant immigration, what those impacts might have been, and how they would have been expressed archaeologically and ethnohistorically (Cordell 1995). It is with this perspective in mind that we can ask what the archaeological records of the presumed donating side, the intermediate areas, and the potential receiving sides tell us about issues of site-unit intrusion, socioeconomic ripples, family vs. village-coordinated movement, punctuated movement, and other possible scenarios (Cordell 1995; Duff and Wilshusen 2000; Haury 1958; Moore 2008; Roney 1995).

Identifying migration archaeologically relies on chronological correlations between donating and receiving sides (Haury 1958), and modeling the northern Rio Grande role in Southwest-wide migrations requires a more precise chronometric framework for both intraregional and interregional comparisons. Although a goal should be to characterize the archaeological record in the northern Rio Grande during periods of regional population movements, such as the tenth, late twelfth, and late thirteenth–early fourteenth centuries, we hope we have made the point that understanding social and demographic dynamics in the preceding, intervening, and subsequent periods is just as important.

Systematic development of a conservative, comprehensive population reconstruction provides a demographic context against which to assess the implications of immigration. The reconstruction presented here is a first step in that process. Like reconstructions produced by Dean, Doelle, and Orcutt (1994), Crown, Orcutt, and Kohler (1996), and Duff and Wilshusen (2000), our effort lacks the finer detail emerging from the northern San Juan (Ortman Varien, and Gripp 2007; Varien et al. 2007). This situation is attributable to the pervasive use of period- and phase-based chronologies in the northern Rio Grande, and better demographic reconstructions will require both new chronological tools and a reassessment of chronological goals. Nonetheless, our reconstruction provides a vastly improved baseline for assessing intraregional population trends during the Developmental period and for projecting them into the Coalition and Classic periods. Those trends provide the backdrop for identifying and assessing population influxes from other regions.

Additional studies of human remains from the northern Rio Grande are needed to assess health, fecundity and morbidity, patterns of movement/settlement, and dietary reliance on domestic versus collected food. Those data can then be compared with similar data from

the San Juan regions to evaluate biological, dietary, and settlement similarities and differences. Although we question the validity of aggregated
craniometric studies, we affirm that biometric analyses, discrete traits,
tooth morphology, adaptive physiological responses, and isotope analyses have much to contribute to questions of population affiliations and
migration models.

Paleoenvironmental reconstructions for the northern Rio Grande do
not always agree on the nature and timing of climatic events and trends
(cf. Allen 2004; Cordell et al. 2007; Dean, Doelle, and Orcutt 1994;
Maxwell 2000; Orcutt 1999; Rose, Dean, and Robinson 1981). A carefully constructed synthesis of northern Rio Grande paleoenvironmental
records, including subregional variation, is therefore necessary, and will
place us in a much stronger position to assess push-pull factors involved
in both intra- and interregional population movements. It appears, for
instance, that subregional climatic variation allowed population expansion into nonriverine and upland settings, and may subsequently have
made those same areas untenable for large populations dependent on
intensive agriculture (Blinman 2007). We note, however, that Anthony
(1990:898) questions the utility of push-pull notions for several reasons,
not the least of which is that "the causes of migratory movement can
be extremely complex, so that in many prehistoric cases it is likely that
the proximate causes can no longer be identified." It may be, then, that
even if reconstructions of conditions in presumed donating and receiving regions suggest complementary paleoenvironmental circumstances
(Ahlstrom, Van West, and Dean 1995; Cordell et al. 2007), they do not
reveal the actual causes of migration or the locations and conditions of
resettlement.

A critical aspect of modeling immigration is the ethnic characterization of proposed immigrants and indigenous peoples. This is perhaps
the most difficult problem to address archaeologically. Recent advances
in the theory and method of ethnic assessments (Clark 2001, 2007a) are
only now being applied, and Wilson's systematic assessment of Galisteo
Black-on-white is a positive example. We expect to find more regionally
unique connections between the formal, informal, and technological
aspects of indigenous Pueblo culture in the northern Rio Grande (Lakatos and Post, in press), which should allow stronger comparisons with
immigrant families, communities, and populations.

Relationships between archaeology, ethnohistory, and ethnography need to be critically examined. Recognizing the problems inherent in historical linguistics, glottochronology, and lexicostatistics, it nonetheless remains imperative that Tanoan language histories be compared with events represented in the archaeological record of the northern Rio Grande in order to address different models for the origins and divergences of the Tanoan languages. The possibility that Tewa diverged from Tiwa around AD 1000, an idea posited by Davis (1959) and Trager (1967) and supported by Ortman (this vol.), appears to us to fit well with patterns of indigenous population growth and expansion in the late Developmental period (contra Ortman, this vol.). Additionally, we suspect that in situ development of Tewa language and culture from the indigenous Tanoan base encouraged the divergence of Tiwa language groups by forming an impediment, reinforced by Keresan immigration beginning in the thirteenth century, to maintaining continuity in Tiwa language and culture. This is Peckham's position in Ford, Schroeder, and Peckham (1972), and it contrasts with Ford's and Schroeder's positions in that paper, which argue for what one might call a "parting of the Tiwa sea" by immigrating Tewa speakers. These potential relationships need to be rigorously examined chronologically and in comparison with paleoenvironmental conditions.

A related example of exploring relationships between archaeology, ethnography, and ethnohistory involves the interplay between trajectories of social organizational change and population growth. Moore and Boyer (2009) have shown how the Tewa seasonal moieties could have developed as an in situ Tanoan social organizational response to internal population growth and a combination of natural and sociocultural limits on population expansion and community fissioning. Importantly, Moore and Boyer's model acknowledges the effects of Keresan immigration into the northern Rio Grande in the thirteenth century. The presence of Keresans on the southern Pajarito Plateau, in the Rio Jemez Valley, and in the Rio Grande Valley south of La Bajada Mesa enhanced the inability of Tewa-basin occupants to really expand their growing population and thereby relieve resource stress. One result was the formation of very large villages and the restructuring of integration mechanisms, including the formation of the seasonal moieties. We suggest that this process was but one manifestation of diversifying trajectories within in situ Tanoan cultural development that began in the late Developmental period—the emerging Tiwa-Tewa split—and were reinforced in subsequent centuries.

While we are confident in our "indigenous perspective" on northern Rio Grande Tanoan cultural development, we are also mindful that continuing research will reveal more evidence of the impacts of panregional Puebloan "turbulence" (*sensu* Lipe 1995) in the region. Cordell's (1995) argument for rippling socioeconomic change is important in this regard, as is Ware and Blinman's (2000) consideration of ritual exchange dynamics between Keres and Tanoan communities.

Finally, recorded Pueblo origin stories must be studied within the contexts of relationships between worldview, history, and mythology. Uncritical or narrowly selective references to origin stories or anthropological interpretations of those stories encourage their inappropriate use. Acknowledging Cordell's (1995:204) warning against using such stories as "unambiguous guides" for interpreting the archaeological record, they can, nonetheless, provide important information about the development of cultural similarity and diversity, intra- and interregional presence and movement of peoples, and perceptions and even definitions of cultural and ethnic identity. That potential will only be realized if we understand that these stories embody different lessons for us than they do for Pueblo peoples, and if we apply methodologies that appropriately relate myth to critical observation (e.g., Barber and Barber 2004; Basso 1996; Boyer 2008).

Conclusions

The archaeology of the northern Rio Grande has traditionally played a passive role in modeling the depopulation of the San Juan regions. While historical clustering of Pueblo peoples suggests an end point for migration, details of northern Rio Grande archaeology, both before and after the migration period, have been underutilized or ignored when developing conventional, donation-side models.

The long tradition of Pueblo cultural development in the northern Rio Grande was quite different from that of the Four Corners. We assert that these trajectories show that the groups living in these areas developed and maintained different cultural identities that were not masked by events in the late thirteenth century.

Historically proffered evidence for direct movement from the northern San Juan is unsupported in light of the material evidence and the weight of data showing northern Rio Grande cultural continuity from the Developmental period through the present. Rather than a nearly empty landscape, the northern Rio Grande was home to a substantial, growing, and expanding indigenous population before the fourteenth century. Occupied by people with distinct material culture, subsistence patterns, and organizational structures, dispersed late Developmental-period villages approached the transition to aggregated communities well before the San Juan regions were abandoned. These patterns represented a response to local conditions and pressures rather than a reaction to immigrants.

Our population reconstruction suggests that immigration was not an essential element of pre–AD 1300 population trends in the northern Rio Grande. This is particularly true for the subregions north of La Bajada Mesa that had substantial and growing populations, while the subregion to the south was the only area available to accommodate substantial immigrant groups. Continuity in architectural forms and features and community organization make it likely that modern Tewa and Tiwa peoples are descended from the indigenous northern Rio Grande population present since at least the Developmental period. Climate change, the oft-considered motivating context for twelfth- and thirteenth-century population movements from the San Juan regions, appears to have encouraged internal movements within the northern Rio Grande as new areas were opened for agricultural settlement (Blinman 2007; Kohler, ed., 2004). Galisteo Black-on-white pottery, frequently cited as evidence for northern San Juan immigration, actually represents a local response to resources in a newly occupied area. Finally, recently proposed human craniometric evidence equating northern San Juan people with the Tewa is problematic because of weaknesses in sampling methodology and the lack of corroborating archaeological and ethnohistorical data.

We do not assert that people from the northern San Juan did not find their way to the northern Rio Grande. Rather, the archaeological evidence suggests that, if northern San Juan immigrants did enter the northern Rio Grande, they did so in groups, probably small in size, that were quickly assimilated and disappeared into existing communities. We suspect that assimilation was made easier because people leaving the northern San Juan were ancestral Keres and entered southern San Juan Keres communities.

While we see no evidence for direct northern San Juan immigration, there is strong evidence for sustained southern San Juan interaction and punctuated immigration along the western fringe of the northern Rio Grande beginning in the late twelfth century. Archaeological evidence from that area reflects transitional cultural and settlement patterns for southern San Juan peoples, and their entry into the northern Rio Grande began well before the northern San Juan was abandoned. Movement through the Rio Puerco and Rio Jemez led to the region between Albuquerque and Cochiti, which coincidentally held the lowest indigenous population and the most available land around AD 1200 and therefore presented the greatest opportunity for successful establishment of immigrant villages. It is also the location of the eastern Keres Pueblos, which retain street-like layouts and southern-oriented kivas (Stubbs 1950) strikingly similar to late Pueblo III villages in the San Juan regions (Lipe and Ortman 2000; Ortman et al. 2000; Windes 2007).

We applaud efforts to solve the problems of northern San Juan depopulation. But the lack of evidence supporting large-scale, direct movement from the northern San Juan to the northern Rio Grande is rarely addressed substantively by models that simply assume this movement occurred. Explaining this lack of evidence should be a major consideration in such models. We contend that framing relevant questions about northern San Juan migrations involves accurately describing the sizes and constituents of northern San Juan groups as they left that region (e.g., assessing the implications of Kuckelman's research presented in this vol.). It also entails identifying the circumstances in which such groups could move into new regions with unfamiliar resource structures and with substantial existing populations, some perhaps culturally related and others probably not (e.g., Anthony 1990:902–905). More rigorous models that accurately incorporate the archaeological and ethnohistorical records of proposed receiving regions, and that formulate and test relevant criteria for identifying immigrant population groups of varying sizes in different regions and circumstances, must be developed. Finally, we suggest that studies of this phenomenon must look closely at intermediate areas that would have been traversed by immigrants as the foci of initial immigration.

Tracking where Pueblo people went as they left the Four Corners is important for understanding events and processes occurring throughout the northern Southwest after AD 1250. Archaeologists have long found intellectual comfort in knowing that those people went to the areas most heavily occupied after AD 1300. Nonetheless, continuing research does not support most models that make the northern Rio Grande receive this thirteenth-century immigration. We need to examine the whole picture, including intermediate regions and the donating and presumed receiving sides, to better understand the dynamics of prehistoric population movements.

13

The Environmental, Demographic, and Behavioral Context of the Thirteenth-Century Depopulation of the Northern Southwest

Jeffrey S. Dean

As a discussant for the Amerind Foundation Seminar "New Light on the Thirteenth-Century Depopulation of the Northern Southwest," I was assigned two seemingly unrelated topics: (1) discuss the environmental considerations raised in these papers, and (2) provide a comparative perspective on the thirteenth-century abandonment of the northern Southwest by discussing the Mesa Verdeans' western neighbors, the Kayenta Anasazi of northern Arizona and southern Utah. Mesa Verdeans and Kayentans confronted a variety of environmental conditions, variations, and changes with similar technologies and subsistence strategies. Their markedly different behavioral responses to these challenges illuminate the range of social processes involved in the cultural and demographic transformations of the 1250–1350 period across the Southwest. Such comparisons help characterize the complex interplay of variations in environment, human demography, and behavior and the complicated web of causes and effects involved in such human transformations.

Originally, I had intended to focus my evaluation of the Amerind Seminar presentations on environmental issues and to offer only a few general comparative observations on Kayenta Branch prehistory. During the course of the meeting, however, I frequently found myself leaping to my feet (metaphorically) to point out that events in the Kayenta area departed significantly from generalizations being made about the central Mesa Verde area. It became apparent that Kayenta behavior at crucial times and under critical circumstances was nearly the opposite of that of the Mesa Verdeans. Indeed, the situation became so extreme (bordering on the outrageous) that James Allison suggested that the Kayentans be dubbed the "anti–eastern Anasazi." As the exceptions accumulated, it became clear that the Kayenta Branch offered contrasts to the Mesa Verde situation that amplified understanding of the human exodus from the Four Corners region around AD 1300. Therefore, I feel justified in expanding the Kayenta discussion into an examination of differing contemporaneous behavioral responses to similar, but not identical, demographic, environmental, and historical pressures in adjacent localities.

Environmental Considerations

Environment has long been recognized as a critical factor in the human occupation of the Southwest (U. Francis Duff 1904:303). Anglo settlers' struggles to scratch out a living from a harsh landscape coupled with their appreciation of Native Americans' subtle adaptations to local environmental conditions impressed early observers with the iron grip that the environment exerted on human survival in this marginal region. Obviously, the same conditions held for the past inhabitants of the region, the material remains of whose activities dotted the countryside. This realization stimulated an archaeological concern for understanding past environments that began in the late 1800s and persists in an intensified form into the present. Depending on one's theoretical leanings and approach to explaining human behavior, the topic of environmental impact on human behavior remains controversial, and it is not surprising that the chapters in this volume express different opinions in this regard. Most scholars should be able to agree, however, that the more we know about the environment and its vagaries, the better able we will be to resolve questions about human interactions with the external world. The ongoing refinement of existing techniques of paleoenvironmental reconstruction and the continuing development of new analytical methods will improve understanding of the environmental stability, variation, and change that affected the inhabitants of the region. Therefore, paleoenvironmental reconstruction will remain an important concern of southwestern archaeology for the foreseeable future.

It comes as no surprise, then, that the present volume includes a number of sophisticated reconstructions of past environmental variability and several efforts to relate past human behavior to these variations. The quality and breadth of these studies is most impressive, eloquent testimony to how much has been learned about past environment in the study area since the publication of the special Mesa Verde–Rio Grande number of the *Journal of Anthropological Archaeology* (Cameron, ed., 1995).

By plotting numbers of tree-ring cutting dates against averaged dendroclimatic reconstructions for the Southwest, Berry and Benson (this vol.) document a positive relationship between tree-cutting activity and favorable (wet) climatic conditions, a relationship first specified for the Mesa Verde area by Burns (1983). In particular, Berry and Benson show a marked regional diminution in the number of cutting dates during the severe droughts of the middle-twelfth and late-thirteenth centuries, two events that loom large throughout this volume. Kohler (this vol.) reports the Village Ecodynamics Project's dendroclimatic reconstruction of high- and low-frequency variation in potential crop yields in the study area. The high-frequency component of the Village Ecodynamics Project's effort modifies Van West's (1994) GIS-based reconstructions to produce more reasonable estimates of past annual crop yields. The most innovative aspect of the Village Ecodynamics Project's analysis is the use of two high-elevation, temperature-sensitive bristlecone-pine tree-ring chronologies—from Almagre Mountain, Colorado, and San Francisco Peaks, Arizona—to add a low-frequency temperature component to the production estimates, an objective pursued by Petersen (1988) in the Mesa Verde area and by Salzer (2000a; Salzer and Kipfmueller 2005) in the Flagstaff area. Despite the acknowledged methodological pitfalls of this approach (Kohler, this vol.), the Village Ecodynamics Project's combined high-low frequency crop-yield reconstruction exhibits considerable explanatory power.

Wright (this vol., 2006) employs a different approach to low-frequency temperature reconstruction. Instead of using tree rings, he relies on the ratio of ponderosa pine to Englemann spruce pollen frequencies in a radiocarbon-dated stratigraphic sequence from this subalpine fen in the La Plata Mountains on the northeastern periphery of the central Mesa Verde area. Despite the lower chronological resolution of Wright's pollen study, his temperature reconstruction resembles the low-frequency aspects of the Village Ecodynamics Project's annually resolved reconstruction (Wright, this vol.: fig. 4.2). The convergence of these independent reconstructions enhances confidence in both. Wright also compares dendroclimatic precipitation reconstructions for the central Mesa Verde area and six other areas (western Mesa Verde, northern Rio Grande, southern Colorado Plateau, Kayenta, Mogollon Rim, and below the Rim) across the region. In addition to characterizing spatial variability in temperature and precipitation, this analysis identifies periods of combined moisture- and temperature-induced stress (Wright, this vol.: fig. 4.3) that can be related to population movements and behavioral changes.

Commendably, the seminar did not neglect anthropogenic environmental impacts as demonstrated by Duff et al.'s (this vol.) analysis of the environmental effects of farming and roof-beam and fuelwood procurement in the vicinity of Shields Pueblo.

The studies reported here and other research define natural and anthropogenic environmental deteriorations that, along with nonenvironmental factors, created serious subsistence stress on the human societies of the area (Kohler, this vol.). These results are incorporated into many of the other chapters in this volume to assess the role of environmental variability in triggering the Mesa Verdean exodus at the end of the thirteenth century and in determining the destinations of the emigrants.

In addition to illuminating the human past, the environmental applications presented in this volume raise important issues concerning the nature of paleoenvironmental reconstructions and the ways in which they can be most effectively related to human behavior, particularly that of the central Mesa Verde study area. Because there is little I can add to or subtract from these presentations, I present here a few observations and cautions that may help clarify or advance research along these lines. Note that most of these remarks refer to paleoenvironmental analysis in general and not specifically to the studies reported in this volume. Two issues are especially important in this regard: (1) conceptual and terminological specificity and (2) careful assessment of the relevance of paleoenvironmental reconstructions to specific archaeological cases.

First, following Mark Varien's call to the Amerind Foundation seminar for greater precision and rigor in archaeological terminology, I argue that environmental considerations in archaeological discourse merit an equal degree of exactitude. Conceptual clarity and consistency are essential to understanding past environmental variations, comparing them coherently across time and space, and relating them to human behavior. Slipshod use of key concepts and terms impedes achieving these goals. For example, the archaeological literature exhibits an unfortunate tendency to conflate *environment* and *climate*, which often obscures or deflects attention from potentially important nonclimatic aspects of the environment. Climate is part of the environment, but not the totality of it. Important nonclimatic factors include fluvial processes, insect infestations, plant diseases, soil depletion, the distributions of natural resources, anthropogenic effects, and many others. Maintaining the distinction between climate and other environmental factors sharpens the focus on all relevant aspects of the environment and is vital to better understanding human-environment relationships.

It is important to recognize fundamental aspects of the temporal structure of the environment. *Stability* exists when the boundary conditions that regulate a prevailing system remain stable. Southwestern climate type has been stable at least since the end of the Altithermal, when atmospheric circulation patterns and other factors that regulate modern climate were established. *Variability* refers to fluctuations within limits established by prevailing boundary conditions. Southwestern climate during the period of interest here has been characterized by fluctuations around means and variances established by stable boundary conditions. Environmental *change* occurs when limiting conditions themselves change to transform one state into another. The many droughts evident in southwestern tree-ring records represent variation, not change. True climate change occurred at the transition from the Pleistocene to the Holocene and may be happening now due to global warming and other anthropogenic causes.

Another important aspect of southwestern environment is the kind of variability represented (Dean 1988b, 1996a, 2000). *Stable* aspects have not changed appreciably over the time period of interest, that is, the last four thousand years or so. Stable features include things such as climate type, bedrock geology, and large-scale topography. Present conditions are adequate indicators of stable features that need not be reconstructed. *Low-frequency* and *high-frequency* aspects of the environment (such as fluvial processes and climate) vary at cycles shorter than the study period. Because present conditions do not accurately reflect past low- and high-frequency conditions, such variations must be reconstructed using various paleoenvironmental techniques. *Episodic* factors (such as earthquakes and volcanic eruptions) exhibit no known periodicity and must be identified in the geologic or archaeological records. Environmental variation has several important attributes in addition to *amplitude* (warm vs. cool, dry vs. wet, etc.). *Temporal* variability captures the rate (gradual or rapid) of change from maximum to minimum values. *Spatial* variability reflects how conditions differed from one place to another. *Coherence* describes the geographical pattern of association among recording stations, that is, which stations behave similarly or differently through time.

There are two basic kinds of paleoenvironmental reconstruction: *qualitative* reconstructions record relative variability in environmental factors, whereas *quantitative* reconstructions produce results in standard units of measurement such as inches of precipitation and degrees of temperature. Consistent application of these or equivalent agreed-upon concepts and terms would significantly clarify archaeological dialogue on environmental matters.

On a larger scale, I think it is bad practice to apply climatic concepts from other parts of the world to the Southwest when we are uncertain as to whether such remote phenomena actually affected the latter region and, if they did, how they were expressed there. Cases in point are the Medieval Warm Period and Little Ice Age, both of which are defined by environmental variations in northern Europe (Hughes and Diaz 1994; Grove 1988). A major drawback in transferring these concepts to the Southwest is the tendency to distort them to fit the southwestern situation by altering both their time spans and the criteria by which they are defined. Although its name implies that the Medieval Warm Period spanned the medieval era, historically placed between AD 500 and 1500, the Medieval Warm Period's creator, H. H. Lamb (1965), confined it to a fairly brief period centered on the twelfth century AD (Hughes and Diaz 1994). Consensus among paleoclimatologists generally restricts the Little Ice Age to around AD 1550–1850 (Bradley 1999:763; Grove 1988:4), a far cry from statements, based on local evidence, that it began as early as the thirteenth century in the Southwest (LeBlanc 1999; Petersen 1988). The unusually cool southwestern climate of the thirteenth century (Petersen 1988; Salzer 2000a; Wright, this vol.: fig. 4.3), however, cannot be shown to be related to the sixteenth-century glacier expansions that define the Little Ice Age, and nothing is to be gained by linking these phenomena. To paraphrase several prominent paleoenvironmentalists: "If you're not talking about glaciers, you're not talking about the Little Ice Age." We in the Southwest are not talking about glaciers, and we should be content simply with identifying abnormally cool periods rather than imposing an extraneous and unnecessary concept on the Southwest.

A related problem is whether the European Medieval Warm Period and Little Ice Age reflect climatic excursions everywhere in the world or whether they are more localized. In fact, neither of these phenomena can be objectively identified as long, continuous deviations from climatic means outside of Europe; rather, these time periods are characterized elsewhere by discontinuous cool episodes interspersed among warmer intervals (Bradley 1999). A comprehensive study of worldwide temperature variation (Mann et al. 1998) failed to generate strong evidence for a global or prolonged Little Ice Age. Salzer's (2000a; Salzer and Kipfmueller 2005) Flagstaff-area temperature reconstruction shows only intermittent cool intervals between 1550 and 1850 and anomalous warmth during the entire eighteenth century. Even if the Medieval Warm Period and Little Ice Age were global phenomena, there is no reason to expect their effects to be similar worldwide (Jansen et al. 2007:468–469). Anomalous warmth or cold in Europe does not necessarily equate to unusually warm or cool conditions in the Southwest any more than an El Niño event produces identical effects everywhere in the world. To conclude, both the Medieval Warm Period and Little Ice Age concepts are sufficiently imprecise and carry so many extraneous connotations that to apply them to the Southwest is confusing at best and misleading at worst. Instead, reliance should be placed on specific paleoenvironmental evidence for the region in question, in this case the Southwest, rather than on dubious connections to exogenous phenomena of uncertain relevance to the issues at hand. Second, care must be taken in applying paleoenvironmental reconstructions to particular archaeological contexts. Such applications must take into account the environmental factors to which each reconstruction technique is sensitive, the temporal and spatial scales and resolution involved, and the original purpose for which the reconstruction was made. Insensitivity to specific environmental factors can limit a technique's applicability to certain kinds of human activity. Because of the analytical techniques and large-scale geographic partitioning used, continental dendroclimatic reconstructions (Cook et al. 2007; Herweijer et al. 2007) commonly lack the spatial resolution necessary to investigate certain topics. Although such studies can identify megadroughts that affected much of North America, they cannot reveal more localized food-production differentials that may have influenced events like the depopulation of the Four Corners area. Most reconstructions are performed to illuminate topics other than human-environment interactions. For example, the vast majority of dendroclimatic reconstructions are undertaken to advance knowledge of climate, and their relevance to specific questions about human behavior may be limited. Knowledge of general atmospheric circulation patterns may be less useful than estimates of how much rain fell on a specific piece of ground in a specified year.

Some ways of relating past human behavior to paleoenvironment are more fruitful than others. The late, lamented SARG taught us that it is fairly unproductive to simply look for matches between environmental perturbations and apparent disruptions in the archaeological record (Dean 1978b). Even when such coincidences exist, the likelihood that the former caused the latter is hard to assess. Rather, progress is made by testing hypotheses based on plausible models linking environmental variability and change to human behavior. Human adaptation to environmental stability, variation, and change results from the complex interplay of environment, human demography, and behavior (Dean 1988b). Similar environmental perturbations do not necessarily trigger identical behavioral responses under any and all demographic and cultural conditions. Unless we have some ideas about which behaviors are likely to succeed in different contexts, we have no way of knowing when observed behavior is an outcome of environmental stresses or some other cause(s). For example, low population levels allow responses to environmental factors different from responses possible with high population levels (as Berry and Benson, and Kohler, note in this volume). Contextual differences such as these may help explain why earlier environmental stresses in the study area did not cause abandonments similar to those associated with the severe environmental degradation of the late thirteenth century. The authors of the chapters in this volume do an excellent job of examining alternative explanations for observed behavior that involve the full range of relevant environmental, demographic, behavioral, and historical factors.

The Kayenta Contrarians

The archaeological attributes (pottery, architecture, site configurations, settlement patterns) that distinguish Kayenta from Mesa Verde are too well documented (Dean 1996b, 2002; Gladwin and Gladwin 1934; Kidder [1924] 1962; McGregor 1941) to require repetition here. Rather, more inferential aspects of past human behavior and organization illuminate human-human and human-environment interactions that help account for the manifest differences in the processes involved in the Mesa Verde and Kayenta emigrations from the Four Corners region.

Before considering the differences, however, the basic similarities between the two situations should be addressed. The Mesa Verde and Kayenta areas were subject to similar (but not identical) environmental conditions, variations, and changes from the beginning of the Holocene to the present (Betancourt 1990; Petersen 1988). In particular, both areas were afflicted with major droughts in the middle twelfth and late thirteenth centuries. Both groups participated (differentially) in the same basic Anasazi cultural tradition that evolved on the southern Colorado Plateau after the adoption of agriculture at the end of the Archaic period. This joint heritage is embodied in comparable settlement trajectories evidenced from pithouse hamlets to large pueblos codified in the Pecos Classification (Kidder 1927) and in various phase sequences. Shared environmental knowledge and similar subsistence technologies were entrained to extract a living from similar assemblages of wild plants and animals and the same suite of crops: corn, beans, squash, and various commensal species. Mesa Verde and Kayenta societies organized households into progressively larger, higher-level units culminating in multivillage communities sometimes linked by "roads" and line-of-sight communications systems. Religious commonalities include the development and use of kivas with analogous configurations, attributes, and features; the association of kivas with groups of domestic structures; and, to a lesser degree, the occasional use of great kivas. Both groups departed the Four Corners region for distant destinations at the end of the thirteenth century. Beyond these commonalities, dissimilarities begin to outweigh the similarities.

Despite abutting one another, the environments of the Mesa Verde and Kayenta areas differ in several important respects. The higher central Mesa Verde area comprises an array of broad, discontinuous uplands separated by relatively narrow southwest- and west-trending drainages. Deep, fertile soils, adequate precipitation, and warm southwestern exposures combine to make the uplands in the central Mesa Verde area the most productive dry-farming locality in the Southwest, both in the remote past and now. The lowlands of this area consist primarily of narrow canyons with constricted bands of alluvium that provide only limited potential for floodplain agriculture. In sharp contrast, the lower-elevation Kayenta environment is characterized by barren, unproductive uplands only locally suitable for intensive farming and by numerous lowland valleys and canyons filled with Holocene sediments suitable for floodplain agriculture. Because Kayenta-area precipitation is considerably lower than that of the Mesa Verde uplands (Wright, this vol.: figs. 4.1 and 4.4), Kayenta farming depends more on alluvial groundwater than on generally insufficient and unreliable precipitation.

Although there can be little doubt that Mesa Verde and Kayenta people shared the same body of environmental knowledge and subsistence practices, different aspects of their technologies were drawn upon to cope with the disparate environments of the two areas. Mesa Verdeans depended primarily on precipitation-controlled dry farming of upland areas, with only limited reliance on floodplain agriculture along the drainages. While floodplain processes were not important in the Mesa Verde uplands, where dry farming prevailed (Varien, this vol.), they were undoubtedly significant in nearby drainages, such as McElmo Canyon. Some of the human conflict evident in the Mesa Verde area in the middle twelfth and late thirteenth centuries could have resulted from competition between upland dwellers and lowlanders displaced by arroyo cutting and alluvial groundwater decretion or from attempts by stressed uplanders to appropriate arable land in the lowlands. In contrast, the Kayentans were masters of the lowland floodplains, where alluvial groundwater rather than precipitation was the primary limiting factor in the agricultural equation (Dean 1969, 2006). Even in the Kayenta uplands, such as those around Navajo Mountain, farming relied less on direct rainfall than on water-management techniques adapted to lowland environments (Lindsay 1961). As a result, the Mesa Verdeans were more vulnerable to high-frequency environmental variability (rainfall) than were the Kayentans, who were more susceptible to low-frequency environmental processes (Dean 1988b, 1996b), such as the rise and fall of alluvial water tables. At times, this situation provided the Kayentans with a greater degree of subsistence stability than that enjoyed by the Mesa Verdeans.

Important demographic differences also distinguish the two areas. The population of the central Mesa Verde area far exceeded that of the Kayenta area. As many as 20,000 people are estimated for the former (Varien, this vol.), while the latter probably never surpassed 7,500 individuals (Dean, Doelle, and Orcutt 1994: fig. 4.2). Population maxima were achieved at different times. Mesa Verde population is estimated to have peaked sometime between 1225 and 1260 (Varien, this vol.), well before the late-thirteenth-century emigration, while Kayenta population probably crested between 1250 and 1285 (Dean 1996b, 2002; Dean, Doelle, and Orcutt 1994), only a few years before the exodus around 1300. Particularly in the eastern part of the central Mesa Verde area, local population densities exceeded those of the Kayenta area, which peaked at places in the Klethla, Long House, and Kayenta valleys (Dean, Lindsay, and Robinson 1978; Haas and Creamer 1993) and on the Rainbow Plateau (Lindsay et al. 1968).

Throughout much of its history, Kayenta society was less complex than that of the central Mesa Verde area. This disparity is reflected in the time lag in Kayenta attainment of levels of social organization that characterized the Pecos Classification periods defined in the Mesa Verde area. Already-existing social divergences began to widen during the Pueblo I period, which began in the Mesa Verde area around AD 700 and in the Kayenta area around AD 850. By AD 900, some Mesa Verdeans were living in extremely large villages composed of numerous residential units (households?) that occupied suites of living and storage chambers incorporated into masonry roomblocks. Households were integrated into larger subvillage and village units by activities that took place in large communal pit structures (great kivas). At roughly the same time, Kayenta households occupied individual habitation units comprising residential pithouses and external, contiguous, slab-lined storage cists. Occasionally, such households were loosely organized into fairly large villages that lacked obvious communal structures. Parenthetically, such structures (great kivas) were present in earlier Basketmaker III villages (Gilpin and Benallie 2000) but disappeared permanently from the Kayenta cultural tradition by Pueblo I.

Differentiation continued into the succeeding Pueblo II period, which began around AD 900 in the east and a century later in the west. Even though both areas were characterized by some disaggregation of large settlements and dispersion of population, the Kayentans took these trends to extremes not evident in the Mesa Verde area. People of both groups inhabited sites exhibiting the classic unit pueblo configuration of an aligned masonry roomblock, kiva, and trashmound (Prudden 1903), but the Kayentans lacked contiguous agglomerations of such units as well as communal features, such as great kivas, for integrating multi-unit communities. Furthermore, the Kayenta population exhibited an almost pathological aversion to aggregation, spacing their habitations almost uniformly across the landscape (Dean, Lindsay, and Robinson 1978: fig. 1), dispersing into empty areas, and expanding beyond the northern and western peripheries of their former territory.

Of greatest importance here are differences that developed during the Pueblo III period as defined in the Mesa Verde archaeological sequence (AD 1100–1300). In the Kayenta area, the Pueblo II pattern persisted until around AD 1150, when it was terminated by major demographic and cultural changes. During a hundred-year "transitional" interval (AD 1150–1250), Kayenta peoples withdrew from the peripheries of their distribution, abandoned numerous upland zones (such as northern Black Mesa) within their "traditional" territory, and began concentrating along well-watered locations in the "heartland." During this interval, they experimented with a wide variety of settlement configurations ranging from small pithouse hamlets to medium-sized plaza-oriented pueblos with various combinations of pithouse residences and masonry habitation and storage chambers. Although "classic" unit pueblos lasted into this period, they were outnumbered by other site configurations. Through it all, the household, either singly or organized into hamlets through activities associated with (usually) one kiva, remained the basic unit of social organization. There is no evidence for larger communities comprising multiple hamlets or villages. These patterns contrast strongly with contemporaneous developments in the Mesa Verde area, which saw the (re)establishment of large, complex sites in which households were integrated into larger kiva-courtyard units, which, in turn, were organized into fairly large villages and multivillage communities.

A true Pueblo III archaeological pattern did not emerge in the Kayenta area until around AD 1250, more than a century after the development of such configurations in the Mesa Verde area. The Kayenta Branch Tsegi Phase (AD 1250–1300) was characterized by the development of medium to large villages, most of which exhibited one of three main configurations: (1) large, rather amorphous pithouse villages; (2) villages composed of room clusters and courtyard complexes; and (3) villages with masonry roomblocks organized around one or more plazas. Despite the size and complexity of some of these villages, the household is universally present in the form of room clusters and courtyard complexes (Dean 1969, 1970; Lindsay 1969) and remained the basic unit of social organization both structurally and behaviorally. Absent from most Kayenta sites were multihousehold groups focused on small plazas containing kivas similar to the kiva-courtyard groups in late Mesa Verde sites. In extremely large Kayenta sites, such as Long House (Dean 2002: fig. 6.13), structural units intermediate between room clusters (households) and entire sites (villages) appear to be small- to medium-sized plaza-oriented pueblos. Typically, kivas are associated with villages as wholes and not with smaller units within villages.

Strong evidence exists throughout the Kayenta area for a four-tier Tsegi Phase settlement organization consisting of (1) residential pueblos, (2) central pueblos that served as foci of (3) communities comprising numerous residential pueblos, and (4) groupings of communities linked by line-of-sight relationships between their central pueblos. Such organizations were apparently fairly loosely structured, and this pattern was short-lived, probably lasting for no more than twenty-five years (1275–1300). Evidence from Tsegi Canyon cliff dwellings indicates a great deal of flexibility in the Kayentans' ability to accommodate the mobility of various constituent social units (Dean 1969). At Kiet Siel, households came and went (and/or were formed and dissolved) with no evident disruption of the overall cohesion of the village, while at Betatakin, both household and village-level behavior are evident. As opposed to the more rigid organization of Pueblo III Mesa Verde society (Hegmon et al. 2008; Kohler, this vol.), extreme adaptability in the face of environmental and social adversity was a hallmark of contemporaneous Kayenta behavior.

Different historical trajectories distinguished the Mesa Verde and Kayenta areas as well. The Kayentans were relatively immune to unifying forces that swept the Anasazi world from time to time. Most notably, they seemed impervious to the expansion of the Chaco Phenomenon in the eleventh and twelfth centuries. Even though the Chacoan colossus lapped up against the southeastern, eastern, and northeastern margins of the Kayenta area, there is little evidence that the Kayentans succumbed to its influence. While aggregation was the word of the day in the east during the Chacoan golden age, extreme dispersal was the Kayenta maxim at the same time. Apart from a few examples along the south-eastern margin of Black Mesa, no Chacoan outlier communities, great houses, or great kivas penetrated the Kayenta heartland, perhaps because of Kayenta avoidance of aggregation. The number of imported Chacoan ceramic vessels found in the Kayenta area can probably be counted on the fingers of two hands. The Kayentans' independence from the highly structured Chacoan system may have allowed them to preserve the behavioral flexibility necessary to withstand subsequent environmental and social perturbations that had more calamitous consequences for the eastern Anasazi, Mesa Verdeans included (Kohler, this vol.).

Resolute independence notwithstanding, there is abundant evidence that Kayenta people maintained relationships with other inhabitants of the region. Kayenta potters participated in the pottery design-style conventions that occasionally spread throughout the Anasazi domain (Plog 1983). Especially after AD 1150, Kayenta and Mesa Verde people interacted in numerous ways, even commingling along their common frontier in southeastern Utah. The most abundant imported pottery in the Kayenta area came from Mesa Verdean sources, although Kayenta pottery is comparatively rare in Mesa Verde sites. The occurrence of towers in three Tsegi Phase contexts—Poncho House (Guernsey 1931), Ruin 8 (Fewkes 1911; Kidder and Guernsey 1919), and Kiet Siel (Dean 1969)—denotes the limited borrowing of a Mesa Verdean architectural form, if not its function. A room executed in Mesa Verde–style masonry and incorporating a Mesa Verde–style doorway suggests the presence of a Mesa Verdean immigrant at Kiet Siel (Dean 1969). But shared pot-tery production and design conventions—exemplified by near identities between Kayenta and Tusayan pottery (Smith 1971) and by white-outlined polychrome painting (Beals, Brainerd, and Smith 1945)—and the sub-sequent movements of migrant groups specify strong Kayenta ties to the south, especially with the Tusayan Branch inhabitants of the Hopi

Mesas area and with Western Pueblo groups along the Mogollon Rim that are absent from the Mesa Verde area. Conversely, Mesa Verde connections to the Rio Grande area to the east (Ortman, this vol.) were not shared by Kayenta people. Such divergent contacts were undoubtedly important determinants of the final destinations of emigrants from the Mesa Verde and Kayenta areas.

The aforementioned environmental, demographic, sociocultural, and historical deviations were probably important elements in the markedly different behavioral responses of Kayenta and Mesa Verde people to the two major episodes of environmental, demographic, and social stress of the Pueblo III period, the middle 1100s and the late 1200s, both of which were characterized by low- and high-frequency environmental deterioration. As developed above, the inhabitants of the Mesa Verde area were especially vulnerable to the high-frequency climatic aspects of this downturn, while the Kayentans were adversely affected by both components of the environmental situation. As documented in this volume and elsewhere (Kuckelman, Lightfoot, and Martin 2002), in the Mesa Verde area, each interval was characterized by a pronounced increase in intra- and intercommunity strife as exemplified by murder, physical combat (warfare), cannibalism, and, ultimately in the thirteenth century, large-scale emigration. These behaviors were undoubtedly occasioned by unfortunate combinations of natural and anthropogenic environmental degradation, high population levels that strained the productive capacities of the reduced amount of land available for exploitation, competition for resources limited by both environmental problems and intergroup antagonisms, and rigid social organization constrained by both internal structure and external pressures (Kohler, this vol.).

Kayenta responses to the stresses of these two periods differed radically from those of the Mesa Verdeans. There is virtually no evidence in the Kayenta area for large-scale violence in either time period. Haas and Creamer (1993) argue that potentially defendable site locations (rock shelters and eminences) and restricted access to parts of some sites indicate the existence of overt conflict occasioned by competition for diminishing resources (food) during the Tsegi Phase. These features, however, can be more parsimoniously explained by other factors (Dean 1996b, 2002). Cliff dwellings are not inherently defensive and, given certain kinds of conflict, can be death traps. Construction on eminences generally involves central pueblos, whose locations are dictated by line-of-sight requirements, rather than ordinary residential pueblos, which do not require such visual connections. Intervisibility itself does not necessarily imply defense for two reasons. First, intervisibility could have served purposes other than defense, such as coordinating communal secular and ceremonial activities. Second, some of the line-of-sight systems are too small (Long House Valley) or too large (Rainbow Plateau, Paiute Mesa) to have served any useful defensive purposes. Access restrictions, such as those at Long House (Dean 2002: fig. 6.13) and Segazlin Mesa (Lindsay et al. 1968), were more likely designed to channel secular and religious traffic away from residential areas and into public places, such as plazas, where communal activities took place.

Other considerations also argue against defense in the Kayenta area. The placement of many sites, such as Betatakin, some distance from and out of sight of the fields would not have been a sensible reaction to the threat of raiders seeking food. Furthermore, the numerous isolated storage rooms, probably used to stockpile seed corn near the fields, would have been totally vulnerable to human predation. Tellingly, domestic water sources (seeps, springs, natural tanks, and reservoirs) are commonly situated outside the walls of both cliff dwellings (Betatakin, Batwoman House, Twin Caves Pueblo [Dean 1969]) and open sites (Long House [Dean 2002], Tower House [Kidder and Guernsey 1919], Red House, Yellow House), not an effective precaution against potential sieges. The vast majority of the many "loopholes" that pierce masonry walls would have been useless in combat because of their severely restricted "fields of fire" and the near impossibility of accurately firing arrows through them. At best, these features could have served as observation ports, often commanding tiny fields of view. The vast majority of sites of both periods are in open, undefendable locations, often far from possible refuges (central pueblos in the Tsegi Phase). Small, isolated field houses and other limited-activity sites located some distance from the nearest residential pueblos are abundant. Finally, the Kayenta area is characterized by a notable lack of evidence for the harsh treatment of people by other humans. Only a few skeletons exhibit injuries that can be attributed to causes other than everyday hazards encountered by people living rough, unsafe lives (Ryan 1977). There were no massacres, battles, or incidents of cannibalism such as those in the Mesa Verde area.

Sites abandoned during the late thirteenth-century emigration from the Kayenta area exhibit radically different abandonment behavior from that seen in the central Mesa Verde, where many sites were clearly vacated hastily and under duress. Tsegi Phase sites are replete with evidence for orderly, programmed abandonment incompatible with hurried departures forced by internal or external strife. The dearth of de facto refuse and portable items indicates methodical, perhaps staged removal of transportable materials. The removal of metates from their bins represents the perpetuation of a traditional Kayenta abandonment behavior that went back at least as far as the Pueblo I period (middle 800s). Sealed granaries at Kiet Siel, Twin Caves Pueblo, and other sites imply intentions to return. Although the idea remains unverifiable, it seems likely that the huge white fir log positioned across the entrance to Kiet Siel represents a deliberate act of closure, a statement of continued ownership, and a warning to others to keep out of the empty pueblo.

Perhaps the most remarkable contrast between the Mesa Verde and Kayenta abandonments of the Four Corners region around AD 1300 is the vast difference in our ability to archaeologically trace the movements of these emigrants in time and space. Except for site-unit intrusions near Gallina Springs and Socorro (Lekson et al. 2002), evidence for Mesa Verde movement into the Rio Grande Valley, though commonly affirmed (Ortman, this vol.), remains controversial (Boyer et al., this vol.; Cameron, this vol.). On the other hand, Kayenta migrants are easily followed through distributions of unique pottery attributes, architectural features, and site layouts. In conformance with evidence indicating premigration ties to other groups, Kayenta movements generally took a southward direction. The majority of the Kayenta migrants undoubtedly joined closely related Tusayan Branch societies in the Hopi Mesas–Antelope Mesa area to the south. Others, however, leapfrogged this area to localities even farther south. In the most famous migration in southwestern archaeology (Haury 1958)—indicated by the presence of Kayenta pottery, local copies of Kayenta pottery, an intrusive pueblo roomblock, a D-shaped kiva, and exogenous human skeletal traits— Kayenta-Tusayan immigrants showed up at Point of Pines below the Mogollon Rim. Other site-unit intrusions, architectural traits, pottery, and a ceremonial cache identify Kayenta immigrants in the Safford (Wasley 1962; Woodson 1999) and San Pedro (Clark 2007a; Di Peso

1958b; Lindsay 1987; Lyons 2003) valleys of southern Arizona, a movement that is now thought to extend into western New Mexico (anonymous 2008; Clark et al. 2008; Vanderpool 2008). The distribution of Kayenta-affiliated pottery forms and attributes—such as rim-perforated plates (Clark 2007a; Lyons 2003) and Tucson Polychrome pottery (Lindsay 1992), which is derived from Kiet Siel Polychrome—denote an even wider spread of Kayenta influence. Finally, "western pueblo" presences in the Grasshopper area (Reid 1989) and Tonto basin (Clark 2001) may identify additional Kayenta southward intrusions. Extreme southern traces of Kayenta influence fade away (become archaeologically invisible) sometime in the fourteenth century.

Two major questions arise from the foregoing comparison of the Kayenta and Mesa Verde abandonments of the Four Corners region at the end of the thirteenth century. First, why did these people, so similar to each other in many ways and, indeed, in sustained contact with each other, respond so differently to the pressures of thirteenth-century life on the Colorado Plateau? Second, why is it so much easier archaeologically to track the Kayenta emigration all the way to southern Arizona (and New Mexico?) than it is to follow the Mesa Verdeans' exodus from the Four Corners? These questions are not unrelated but are treated separately for clarity.

The first question can be simply answered with two words: stability and flexibility. For long periods of time (for example, ca. AD 400–750, 925–1250, 1500–1880), floodplain aggradation and high alluvial water tables provided Kayenta-area farmers (Anasazi and Navajo alike) with a degree of subsistence stability unmatched in the Mesa Verde area, where the majority of the population depended on highly variable precipitation. Due to higher elevations, the Mesa Verdeans might also have been more vulnerable to depressed temperatures, although cold-air drainage might have impeded farming in the Kayenta lowlands. Even in times characterized by arroyo cutting and groundwater decretion (ca. AD 250–400, 750–925, 1250–1500, 1880–present), floodplain farming provided a degree of subsistence stability for limited numbers of Kayentans (and Navajos), who occupied localities suitable for agriculture given these conditions. Once floodplain degradation began around 1250, Kayenta agriculture became more dependent on insufficient and unreliable precipitation, and not long afterward, these people left the region. Significantly, the majority of the Kayenta emigrants probably went first to the Hopi Mesas area, where low-frequency environmental processes sustained greater subsistence stability than was then available in the Kayenta heartland (Dean 1966, 1969; Hack 1942).

A high degree of behavioral and social flexibility provided Kayentans with a level of adaptive stability not evident in the central Mesa Verde area (Kohler, this vol.). Kayenta settlement location was commonly adjusted to low-frequency floodplain conditions. During periods of aggradation and water-table accretion, especially during the 925–1250 period, Kayenta settlements were dispersed widely across the landscape. During periods of floodplain degradation, settlement was concentrated in localities suitable for farming, given arroyo cutting and depressed alluvial groundwater levels. As a result, Pueblo I (850–1000) and Tsegi Phase (1250–1300) sites commonly occur together in the same places, many of which, not coincidently, are currently farmed by Navajos. As long as population did not exceed levels that could be supported by these special localities, subsistence stress would have been manageable. Such levels were reached only after 1200 and became a problem only after the inception of floodplain degradation after 1250. Thus, during the Tsegi Phase, access to agricultural resources (mainly arable land) was limited by the natural environment rather than social factors similar to those that constrained Mesa Verdean access to such resources (Kohler, this vol.).

Organizational flexibility also characterized the Kayentans through-out their history. Aggregation into large settlements occurred during the Pueblo I period and the Tsegi Phase, when floodplain processes limited the distribution of farmable locations. As soon as aggradation reopened the entire floodplains to farming during the Pueblo II period, the large Pueblo I communities dissolved into smaller, widely dispersed unit-pueblo configurations. The social arrangements that allowed large Pueblo I communities to exist gave way to different arrangements appropriate for small, dispersed communities. During the Transition period (1150–1250), which occurred during a major drought and a secondary low-frequency environmental regression, a variety of social arrangements, ranging from small pithouse hamlets to medium-sized plaza-oriented pueblos, prevailed, a further outcome of Kayentan social plasticity. By 1250, these organizational experiments had crystallized into the completely different, more complex, but not totally homogeneous Tsegi Phase pattern. The one constant through all these transformations was the integrity of the household, which was the basic building block of all Kayenta social configurations from the Basketmaker III period through the Tsegi Phase. From AD 600 through 1300, Kayentans exhibited an extraordinary aptitude for organizing households in an amazing number of ways.

Kayenta social flexibility was founded on the ability to maintain a basic unit of organization, the household, and merge it with other households, into a variety of larger, more inclusive entities as circumstances warranted. At the same time, the Kayenta people retained the ability to reconfigure the larger units by recombining their constituent parts and to deconstruct them into smaller components. This social adaptability not only allowed the people to survive in a harsh and unpredictable environment, it also facilitated the integration of post-1300 Kayenta immigrants into established communities and already inhabited areas across much of the western Southwest. Kayentans could travel as individual households or various combinations of households and reform these units as required by local circumstances.

Several factors may account for the Kayentans' ability to retain such adaptive flexibility for nearly a millennium. First, such fluidity was probably necessary for survival in the marginal and unreliable environments of the western Anasazi area. Second, the integrity and independence of the household provided a solid organizational foundation for Kayenta society. The evident aversion to aggregation and consequent centrifugal settlement history probably reflect the organizational strength of the household. Third, the Kayentans' relative isolation from contemporaneous groups, whether self-imposed or fortuitous, made them relatively impervious to more complex and rigid organizational principles emanating from Mesa Verdean and Chacoan centers. The fact that the Kayentans were not drawn into the Chacoan sphere of influence may have saved them from the disastrous sociocultural inflexibility that afflicted the Pueblo III Mesa Verdeans. Finally, and totally subjectively, the Kayenta people seem to me to evince a certain truculent resistance to outside ideas and pressures that did, perhaps, make them true contrarians determined to maintain their own identity in defiance of other people.

Many of the factors cited above in connection with the first question obviously also apply to the second question: Why can Kayenta migrants, unlike those from Mesa Verde, be traced over such long distances and time spans? Another factor, brought up at the seminar by John Ware, is the high probability that the Kayentans maintained their kinship system and its attendant social relationships through the environmental, demographic, and social upheavals of the late thirteenth and early fourteenth centuries. Kinship affiliations likely strengthened pre-1300 ties with societies to the south, helped determine the destinations of Kayenta migrants, and facilitated the integration of immigrant Kayenta households and larger units into existing communities. Strong kin relations, responsibilities, and markers also would have helped perpetuate the settlement, architectural, and pottery continuities that allow archaeologists to recognize Kayenta immigrants in postmigration contexts. Finally, a separate language may have played an important role in maintaining the Kayenta kinship system and marker traits, ensuring the cohesion of migrant Kayenta groups, such as those evident at Goat Hill (Woodson 1999) and in the San Pedro Valley (Di Peso 1958a), and integrating Kayenta immigrants into host communities, especially the closely related Tusayan Branch groups of the Hopi Mesas area.

Conclusion

The deliberations of the Amerind Foundation seminar go a long way toward resolving many of the ambiguities associated with the depopulation of the Mesa Verde area at the end of the thirteenth century. Highly sophisticated and problem-directed paleoenvironmental reconstructions illuminate many aspects of the natural world that would have impacted the people of the area, as well as the environmental effects of human behavior. At the same time, detailed archaeological studies elucidate the demographic and behavioral dimensions of the Mesa Verdean departure for, hopefully, better places to carry on their way of life. This volume brings these considerations to life and leaves us hungering for more. Fortunately, as is commonly the case, more questions than answers were generated by the seminar, and plenty remains to be done before we achieve a complete understanding of the massive depopulation of the northern Southwest.

Acknowledgments

Special thanks are due to Tim Kohler, Aaron M. Wright, and Mark Varien for convening two sessions entitled "New Light on the Thirteenth-Century Depopulation of the Northern Southwest"—one as a symposium at the seventy-second annual meeting of the Society for American Archaeology in April 2007, the other as a special seminar held at the Amerind Foundation in February 2008—and for inviting me to participate in both. As usual, John Ware and his capable staff at the Amerind Foundation provided an unmatched venue for formal deliberations and for after- and before-hours discussions that roved over numerous issues, both relevant and tangential to the seminar. Finally, I thank the other participants in the seminar who enlightened me on finer points of southwestern archaeology too numerous to mention.

14

Advances in Understanding the Thirteenth-Century Depopulation of the Northern Southwest

Catherine M. Cameron

In the two decades since David Anthony's (1990) "Baby and the Bathwater" article redirected our attention to migration, archaeologists have become increasingly sophisticated in their understanding of prehistoric population movement (see, for example, Bellwood and Renfrew 2002). This is especially true in the Southwest, where some scholars never quit studying migration (Dean 1969, 1970; Reid 1989) and where its revival has been warmly embraced. Certainly, the depopulation of the northern San Juan region has been a key research focus since the late nineteenth century. The "abandoned" cliff dwellings of Mesa Verde and adjacent areas have arguably colored our perception of prehispanic southwestern people and have also provided the public with one of its most popular "mysteries."

Although the depopulation of the northern San Juan region has never left archaeological center stage, the chapters in this volume provide a significant leap forward in our understanding of this episode of southwestern prehistory. This is so for several reasons. First, recent developments in climatic reconstruction in the northern San Juan, presented here, allow a very precise reconstruction of the environmental situation facing people in the thirteenth century. We have a less refined understanding of the paleoenvironment in other areas to which northern San Juan peoples may have migrated, such as the northern Rio Grande region, but advances have been made there, too. Second, the authors in this volume explore patterns on a very large scale, recognizing that the Southwest was in some ways a single large region, and that environmental change or population movement in one area had downstream effects on others. Third, the authors have recognized that single factors, such as drought or warfare, are insufficient as explanations for the northern San Juan depopulation and explore the complex interaction of environmental, social, and demographic factors to develop models for why and how depopulation took place, as well as its effect on other parts of the Southwest.

The success of this volume is in part a result of collaboration among scholars who have conducted research in southwestern Colorado for several decades. This collaboration began with the highly productive Dolores Archaeological Project of the late 1970s and 1980s, directed by David Breternitz of the University of Colorado. The Dolores Archaeological Project involved the collaboration of William Lipe and Timothy Kohler of Washington State University. In the early 1980s, the Crow Canyon Archaeological Center emerged as an institute for research and public education, and by the 1990s, it was the primary archaeological entity in southwestern Colorado. Crow Canyon Archaeological Center involved—as employees, research associates, or consultants—many former Dolores Archaeological Project personnel (including this volume's authors Eric Blinman, Tim Kohler, Kristin Kuckelman, Bill Lipe, Mark Varien, and Dean Wilson) and continued the productive collaboration with Washington State University. Crow Canyon Archaeological Center and Washington State University (as well as other southwestern universities, especially Arizona State University) have also trained a new generation of prominent archaeologists whose work is found in this volume (Donna Glowacki, Scott Ortman, Susan Ryan, and Aaron M. Wright). Jointly, the two institutions created the Village Ecodynamics Project, which developed much of the data for the central Mesa Verde region presented in these chapters.

This volume also includes the contributions of scholars with expertise outside southwestern Colorado, which creates the proper large scale for understanding the depopulation of the northern San Juan. Perhaps most exciting are links with the Coalescent Communities Database (Hill, Clark, and Doelle, this vol.), a compilation of data on sites throughout the Southwest that date to the thirteenth through the eighteenth centuries. The Coalescent Communities Database was developed by scholars from the Center for Desert Archaeology in Tucson (another prolific private archaeological institute) and by David Wilcox of the Museum of Northern Arizona. It incorporates information from the southern Southwest as well as the northern Southwest. Bringing together Village Ecodynamics Project and Coalescent Communities Database scholars and databases in this volume allows an examination of population dynamics on a very large scale that is essential to the complete understanding of southwestern historical processes. Berry and Benson (this vol.) use tree-ring data from the northern Southwest to provide a different but complementary view of large-scale population dynamics. The contributions of James Allison and a group of researchers from the northern Rio Grande are also critical to the success of this volume. Allison's contribution focuses on what was once called the "Northern Periphery" of the Southwest, linking developments, including depopulation, in that region to larger patterns in other parts of the Southwest. The expertise of Boyer and others in the northern Rio Grande region provides an essential balance to the assumptions of northern San Juan archaeologists concerning migrants' destinations after they left the northern San Juan region.

My goal is to highlight the advances this volume makes in understanding the northern San Juan depopulation and the effect of this process on other regions. I point out some gaps and contradictions in our knowledge of the process and suggest directions for further research. I begin by summarizing the volume's cogent argument for the causes of the depopulation of the northern San Juan region, including environmental, demographic, and social factors emphasized by different authors. Next, I look at the other side of the depopulation—migration to new areas. Here is where archaeological interpretations conflict. Northern San Juan archaeologists assume migration to the northern Rio Grande, while northern Rio Grande archaeologists, represented here by archaeologists from the Office of Archaeological Studies, Museum of New Mexico (including Eric Blinman, who attended the Amerind seminar on which this volume is based), question the assumption that many migrants from the north entered their region. The biggest problem for archaeologists is identifying immigrants in the archaeological record, and I review the contributions of the authors in this volume toward solving this problem. Finally, I suggest that we might advance our understanding of the depopulation through study of the size and composition of migratory groups, as well as their status relative to native populations in the destination area (topics that have not been ignored by the authors of this volume; see, for example, Lyons, Hill, and Clark 2005; also Anschuetz and Wilshusen 2010; Bernardini and Fowles, in press; Clark and Laumbach, in press; Mills, in press; Ortman and Cameron, in press; Stone 2003; Stone and

Lipe, in press). Exploring these factors should improve our understanding of why we sometimes see migrants in the archaeological record and why at other times we do not, as well as helping us recognize the important effects that migrants have on the areas they enter.

Depopulation: Why Did They Leave?

Authors in this volume seem to agree that the depopulation was multicausal and present accounts that vary in their emphasis on environmental variability, human impact on the environment, demographic changes, and social factors (see especially chapters by Duff, Adams, and Ryan; Berry and Benson; Glowacki; Kohler; Kuckelman; Varien; and Wright). The chapters are informed by cutting-edge environmental and paleodemographic reconstructions that are perhaps the most novel contributions of this volume and that expand on reconstructions presented elsewhere (Kohler et al. 2008; Varien et al. 2007). The chapters also present carefully researched and reasoned arguments that social factors were also decisive causes for the depopulation. I will touch only briefly on the environmental reconstructions (which are addressed more fully by Dean's chapter in this volume) and then highlight the different but complementary perspectives of several authors who offer multicausal explanations for the northern San Juan depopulation.

More than a decade ago, Van West's (1994) important study of maize productivity in the northern San Juan region concluded that, while environmental conditions in the northern San Juan were extremely challenging during the late 1200s, they did not require the complete depopulation of the area. Her study caused a useful shift in focus to social and other factors in explaining the depopulation (for example, Cameron 1995; Cameron, ed., 1995; Lekson et al. 2002:94–96; Lipe 1995; Lipe and Varien 1999b:342). Using a wealth of new and innovative data, this volume profitably returns the focus to the environment (see especially chapters by Berry and Benson, Kohler, and Wright) and the effect of environmental change on subsistence (see chapters by Duff Adams, and Ryan and Kuckelman). Environmental variability clearly played a role in depopulation, and the volume presents a refined and admirably broad view of environmental conditions, especially in the central Mesa Verde region but also in the Southwest more generally.

The sophisticated paleodemographic reconstructions presented here involve nested geographic scales. At the smallest geographic scale is the unparalleled database compiled by the Village Ecodynamics Project for the central Mesa Verde region that permits the highly refined population estimates used by many of the authors in the volume (see especially Kohler, Glowacki, Varien). At a larger scale, Glowacki's demographic reconstruction of the northern San Juan region has transformed our understanding of regional population movements in the thirteenth century. Berry and Benson shift the focus outward to the southern Colorado Plateau and northern Rio Grande regions (see fig. 3.1). They equate tree-ring cutting dates with population for different regions, providing a less precise but still useful method of looking at where and when population concentrations occur. At the largest scale is the Coalescent Communities Database, discussed by Hill and colleagues, which covers most of the Southwest and uses a comprehensive site database. The combination of scales at which paleodemography is reconstructed, combined with careful environmental reconstructions, allow the authors to explore the articulation between environmental change and population movements.

Berry and Benson's analysis of tree-ring dates demonstrates the influence of the environment on human behavior by showing that low numbers of cutting dates overlap temporally and spatially with climatic downturns and high numbers of cutting dates with favorable conditions. For the northern San Juan, both Wright and Kohler use the most recent paleoclimatic data to reconstruct the region's conditions. Interestingly, Kohler's reconstruction for the central Mesa Verde region revisits Van West's work and finds projected maize-productivity figures that are considerably lower than those Van West proposed.

Although the authors of the volume agree that the depopulation was multicausal, they differ in the causal factors they stress. Kohler and Glowacki offer slightly different, but complementary, explanations. For example, Kohler places somewhat more emphasis on environmental change and human impacts on the environment, while Glowacki emphasizes social factors. Kohler sees a downturn in the environment during the first half of the 1200s as causing populations to leave less-favored parts of the northern San Juan region for the central Mesa Verde area, which by the second quarter of the thirteenth century had became a refugium. Population build-up had impacts on the environment, resulting in further declines in the availability of large mammals and accentuating an earlier switch to turkey as a source of protein. Humans and turkeys both relied on maize, putting an additional strain on uncertain maize production. Chapters by Duff, Adams, and Ryan and Kuckelman provide supporting evidence for Kohler's reconstruction. Duff, Adams and Ryan show that residents of Shields Pueblo likely also depleted certain plants and animals in the area around the site. By the late 1270s and early 1280s, residents of both Shields Pueblo and especially nearby Sand Canyon Pueblo seem to have been stressed. At Sand Canyon Pueblo by this time, residents had resorted to the use of wild plants and animals, and the final residents of this community met a violent end (Kuckelman, this vol.). However, Duff, Adams, and Ryan emphasize that the environmental changes they have documented "do not evidence major disruptions that would have necessitated emigration" and point to the importance of social processes in explaining the depopulation.

Glowacki (2006, this vol.) has established that subregions in the northern San Juan had different histories of population movement and that some parts of the region were depopulated well before the late thirteenth century. The far northeastern part of the region around the Chimney Rock great house was depopulated by the mid-twelfth century, if not before (Eddy 1977; Varien et al. 1996). During the Pueblo III period, depopulation had a west-to-east trend, with areas to the west in southeastern Utah depopulated before the central Mesa Verde region. Glowacki and Kohler seem to differ in the causal mechanisms for the depopulation of the western part of the northern San Juan region. Whereas Kohler emphasizes a mid-thirteenth-century environmental downturn and suggests that migrants from the west must have been desperate because they were moving into an area where only poor land was available, Glowacki uses this same information to suggest that social factors, rather than environmental pressures, prompted the move.

Kohler and Glowacki also differ—although in compatible ways—in their assessment of social factors that caused depopulation in the northern San Juan region. Kohler points out that the large communities that developed in the northern San Juan region during the 1200s created strong institutions that linked social groups, such as lineages and clans, together. With deteriorating social and environmental conditions in the mid-1200s, large communities ceased to be the best settlement option but social ties made community decomposition difficult. Because of these social ties and because of population packing the landscape, it was difficult for smaller groups to extricate themselves and relocate to areas where life would be easier (see also Benson, Peterson, and Stein 2007). Another reason small groups could not move out on their own was the dramatic increase in conflict that developed in the late thirteenth century, likely the result of competition for resources.

Glowacki argues that a ritual transformation was taking place in the eastern part of the northern San Juan region in the mid- to late 1200s, and that population aggregation and continued immigration throughout this period may have led to a social breakdown that resulted in emigration as early as the 1260s. Like Kohler, she points to evidence of violence, which became most pronounced in the late thirteenth century just before the area was completely depopulated. Also like Kohler, she emphasizes the importance of social ties, pointing out that once emigration from the region began, the difficulty of maintaining social coherence would have been an added impetus to leave.

Glowacki places the ritual transformation she proposes in a wider historical context, arguing that it relates to the changing role of Chaco Canyon and Aztec Ruins, as well as to the ways in which Chacoan ideology played out in northern San Juan society. She points to long-established connections between Chaco Canyon and the northern San Juan region that some scholars have argued involved movement back and forth between these two regions (Cameron 2005; Cameron and Duff 2008; Judge 1989; Lekson 1999; Wilshusen and Van Dyke 2006). She proposes that the depopulation of the northern San Juan region may have been the result of the ultimate rejection of Chacoan ideology, and that migration was undertaken at least in part to shed any remnant of Chacoan or Aztecan influence (see also Lekson [1999], who argues that the depopulation of the northern San Juan was the result of the rejection of Chacoan traditions and the fall of Aztec). As discussed below, this proposal has important implications for explaining the lack of continuity in cultural practices in the places where northern San Juan migrants eventually settled.

Authors in the volume see violence as an important factor in the depopulation. Varien provides historical context for arguments about warfare in the northern San Juan region and emphasizes the extent to which intercommunity violence might have been destructive to farmers trying to cope with difficult environmental conditions. Coercive force emanating from the massive Aztec complex may have been a factor in the significant increase in violence evident during the thirteenth century (Cameron and Duff 2008; Glowacki 2006; Kohler and Turner 2006; Lekson 1999, 2002). Varien notes that warfare may have decreased the numbers of people who ultimately left the northern San Juan region (see also Lipe, this vol.), and I believe that this is an observation that deserves more study, as not only may population numbers have been diminished—the composition of the remaining population may also have changed (see below). LeBlanc (2002) notes that warfare in forager and farmer societies often results in the death of more than 25 percent of males, with many women and children taken captive (see also Cameron 2008, 2009; Kohler and Turner 2006; Martin 2008). The implications for the northern San Juan region are that after decades of warfare, migrant groups leaving the northern San Juan region would likely be of a very different composition than those of earlier periods. For example, community-sized migrant groups might represent conglomerations of a few successful male combatants and many captive women and children, rather than tightly knit, culturally intact communities. As discussed below, these different compositions likely had impacts on the archaeological visibility of migrants.

Migration: Where Did They Go?

We seem to be getting closer to an understanding of the reasons for the depopulation of the northern San Juan region, but there is less agreement concerning migrant destinations. Glowacki makes the important point that migrants from the northern San Juan almost certainly left for a variety of different destinations via different routes. Although archaeologists can agree on some destinations, there is strong disagreement about others, especially the northern Rio Grande. In this volume, Hill and his colleagues and Berry and Benson provide broad demographic views of Southwest population movements, while Ortman and Boyer and his colleagues provide strongly contrasting views of the evidence for migration from the northern San Juan to the northern Rio Grande.

As Varien notes, more than forty years ago, Emma Lou Davis (1964, 1965) stressed the interconnectedness of the Southwest and that population shifts could have regionwide effects. This important point was lost during the years in which migration was proscribed as a research focus, but Hill and his colleagues demonstrate that population movement is the *rule* in the Southwest and emphasize that environmental, demographic, or social change in one part of the Southwest can have dramatic impacts on other parts. They use the Coalescent Communities Database to capture demographic snapshots of the Southwest at fifty-year intervals from the thirteenth through the fifteenth centuries. Hill and colleagues see growth in population in the northern Rio Grande and Zuni areas as the northern San Juan region is depopulated. They argue that the immigration of Pueblo people into the southern Southwest (see also Clark 2001; Hill et al 2004; Lyons, Hill, and Clark 2005; Stark, Clark, and Elson 1995) as a result of the depopulation of the northern Southwest was a catalyst for a series of demographic and social upheavals that ended with the collapse of the Classic-period Hohokam. The demographic trends presented by Hill and colleagues are an interesting complement to Berry and Benson's tree-ring based patterns, and an overlay of the two datasets could be informative. Especially intriguing would be the inclusion of demographic information from the Fremont area compiled by Allison. This would allow a better understanding of how the Fremont area affected, or was affected by, Southwest population movements.

There is an intriguing contrast between the visibility of migrants in central and southern Arizona and those in central New Mexico that is at the heart of the disagreement between northern San Juan and northern Rio Grande archaeologists. Archaeologists in central and southern Arizona and west-central New Mexico seem to have no difficulty in accepting migrants from the northern Southwest, and this may in part be because of several well-known site-unit intrusions from the Kayenta region. The Maverick Mountain enclaves at Point of Pines (Haury 1958; Stone 2003), Reeve Ruin (DiPeso 1958a, 1958b), Goat Hill (Woodson 1999), and Davis Ranch Ruin all display unambiguous evidence that people from northeastern Arizona moved south. The impact of less-obvious migrants into areas such as the Tonto basin (see also Clark 2001; Stark, Clark, and Elson 1995) have been carefully studied by archaeologists there. Similarly, for west-central New Mexico, Varien discusses three site-unit intrusions from the northern San Juan region: Pinnacle Ruin (Lekson et al. 2002), Gallinas Springs, and the Roadmap Site (although none of these sites has as clear a migratory signal as the Kayenta sites).

In the northern Rio Grande region, however, the situation is different, as illustrated in this volume by the disparate views presented in the chapter by Ortman and that by Boyer and colleagues. Ortman's four-field approach provides a convincing set of arguments for the movement of people from the northern San Juan region into the northern Rio Grande. Skeletal evidence suggests that these migrants did not mingle with local residents of the northern Rio Grande, but moved in as sizable groups and established large, separate communities. Ortman sees these people as ancestral Tewa. In contrast, Boyer and others see migration of some *southern* San Juan peoples into the Middle Rio Puerco region and, in a sort of ripple effect, ultimately into the northern Rio Grande (see also Roney 1995). This team offers evidence for "punctuated" immigration from the southern San Juan region into the western fringes of the northern Rio Grande region beginning in the late twelfth century but sees no necessity to invoke "evidence for direct northern San Juan immigration" to explain NRG demographic trends. Yet even their own population estimates, which are lower than those developed by other scholars, show a significant increase during the AD 1200s that almost doubles the northern Rio Grande population (Boyer et al. fig. 12.3).

Varien, like Boyer and colleagues, examines population trends in the San Juan basin for evidence of northern San Juan migrants moving through this area. His conclusions provide a somewhat different interpretation of demographics there. Although he believes that as many as ten thousand people left the northern San Juan region (about the size of the maximum thirteenth-century northern Rio Grande population increase estimated by Boyer and colleagues), he shows that populations in *both* the northern San Juan and the San Juan basin were rising during the middle part of the thirteenth century. In other words, the San Juan basin may already have had a significant population. Furthermore, Varien notes that even if all of the residents of the San Juan basin had come from the northern San Juan, they could not have accounted for the total number of people who left that region. He points out, however, that both the northern San Juan region and the San Juan basin shared a generally similar material culture, meaning that migrants from both areas moving into the northern Rio Grande might be difficult to distinguish.

The contrasting viewpoints of Ortman and Boyer and colleagues epitomize a long-standing conundrum relating to the depopulation of the northern San Juan region. Archaeologists from the northern San Juan region see people leaving, while many archaeologists from the northern Rio Grande, in spite of huge population increases coinciding with northern depopulation, see few migrants entering their territory. Population dynamics presented by Hill and colleagues, as well as others (for example, compare Varien et al. [1996] with Crown, Orcutt, and Kohler [1996]; see also Boyer et al., this vol.: fig. 12.3) and ceramic stylistic similarities make the northern Rio Grande region a very likely destination. Unfortunately, the archaeological record in the northern Rio Grande region lacks, to date, obvious site-unit intrusions like those that Kayenta migrants left in southern Arizona (see Boyer et al., this vol. and Lipe, this vol.). The lack of obvious cultural traits typical of the northern San Juan has prevented archaeologists in the northern Rio Grande from accepting many northern San Juan migrants into their region. As discussed below, however, apparent absence of migrants in the northern Rio Grande may simply reflect our inability to see them.

Seeing Migrants: How Did They Go?

Lack of agreement about migration destinations indicates that we need to refine our methods for "seeing" migrants in the archaeological record. This involves exploring in more detail the conditions under which people either maintain the cultural practices of their homeland or discard or change them. Part of this process entails assessing the size and composition of the migrating group, the size and nature of the communities in the destination area, and interactions between native and migrant populations. This volume presents somewhat variable views of the size of the groups that left the northern San Juan region, and small group size is used by some authors to explain the lack of site-unit intrusions in the northern Rio Grande region. The authors make intriguing suggestions that migrants purposely shed the cultural practices of their homeland, but we should also consider other factors, such as gender selectivity for migrants and migrant/native status differentials (see Lipe, this vol.).

At least since Mera (1935), archaeologists have noted similarities in ceramic styles between the northern San Juan region and the northern Rio Grande region, and these similarities have set up the expectation that northern San Juan peoples relocated to the northern Rio Grande during the thirteenth century. But the extent and meaning of ceramic similarity is under debate. In a recent examination of this question, Cordell and her colleagues (2007) argue that ceramic style and type similarities signify long-term social interactions that facilitated migration between the two regions. In contrast, Boyer and others (this vol.) acknowledge a broad flow of stylistic information across the northern Southwest but see significant differences between northern San Juan and Rio Grande types, especially in technological characteristics, that they feel argues against use of ceramic similarities to document migration.

Moving beyond ceramics, Lipe catalogs other differences between the northern San Juan and northern Rio Grande regions in habitation units, settlement layout, and artifact types. He establishes the large number of cultural practices (evident in archaeological remains) that did not "make the trip" between the two areas when the northern San Juan became depopulated. Kayenta migrants to central and southern Arizona retained both architectural and ceramic practices typical of their homeland, but similarly strong signatures of northern San Juan migrants are not found in the northern Rio Grande—or elsewhere, a point made by both Lipe (this vol.) and Varien (this vol.).

Some northern Rio Grande archaeologists argue that few migrants ever moved directly into their region from the northern San Juan. Northern San Juan archaeologists believe that people from their region *did* move to the northern Rio Grande and have developed arguments for the lack of site-unit intrusions there. These arguments have centered primarily on the size of migrant groups. Scholars suggest that families or households were the most common migratory unit; they argue that during times of economic downturn and environmental distress, these small groups of migrants would have been incorporated into native populations, leaving little evidence of their presence in the archaeological record (Cordell 1995; Cordell et al. 2007; Kohler 1993; Lipe, this vol.). Cordell and colleagues (2007) suggest that ceramic similarities indicate that these two regions were part of a large, long-term risk-sharing pool and that their long-term relationship facilitated migration between the two areas.

Small group size and integration into existing communities has been a long-established explanation for the lack of obvious northern San Juan migrant communities in the northern Rio Grande, and this migratory pattern almost certainly accounts for some of the prehispanic population movement in the Southwest. However, there is also evidence for larger migrant groups. In a recent study of Hopi oral traditions, Bernardini (2005) suggests that the subclan was the common unit of migration, defining the subclan as the members of a specific clan residing in a single village. Pueblo origin accounts frequently discuss the movement of entire communities, and archaeologists have found communities made up exclusively of migrants in southern Arizona (Di Peso 1958a, 1958b; Woodson 1999) and west-central New Mexico (Lekson et al. 2002). Chapters in this volume also present evidence that large, community-sized groups left the northern San Juan region and established themselves in the northern Rio Grande. Glowacki (this vol.) points to the rapidity with which the eastern part of the northern San Juan region was depopulated and suggests that migrants left in large groups. Similarly, Varien proposes that small, kin-based groups may have left the northern San Juan early but that later in the thirteenth century, migration was undertaken by large social groups. Ortman's skeletal data indicate that northern San Juan migrants formed communities that were separate from northern Rio Grande natives, also suggesting that they arrived in community-sized groups.

If migrants moved as community-sized groups and established independent towns, it is far more difficult to understand why they did not continue the cultural practices of their homeland. A sizable independent community should be under far less pressure to adopt local cultural practices than would a few families trying to adjust to living with members of a culturally different group. Yet habitation units, site layouts, and kiva styles in the northern Rio Grande are different from those in the northern San Juan region (Lipe, this vol.). The proposal that migrants were intentionally shedding traditional cultural practices related to their Chacoan past (Glowacki, this vol.; Lekson 1999, 2002) is important. Lipe adds that migrants may also have been attracted to newly emerging religious practices and community organization in the northern Rio Grande (see also Lipe 1995). Significantly, Lipe believes that migrants may even have been involved with the development of these new social forms. Lipe points out that community and other patterns in the northern Rio Grande were in flux during the period when evidence suggests that northern San Juan migrants were arriving, so there is not a clear set of northern Rio Grande cultural practices that northern San Juan migrants could have adopted. Furthermore, even if migrants entered the northern Rio Grande in community-sized groups, they were still entering an ethnically and linguistically diverse region where "blending in" might have been socially or politically useful (see Lipe, this volume, for expectations for when migrants might "stand out" versus blend in). For these reasons, perhaps we should not be surprised that northern San Juan cultural practices were not duplicated in the northern Rio Grande region in a time of significant social change.

The Future: More Work to Do

The authors of this volume have presented a cogent set of arguments for why we might not see northern San Juan migrants in the archaeological record even if they arrived in large groups, but I believe it is in regard to destination areas that we still have much work to do in understanding migration. We need to explore the reasons for the variable visibility of migrants in the archaeological record and especially understand their impact on native populations. This is a large topic that is just beginning to be addressed by archaeologists (Burmeister 2000; Cameron, in press; Lyons, Hill, and Clark 2005; Ortman and Cameron, in press; Stone 2003). I suggest that it is not just the size of migrant groups, but their composition and (a directly related factor) their status in relation to natives that may have the greatest effect on archaeological visibility (Cameron, in press). Here, I offer a few brief observations on the implications of these factors for seeing migrants in the archaeological record.

Southwest archaeologists tend to assume that small migrant groups were composed of families or households. The composition of mid-sized or large groups is rarely discussed, but again, they are likely assumed to be composed of households. There is reason to question whether this is always the case, however, and gender- and age-imbalanced migrant groups might have been common. For example, there is evidence that during times of stress, households decompose (anonymous n.d.).

An historical account from Hopi tells about the "starving time" that apparently occurred during the late eighteenth or early nineteenth century. According to this account, when times got tough, the nuclear family disintegrated—old people were dispatched, some children were sold to the Zuni, while other women and children walked to the Rio Grande to sell themselves as slaves to the Spanish. The men also dispersed. Some people eventually returned; others never did. This example indicates that we should consider the possibility that households often did *not* move together, and that small groups of migrants might have been of a single sex or might have consisted of related women and their children. Gender imbalances might also have characterized migrant groups of other sizes. As discussed above, decades of warfare may have seriously depressed the male population, leaving women and children to make up a greater proportion of even mid-sized or large migrant groups.

We should consider how group size and gender composition affected migrant status in relation to natives when migrants reached their destination. Lipe (this vol.) believes that northern Rio Grande leaders may have been actively recruiting people to join developing large villages and that these villages had established social institutions capable of integrating newcomers. But there were very likely differences in how small groups of desperate women and children were accepted into an ongoing community in comparison to the acceptance accorded a large, intact, or possibly even high-status household. These women and children might have felt compelled to adopt cultural practices typical of the communities they joined. Even large or mid-sized migrant groups that were composed of significant numbers of remnant or captive women and children might also have been constrained in the degree to which they could (or perhaps would choose to) function as a culturally distinct group after moving to a new region.

Clearly, we should expect differences in the extent to which groups of different sizes and composition were able to express homeland cultural practices and, as a result, how they might differ in terms of archaeological visibility. A recent study by Lowell (2007) suggests some of the archaeological signatures of migrant gender imbalance that we might look for. Lowell (2007) proposes that migrants to Grasshopper Pueblo were primarily female war refugees. She shows that these women brought gender-linked cultural practices, such as pottery style and hearth-construction methods, while male-linked traits, such as projectile-point type and kiva construction methods, continued according to native practices. Similar interpretations might usefully be applied to the northern Rio Grande. For example, archaeologists searching for northern San Juan migrants in the northern Rio Grande have noted the post–Middle Coalition absence of the small "household kivas" typical of the northern San Juan region (Dutton 1964; Lipe 1995, this vol.—although Lipe, this vol., disagrees with this proposal). While the suggestion that migrants were intentionally shedding cultural practices is a good one, we should also consider the possibility that the males who might have constructed typical northern San Juan kivas were uncommon migrants. Furthermore, the similarity of ceramic styles throughout the northern Southwest could be explained by the widespread trade of captive women (as suggested by Trigger 1976:159–161) rather than efforts at risk minimization.

Conclusions

The chapters in this volume offer a new look at the depopulation of the northern Southwest, and one that is informed by significant advances in our understanding of environmental, demographic, and social conditions throughout the Southwest during the late prehispanic period. The authors agree that the depopulation of the northern San Juan region was multicausal, involving a suite of environmental and climatic alterations, demographic changes, and social factors. Environmental downturns in the northern San Juan region and throughout the Southwest, as well as ritual transformations in the central Mesa Verde region, resulted in population concentration in this area. Evidence of human impacts on an already fragile landscape is apparent by the mid- to late 1200s. Warfare and violence was likely a result of unprecedented population growth and competition for scarce resources, and violence likely resulted in an inability to use farming land in the most efficient manner, causing more hardship. Large, aggregated communities developed strong institutions that linked together social groups such as lineages and clans. When hard times came and large communities ceased to be the best settlement option, social ties, population growth, and increased levels of conflict made community decomposition difficult. Because of these social ties, population packing, and the threat of violence, it was difficult for smaller groups to extricate themselves and relocate to areas where life would be easier. Deteriorating environmental and social conditions may have led people to repudiate long-held social and ritual traditions associated with the ancient Chacoan regional system. Knowledge of powerful social developments elsewhere may have been the impetus necessary for the final removal of all population from the northern San Juan.

Although there is general agreement about the causes of depopulation, arguments develop in determining where migrants went. This is especially true in considering whether northern San Juan migrants are responsible for the large spike in population in the northern Rio Grande during the later thirteenth century. The demographics are telling: population levels declined in the northern San Juan at approximately the same time those in the northern Rio Grande rose. Yet some northern Rio Grande archaeologists see few, if any, northern San Juan migrants entering their territory. Northern San Juan archaeologists look for ways to explain the lack of site-unit intrusions. Some of these explanations include small group size and integration with ongoing northern Rio Grande populations, intentional discard of traditional cultural practices, and the social state of flux in the northern Rio Grande that resulted in a new social order developed by both natives and migrants.

The lack of site-unit intrusions in the northern Rio Grande is underlined by the presence of a number of site-unit intrusions in central and southern Arizona where migrants came from the Kayenta region. At the Amerind seminar during which this volume was developed, Jeff Dean observed that Kayenta people were less stressed by an ongoing drought and less beset by violence than were the northern San Juan populations. In other words, Kayenta migrations were made by people who chose to maintain their identity, while the northern San Juan migrations were made by groups wracked by violence and a failed social system. As a result, northern San Juan migrants abandoned homeland cultural practices as they departed.

Dean's suggestion is important, and I argue that we should follow up on his observation. Future research should examine both the size and the composition of migrant groups that left the northern San Juan, as well as their status in relation to natives in destination areas. I believe that we may find migrant groups with significant gender imbalances, as well as different statuses vis-à-vis native groups. Different group compositions and statuses result in a differential ability or desire of migrants to continue homeland practices. When homeland practices are discontinued, migrants disappear from the archaeological record.

REFERENCES CITED

Abbott, David R. 2000. *Ceramics and Community Organization among the Hohokam.* University of Arizona Press, Tucson.

Abbott, David R. (editor). 2003. *Centuries of Decline during the Hohokam Classic Period at Pueblo Grande.* University of Arizona Press, Tucson.

Abbott, David R., and Michael S. Foster. 2003. Site Structure, Chronology, and Population. In *Centuries of Decline during the Hohokam Classic Period at Pueblo Grande*, edited by David R. Abbott, pp. 24–47. University of Arizona Press, Tucson.

Abbott, David R., and David A. Gregory. 1988. Hohokam Ceramic Wares and Types. In *The 1982–1984 Excavations at Las Colinas: Material Culture*, edited by David R. Abbott, Kim E. Beckwith, Patricia L. Crown, R. Thomas Euler, David A. Gregory, J. Ronald London, Marylin B. Saul, Larry A. Schwalbe, Mary Bernard-Shaw, Christine R. Szuter, and Arthur W. Vokes, pp. 5–28. Arizona State Museum Archaeological Series, no. 162(4). Arizona State Museum, University of Arizona, Tucson.

Adams, David K., and Andrew C. Comrie. 1997. The North American Monsoon. *Bulletin of the American Meteorological Society* 78:2197–2213.

Adams, E. Charles. 1991. *The Origin and Development of the Pueblo Katsina Cult.* University of Arizona Press, Tucson.

Adams, E. Charles, and Andrew I. Duff (editors). 2004. *The Protohistoric Pueblo World, AD 1275–1600.* University of Arizona Press, Tucson.

Adams, Karen R. 1999. Macrobotanical Remains. In *The Sand Canyon Archaeological Project: Site Testing*, edited by M. Varien, chapter 16. Crow Canyon Archaeological Center, Cortez, Colorado. http://www.crowcanyon.org/ResearchReports/SiteTesting/start.asp, (accessed July 10, 2008).

———. 2004. Plant Use at Shields Pueblo. In *Communities through Time: The Archaeology of Shields Pueblo (5MT3807), Montezuma County, Colorado*, edited by A. Duff and S. Ryan. Manuscript on file, Crow Canyon Archaeological Center, Cortez, Colorado.

———. 2006. Pollen Analysis from Shields Pueblo. In *Communities through Time: The Archaeology of Shields Pueblo (5MT3807), Montezuma County, Colorado*, edited by A. Duff and S. Ryan. Manuscript on file, Crow Canyon Archaeological Center, Cortez, Colorado.

———. 2008. Anthropogenic Ecology in the American Southwest: The Plant Perspective. Paper presented at "Movement, Connectivity, and Landscape Change," the Twentieth Anniversary Southwest Symposium, Arizona State University, Tempe.

Adams, Karen R., and Vandy E. Bowyer. 2002. Sustainable Landscape: Thirteenth-Century Food and Fuel Use in the Sand Canyon Locality. In *Seeking the Center Place: Archaeology and Ancient Communities in the Mesa Verde Region*, edited by Mark D. Varien and Richard H. Wilshusen, pp. 123–142. University of Utah Press, Salt Lake City.

Adams, Karen R., Kristin A. Kuckelman, and Vandy E. Bowyer. 2007. Archaeobotanical Remains. In *The Archaeology of Sand Canyon Pueblo: Intensive Excavations at a Late-Thirteenth-Century Village in Southwestern Colorado* [HTML title], edited by Kristin A. Kuckelman. http://www.crowcanyon.org/ResearchReports/SandCanyon/Text/scpw_archaeobotanicalremains.asp (accessed February 2, 2008).

Adams, Karen R., Cathryn M. Meegan, Scott G. Ortman, R. Emerson Howell, Lindsay C. Werth, Deborah A. Muenchrath, Michael K. O'Neill, and Candice A. C. Gardner. 2006. MAÍS (Maize of American Indigenous Societies) Southwest: Ear Descriptions and Traits that Distinguish 27 Morphologically Distinct Groups of 123 Historic USDA Maize (*Zea mays* L. spp. *mays*) Accessions and Data Relevant to Archaeological Subsistence Models. Manuscript in the possession of Karen R. Adams.

Adams, Karen R., and Kenneth L. Petersen. 1999. Environment. In *Colorado Prehistory: A Context for the Southern Colorado River Basin*, edited by William D. Lipe, Mark D. Varien, and Richard H. Wilshusen, pp. 14–50. Colorado Council of Professional Archaeologists, Denver.

Adler, Michael. 1989. Ritual Facilities and Social Integration in Nonranked Societies. In *The Architecture of Social Integration in Prehistoric Pueblos*, edited by William D. Lipe and Michelle Hegmon, pp. 35–52. Crow Canyon Archaeological Center, no. 1, Cortez, Colorado.

———. 1990. Communities of Soil and Stone: An Archaeological Investigation of Population Aggregation among the Mesa Verde Region Anasazi, AD 900–1300. Unpublished PhD dissertation, Department of Anthropology, University of Michigan, Ann Arbor.

———. 1992. The Upland Survey. In *The Sand Canyon Archaeological Project: A Progress Report*, edited by William D. Lipe, pp. 11–23. Occasional Papers of the Crow Canyon Archaeological Center, no. 2. Cortez, Colorado.

———. 1993. Why Is a Kiva? New Interpretations of Prehistoric Social Integrative Architecture in the Northern Rio Grande Region of New Mexico. *Journal of Anthropological Research* 49:319–346.

———. 1994. Population Aggregation and the Anasazi Social Landscape. In *The Ancient Southwestern Community: Models and Methods for the Study of Prehistoric Social Organization*, edited by W. H. Wills and R. D. Leonard, pp. 85–101. University of New Mexico Press, Albuquerque.

———. 1996a. The Great Period: The Pueblo World during the Pueblo III Period, AD 1150 to 1350. In *The Prehistoric Pueblo World, AD 1150–1350*, edited by Michael A. Adler, pp. 1–10. University of Arizona Press, Tucson.

———. 1996b. Land Tenure, Archaeology, and the Ancestral Pueblo Social Landscape. *Journal of Anthropological Archaeology* 15:337–371.

———. 2007. The Architecture of Pottery Mound Pueblo. In *New Perspectives on Pottery Mound Pueblo*, edited by P. Schaafsma, pp. 29–54. University of New Mexico Press, Albuquerque.

Adler, Michael A. (editor). 1996. *The Prehistoric Pueblo World, AD 1150–1350*. University of Arizona Press, Tucson.

Adler, Michael A., and Herbert W. Dick, editors. 1999. *Picuris Pueblo through Time: Eight Centuries of Change at a Northern Rio Grande Pueblo*. William P. Clements Center for Southwest Studies, Southern Methodist University, Dallas.

Adler, Michael, and Amber Johnson. 1996. Appendix: Mapping the Puebloan Southwest. In *The Prehistoric Pueblo World, AD 1150–1350*, edited by Michael A. Adler, pp. 255–272. University of Arizona Press, Tucson.

Adler, Michael A., and Mark D. Varien. 1994. The Changing Face of the Community in the Mesa Verde Region, AD 1000–1300. In *Proceedings of the Anasazi Symposium 1991*, compiled by Jack E. Smith and Art Hutchinson, pp. 83–97. Mesa Verde Museum Association, Inc., Mesa Verde National Park, Colorado.

Ahlstrom, Richard V. N. 1985. The Interpretation of Archaeological Tree-Ring Dates. Unpublished PhD dissertation, Department of Anthropology, University of Arizona, Tucson.

Ahlstrom, Richard V. N., Jeffrey S. Dean, and William J. Robinson. 1991. Evaluating Tree-Ring Interpretations at Walpi Pueblo, Arizona. *American Antiquity* 56:628–644.

Ahlstrom, Richard V. N., Carla R. Van West, and Jeffrey S. Dean. 1995. Environmental and Chronological Factors in the Mesa Verde–Northern Rio Grande Migration. *Journal of Anthropological Archaeology* 14:125–142.

Aikens, C. Melvin. 1965. *Excavations in Southwest Utah*. Anthropological Papers, no. 79. University of Utah, Salt Lake City.

———. 1966. *Virgin-Kayenta Cultural Relationships*. Anthropological Papers, no. 79. University of Utah, Salt Lake City.

Akins, Nancy J. 1986. *A Biocultural Approach to Human Burials from Chaco Canyon, New Mexico*. Reports of the Chaco Center 9. Branch of Cultural Research, Department of the Interior, National Park Service, Santa Fe, New Mexico.

———. 1995. Contrasting Gender Roles in the Galisteo and San Juan Basins of New Mexico. Paper presented in the symposium "Women's Bodies, Women's Lives: Biological Indicators of Labor and Occupational Stress," sixty-fifth annual meeting of the American Association for Physical Anthropologists, Oakland.

———. 2008a. Utilization of Fauna. In *Excavations along NM 22: Agricultural Adaptation from AD 500 to 1900 in the Northern Santo Domingo Basin, Sandoval County, New Mexico*, vol. 2: *Major Site Excavations at LA 265, LA 6169, LA 6170, and LA 6171*, compiled by S. Post and R. Chapman. Archaeology Notes 385. Office of Archaeological Studies, Museum of New Mexico, Santa Fe.

———. 2008b. Making a Living in the Upper Rio Grande Area: Health and Mobility in Prehistoric Population of Northern New Mexico. Paper presented in the symposium "Southwestern Bioarchaeology in 2008: Current Themes, Issues, and Research Trajectories," seventy-third annual meeting of the Society for American Archaeology, Vancouver, British Colombia.

———. 2008c. Human Skeletal Remains. *Excavations along NM 22: Agricultural Adaptation from AD 500 to 1900 in the Northern Santo Domingo Basin, Sandoval County*, compiled by S. Post and R. Chapman. Archaeology Notes 385. Office of Archaeological Studies, Museum of New Mexico, Santa Fe.

———. 2009. Overview of the Pojoaque Corridor Fauna. In *Land, Settlement, and Community in the Southern Tewa Basin*, vol. 3, edited by J. L. Boyer and S. A. Lakatos (draft, in preparation). Office of Archaeological Studies, Museum of New Mexico, Santa Fe.

Akins, Nancy L., Steven A. Lakatos, and Jeffrey L. Boyer. 2003. *Preliminary Results of Data Recovery Investigations at LA 391 and Emergency Data Recovery Investigations at LA 388, US 84/285 Santa Fe to Pojoaque Corridor, Santa Fe County, New Mexico*. Archaeology Notes 328. Office of Archaeological Studies, Museum of New Mexico, Santa Fe.

Allen, Craig D. 2004. Ecological Patterns and Environmental Change in the Bandelier Landscape. In *Archaeology of Bandelier National Monument: Village Formation on the Pajarito Plateau, New Mexico*, edited by Timothy A. Kohler, pp. 19–68. University of New Mexico Press, Albuquerque.

Allen, Joseph, W. 1971. *The Pueblo Alamo Project: Archaeological Salvage at the Junction of U.S. 85 and U.S. 285 South of Santa Fe, New Mexico*. Laboratory of Anthropology Notes 86. Museum of New Mexico, Santa Fe.

Allison, James R. 1990. Anasazi Subsistence in the Saint George Basin, Southwestern Utah. Unpublished master's thesis, Department of Anthropology, Brigham Young University, Provo, Utah.

————. 1996. Comments on the Impacts of Climatic Variability and Population Growth on Virgin Anasazi Cultural Development. *American Antiquity* 61:414–418.

————. 2000. Craft Specialization and Exchange in Small-Scale Societies: A Virgin Anasazi Case Study. Unpublished PhD dissertation, Department of Anthropology, Arizona State University, Tempe.

————. 2002. *Archaeological Excavations at the Salt Lake Airport*. Research Report, no. 02-23. Baseline Data, Orem, Utah.

————. 2005. Virgin Anasazi Radiocarbon Chronology. Paper presented at the Three Corners Conference, Las Vegas, Nevada.

————. 2008. Shinarump Red Ware and Other Red Ware Pottery North and West of the Colorado River. *Pottery Southwest* 27(1): 21–34.

Allison, James R., Judi L. Cameron. Arlene Colman, and Quint A. Colman. 2000. *Test Excavations at 42DV2, a Late Prehistoric and Archaic Site in the Jordan River Delta, Davis County, Utah*. Research Report, no. 97-20. Baseline data, Orem, Utah.

Allison, James R., and Arlene Colman. 1998. Ceramic Analysis. In *Excavation/Mitigation Report, Three Sites near Hildale, Utah: 42Ws 2195, 42Ws 2196, AZ B:1:35 (BLM) (Reservoir Site)*, compiled by Asa S. Nielson, pp. 9.1–9.70. Research Report, no. U98-8. Baseline Data, Orem, Utah.

Allison, James R., Cathryn M. Meegan, and Shawn S. Murray. 2008. Archaeology and Archaeobotany of Southern Paiute Horticulture in the Saint George Basin, Southwestern Utah. *Kiva* 73(4): 417–449.

Allison, Paul D. 2001. *Missing Data*. Quantitative Applications in the Social Sciences 07-136. Sage Publications, Thousand Oaks, California.

Allison, Penelope M. 1999. Introduction. In *The Archaeology of Household Activities*, edited by P. M. Allison, pp. 1–18. Routledge, New York.

Ambler, J. Richard. 1966. *Caldwell Village and Fremont Prehistory*. Anthropological Papers, no. 84. University of Utah, Salt Lake City.

Ambler, J. Richard, and Mark Q. Sutton. 1989. The Anasazi Abandonment of the San Juan Drainage and the Numic Expansion. *North American Archaeologist* 10:39–53.

Amsden, Charles A. 1931. Part One: Black-on-white Ware. In *The Pottery of Pecos*, vol. 1, by A. V. Kidder, pp. 17–72. Yale University Press, New Haven.

Andrade, Edward R., and William D. Sellers. 1988. El Niño and Its Effects on Precipitation in Arizona and Western New Mexico. *Journal of Climate* 8:403–410.

Anonymous. n.d. The Starving Time. In Part III, Hopi. Manuscript on file, Huntington Library, Pasadena, California. Note: This is an account written by an Indian agent of his life at the Hopi villages. It apparently dates to the mid-1800s.

Anonymous. 2008. Come Together? *Preservation Archaeology News* (Summer 2008): 1, 4–5.

Anschuetz, Kurt F. 2005. Landscapes as Memory: Archaeological History to Learn From and to Live By. In *Engaged Anthropology: Essays in Honor of Richard I. Ford*, edited by Michelle Hegmon and Sunday Eiselt, pp. 52–72. Museum of Anthropology, University of Michigan, Ann Arbor.

Anschuetz, Kurt F., John C. Acklen, and David V. Hill. 1997. Prehistoric Overview. In *Ole Volume I: Context*, edited by J. C. Acklen, pp. 71–118. TRC Mariah Associates and Public Service Company of New Mexico, Albuquerque.

Anschuetz, Kurt, and Richard H. Wilshusen. Ensouled Places: Ethnogenesis and the Making of the Dinétah and Tewa Basin Landscapes. In *Changing Histories, Landscapes, and Perspectives: The 20th Anniversary Southwest Symposium*, edited by Margaret Nelson and Colleen Strawhacker. University Press of Colorado, Boulder.

Anthony, David W. 1990. Migration in Archaeology: The Baby and the Bathwater. *American Anthropologist* 92:895–914.

Anyon, Roger, and Steven A. LeBlanc. 1980. The Architectural Evolution of Mogollon-Mimbres Communal Structures. *Kiva* 45:253–277.

Arakawa, Fumiyasu. 2006. Lithic Raw Material Procurement and the Social Landscape in the Central Mesa Verde Region, AD 600–1300. Unpublished PhD dissertation, Department of Anthropology, Washington State University, Pullman.

Arnon, Nancy S., and W. W. Hill. 1979. Santa Clara Pueblo. In *Handbook of North American Indians*, vol. 9: *Southwest*, edited by A. Ortiz, pp. 296–307. Smithsonian Institution, Washington, DC.

Bahr, Donald M. 1971. Who Were the Hohokam? The Evidence from Pima-Papago Myths. *Ethnohistory* 18(3): 245–266.

Bahr, Donald M. (editor). 2001. *O'odham Creation and Related Events, As Told to Ruth Benedict in 1927 in Prose, Oratory, and Song*. University of Arizona Press, Tucson.

Bahr, Donald M., Juan Smith, William Smith Allison, and Julian D. Hayden. 1994. *The Short, Swift Time of Gods on Earth: The Hohokam Chronicles*. University of California Press, Berkeley.

Baillie, M.G.L. 1982. *Tree-Ring Dating and Archaeology*. University of Chicago Press, Chicago.

Bannister, Bryant. 1962. The Interpretation of Tree-Ring Dates. *American Antiquity* 27:508–514.

———. 1963. Dendrochronology. In *Science in Archaeology*, edited by D. Brothwell and E. Higgs, pp. 161–176. Basic Books, New York.

Barber, Elizabeth W., and Paul T. Barber. 2004. *When They Severed Earth from Sky: How the Human Mind Shapes Myth*. Princeton University Press, Princeton.

Barry, Roger G., and Richard J. Chorley. 2003. *Atmosphere, Weather and Climate*. 8th ed. Routledge, London.

Basso, Keith H. 1996. *Wisdom Sits in Places: Landscape and Language among the Western Apache*. University of New Mexico Press, Albuquerque.

Beals, Ralph L., George W. Brainerd, and Watson Smith. 1945. *Archaeological Studies in Northeast Arizona*. University of California Publications in American Archaeology and Ethnology, vol. 44, no. 1. University of California Press, Berkeley and Los Angeles.

Bellorado, Benjamin. 2007. Breaking Down the Models: Reconstructing Prehistoric Subsistence Agriculture in the Durango District of Southwestern Colorado. Unpublished master's thesis, Department of Anthropology, Northern Arizona University, Flagstaff.

Bellwood, Peter S. 2005. *First Farmers: The Origins of Agricultural Societies*. Blackwell Publishing, Oxford.

Bellwood, Peter S., and Colin Renfrew. 2002. *Examining the Farming/Language Dispersal Hypothesis*. McDonald Institute Monographs. Oxbow Books, Oxford.

Benson, Larry V., Michael S. Berry, Edward A. Jolie, Jerry D. Spangler, David W. Stahle, and Eugene M. Hattori. 2007. Possible Impacts of Early 11th-, Middle 12th-, and Late-13th-Century Droughts on Western Native Americans and the Mississippian Cahokians. *Quaternary Science Reviews* 26:336–350.

Benson, Larry V., Kenneth Petersen, and John Stein. 2007. Anasazi (Pre-Columbian Native-American) Migrations during the Middle-12th and Late-13th Centuries: Were They Drought Induced? *Climatic Change* 83(1–2): 187–213.

Berlin, G. Lennis, J. Richard Ambler, Richard H. Hevly, and Gerald G. Shaber. 1977. Identification of a Sinagua Agricultural Field by Aerial Thermography, Soil Chemistry, Pollen/Plant Analysis, and Archaeology. *American Antiquity* 42:588–600.

Bernardini, Wesley. 1996. Transitions in Social Organization: A Predictive Model from Southwestern Colorado. *Journal of Anthropological Archaeology* 15:372–402.

———. 2005. *Hopi Oral Tradition and the Archaeology of Identity.* University of Arizona Press, Tucson.

Bernardini, Wesley, and Severin Fowles. In press. Becoming Hopi, Becoming Tewa: Two Pueblo Histories of Movement. In *Changing Histories, Landscapes, and Perspectives: The 20th Anniversary Southwest Symposium*, edited by Margaret Nelson and Colleen Strawhacker. University Press of Colorado, Boulder.

Berry, Michael S. 1982. *Time, Space, and Transition in Anasazi Prehistory.* University of Utah Press, Salt Lake City.

Berry, Michael S., and Claudia F. Berry. 2001. *An Archaeological Analysis of the Prehistoric Fremont Culture for the Purpose of Assessing Cultural Affiliation with Nine Claimant Tribes.* Report prepared for the Bureau of Reclamation, Upper Colorado Regional Office, Salt Lake City, Utah.

Betancourt, Julio L. 1990. Late Quaternary Biogeography of the Colorado Plateau. In *Packrat Middens: The Last 40,000 Years of Biotic Change*, edited by Julio L. Betancourt, Thomas R. Van Devender, and Paul S. Martin, pp. 259–292. University of Arizona Press, Tucson.

Betancourt, Julio L., Jeffrey S. Dean, and H. M. Hull. 1986. Prehistoric Long-Distance Transport of Construction Beams, Chaco Canyon, New Mexico. *American Antiquity* 51:370–374.

Bice, Richard A. 1994. Some Thoughts on the Naming and Dating of San Ignacio Black-on-white Pottery (Late Chaco-McElmo Black-on-white) in the North Central Region of New Mexico. In *Artifacts, Shrines, and Pueblos: Papers in Honor of Gordon Page*, edited by M. Duran and D. Kirkpatrick, pp. 27–40. Archaeological Society of New Mexico, Albuquerque.

Bice, Richard A., Phyllis S. Davis, and William M. Sundt. 1998. *The AS-8 Pueblo and the Cañada de las Milpas: A Pueblo III Complex in North-Central New Mexico.* Albuquerque Archaeological Society, Albuquerque.

Bice, Richard A., and William M. Sundt. 1972. *Prieta Vista: A Small Pueblo III Ruin in North-Central New Mexico.* Albuquerque Archaeological Society, Albuquerque.

Billman, Brian R. 2008. An Outbreak of Violence and Raiding in the Central Mesa Verde Region in the 12th Century AD. In *Social Violence in the Prehispanic American Southwest*, edited by Deborah L. Nichols and Patricia L. Crown, pp. 41–69. University of Arizona Press, Tucson.

Billman, Brian R., Patricia M. Lambert, and Banks L. Leonard. 2000. Cannibalism, Warfare, and Drought in the Mesa Verde Region during the Twelfth Century AD. *American Antiquity* 65:145–178.

Bintliff, John. 2007. Emergent Complexity in Settlement Systems and Urban Transformation. In *Historische Geographie der Alten Welt: Grundlagen Erträge, Perspektiven. Festausgabe für Eckart Olshausen*, edited by U. Fellmeth, P. Guyot, and H. Sonnabend, pp. 43–82. Spudasmata (114). Hildesheim, Zürich.

Biondi, Franco, D. L. Perkins, D. R. Cayan, and M. K. Hughes. 1999. July Temperature during the Second Millenium Reconstructed from Idaho Tree-Rings. *Geophysical Research Letters* 26:1445–1448.

Blackburn, Fred M. 2006. *The Wetherills: Friends of Mesa Verde.* The Durango Herald Small Press, Durango, Colorado.

Blanchette, R. A. 2000. A Review of Microbial Deterioration Found in Archaeological Wood from Different Environments. *International Biodeteriorations and Biodegradation* 46:189–204.

Blinman, Eric. 2000. The Foundations, Practice, and Limitations of Ceramic Dating in the American Southwest. In *It's About Time*, edited by S. E. Nash, pp. 41–59. University of Utah Press, Salt Lake City.

———. 2007. Can't Grow Corn There Today: Climate Change and the Culture History of the Galisteo Basin. Paper presented at the eightieth Pecos Conference, Pecos National Historic Park, New Mexico.

Bloom, L. B. 1934. Note on the Penalosa Map. *New Mexico Historical Review* 9(2): 228–230.

Bowser, Brenda J. 2002. The Perceptive Potter: An Ethnoarchaeological Study of Pottery, Ethnicity, and Political Action in Amazonia. Unpublished PhD dissertation, Department of Anthropology, University of California, Santa Barbara.

Boyd, Robert, and Peter J. Richerson. 1985. *Culture and the Evolutionary Process.* University of Chicago Press, Chicago.

———. 2009. Voting with Your Feet: Payoff-Biased Migration and the Evolution of Group-Beneficial Behavior. *Journal of Theoretical Biology* 257:331–339.

Boyer, Jeffrey L. 1994. Occupying the Taos Frontier: The Valdez Phase and Valdez Phase Sites. In *Studying the Taos Frontier: The Pot Creek Data Recovery Project*, by J. L. Boyer, J. L. Moore, D. F. Levine, L. Mick-O'Hara, and M. S. Toll, pp. 379–424. Archaeology Notes, no. 68. Office of Archaeological Studies, Museum of New Mexico, Santa Fe.

———. 1995. Anasazi Communities on the Taos Frontier: Introduction to Data Recovery on Blueberry Hill. In *The Blueberry Hill Road Testing Project: Results of Archaeological Test Investigations at 20 Sites and a Plan for Data Recovery Investigations at 12 Sites along Blueberry Hill Road, Taos County, New Mexico*, edited by J. L. Boyer and S. O. Urban. Archaeology Notes 182 (manuscript). Office of Archaeological Studies, Museum of New Mexico, Santa Fe.

———. 1997. *Dating the Valdez Phase: Chronometric Reevaluation of the Initial Anasazi Occupation of North-Central New Mexico.* Archaeology Notes 164. Office of Archaeological Studies, Museum of New Mexico, Santa Fe.

———. 2000. It Takes a Village to Dig a Kiva: Archaeological and Ethnohistorical Evidence for the Formation of Early Puebloan Communities in the Northern Rio Grande. Paper presented in the Summer Colloquium Series. Fort Burgwin Research Center, Taos, NM.

———. 2001. LA 391: The Mera Community Center Site. In *US 84/285 Santa Fe to Pojoaque Corridor: Preliminary Results of Data Recovery Investigations at Five Sites Near Cuyamungue, Santa Fe County, New Mexico*, by J. Boyer, J. Moore, and S. A. Lakatos, pp. 22–32. Archaeology Notes, no. 296. Office of Archaeological Studies, Museum of New Mexico, Santa Fe.

———. 2002. It Takes a Village to Have a Plaza: An Argument for Early Puebloan Community Integration in the Northern Rio Grande. Paper presented in the symposium "Roadside Archaeology and History in New Mexico," sixth annual meeting of the Society for American Archaeology, Denver.

Boyer, Jeffrey L. 2008. North People and South People: Ethnohistorical and Archaeo-logical Evidence for the Origins and Organization of Taos Pueblo. In *Chasing Chaco and the Southwest: Papers in Honor of Frances Joan Mathien*, edited by R. Wiseman, T. O'Laughlin, C. Snow, and C. Travis, pp. 19–35. Papers of the Archaeological Society of New Mexico, vol. 34. Albuquerque.

Boyer, Jeffrey L., Nancy J. Akins, and Jessica Badner. 2002. *Preliminary Report on Human Burials Recovered from LA 391, US 84/285 Santa Fe to Pojoaque Corridor, Santa Fe County, New Mexico.* Report on file at the Office of Archaeological Studies, Museum of New Mexico, Santa Fe.

Boyer, Jeffrey L., and Steven A. Lakatos. 2008. The Puebloan Prehistory of the Northern Rio Grande. Paper circulated at the Amerind Foundation Seminar on the Depopulation of the Northern San Juan Region, February 23–27, 2008.

Boyer, Jeffrey L., James L. Moore, and Steven A. Lakatos. 2001. US 84/285 Santa Fe to Pojoaque Corridor: Preliminary Results of Data Recovery Investigations at Five Sites Near Cuyamungue, Santa Fe County, New Mexico. Archaeology Notes, no. 296. Office of Archaeological Studies, Museum of New Mexico, Santa Fe.

Bradfield, Maitland. 1971. *The Changing Patterns of Hopi Agriculture.* Occasional Paper, no. 30. Royal Anthropological Institute of Great Britain and Ireland, London.

Bradley, Bruce A. 1992. Excavations at Sand Canyon Pueblo. In *The Sand Canyon Archaeo-logical Project: A Progress Report*, edited by William D. Lipe, pp. 79–97. Occasional Papers of the Crow Canyon Archaeological Center, no. 2. Cortez, Colorado.

———. 1993. Planning, Growth, and Functional Differentiation at a Prehistoric Pueblo: A Case Study from SW Colorado. *Journal of Field Archaeology* 20(1): 23–42.

———. 1996. Pitchers to Mugs: Chacoan Revival at Sand Canyon Pueblo. *Kiva* 61:241–256.

Bradley, Cynthia S. 2002. Thoughts Count: Ideology and the Children of Sand Canyon Pueblo. In *Children in the Prehistoric Puebloan Southwest*, edited by Kathryn A. Kamp, pp. 169–195. University of Utah Press, Salt Lake City.

Bradley, Raymond S. 1999. *Paleoclimatology: Reconstructing Climates of the Quaternary.* 2d ed. Academic Press, San Diego.

Braun, David P., and Stephen Plog. 1982. Evolution of Tribal Social Networks: Theory and Prehistoric North American Evidence. *American Antiquity* 47:504–525.

Breternitz, David A. 1966. *An Appraisal of Tree-Ring Dated Pottery in the Southwest.* Anthro-pological Papers of the University of Arizona, no. 10. University of Arizona Press, Tucson.

Breternitz, David A., Arthur H. Rohn, and Elizabeth A. Morris. 1974. *Prehistoric Ceramics of the Mesa Verde Region.* Museum of Northern Arizona, Ceramic Series, no. 5. Northern Arizona Society of Science and Art, Inc., Flagstaff.

Brew, John O. 1943. On the Pueblo IV and on the Katchina-Tlaloc Relations. In *El norte de Mexico y el sur de Estados Unidos: Tercera reunión de Mesa Redonda Sobre Problemas Antropologicos de Mexico y Centro América*, pp. 241–245. Sociedad Mexicana de Antro-pologia, México, D.F.

Brisbin, Joel M., Donna M. Glowacki, and Kay E. Barnett. 2008. Spruce Tree House 2007 Summary of Architectural Documentation: Structures and Social Organization in a Thirteenth Century Cliff Dwelling, Mesa Verde National Park, Colorado. Manuscript on file at Mesa Verde National Park, Colorado.

Brown, David P., and Andrew C. Comrie. 2002. Sub-Regional Seasonal Precipitation Linkages to SOI and PDO in the Southwest United States. *Atmospheric Science Letters* 3:94–102.

Brown, G. M., Thomas C. Windes, and Peter J. McKenna. 2008. Animas Anamnesis: Aztec Ruins, or Anasazi Capital. In *Salmon Ruins Working Conference Proceedings*, edited by P. F. Reed. University of Utah Press, Salt Lake City.

Brunson, Judy Lynn. 1989. *The Social Organization of the Los Muertos Hohokam: A Reanalysis of Cushing's Hemenway Expedition Data*. PhD dissertation, Department of Anthropology, Arizona State University, Tempe. Proquest, Ann Arbor.

Buck, Caitlin E., James B. Kenworthy, Cliff D. Litton, and Adrian F. M. Smith. 1991. Combining Archaeological and Radiocarbon Information: A Bayesian Approach to Calibration. *Antiquity* 65:808–821.

Burmeister, Stefan. 2000. Archaeology and Migration: Approaches to an Archaeological Proof of Migration. *Current Anthropology* 41:539–567.

Burns, Barney T. 1983. Simulated Anasazi Storage Behavior Using Crop Yields Reconstructed from Tree Rings, AD 652–1968. 2 vols. PhD dissertation, University of Arizona. University Microfilms International, Ann Arbor.

Bussey, Stanley D. 1968. Excavations at LA 6462, The North Bank Site. In *Cochiti Dam Archaeological Salvage Project*, Part 1: *Report on the 1963 Season*, assembled by C. Lange, pp. 5–12. Research Records, no. 6. Museum of New Mexico, Santa Fe.

Cameron, Catherine M. 1990. The Effect of Varying Estimates of Pit Structure Use-Life on Prehistoric Population Estimates in the American Southwest. *Kiva* 55:155–166.

———. 1995. Migration and the Movement of Southwestern Peoples. *Journal of Anthropological Archaeology* 14:104–124.

———. 2005. Exploring Archaeological Cultures in the Northern Southwest: What Were Chaco and Mesa Verde? *Kiva* 70(3): 227–254.

———. 2008. Captives in Prehistory: Agents of Social Change. In *Invisible Citizens: Captives and Their Consequences*, edited by Catherine M. Cameron, University of Utah Press.

———. In press. Captives and Culture Change: Implications for Archaeologists. *Current Anthropology*.

Cameron, Catherine M. (editor). 1995. Special Issue: Migration and the Movement of Southwestern Peoples. *Journal of Anthropological Archaeology* 14:99–250.

Cameron, Catherine M., and Andrew I. Duff. 2008. History and Process in Village Formation: Context and Contrasts from the Northern Southwest. *American Antiquity* 73:29–58.

Campbell, Lyle. 1998. *Historical Linguistics: An Introduction*. MIT Press, Cambridge.

Campbell, Lyle, and Terrence Kaufman. 1976. A Linguistic Look at the Olmecs. *American Antiquity* 41:80–89.

Carlson, Ingrid K., Angela Linse, and Timothy A. Kohler. 1990. Excavations in Area 2. In *Bandelier Archaeological Excavation Project: Summer 1989 Excavations at Burnt Mesa Pueblo*, edited by Timothy A. Kohler, pp. 49–74. Reports of Investigations 62. Washington State University, Pullman.

Carr, Christopher. 1995. A Unified Middle-Range Theory of Artifact Design. In *Style, Society and Person: Archaeological and Ethnological Perspectives*, edited by Christopher Carr and Jill E. Neitzel, pp. 171–258. Plenum Press, New York.

Carson, E. Ann. 2006. Maximum Likelihood Estimation of Human Craniometric Heritabilities. *American Journal of Physical Anthropology* 131:169–180.

Cashdan, Elizabeth (editor). 1990. *Risk and Uncertainty in Tribal and Peasant Economies.* Westview Press, Boulder.

Cattanach, George S., Jr. 1980. *Long House, Mesa Verde National Park, Colorado.* National Park Service, Washington, DC.

Cavalli-Sforza, L. L., and M. W. Feldman. 1972. *Cultural Transmission and Evolution: A Quantitative Approach.* Princeton University Press, Princeton.

Charles, Mona C., and Sally J. Cole. 2006. Chronology and Cultural Variation in Basketmaker II. *Kiva* 72:167–216.

Cheverud, James M. 1988. A Comparison of Genetic and Phenotypic Correlations. *Evolution* 42:958–968.

Christen, J. Andre. 1994. Bayesian Interpretation of ¹⁴C Results. Unpublished PhD thesis, University of Nottingham, Nottingham, UK.

Churchill, Melissa J. (editor). 2002. *The Archaeology of Woods Canyon Pueblo: A Canyon-Rim Village in Southwestern Colorado.* http://www.crowcanyon.org/woodscanyon (accessed August 15, 2008).

Churchill, Melissa J., Kristin A. Kuckelman, and Mark D. Varien. 1998. Public Architecture in the Mesa Verde Region, AD 900 to 1300. Paper presented at the sixty-third annual meeting of the Society for American Archaeology, Seattle.

Clark, Jeffery J. 2001. *Tracking Prehistoric Migrations: Pueblo Settlers among the Tonto Basin Hohokam.* Anthropological Papers of the University of Arizona, no. 65. University of Arizona Press, Tucson.

————. 2007a. A San Pedro Valley Perspective on Ancestral Pueblo Migration in the Hohokam world. In *The Hohokam Millennium*, edited by Suzanne K. Fish and Paul R. Fish, pp. 99–108. School for Advanced Research Press, Santa Fe.

————. 2007b. Archaeological Concepts for Assessing Mogollon-Zuni Connections. In *Zuni Origins: Toward a New Synthesis of Southwestern Archaeology*, edited by D. Gregory and D. Wilcox, pp. 39–48. University of Arizona Press, Tucson.

————. 2007c. *Precontact Population Decline and Coalescence in the Southern Southwest.* Final Report for National Science Foundation Project, no. 0342661.

Clark, Jeffery J., and Karl W. Laumbaugh. In press. Pueblo Migrations in the Southern Southwest: Perspectives from Arizona and New Mexico. In *Changing Histories, Landscapes, and Perspectives: The 20th Anniversary Southwest Symposium*, edited by Margaret C. Nelson and Colleen A. Strawhacker.

Clark, Jeffery J., M. Kyle Woodson, and Mark C. Slaughter. 2004. Those Who Went to the Land of the Sun: Puebloan Migrations into Southeastern Arizona. In *The Archaeology of a Land Between: Regional Dynamics in the History and Prehistory of Southeastern Arizona*, edited by Henry D. Wallace. University of New Mexico Press, Albuquerque.

Coffey, Grant D., and Kristin A. Kuckelman. 2006. Report of 2005 Research at Goodman Point Pueblo (Site 5MT604), Montezuma County, Colorado. http://www.crowcanyon .org/ResearchReports/GoodmanPoint/interim_reports/2005/Text_2005.html (accessed July 7, 2008).

Cole, Sarah. 2007. Population Dynamics and Sociopolitical Instability in the Central Mesa Verde Region, AD 600–1280. Unpublished master's thesis, Department of Anthropology, Washington State University, Pullman, Washington.

Collins, Susan M. 1975. Prehistoric Rio Grande Settlement Patterns and the Inference of Demographic Change. Unpublished PhD dissertation, Department of Anthropology, University of Colorado, Boulder.

Colson, Elizabeth. 1980. In Good Years and in Bad: Food Strategies of Self-Reliant Societies. *Journal of Anthropological Research* 35:1–29.

Colton, Harold S. 1939. *Prehistoric Culture Units and Their Relationships in Northern Arizona.* Museum of Northern Arizona Bulletin 17. Northern Arizona Society of Science and Art, Flagstaff.

Colton, Harold S., and Lyndon L. Hargrave. 1937. *Handbook of Northern Arizona Pottery Wares.* Museum of Northern Arizona Bulletin 11. Northern Arizona Society of Science and Art, Flagstaff.

Coltrain, Joan Brenner. 1996. Stable Carbon and Radioisotope Analysis. In *Steinaker Gap: An Early Fremont Farmstead,* edited by R. K. Talbot and L. D. Richens, pp. 115–122. Museum of Peoples and Cultures Occasional Papers, no. 2. Brigham Young University, Provo.

———. 1997. Fremont Economic Diversity: A Stable Carbon Isotope Study of Formative Subsistence Practices in the Eastern Great Basin. Unpublished PhD dissertation, Department of Anthropology, University of Utah, Salt Lake City.

Coltrain, Joan Brenner, and Steven W. Leavitt. 2002. Climate and Diet in Fremont Prehistory: Economic Variability and Abandonment of Maize Agriculture in the Great Salt Lake Basin. *American Antiquity* 67:453–485.

Coltrain, Joan Brenner, and Thomas W. Stafford Jr. 1999. Stable Carbon Isotopes and Great Salt Lake Wetlands Diet: Toward an Understanding of the Great Basin Formative. In *Prehistoric Lifeways in the Great Basin Wetlands: Bioarchaeological Reconstruction and Interpretation,* edited by Brian E. Hemphill and Clark Spencer Larsen, pp. 55–83. University of Utah Press, Salt Lake City.

Cook, Edward R. 2006. Tree-Ring Reconstructions of North American Drought: The Current State and Where Do We Go from Here? Paper presented at "Epic Droughts of the Last Two Millennia," the twenty-second Pacific Climate Workshop, Pacific Grove, California.

Cook, Edward R., Keith R. Griffa, David M. Meko, Donald S. Graybill, and Gary Funkhouser. 1995. The "Segment Length Curse" in Long Tree-Ring Chronology Development for Paleoclimatic Studies. *The Holocene* 5:229–237.

Cook, Edward R., Richard Seager, Mark A. Cane, and David W. Stahle. 2007. North American Drought: Reconstructions, Causes, and Consequences. *Earth Science Reviews* 81:93–134.

Cook, Edward R., Connie A. Woodhouse, C. Mark Eakin, David M. Meko, and David W. Stahle. 2004. Long-Term Aridity Changes in the Western United States. *Science* 306: 1015–1018.

Cordell, Linda S. 1979. *A Cultural Resources Overview of the Middle Rio Grande Valley, New Mexico.* U.S. Dept. of Agriculture, Forest Service, Southwest Region, Albuquerque; and U.S. Dept. of the Interior, Bureau of Land Management, New Mexico State Office, Santa Fe.

———. 1995. Tracing Migration Pathways from the Receiving End. *Journal of Anthropological Archaeology* 14:203–211.

———. 1997. *Archaeology of the Southwest.* Academic Press, New York.

———. 2000. Aftermath of Chaos in the Pueblo Southwest. In *Environmental Disaster and the Archaeology of Human Response,* edited by Garth Bawden and Richard M. Reycraft, pp. 179–193. Maxwell Museum of Anthropology, Anthropological Papers, no. 7. University of New Mexico, Albuquerque.

Cordell, Linda S., Carla R. Van West, Jeffrey S. Dean, and Deborah A. Muenchrath. 2007. Mesa Verde Settlement History and Relocation: Climate Change, Social Networks, and Ancestral Pueblo Migration. *Kiva* 72:379–405.

Corruccini, Robert S. 1972. The Biological Relationships of Some Prehistoric and Historic Pueblo Populations. *American Journal of Physical Anthropology* 37:373–388.

Creamer, Winifred. 1993. *The Architecture of Arroyo Hondo Pueblo, New Mexico*. Arroyo Hondo Archaeological Series, no. 7. School of American Research, Santa Fe.

Creamer, Winifred, and Jonathan Haas. 2003. Villages before Aggregation: The Merrigan Site (LA 110971), a Developmental Period Hamlet, El Rancho, New Mexico. *Fieldiana: Anthropology*, new series, 35. Field Museum of Natural History, Chicago.

Crow Canyon Archaeological Center. 2004. *The Sand Canyon Pueblo Database*. http://www.crowcanyon.org/ResearchReports/dbw/dbw_chooser.asp?Site=5MT765 (accessed February 2, 2008).

———. 2008. *The Crow Canyon Archaeological Center Research Database*. http://www.crowcanyon.org/researchdatabase (accessed July 10, 2008).

Crowley, Thomas J. 2000. Causes of Climate Change over the Past 1000 Years. *Science* 289:270–277.

Crown, Patricia L. 1981. Analysis of the Las Colinas Ceramics. In *The 1968 Excavations at Mound 8, Las Colinas Ruins Group, Phoenix, Arizona*, edited by Laurens C. Hammack and Alan P. Sullivan, pp. 87–169. Arizona State Museum Archaeological Series, no. 154. Arizona State Museum, University of Arizona, Tucson.

———. 1987. Classic Period Hohokam Settlement and Land Use in the Casa Grande Ruins Area, Arizona. *Journal of Field Archaeology* 14:147–162.

———. 1991. Evaluating the Construction Sequence and Population of Pot Creek Pueblo. *American Antiquity* 56:291–314.

———. 1994. *Ceramics and Ideology: Salado Polychrome Pottery*. University of New Mexico Press, Albuquerque.

Crown, Patricia L., Janet D. Orcutt, and Timothy A. Kohler. 1996. Pueblo Cultures in Transition: The Northern Rio Grande. In *The Prehistoric Pueblo World, AD 1150–1350*, edited by Michael A. Adler, pp. 188–204. University of Arizona Press, Tucson.

Crown, Patricia L., Larry A. Schwalbe, and J. Ronald London. 1988. X-Ray Fluorescence Analysis of Materials Variability in Las Colinas Ceramics. In *The 1982–1984 Excavations at Las Colinas: Material Culture*, pp. 29–71. Arizona State Museum Archaeological Series, no. 162(4). Arizona State Museum, University of Arizona, Tucson.

Daly, Christopher, Ronald P. Neilson, and Donald L. Phillips. 1994. A Statistical-Topographic Model for Mapping Climatological Precipitation over Mountainous Terrain. *Journal of Applied Meteorology* 33:140–158.

Damon, Paul E., J. C. Lerman, and A. Long. 1978. Temporal Fluctuations of Atmospheric ^{14}C: Causal Factors and Implications. *Annual Review of Earth and Planetary Science* 6:457–494.

Damp, Jonathan E., Stephen A. Hall, and Susan J. Smith. 2002. Early Irrigation on the Colorado Plateau near Zuni Pueblo, New Mexico. *American Antiquity* 67:665–676.

Danson, Edward B. 1957. *An Archaeological Survey of West Central New Mexico and East Central Arizona*. Papers of the Peabody Museum of American Archaeology and Ethnology, Harvard University, vol. 54, no. 1. Cambridge, Mass.

David, Nicholas, Judy Sterner, and Kodzo Gavua. 1988. Why Pots Are Decorated. *Current Anthropology* 29:365–389.

Davis, Emma Lou. 1964. Anasazi Mobility and Mesa Verde Migrations. Unpublished PhD dissertation, Department of Anthropology, University of California at Los Angeles.

————. 1965. Small Pressures and Cultural Drift as Explanations for Abandonment of the San Juan Area, New Mexico and Arizona. *American Antiquity* 30:353–355.

Davis, Emma Lou, and James H. Winkler. 1959. A Late Mesa Verde Site in the Rio Puerco Valley. *El Palacio* 66(3): 92–100.

Davis, Irvine. 1959. Linguistic Clues to Northern Rio Grande Prehistory. *El Palacio* 66(3): 73–84.

————. 1989. A New Look at Aztec-Tanoan. In *General and Amerindian Ethnolinguistics: In Remembrance of Stanley Newman*, edited by Mary Ritchie Key and Henry M. Hoenig-swald, pp. 365–379. Mouton de Gruyter, Berlin and New York.

Dean, Jeffrey S. 1966. The Pueblo Abandonment of Tsegi Canyon, Northeastern Arizona. Paper presented at the thirty-first annual meeting of the Society for American Archaeology, Reno.

————. 1969. *Chronological Analysis of Tsegi Phase Sites in Northeastern Arizona*. Papers of the Laboratory of Tree-Ring Research, no. 3, University of Arizona Press, Tucson.

————. 1970. Aspects of Tsegi Phase Social Organization: A Trial Reconstruction. In *Reconstructing Prehistoric Pueblo Societies*, edited by William A. Longacre, pp. 140–174. University of New Mexico Press, Albuquerque.

————. 1978a. Tree-Ring Dating in Archeology. In Anthropological Papers, no. 99, pp. 129–163. University of Utah, Salt Lake City.

————. 1978b. An Evaluation of the Initial SARG Research Design. In *Investigations of the Southwestern Anthropological Research Group: An Experiment in Archaeological Cooperation: The Proceedings of the 1976 Conference*, edited by Robert C. Euler and George J. Gumerman, pp. 103–117. Museum of Northern Arizona, Flagstaff.

————. 1986. Dendrochronology. In *Dating and Age Determination of Biological Materials*, edited by M. R. Zimmerman and J. I. Angel, pp. 126–165. Croom Helm, London.

————. 1988a. Dendrochronology and Paleoenvironmental Reconstruction on the Colorado Plateaus. In *The Anasazi in a Changing Environment*, edited by George J. Gumerman, pp. 119–167. Cambridge University Press, Cambridge.

————. 1988b. A Model of Anasazi Behavioral Adaptation. In *The Anasazi in a Changing Environment*, edited by George J. Gumerman, pp. 25–44. Cambridge University Press, Cambridge.

————. 1996a. Demography, Environment, and Subsistence Stress. In *Evolving Complexity and Environmental Risk in the Prehistoric Southwest*, edited by Joseph A. Tainter and Bonnie Bagley Tainter, pp. 25–56. Santa Fe Institute Studies in the Sciences of Complexity, Proceedings, vol. 24. Addison-Wesley Publishing Company, Reading, Massachusetts.

————. 1996b. Kayenta Anasazi Settlement Transformations in Northeastern Arizona, AD 1150 to 1350. In *The Prehistoric Pueblo World, AD 1150–1350*, edited by Michael A. Adler, pp. 29–47. University of Arizona Press, Tucson.

————. 1997. Dendrochronology. In *Chronometric Dating in Archaeology*, edited by R. E. Taylor and M. J. Aitken, pp. 31–64. Plenum Press, New York.

————. 2000. Complexity Theory and Sociocultural Change in the American Southwest. In *The Way the Wind Blows: Climate, History, and Human Action*, edited by Roderick J. McIntosh, Joseph A. Tainter, and Susan Keech McIntosh, pp. 89–118. Columbia University Press, New York.

Dean, Jeffrey S. 2002. Late Pueblo II–Pueblo III in Kayenta-Branch Prehistory. In *Prehistoric Culture Change on the Colorado Plateau: Ten Thousand Years on Black Mesa*, edited by Shirley Powell and Francis E. Smiley, pp. 121–157. University of Arizona Press, Tucson.

———. 2006. Subsistence Stress and Food Storage at Kiet Siel, Northeastern Arizona. In *Environmental Change and Human Adaptation in the Ancient American Southwest*, edited by David E. Doyel and Jeffrey S. Dean, pp. 160–179. University of Utah Press, Salt Lake City.

Dean, Jeffrey, William Doelle, and Janet Orcutt. 1994. Adaptive Stress, Environment, and Demography. In *Themes in Southwest Prehistory*, edited by George J. Gumerman, pp. 53–86. School of American Research Press, Santa Fe, New Mexico.

Dean, Jeffrey S., Robert E. Euler, George J. Gumerman, Fred Plog, Richard H. Hevly, and Thor N. V. Karlstrom. 1985. Human Behavior, Demography, and Paleoenvironment on the Colorado Plateaus. *American Antiquity* 50:537–554.

Dean, Jeffrey S., and Gary S. Funkhouser. 1995. Dendroclimatic Reconstructions for the Southern Colorado Plateau. In *Proceedings of the Workshop, Climate Change in the Four Corners and Adjacent Regions: Implications for Environmental Restoration and Land-Use Planning*, edited by W. Joseph Waugh, Kenneth L. Petersen, Peter E. Wigand, B. D. Louthan, and R. D. Walker, pp. 85–104. U.S. Department of Energy, Grand Junction Projects Office, Grand Junction, CO.

———. 2004. Dendrochronology and Fluvial Chronology in Chaco Canyon, Appendix A. In *Relation of "Bonito" Paleo-Channels and Base-Level Variations to Anasazi Occupation, Chaco Canyon, New Mexico*, edited by E. R. Force, R. G. Vivian, T. C. Windes, and J. S. Dean, pp. 39–41. Arizona State Museum Archaeological Series 194, Tucson.

Dean, Jeffrey S., George J. Gumerman, Joshua M. Epstein, Robert L. Axtell, Alan C. Swedlund, Miles T. Parker, and Stephen McCarroll. 2000. Understanding Anasazi Culture Change through Agent-Based Modeling. In *Dynamics in Human and Primate Societies: Agent-Based Modeling of Social and Spatial Processes*, edited by Timothy A. Kohler and George J. Gumerman, pp. 179–205. Oxford University Press, New York.

Dean, Jeffrey S., Alexander J. Lindsay Jr., and William J. Robinson. 1978. Prehistoric Settlement in Long House Valley, Northeastern Arizona. In *Investigations of the Southwestern Anthropological Research Group: An Experiment in Archaeological Cooperation; The Proceedings of the 1976 Conference*, edited by Robert C. Euler and George J. Gumerman, pp. 25–44. Museum of Northern Arizona, Flagstaff.

Dean, Jeffrey S., and William J. Robinson. 1977. *Dendroclimatic Variability in the American Southwest, AD 680 to 1970*. Laboratory of Tree-Ring Research, University of Arizona, Tucson. U.S. Department of Commerce, National Technological Information Service PB-266 340, Springfield, Virginia.

———. 1978. *Expanded Tree-Ring Chronologies for the Southwestern United States*. Chronology Series 3. Laboratory of Tree-Ring Research, University of Arizona, Tucson.

Dean, Jeffrey S., and Carla R. Van West. 2002. Environment-Behavior Relationships in Southwestern Colorado. In *Seeking the Center Place: Archaeology and Ancient Communities in the Mesa Verde Region*, edited by Mark D. Varien and Richard H. Wilshusen, pp. 81–99. University of Utah Press, Salt Lake City.

Dean, Jeffrey S., and R. L. Warren. 1983. Dendrochronology. In *The Architecture and Dendrochronology of Chetro Ketl, Chaco Canyon, New Mexico*, edited by S. H. Lekson, pp. 105–240. National Park Service Reports of the Chaco Center, no. 6, Albuquerque.

Dean, Patricia. 1992. *Prehistoric Pottery in the Northeastern Great Basin: Problems in the Classification and Archaeological Interpretation of Undecorated Fremont and Shoshoni Wares.*

PhD dissertation, University of Oregon, Eugene. University Microfilms International, Ann Arbor.

Decker, Kenneth W., and Larry L. Tieszen. 1989. Isotopic Reconstructions of Mesa Verde Diet from Basketmaker III to Pueblo III. *Kiva* 55:33–47.

Demarest, Arthur. 2004. *Ancient Maya: The Rise and Fall of a Rainforest Civilization.* Cambridge University Press, Cambridge.

Dickson, D. Bruce, Jr. 1975. Settlement Pattern Stability and Change in the Middle Northern Rio Grande Region, New Mexico: A Test of Some Hypotheses. *American Antiquity* 40:159–171.

——. 1979. *Prehistoric Pueblo Settlement Patterns: The Arroyo Hondo, New Mexico, Site Survey.* School of American Research, Santa Fe, New Mexico.

Di Peso, Charles C. 1958a. *The Reeve Ruin of Southeastern Arizona: A Study of a Prehistoric Western Pueblo Migration into the Middle San Pedro Valley.* The Amerind Foundation, no. 8. The Amerind Foundation, Inc., Dragoon, Arizona.

——. 1958b. Western Pueblo Intrusion into the San Pedro Valley. *Kiva* 23:12–16.

Dodd, Walter A., Jr. 1982. *Final Year Excavations at the Evans Mound Site.* Anthropological Papers, no. 106. University of Utah, Salt Lake City.

Doelle, William H. 2000. Tonto Basin Demography in a Regional Perspective. In *Salado*, edited by Jeffrey S. Dean, pp. 81–105. Amerind Foundation New World Studies Series, no. 4. Amerind Foundation, Dragoon, AZ, and University of New Mexico Press, Albuquerque.

Doelle, William H., and Henry D. Wallace. 1991. The Changing Role of the Tucson Basin in the Hohokam Regional System. In *Exploring the Hohokam: Prehistoric Desert Peoples of the American Southwest*, edited by George J. Gumerman, pp. 279–345. Amerind Foundation New World Studies Series, no. 1. Amerind Foundation, Dragoon, Arizona, and University of New Mexico Press, Albuquerque.

Douglass, Andrew E. 1914. A Method of Estimating Rainfall by the Growth of Trees. In *The Climatic Factor as Illustrated in Arid America*, edited by E. Huntington, pp. 101–121. Carnegie Institute of Washington Publication 192. Washington, DC.

——. 1921. Dating Our Prehistoric Ruins. *Natural History* 21:27–30.

——. 1929. The Secret of the Southwest Solved by Talkative Tree Rings. *National Geographic* 56:737–770.

Doyel, David E. 1974. *Excavations in the Escalante Ruin Group, Southern Arizona.* Arizona State Museum Archaeological Series, no. 37. Arizona State Museum, University of Arizona, Tucson.

Dozier, Edward P. 1954. *The Hopi-Tewa of Arizona.* University of California Publications in American Archaeology and Ethnology 44(3): 259–376. University of California Press, Berkeley.

——. 1970. *The Pueblo Indians of North America.* Holt, Rinehart and Winston, Inc., New York.

Drèze, Jean, and Amartya Sen. 1989. *Hunger and Public Action.* Clarendon Paperbacks, Oxford.

Driver, Jonathan C. 1996. Social Complexity and Hunting Systems in Southwestern Colorado. In *Debating Complexity: Proceedings of the Twenty-Sixth Annual Chacmool Conference*, edited by D. A. Meyer, P. C. Dawson, and D. T. Hanna, pp. 364–374. Archaeological Association of the University of Calgary, Calgary, Alberta.

——. 2002. Faunal Variation and Change in the Northern San Juan Region. In *Seeking the Center Place: Archaeology and Ancient Communities in the Mesa Verde Region*, edited by Mark D. Varien and Richard H. Wilshusen, pp. 143–160. University of Utah Press, Salt Lake City.

Driver, Jonathan C., Michael J. Brand, Lianne Lester, and Natalie D. Munro. 1999. Faunal Studies. In *The Sand Canyon Archaeological Project: Site Testing*, edited by M. Varien, chapter 18. Crow Canyon Archaeological Center, Cortez, Colorado. http://www .crowcanyon.org/ResearchReports/SiteTesting/start.asp (accessed July 10, 2008).

Drossel, Barbara. 2001. Biological Evolution and Statistical Physics. *Advances in Physics* 50:209–295.

Duff, Andrew I. 1998. The Process of Migration in the Late Prehistoric Southwest. In *Migration and Reorganization: The Pueblo IV Period in the American Southwest*, edited by Katherine Spielmann, pp. 31–52. Anthropological Research Papers, no. 51. Arizona State University, Tempe.

———. 2002. *Western Pueblo Identities: Regional Interaction, Migration, and Transformation*. University of Arizona Press, Tucson.

———. 2006a. Research Design and Field Objectives—Communities through Time: Cooperation, Conflict, and Migration. In *Communities through Time: The Archaeology of Shields Pueblo (5MT3807), Montezuma County, Colorado*, edited by Andrew Duff and Susan Ryan. Manuscript on file, Crow Canyon Archaeological Center, Cortez, Colorado.

———. 2006b. Chronology: Shields Pueblo through Time. In *Communities through Time: The Archaeology of Shields Pueblo (5MT3807), Montezuma County, Colorado*, edited by Andrew Duff and Susan Ryan. Manuscript on file, Crow Canyon Archaeological Center, Cortez, Colorado.

———. 2006c. Synthesis: The Shields Pueblo Community through Time. In *Communities through Time: The Archaeology of Shields Pueblo (5MT3807), Montezuma County, Colorado*, edited by Andrew Duff and Susan Ryan. Manuscript on file, Crow Canyon Archaeological Center, Cortez, Colorado.

Duff, Andrew I., and Susan C. Ryan. 1999. The 1998 Field Season at Shields Pueblo (5MT3807), Montezuma County, Colorado. http://www.crowcanyon.org/ResearchReports/ Shields/Shields1998season/Shields_1998.asp (accessed July 10, 2007).

———. 2000. The 1999 Field Season at Shields Pueblo (5MT3807), Montezuma County, Colorado. http://www.crowcanyon.org/ResearchReports/Shields/Shields1999season/ Shields_1999_Start.asp (accessed July 10, 2007).

———. 2001. The 2000 Field Season at Shields Pueblo (5MT3807), Montezuma County, Colorado. http://www.crowcanyon.org/ResearchReports/Shields/Shields2000season/ Shields_2000_text.asp (accessed July 10, 2007).

Duff, Andrew I., and S. C. Ryan (editors). 2006. *Communities through Time: The Archaeology of Shields Pueblo (5MT3807), Montezuma County, Colorado*. Manuscript on file, Crow Canyon Archaeological Center, Cortez, Colorado.

Duff, Andrew I., and Richard H. Wilshusen. 2000. Prehistoric Population Dynamics in the Northern San Juan Region, AD 950–1300. *Kiva* 66:167–190.

Duff, U. Francis. 1904. Some Exploded Theories Concerning Southwestern Archaeology. *American Anthropologist* 6:303–306.

Durand, Stephen R., and Larry L. Baker. 2003. Population, Settlement Patterns, and Paleoenvironment: Culture Change in the Middle Rio Puerco Valley. In *Prehistory of the Middle Rio Puerco Valley, Sandoval County, New Mexico*, edited by Larry L. Baker and Stephen R. Durand, pp. 179–189. Archaeological Society of New Mexico Special Publication, no. 3.

Dutton, Bertha. 1964. Las Madres in the Light of Anasazi Migrations. *American Antiquity* 29:449–454.

Eddy, Frank W. 1977. *Archaeological Investigations at Chimney Rock Mesa, 1970–1972.* Memoirs of the Colorado Archaeological Society, no. 1. Colorado Archaeological Society, Boulder.

Eddy, John A. 1977. Climate and the Changing Sun. *Climate Change* 1:173–190.

Edelman, Sandra A. 1979. San Ildefonso Pueblo. In *Handbook of North American Indians,* vol. 9: *Southwest,* edited by A. Ortiz, pp. 308–316. Smithsonian Institution, Washington, DC.

Edelman, Sandra A., and Alfonso Ortiz. 1979. Tesuque Pueblo. In *Handbook of North American Indians,* vol. 9: *Southwest,* edited by A. Ortiz, pp. 330–335. Smithsonian Institution, Washington, DC.

Eliade, Mircea. 1987. *The Sacred and the Profane: The Nature of Religion.* Harcourt, Inc., San Diego.

———. 1991. *Images and Symbols: Studies in Religious Symbolism.* Princeton University Press, Princeton.

Ellis, Florence H. 1964. Archaeological History of Nambe Pueblo, 14th Century to the Present. *American Antiquity* 30:34–42.

———. 1967. Where Did the Pueblo People Come From? *El Palacio* 74(3): 35–43.

———. 1974. Nambe: Their Past Agricultural Use of Territory. Prepared for the USDI, Bureau of Indian Affairs. Manuscript on file, New Mexico State Engineer Office, Santa Fe.

———. 1975. Life in the Tesuque Valley and Elsewhere in the Santa Fe Area during the Pueblo II Stage of Development. *Awanyu* 3(2): 27–49.

El-Najjar, Mahmoud Y. 1978. Southwestern Physical Anthropology: Do the Cultural and Biological Parameters Correspond? *American Journal of Physical Anthropology* 48:151–158.

———. 1981. A Comparative Study of Facial Dimensions at Gran Quivira. In *Contributions to Gran Quivira Archaeology,* edited by Alden C. Hayes, pp. 157–159. Publications in Archeology, vol. 17. Department of the Interior, National Park Service, Washington, DC.

———. 1986. The Biology and Health of the Prehistoric Inhabitants of Canyon de Chelly. In *Archaeological Investigations at Antelope House,* edited by Don P. Morris, pp. 206–220. Department of the Interior, National Park Service, Washington, DC.

Elson, Mark D. 1998. *Expanding the View of Hohokam Platform Mounds: An Ethnographic Perspective.* Anthropological Papers of the University of Arizona, no. 63. University of Arizona Press, Tucson.

English, Nathan B., Julio L. Betancourt, Jeffrey S. Dean, and Jay Quade. 2001. Strontium Isotopes Reveal Distant Sources of Archaeological Timber in Chaco Canyon, New Mexico. *Proceedings of the National Academy of Sciences* 98:11891–11896.

Erwin, Douglas H. 2006. *Extinction: How Life on Earth Nearly Ended 250 Million Years Ago.* Princeton University Press, Princeton, New Jersey.

Euler, Robert E., George J. Gumerman, Thor N. V. Karlstrom, Jeffrey S. Dean, and Richard H. Hevley. 1979. The Colorado Plateaus: Cultural Dynamics and Paleoenvironment. *Science* 205:1089–1101.

Ezzo, J. A. 1993. *Human Adaptation at Grasshopper Pueblo, Arizona.* International Monographs in Prehistory, Archaeological Series, no. 4. University of Michigan, Ann Arbor.

Fairley, Helen C. 1989. Culture History. In *Man, Models, and Management: An Overview of the Archaeology of the Arizona Strip and the Management of Its Cultural Resources,* by Jeffrey H. Altschul and Helen C. Fairley, pp. 85–152. Report submitted to the USDA Forest Service and the USDI Bureau of Land Management by Statistical Research, Plateau Archaeology, and Dames and Moore.

Fauconnier, Gil. 1997. *Mappings in Thought and Language.* Cambridge University Press, Cambridge.

Fauconnier, Gil, and Mark Turner. 1994. *Conceptual Projection and Middle Spaces.* Report 9401, University of California, San Diego, Department of Cognitive Science, La Jolla.

Fewkes, Jesse Walter. 1911. *Preliminary Report on a Visit to the Navaho National Monument, Arizona.* Bureau of American Ethnology Bulletin 50. Washington.

———. 1919. *Prehistoric Villages, Castles, and Towers of Southwestern Colorado.* Smithsonian Institution, Washington, DC.

Field, Julie S. 2004. Environmental and Climatic Considerations: A Hypothesis for Conflict and the Emergence of Social Complexity in Fijian Prehistory. *Journal of Anthropological Archaeology* 23:79–99.

Fiero, Kathleen. 1999. *Balcony House: A History of a Cliff Dwelling.* Mesa Verde National Park Archeological Research Series Number 8-A. Mesa Verde Museum Association, Inc., Mesa Verde National Park, Colorado.

Fink, T. Michael. 1991. Prehistoric Irrigation Canals and Their Possible Impact on Hohokam Health. In *Prehistoric Irrigation in Arizona*, edited by Cory Dale Breternitz, pp. 61–88. Soil Systems Publications in Archaeology, no. 17. Soil Systems, Inc., Phoenix.

Fink, T. Michael, and Charles F. Merbs. 1991. Hohokam Paleonutrition and Paleopathology: A Search for Correlates. *Kiva* 56:293–318.

Firor, James. 1993. *Stabilization Assessment of Site AZ B:1:102(BLM)/2MO869 Colorado City, Arizona.* Report submitted to the Bureau of Land Management, Arizona Strip District. Alpine Archaeological Consultants, Montrose, Colorado.

Fish, Suzanne K., and Paul R. Fish. 1992. Prehistoric Landscapes of the Sonoran Desert Hohokam. *Population and Environment* 13:269–283.

Fish, Suzanne K., Paul R. Fish, and John H. Madsen. 1990. Analyzing Regional Agriculture: A Hohokam Example. In *The Archaeology of Regions: A Case for Full Coverage Survey*, edited by Suzanne K. Fish and Stephen A. Kowalewski, pp. 189–218. Smithsonian Institution Press, Washington, DC.

Fish, Suzanne K., and Gary P. Nabhan. 1991. Desert as Context: The Hohokam Environment. In *Exploring the Hohokam: Prehistoric Desert Peoples of the American Southwest*, edited by George J. Gumerman, pp. 29–60. Amerind Foundation New World Studies Series, no. 1. Amerind Foundation, Dragoon, AZ, and University of New Mexico Press, Albuquerque.

Force, Eric, and Wayne Howell. 1997. *Holocene Depositional History and Anasazi Occupation in McElmo Canyon, Southwestern Colorado.* Arizona State Museum Archaeological Series 188. University of Arizona Press, Tucson.

Ford, Richard I., Albert H. Schroeder, and Stewart L. Peckham. 1972. Three Perspectives on Puebloan Prehistory. In *New Perspectives on the Pueblos*, edited by Alfonso Ortiz, pp. 19–39. University of New Mexico Press, Albuquerque.

Fowler, Andrew P., and John R. Stein. 1992. Anasazi Great Houses in Space, Time, and Paradigm. In *Anasazi Regional Organization and the Chaco System*, edited by D. E. Doyel, pp. 101–122. Maxwell Museum of Anthropology Anthropological Paper, no. 5, Albuquerque.

Fowler, Andrew P., John R. Stein, and Roger Anyon. 1987. *An Archaeological Reconnaissance of West-Central New Mexico: The Anasazi Monuments Project.* Report submitted to the State of New Mexico Office of Cultural Affairs, Historic Preservation Division, Santa Fe.

Fowler, Catherine S. 1983. Some Lexical Clues to Uto-Aztecan Prehistory. *International Journal of American Linguistics* 49:224–257.

Fowler, Don D., and Jesse D. Jennings. 1982. Great Basin Archaeology: A Historical Overview. In *Man and Environment in the Great Basin*, edited by David B. Madsen and James F. O'Connell, pp. 105–120. Society for American Archaeology Papers, no. 2. Washington, DC.

Fowles, Severin. 2004a. Tewa versus Tiwa: Northern Rio Grande Settlement Patterns and Social History, AD 1275–1540. In *The Protohistoric Pueblo World, AD 1275–1600*, edited by E. Charles Adams and Andrew Duff, pp. 17–25. University of Arizona Press, Tucson.

———. 2004b. The Making of Made People: The Prehistoric Evolution of Hierocracy among the Northern Tiwa of New Mexico. Unpublished PhD dissertation, Department of Anthropology, University of Michigan, Ann Arbor.

Fox, Robin. 1967. *The Keresan Bridge: A Problem in Pueblo Ethnology*. London School of Economics Monographs on Social Anthropology, no. 35. The Athlone Press, New York.

Frank, Barbara W., and Richard A. Thompson. 1995. *Fifth Interim Report: The 1994 SUU Field School Excavations at the Corngrower Site, AZ B:1:102 (BLM), Colorado City Arizona*. Report on file, Bureau of Land Management Arizona Strip District Office, Saint George, Utah.

Frantz, Don, and Donna Gardner. 1995. Southern Tiwa Lexicon: Isleta. Manuscript in possession of the author.

Frisbie, Theodore R. 1967. *The Excavation and Interpretation of the Artificial Leg Basketmaker III–Pueblo I Sites near Corrales, New Mexico*. Unpublished masters' thesis, Department of Anthropology, University of New Mexico, Albuquerque.

Fye, Falko K., David W. Stahle, and Edward R. Cook. 2003. Paleoclimatic Analogs to Twentieth-Century Moisture Regimes across the United States. *Bulletin of the American Meteorological Society* 84:901–909.

Geertz, Clifford. 2005. Very Bad News. Review in *The New York Review of Books*, 52 (5), March.

Gibbs, Raymond W., Jr. 1994. *The Poetics of Mind: Figurative Language, Thought, and Understanding*. Cambridge University Press, Cambridge.

Gilman, Patricia A. 1987. Architecture as Artifact: Pit Structures and Pueblos in the American Southwest. *American Antiquity* 52:538–564.

Gilpin, Dennis, and Larry Benallie Jr. 2000. Juniper Cove and Early Community Structure West of the Chuska Mountains. In *Foundations of Anasazi Culture: The Basketmaker-Pueblo Transition*, edited by Paul F. Reed, pp. 161–173. University of Utah Press, Salt Lake City.

Gilpin, Dennis, Susan E. Perlman, Louise M. Senior, and Lynn A. Neal. 2002. Cultural Affiliation Study for Canyons of the Ancients National Monument, Southwest Colorado. Report prepared for the Bureau of Land Management, Canyons of the Ancients National Monument, and Anasazi Heritage Center. Two Rivers Report, no. TR-01.

Gish, Jannifer W. 1999. Pollen Results. In *The Sand Canyon Archaeological Project: Site Testing*, edited by Mark D. Varien, chapter 17. Crow Canyon Archaeological Center, Cortez, Colorado. http://www.crowcanyon.org/ResearchReports/SiteTesting/start.asp (accessed July 7, 2008).

Gladwin, Winifred, and Harold S. Gladwin. 1934. *A Method for Designation of Cultures and Their Variations*. Medallion Papers, no. 15. Gila Pueblo, Globe, AZ.

Glock, Waldo S. 1937. *Principles and Methods of Tree-Ring Analysis*. Carnegie Institution of Washington Publication 486, Washington, DC.

Glowacki, Donna M. 2001. Yucca House (5MT5006) Mapping Project Report. Unpublished report on file, Crow Canyon Archaeological Center and Mesa Verde National Park, Colorado.

————. 2006. The Social Landscape of Depopulation: The Northern San Juan, AD 1150–1300. Unpublished PhD dissertation, Department of Anthropology, Arizona State University, Tempe.

————. 2007. The Social Landscape of the 13th Century Depopulation of the Northern San Juan. Paper presented in the symposium "New Light on the Thirteenth-century Depopulation of the Northern Southwest" at the annual meeting of the Society for American Archaeology, Austin, Texas.

————. 2009. Religion and the Mesa Verde Migrations. Paper presented at the Amerind Seminar "Religious Ideologies in the Pueblo Southwest, AD 1250–1540," April 1–5, Dragoon, AZ.

Goodrich, Gregory B. 2007. Influence of the Pacific Decadal Oscillation on Winter Precipitation and Drought during Years of Neutral ENSO in the Western United States. *Weather and Forecasting* 22:116–124.

Graumlich, Lisa J. 1993. A 1000-Year Record of Temperature and Precipitation in the Sierra Nevada. *Quaternary Research* 39:249–255.

Graybill, Donald A. 1983. Graybill-Almagre Mountain B—PIAR–ITRDB CO524. http://www.ncdc.noaa.gov/paleo/metadata/noaa-tree-3339.html (accessed June 10, 2002).

Graybill, Donald A., David A. Gregory, Gary S. Funkhouser, and Fred L. Nials. 2006. Long-Term Streamflow Reconstructions, River Channel Morphology, and Aboriginal Irrigation Systems along the Salt and Gila Rivers. In *Environmental Change and Human Adaptation in the Ancient American Southwest*, edited by David E. Doyel and Jeffrey S. Dean, pp. 69–123. University of Utah Press, Salt Lake City.

Grayson, Donald K. 2001. The Archaeological Record of Human Impacts on Animal Populations. *Journal of World Prehistory* 15:1–68.

Green, Dee F. 1961. *Archaeological Investigations at the G. M. Hinckley Farm Site, Utah County, Utah*. Brigham Young University Press, Provo, Utah.

Green, Ernestine L. 1976. Valdez Phase Occupation near Taos, New Mexico. Report no. 10, Fort Burgwin Research Center, Taos.

Gregory, David A. 1991. Form and Variation in Hohokam Settlement Patterns. In *Chaco and Hohokam: Prehistoric Regional Systems in the American Southwest*, edited by Patricia L. Crown and W. James Judge, pp. 159–193. School of American Research Press, Santa Fe.

Grissino-Mayer, Henri D. 1996. A 2129 Year Reconstruction of Precipitation for Northwestern New Mexico, USA. In *Tree Rings, Environment, and Humanity: Proceedings of the International Conference, Tucson, Arizona, 17–21 May 1994*, edited by Jeffrey S. Dean, David M. Meko, and Thomas W. Swetnam, pp. 191–204. Radiocarbon, Department of Geosciences, University of Arizona, Tucson.

Grove, Jean M. 1988. *The Little Ice Age*. Methuen, London and New York.

Guernsey, Samuel J. 1931. *Explorations in Northeastern Arizona: Report on the Archaeological Fieldwork of 1920–1923*. Papers of the Peabody Museum of American Archaeology and Ethnology, Harvard University, vol. 12, no. 1. Cambridge.

Guernsey, Samuel J., and Alfred V. Kidder. 1921. *Basket-Maker Caves of Northeastern Arizona*. Papers of the Peabody Museum of American Archaeology and Ethnology 12(1). Cambridge.

Gumerman, George J. (editor). 1988. *The Anasazi in a Changing Environment*. Cambridge University Press, Cambridge.

Gumerman, George J., and Jeffrey S. Dean. 1989. Prehistoric Cooperation and Competition in the Western Anasazi Area. In *Dynamics of Southwest Prehistory*, edited by L. S. Cordell and G. J. Gumerman, pp. 99–148. Smithsonian Institution Press, Washington, DC.

Haas, Jonathan, and Winifred Creamer. 1993. Stress and Warfare among the Prehistoric Kayenta Anasazi of the Thirteenth Century A.D. *Fieldiana: Anthropology* 21. Field Museum of Natural History, Chicago.

Hack, John T. 1942. *The Changing Physical Environment of the Hopi Indians of Arizona*. Reports of the Awatovi Expedition Peabody Museum, Harvard University, no. 1. Papers of the Peabody Museum of American Archaeology and Ethnology 35(1). Harvard University Press, Cambridge.

Hale, Kenneth L. 1962. Jemez and Kiowa Correspondences in Reference to Kiowa-Tanoan. *International Journal of American Linguistics* 28(1): 1–5.

———. 1967. Toward a Reconstruction of Kiowa-Tanoan Phonology. *International Journal of American Linguistics* 33:112–120.

Hale, Kenneth, and David Harris. 1979. Historical Linguistics and Archeology. In *Handbook of North American Indians*, vol. 9: *Southwest*, edited by Alfonso Ortiz, pp. 170–177. Smithsonian Institution, Washington, DC.

Halstead, Paul, and John O'Shea. 1989. Introduction: Cultural Responses to Risk and Uncertainty. In *Bad Year Economics: Cultural Responses to Risk and Uncertainty*, edited by Paul Halstead and John O'Shea, pp. 1–7. New Directions in Archaeology. Cambridge University Press, Cambridge.

Hantman, Jeffrey L. 1983. Social Networks and Stylistic Distributions in the Prehistoric Plateau Southwest. Unpublished PhD dissertation, Arizona State University, Tempe.

Harbottle, Garman, and Phil C. Weigand. 1992. Turquoise in Pre-Columbian America. *Scientific American* (Feb.): 78–85.

Hargrave, Lyndon L. 1970. *Mexican Macaws: Comparative Osteology and Survey of Remains from the Southwest*. Anthropological Papers of the University of Arizona, no. 20. University of Arizona Press, Tucson.

Harrington, Carobeth Tucker. 1920. Isleta Language: Texts and Analytical Vocabulary. In *Harrington Papers*, microfilm edition, part 4: *Southwest*, reel 36, frames 399–516. Kraus International, New York.

Harrington, John P. 1909. Notes on the Piro Language. *American Anthropologist* 11:563–594.

———. 1910. An Introductory Paper on the Tiwa Language, Dialect of Taos, New Mexico. *American Anthropologist* 12:11–48.

———. 1916. The Ethnogeography of the Tewa Indians. *Bureau of American Ethnology*, 29:29–618. U.S. Government Printing Office, Washington, DC.

———. 1928. *Vocabulary of the Kiowa Language*. Bureau of American Ethnology Bulletin 84. U.S. Government Printing Office, Washington, DC.

Harris, A. J., James Schoenwetter, and A. H. Warren. 1967. *An Archaeological Survey of the Chuska Valley and the Chaco Plateau, New Mexico*. Part 1: *Natural Science Studies*. Research Records, no. 4, Museum of New Mexico, Albuquerque.

Hartman, Dana. 1988. Paleodemography. In *Hohokam Settlement along the Slopes of the Picacho Mountains: Synthesis and Conclusions*, edited by Richard Ciolek-Torrello, and David Wilcox, pp. 220–243. Museum of Northern Arizona Research Paper 36(6). Museum of Northern Arizona, Flagstaff.

Haury, Emil W. 1945. *The Excavation of Los Muertos and Neighboring Ruins in the Salt River Valley, Southern Arizona.* Papers of the Peabody Museum of American Archaeology and Ethnology, vol. 24(1). Harvard University, Cambridge, Massachusetts.

——. 1958. Evidence at Point of Pines for a Prehistoric Migration from Northern Arizona. In *Migrations in New World Culture History*, edited by Raymond H. Thompson, pp. 1–6. University of Arizona Science Bulletin, no. 27. University of Arizona Press, Tucson.

——. 1976. *The Hohokam: Desert Farmers and Craftsmen.* University of Arizona Press, Tucson.

Hayden, Irwin. 1930. Mesa House. In *Archaeological Explorations in Southern Nevada*, pp. 26–92. Southwest Museum Papers, no. 4. Southwest Museum, Los Angeles.

Hayes, Alden C. 1981. A Survey of Chaco Canyon Archaeology. In *Archaeological Surveys of Chaco Canyon*, edited by Alden C. Hayes, David M. Brugge, and W. James Judge, pp. 1–68. Publications in Archaeology 18A, Chaco Canyon Studies. National Park Service, U.S. Department of the Interior, Washington, DC.

Hays-Gilpin, Kelley. 2008. Life's Pathways: Geographic Metaphors in Ancestral Puebloan Material Culture. In *Archaeology without Borders: Contact, Commerce and Change in the U.S. Southwest and Northwestern Mexico*, edited by Laurie D. Webster and Maxine E. McBrinn, pp. 257–270. University Press of Colorado, Boulder.

Hegmon, Michelle. 1989. Social Integration and Architecture. In *The Architecture of Social Integration in Prehistoric Pueblos*, edited by William D. Lipe and Michelle Hegmon, pp. 5–14. Occasional Paper no. 1. Crow Canyon Archaeological Center, Cortez, Colorado.

——. 1991. Six Easy Steps to Dating Pueblo III Ceramic Assemblages: Working Draft. Manuscript on file, Crow Canyon Archaeological Center, Cortez, Colorado.

Hegmon, Michelle, Margaret C. Nelson, and Susan Ruth. 1998. Abandonment, Reorganization, and Social Change: Analysis of Pottery and Architecture from the Mimbres Region. *American Anthropologist* 100:148–162.

Hegmon, Michelle, Matthew A. Peeples, Ann P. Kinzig, Stephanie Kulow, Cathryn M. Meegan, and Margaret C. Nelson. 2008. Social Transformation and Its Human Costs in the Prehispanic U.S. Southwest. *American Anthropologist* 110:313–324.

Henderson, Junius, and John Peabody Harrington. 1914. *Ethnozoology of the Tewa Indians.* Government Printing Office, Washington, DC.

Henderson, T. Kathleen. 1995. Land Use and Community Organization at the Head of the Scottsdale Canal System. In *Archaeology at the Head of the Scottsdale Canal System*, vol. 3: *Canal and Synthetic Studies*, edited by Mark R. Hackbarth, T. Kathleen Henderson, and Douglas B. Craig, pp. 145–153. Anthropological Papers, no. 95-1(3). Northland Research, Inc., Flagstaff, Arizona.

Hendon, Julia A. 2000. Having and Holding: Storage, Memory, Knowledge, and Social Relations. *American Anthropologist* 102:42–53.

Herweijer, Celine, Richard Seager, Edward R. Cook, and Julien Emile-Geay. 2007. North American Droughts of the Last Millennium from a Gridded Network of Tree-Ring Data. *Journal of Climate* 20:1353–1376.

Hester, James J. 1962. *Early Navajo Migrations and Acculturation in the Southwest.* Museum of New Mexico Papers in Anthropology, no. 6. Santa Fe.

Hewett, Edgar L. *1908. Les communautés anciennes dans le désert américain: Recherches archéologiques sur la distribution et l'organisation sociale des anciennes populations au sudoest des États-Unis et au nord du Mexique.* Librairie Kundig, Geneva.

Hibben, Frank C. 1937. *Excavation of the Riana Ruin and Chama Valley Survey.* University of New Mexico Bulletin, Anthropological Series 2(1). University of New Mexico Press, Albuquerque.

Higgins, R. Wayne, Y. Chen, and Arthur V. Douglas. 1999. Interannual Variability of the North American Warm Season Precipitation Regime. *Journal of Climate* 12:653–680.

Hill, J. Brett. 2008. Hohokam Population Collapse in the Lower Salt River Valley. In *Archaeology Southwest* 21(4): 15–16.

Hill, J. Brett, Jeffery J. Clark, William H. Doelle, and Patrick D. Lyons. 2004. Prehistoric Demography in the Southwest: Migration, Coalescence and Hohokam Population Decline. *American Antiquity* 69:689–716.

Hill, James N. 1970. *Broken K Pueblo: Prehistoric Social Organization in the American Southwest.* Anthropological Papers of the University of Arizona, no. 18. University of Arizona Press, Tucson.

Hill, Jane H. 2001. Proto-Uto-Aztecan: A Community of Cultivators in Central Mexico? *American Anthropologist* 103:913–934.

———. 2008a. The Zuni Language in Southwestern Areal Context. In *Zuni Origins: Toward a New Synthesis of Southwestern Archaeology,* edited by David A. Gregory and David R. Wilcox, pp. 22–38. University of Arizona Press, Tucson.

———. 2008b. Northern Uto-Aztecan and Kiowa-Tanoan: Evidence of Contact between the Proto-Languages? *International Journal of American Linguistics* 74(2): 155–188.

Hinsley, Curtis M., and David R. Wilcox (editors). 2002. *Frank Hamilton Cushing and the Hemenway Southwestern Archaeological Expedition, 1886–1889.* Vol. 2: *The Lost Itinerary of Frank Hamilton Cushing.* Southwest Center Series. University of Arizona Press, Tucson.

Historic American Buildings Survey/Historic American Engineering Record (HABS/HAER), Prints and Photograph Division. 1934. *Kiva, Nambe, Santa Fe County, NM.* American Memory from the Library of Congress. http://memory.loc.gov/pnp/habshaer/nm/nm0000/nm0049/sheet/00001a.tif (accessed November 15, 2005).

Hockett, Bryan Scott. 1998. Sociopolitical Meaning of Faunal Remains from Baker Village. *American Antiquity* 63:289–302.

Hodge, Frederick Webb. 1912. *Handbook of American Indians North of Mexico.* Bureau of American Ethnology Bulletin 30. Smithsonian Institution, Washington, DC.

Holmer, Richard N., and Dennis G. Weder. 1980. Common Post-Archaic Projectile Points of the Fremont Area. In *Fremont Perspectives,* edited by David B. Madsen, pp. 55–68. Antiquities Section Selected Papers, no. 16. Utah State Historical Society, Salt Lake City.

Holmes, William H. 1878. Report on the Ancient Ruins of Southwestern Colorado, Examined during the Summers of 1875 and 1876. In *Tenth Annual Report of the U.S. Geological and Geographical Survey of the Territories for 1876,* pp. 382–408. Geological Survey, Washington, DC.

Hopi Dictionary Project (compiler). 1998. *Hopi Dictionary: A Hopi–English Dictionary of the Third Mesa Dialect.* University of Arizona Press, Tucson.

Howard, Jerry B. 1991. Charting the Past: Mapping the Prehistoric Canals and Sites of the Salt River Valley. In *The Operation and Evolution of an Irrigation System: The East Papago Canal Study,* edited by J. B. Howard and G. Huckleberry, pp. 2.1–2.19. Soil Systems Publications in Archaeology, no. 18, Soil Systems, Inc., Phoenix.

Hoyt, Douglas V., and Kenneth H. Schatten. 1997. *The Role of the Sun in Climate Change.* Oxford University Press, Oxford.

Huckleberry, Gary A., and Brian R. Billman. 1998. Floodwater Farming, Discontinuous Ephemeral Streams, and Puebloan Abandonment in Southwestern Colorado. *American Antiquity* 63:595–616.

Hughes, Malcolm K., and Henry F. Diaz (editors). 1994. *The Medieval Warm Period*. Kluwer Academic Publishers, Dordrecht.

Hunt, L. A., W. Yan, and Gregory S. McMaster. 2003. Simulating Response to Temperature. In *Modeling Temperature Response in Wheat and Maize: Proceedings of a Workshop*, Centro Internacional de Mejoramiento de Maíz y Trigo, El Batán, Mexico, April 23–25, 2001. NRG-GIS Series 03-01. CIMMYT, México, D.F.

Hurst, Winston B. 2003. Typological Analysis of Ceramics from the Middle Rio Puerco of the East. In *Prehistory of the Middle Rio Puerco Valley, Sandoval County, New Mexico*, edited by L. Baker and S. Durand, pp. 55–117. Archaeological Society of New Mexico, Special Publication no. 3. Eastern New Mexico University, Portales.

Ingersoll, Ernest. 1874. Ruins in Southwestern Colorado. *New York Tribune* 3 November.

Jackson, William H. 1876. Ancient Ruins in Southwestern Colorado. In *Annual Report of the United States Geological and Geographical Survey of the Territories, Embracing Colorado and Parts of Adjacent Territories; Being a Report of Progress of the Exploration for the Year 1874*, edited by F. V. Hayden, pp. 367–381. Government Printing Office, Washington, DC.

Janetski, Joel C., and Grant C. Smith. 2007. *Hunter-Gatherer Archaeology in Utah Valley*. Museum of Peoples and Cultures, Occasional Paper no. 12. Brigham Young University, Provo, Utah.

Jansen, E., J. Overpeck, K. R. Briffa, J. C. Duplessy, F. Joos, V. Masson-Delmotte, D. Olago, B. Otto-Bliesner, W. R. Peltier, S. Rahmstorf, R. Ramesh, D. Raynaud, D. Rind, O. Solomina, R. Villalba, and D. Zhang. 2007. Paleoclimate. In *Climate Change 2007: The Physical Science Basis*. Contributions of Working Group I to the Fourth Assessment Report of the Intergovernmental Panel on Climate Change, edited by S. Solomon, D. Qin, M. Manning, Z. Chen, M. Marquis, K. B. Averyt, M. Tignor, and H. L. Miller, pp. 433–498. Cambridge University Press, Cambridge.

Janssen, Marco A., Timothy A. Kohler, and Marten Scheffer. 2003. Sunk-Cost Effects Made Ancient Societies Vulnerable to Collapse. *Current Anthropology* 44:722–728.

Jeançon, Jean A. 1923. *Excavations in the Chama Valley, New Mexico*. Bureau of American Ethnology Bulletin 81. Government Printing Office, Washington.

———. 1925. Primitive Coloradoans. *The Colorado Magazine* 2(1): 35–40.

———. 1929. Archaeological Investigations in the Taos Valley, New Mexico during 1920. *Smithsonian Miscellaneous Collections* 81(12): 1–21. Washington.

———. n.d. The Personal Papers of Jean Allard Jeançon. Manuscripts on file, Denver Public Library.

Jen, Erica. 2005. Stable or Robust? What's the Difference? In *Robust Design: A Repertoire of Biological, Ecological, and Engineering Case Studies*, pp. 1–20. Santa Fe Institute Studies in the Sciences of Complexity. Oxford University Press, Oxford.

Jennings, Jesse D., and Edward Norbeck. 1955. Great Basin Prehistory: A Review. *American Antiquity* 21:1–11.

Jett, Stephen C. 1964. Pueblo Indian Migrations: An Evaluation of the Possible Physical and Cultural Determinants. *American Antiquity* 29:281–300.

Johnson, C. David. 2003. Mesa Verde Region Towers: A View from Above. *Kiva* 68: 323–340.

———. 2006. Critical Natural Resources in the Mesa Verde Region, AD 600–1300: Distribution, Use, and Influence on Puebloan Settlement. Unpublished PhD dissertation, Department of Anthropology, Washington State University, Pullman.

———. 2008. Investigating the Consequences of Long-term Human Predation of *r*-Selected Species: Experiments in the Upland Southwest. Southwest Symposium paper, Tempe, Arizona.

Johnson, C. David, Timothy A. Kohler, and Jason Cowan. 2005. Modeling Historical Ecology, Thinking about Contemporary Systems. *American Anthropologist* 107:96–108.

Johnson, Gregory A. 1979. Information Sources and the Development of Decision-Making Organizations. In *Social Archaeology: Beyond Subsistence and Dating*, edited by C. L. Redman, M. J. Berman, E. V. Curtin, W. T. Langhorne Jr., N. M. Versaggi, and J. C. Wanser, pp. 87–112. Academic Press, New York.

———. 1982. Organizational Structure and Scalar Stress. In *Theory and Explanation in Archaeology: The Southampton Conference*, edited by C. Renfrew, M. J. Rowlands, and B. A. Segraves, pp. 389–421. Academic Press, New York.

Jones, Phil D., and Roy Thompson. 2003. Instrumental Records. In *Global Change in the Holocene*, edited by Anson Mackay, Rick Battarbee, John Birks, and Frank Oldfield, pp. 140–158. Hodder Arnold, London.

Judd, Neil M. 1919. *Archaeological Investigations at Paragonah, Utah*. Miscellaneous Collections 70(3): 1–22. Smithsonian Institution, Washington, DC.

———. 1926. *Archaeological Observations North of the Rio Colorado*. Bureau of American Ethnology, Bulletin 82, Washington, DC.

Judge, W. James. 1989. Chaco Canyon-San Juan Basin. In *Dynamics of Southwest Prehistory*, edited by L. S. Cordell and G. J. Gumerman, pp. 1–12. Smithsonian Institution Press, Washington, DC.

Kakos, Peter J. 2003. Living in the Zone: Basketmaker Food Packages, Hormonal Responses, and the Effects on Population Growth. In *Anasazi Archaeology at the Millenium: Proceedings of the Sixth Occasional Anasazi Symposium*, edited by Paul Reed, pp. 35–47. Center for Desert Archaeology, Tucson.

Karlstrom, Thor N. V. 1988. Alluvial Chronology and Hydrologic Change of Black Mesa and Nearby Regions. In *The Anasazi in a Changing Environment*, edited by George J. Gumerman, pp. 45–91. Cambridge University Press, Cambridge.

Katzenberg, M. Anne. 1995. Report on Bone Chemistry Studies from the Sand Canyon Locality. Manuscript on file, Crow Canyon Archaeological Center, Cortez, Colorado.

———. 1999. Human Skeletal Remains. In *The Sand Canyon Archaeological Project: Site Testing*, edited by Mark D. Varien, chap. 19. http://www.crowcanyon.org/sitetesting (accessed May 29, 2008).

Kenzle, Susan C. 1997. Enclosing Walls in the Northern San Juan: Sociophysical Boundaries and Defensive Fortifications. *Journal of Field Archaeology* 24:195–210.

Kerr, Richard A. 2000. A North Atlantic Climate Pacemaker for the Centuries. *Science* 288:1984–1986.

Kidder, Alfred V. [1924] 1962. *An Introduction to the Study of Southwestern Archaeology, with a Preliminary Account of the Excavations at Pecos*. Department of Archaeology, Phillips Academy, Andover. Yale University Press, New Haven, CT. Originally published 1924; reprinted with a new introductory chapter by Yale University Press, 1962.

———. 1927. Southwestern Archaeological Conference. *Science* 66:489–491.

———. 1932. *The Artifacts of Pecos*. Papers of the Southwestern Expedition, no. 6. Published for Phillips Academy by the Yale University Press, New Haven.

Kidder, Alfred V. 1958. *Pecos, New Mexico: Archaeological Notes.* Papers of the Robert S. Peabody Foundation for Archaeology, vol. 5. Phillips Academy, Andover, Mass.

Kidder, Alfred V., and Samuel J. Guernsey. 1919. *Archaeological Explorations in Northeastern Arizona.* Bureau of American Ethnology Bulletin 65, Washington.

Kiladis, George N., and Henry F. Diaz. 1989. Global Climate Anomalies Associated with Extremes of the Southern Oscillation. *Journal of Climate* 2:1069–1090.

Kilby, J. David. 1997. A Geoarchaeological Analysis of Ten Pueblo III Pit Structures in the Sand Canyon Locality, Southwest Colorado. Unpublished master's thesis, Department of Anthropology, Eastern New Mexico State University, Portales.

Kintigh, Keith W. 1994. Chaco, Communal Architecture, and Cibola Aggregation. In *The Ancient Southwestern Community: Models and Methods for the Study of Prehistoric Social Organization,* edited by W. H. Wills and Robert D. Leonard, pp. 131–140. University of New Mexico Press, Albuquerque.

Kintigh, Keith W., Donna M. Glowacki, and Debra L. Huntley. 2004. Long-Term Settlement History and the Emergence of Towns in the Zuni Area. *American Antiquity* 69:432–456.

Kirch, Patrick V., and Roger C. Green. 2001. *Hawaiki, Ancestral Polynesia: An Essay in Historical Anthropology.* Cambridge University Press, Cambridge.

Knight, Troy A., David M. Meko, and Christopher H. Baisan. 2010. A Bimillennial-Length Tree-Ring Reconstruction of Precipitation for the Tavaputs Plateau, Northeastern Utah. *Quaternary Research* 73(1): 107–117.

Kohler, Timothy A. 1992. Prehistoric Human Impact on the Environment in the Upland North American Southwest. *Population and Environment: A Journal of Interdisciplinary Studies* 13:255–268.

————. 1993. News from the Northern American Southwest: Prehistory on the Edge of Chaos. *Journal of Archaeological Research* 1:267–321.

————. 2000. The Final 400 Years of Prehispanic Agricultural Society in the Mesa Verde Region. *Kiva* 66:191–204.

————. 2007. Testing Optimality in Site Location in the Archaeological Record: Local Examination of a Global Question. Invited paper for panel entitled "Computational Models in Anthropology: What Are They Good For, and Why Should You Care?" 106th annual meeting of the American Anthropological Association, November 28–December 2, Washington, DC.

Kohler, Timothy A. (editor). 2004. *Archaeology of Bandelier National Monument: Village Formation on the Pajarito Plateau, New Mexico.* University of New Mexico Press, Albuquerque.

Kohler, Timothy A., Sarah Cole, and Stanca M. Ciupe. 2009. Population and Warfare: A Test of the Turchin Model in Pueblo Societies. In *Pattern and Process in Cultural Evolution,* edited by S. Shennan, pp. 277–295. University of California Press, Berkeley.

Kohler, Timothy A., Matt Pier Glaude, Jean-Pierre Bocquet-Appel, and Brian M. Kemp. 2008. The Neolithic Demographic Transition in the U.S. Southwest. *American Antiquity* 73:645–669.

Kohler, Timothy A., Sarah A. Herr, and Matthew J. Root. 2004. The Rise and Fall of Towns on the Pajarito (AD 1375–1600). In *Archaeology of Bandelier National Monument: Village Formation on the Pajarito Plateau, New Mexico,* edited by Timothy A. Kohler, pp. 215–264. University of New Mexico Press, Albuquerque.

Kohler, Timothy A., C. David Johnson, Mark Varien, Scott Ortman, Robert Reynolds, Ziad Kobti, Jason Cowan, Kenneth Kolm, Schaun Smith, and Lorene Yap. 2007. Settlement

Ecodynamics in the Prehispanic Central Mesa Verde Region. In *The Model-Based Archaeology of Socionatural Systems*, edited by Timothy A. Kohler and Sander van der Leeuw, pp. 61–104. SAR Press, Santa Fe.

Kohler, Timothy A., and Meredith Matthews. 1988. Long-Term Anasazi Land Use and Forest Reduction: A Case Study from Southwest Colorado. *American Antiquity* 53:537–564.

Kohler, Timothy A., Robert P. Powers, and Janet D. Orcutt. 2004. Bandelier from Hamlets to Towns. In *Archaeology of Bandelier National Monument: Village Formation on the Pajarito Plateau, New Mexico*, edited by Timothy A. Kohler, pp. 293–303. University of New Mexico Press, Albuquerque.

Kohler, Timothy A., and Charles Reed. In press. Explaining the Structure and Timing of Formation of Pueblo I Villages in the Northern U.S. Southwest. In *Sustainable Lifeways: Cultural Persistence in an Ever-Changing Environment*, edited by Naomi F. Miller, Katherine M. Moore, and Kathleen Ryan. University of Pennsylvania Museum of Archaeology and Anthropology, Philadelphia.

Kohler, Timothy A., and Matthew J. Root. 2004a. The First Hunter/Farmers on the Pajarito Plateau (AD 1150–1250). In *Archaeology of Bandelier National Monument: Village Formation on the Pajarito Plateau, New Mexico*, edited by Timothy A. Kohler, pp. 117–172. University of New Mexico Press, Albuquerque.

———. 2004b. The Late Coalition and Earliest Classic on the Pajarito Plateau (AD 1250–1375). In *Archaeology of Bandelier National Monument: Village Formation on the Pajarito Plateau, New Mexico*, edited by Timothy A. Kohler, pp. 173–213. University of New Mexico Press, Albuquerque.

Kohler, Timothy A., and Matthew J. Root (editors). 1992. *Bandelier Archaeological Excavation Project: Summer 1990 Excavations at Burnt Mesa Pueblo and Casa del Rito*. Department of Anthropology Reports of Excavations, no. 64. Washington State University, Pullman, Washington.

Kohler, Timothy A., and Kathryn K. Turner. 2006. Raiding for Women in the Pre-Hispanic Northern Pueblo Southwest? *Current Anthropology* 47:1035–1045.

Kohler, Timothy A., Stephanie VanBuskirk, and Samantha Ruscavage-Barz. 2004. Vessels and Villages: Evidence for the Conformist Transmission in Early Village Aggregations on the Pajarito Plateau, New Mexico. *Journal of Anthropological Archaeology* 23:100–118.

Kohler, Timothy A., and Carla R. Van West. 1996. The Calculus of Self-Interest in the Development of Cooperation: Sociopolitical Development and Risk among the Northern Anasazi. In *Evolving Complexity and Environmental Risk in the Prehistoric Southwest*, edited by Joseph Tainter and Bonnie Bagley Tainter, pp. 169–196. Santa Fe Institute Studies in the Sciences of Complexity vol. 24, Addison-Wesley, Boston.

Kohler, Timothy A., and Mark D. Varien. In press. A Scale Model of Seven Hundred Years of Farming Settlements in Southwestern Colorado. In *Becoming Villagers*, edited by Matthew S. Bandy and Jake R. Fox. University of Arizona Press, Tucson.

Kohler, Timothy A., Mark D. Varien, Aaron M. Wright, and Kristin A. Kuckelman. 2008. Mesa Verde Migrations: New Archaeological Research and Computer Simulation Suggest Why Ancestral Puebloans Deserted the Northern Southwest United States. *American Scientist* 96:146–153.

Konigsberg, Lyle W., and Jane E. Buikstra. 1995. Regional Approaches to the Investigation of Past Human Biocultural Structure. In *Regional Approaches to Mortuary Analysis*, edited by Lane Beck, pp. 191–219. Plenum Press, New York.

Konigsberg, Lyle W., and Stephen D. Ousley. 1995. Multivariate Quantitative Genetics of Anthropometric Traits from the Boas Data. *Human Biology* 67:481–498.

Kosse, Krisztina. 1989. Group Size and Societal Complexity: Thresholds in the Long-Term Memory. *Journal of Anthropological Archaeology* 9:275–303.

Kovecses, Zoltan. 2002. *Metaphor: A Practical Introduction*. Oxford University Press, New York.

Krakauer, David C. 2004. Robustness in Biological Systems—A Provisional Taxonomy. In *Complex Systems Science in Biomedicine*, edited by T. S. Dreisboeck and J. Yasha Kresh, pp. 183–205. Kluwer Academic Press, Dordrecht.

Krakauer, David C., and J. B. Plotkin. 2005. Principles and Parameters of Molecular Robustness. In *Robust Design: A Repertoire for Biology, Ecology, and Engineering*, edited by Erica Jen, pp. 71–103. Oxford University Press, New York.

Kramer, Kathryn. 2002. Sex Ratios and Warfare in the Prehistoric Puebloan Southwest. Unpublished master's thesis, Department of Anthropology, Washington State University, Pullman.

Kroskrity, Paul V. 1993. *Language, History, and Identity: Ethnolinguistic Studies of the Arizona Tewa*. University of Arizona Press, Tucson.

Kuckelman, Kristin A. 2000. The Final Days of Castle Rock Pueblo. In *The Archaeology of Castle Rock Pueblo: A Thirteenth-Century Village in Southwestern Colorado*, edited by Kristin A. Kuckelman. http://www.crowcanyon.org/castlerock (accessed June 20, 2008).

———. 2002. Thirteenth-Century Warfare in the Central Mesa Verde Region. In *Seeking the Center Place: Archaeology and Ancient Communities in the Mesa Verde Region*, edited by Mark D. Varien and Richard H. Wilshusen, pp. 233–253. University of Utah Press, Salt Lake City.

———. 2003. Structural Burning in the Ancient Puebloan Northern Southwest. Paper presented at the sixty-eighth annual meeting of the Society for American Archaeology, Milwaukee.

———. 2006. Ancient Violence in the Mesa Verde Region. In *The Mesa Verde World*, edited by David G. Noble, pp. 127–136. School of American Research Press, Santa Fe.

———. 2007a. Summary and Conclusions. In *The Archaeology of Sand Canyon Pueblo: Intensive Excavations at a Late-Thirteenth-Century Village in Southwestern Colorado* [HTML title], edited by Kristin A. Kuckelman. http://www.crowcanyon.org/sandcanyon (accessed January 29, 2008).

———. 2007b. Catalysts of the Thirteenth-Century Depopulation of Sand Canyon Pueblo and the Central Mesa Verde Region. Paper presented in the symposium "New Light on the Thirteenth-Century Depopulaton of the Northern Southwest" at the annual meeting of the Society for American Archaeology, Austin.

———. In press. The Depopulation of Sand Canyon Pueblo, a Large Ancestral Pueblo Village in Southwestern Colorado. *American Antiquity*.

Kuckelman, Kristin A. (editor). 2000. *The Archaeology of Castle Rock Pueblo: A Thirteenth-Century Village in Southwestern Colorado*. http://www.crowcanyon.org/castlerock (accessed August 15, 2008).

———. 2007. *The Archaeology of Sand Canyon Pueblo: Intensive Excavations at a Late-Thirteenth-Century Village in Southwestern Colorado*. http://www.crowcanyon.org/sandcanyon (accessed July 10, 2008).

Kuckelman, Kristin A., Bruce A. Bradley, Melissa J. Churchill, and James H. Kleidon. 2007. A Descriptive and Interpretive Summary of Excavations, by Architectural Block. In

The Archaeology of Sand Canyon Pueblo: Intensive Excavations at a Late-Thirteenth-Century Village in Southwestern Colorado, edited by Kristin A. Kuckelman. http://www.crowcanyon.org/sandcanyon (accessed February 2, 2008).

Kuckelman, Kristin A., and Grant D. Coffey. 2007. Report of 2006 Research at Goodman Point Pueblo (Site 5MT604) Montezuma County, Colorado. http://www.crowcanyon.org/ResearchReports/GoodmanPoint/interim_reports/2006/Text_2006.asp (accessed July 7, 2008).

Kuckelman, Kristin A., Grant D. Coffey, and Steve R. Copeland. 2009. Interim Descriptive Report of Research at Goodman Point Pueblo (5MT604), Montezuma County, Colorado, 2005–2008. http://crowcanyon.org/ResearchReports/GoodmanPoint/interim_reports/2005_2008/GPP_interim_report_2005_2008.pdf (accessed March 1, 2009).

Kuckelman, Kristin A., Ricky R. Lightfoot, and Debra L. Martin. 2000. Changing Patterns of Violence in the Northern San Juan Region. *Kiva* 66:147–166.

———. 2002. The Bioarchaeology and Taphonomy of Violence at Castle Rock and Sand Canyon Pueblos, Southwestern Colorado. *American Antiquity* 67:486–513.

Kuckelman, Kristin A., and Debra L. Martin. 2007. Human Skeletal Remains. In *The Archaeology of Sand Canyon Pueblo: Intensive Excavations at a Late-Thirteenth-Century Village in Southwestern Colorado,* edited by Kristin A. Kuckelman. http://www.crowcanyon.org/sandcanyon (accessed February 2, 2008).

Kulischek, Jeremy. 2006. Population and Settlement Trends in the Jemez Province, AD 1250 to 1600. Paper presented at the seventy-first annual meeting of the Society for American Archaeology, San Juan, Puerto Rico.

Kurath, Gertrude P., with Antonio Garcia. 1969. *Music and Dance of the Tewa Pueblos.* Museum of New Mexico Research Record 8. Santa Fe.

Kwiatkowski, Scott M. 2003. Evidence for Subsistence Problems. In *Centuries of Decline during the Hohokam Classic Period at Pueblo Grande,* edited by David R. Abbott, pp. 48–69. University of Arizona Press, Tucson.

Lakatos, Steven A. 2003. Pit Structure Architecture of the Developmental Period (AD 600–1200). In *Anasazi Archaeology at the Millenium: Proceedings of the Sixth Occasional Anasazi Symposium,* edited by Paul F. Reed, pp. 49–56. Center for Desert Archaeology, Tucson, AZ.

———. 2006. *Cultural Continuity in the Northern Rio Grande Valley of New Mexico, AD 600–AD 1200.* Unpublished master's thesis, Department of Behavioral Science, New Mexico Highlands University, Las Vegas.

———. 2007. Cultural Continuity and the Development of Integrative Architecture in the Northern Rio Grande Valley of New Mexico, AD 600–1200. *Kiva* 73:31–66.

———. 2009. Identity and Demography in the Northern Rio Grande Valley of New Mexico (A.D. 600–1200). Paper presented in the symposium "Puebloan Prehistory: Research Themes in the Northern Rio Grande" during the New Mexico Archeological Council Fall Conference, The Middle and Northern Rio Grande, November 14, 2009. Maxwell Museum of Anthropology, University of New Mexico, Albuquerque.

Lakatos, Steven A., and Stephen S. Post. In press. Interaction, Accommodation, and Continuity among Early Communities in the Northern Rio Grande Valley, AD 200–900. In *Southwest Pithouse Communities, AD 200–900,* edited by S. Herr and L. C. Young. University of Arizona Press, Tucson.

Lakoff, George. 1987. *Women, Fire, and Dangerous Things: What Categories Reveal about the Mind.* University of Chicago Press, Chicago.

Lakoff, George. 1993. The Contemporary Theory of Metaphor. In *Metaphor and Thought*, edited by Andrew Ortony, pp. 202–251. 2d ed. Cambridge University Press, Cambridge.

Lakoff, George, and Mark Johnson. 1980. *Metaphors We Live By*. University of Chicago Press, Chicago.

———. 1999. *Philosophy in the Flesh: The Embodied Mind and its Challenge to Western Thought*. Basic Books, New York.

Lamb, Hubert H. 1965. The Early Medieval Warm Epoch and its Sequel. *Palaeogeography, Palaeoclimatology, Palaeoecology* 1:13–37.

———. 1977. *Climate: Past, Present, and Future*. Methuen, London.

Lambert, Patricia M. 1999. Human Skeletal Remains. In *The Puebloan Occupation of the Ute Mountain Piedmont*, vol. 5: *Environmental and Bioarchaeological Studies*, edited by B. R. Billman, pp. 111–161. Soil Systems Publications in Archaeology, no. 22. Soil Systems, Phoenix.

Lang, Richard W., and Arthur H. Harris. 1984. *The Faunal Remains from Arroyo Hondo Pueblo, New Mexico*. School of American Research Press, Santa Fe.

Lange, Charles H. 1968. Excavations at LA 6455, The Alfred Herrera Site. In *Cochiti Dam Archaeological Salvage Project, Part 1: Report on the 1963 Season*, assembled by C. Lange, pp. 73–110. Research Records, no. 6. Museum of New Mexico, Santa Fe.

Larson, Daniel O., and Joel Michaelsen. 1990. Impacts of Climatic Variability and Population Growth on Virgin Branch Anasazi Cultural Developments. *American Antiquity* 55:227–249.

Larson, Daniel O., Hector Neff, Donald A. Graybill, Joel Michaelsen, and Elizabeth Ambos. 1996. Risk, Climatic Variability, and the Study of Southwestern Prehistory: An Evolutionary Perspective. *American Antiquity* 61:217–241.

Laski, Vera. 1959. *Seeking Life*. American Folklore Society, Philadelphia, PA.

LeBlanc, Stephen A. 1989. Cibola, Shifting Cultural Boundaries. In *Dynamics of Southwest Prehistory*, edited by Linda S. Cordell and George J. Gumerman, pp. 337–370. Smithsonian Institution Press, Washington, DC.

———. 1999. *Prehistoric Warfare in the American Southwest*. University of Utah Press, Salt Lake City.

———. 2002. Conflict and Language Dispersal: Issues and a New World Example. In *Examining the Farming/Language Dispersal Hypothesis*, edited by Peter Bellwood and Colin Renfrew, pp. 357–368. McDonald Institute Monographs, Oxbow Books, Oxford.

Lekson, Stephen H. 1983. Dating the Hubbard Tri-wall and other Tri-wall Structures. *Southwest Lore* 49(4): 15–23.

———. 1984. *Great Pueblo Architecture of Chaco Canyon, New Mexico*. University of New Mexico Press, Albuquerque. National Park Service, U.S. Dept. of the Interior.

———. 1988. The Idea of the Kiva in Anasazi Archaeology. *Kiva* 53(3): 213–234.

———. 1997. Points, Knives, and Drills of Chaco Canyon. In *Ceramics, Lithics, and Ornaments of Chaco Canyon*, edited by F. Mathien, pp. 659–697. Publications in Archaeology, 18c, Chaco Canyon Studies. USDI National Park Service, Santa Fe, New Mexico.

———. 1999. *The Chaco Meridian: Centers of Political Power in the Ancient Southwest*. AltaMira Press, Walnut Creek, California.

———. 2002. War in the Southwest, War in the World. *American Antiquity* 67:607–624.

Lekson, Stephen H., and Catherine M. Cameron. 1995. The Abandonment of Chaco Canyon, the Mesa Verde Migrations, and the Reorganization of the Pueblo World. *Journal of Anthropological Archaeology* 14:184–202.

Lekson, Stephen H., Curtis P. Nepstadt-Thornberry, Brian E. Yunker, Toni S. Laumbach, David P. Cain, and Karl W. Laumbach. 2002. Migrations in the Southwest: Pinnacle Ruin, Southwestern New Mexico. *Kiva* 68:73–102.

Lightfoot, Kent G. 1984. *Prehistoric Political Dynamics: A Case Study from the American Southwest*. Northern Illinois University Press, DeKalb.

Lightfoot, Ricky R. 1993. Synthesis. In *The Duckfoot Site*, vol. 1: *Descriptive Archaeology*, edited by Ricky R. Lightfoot and Mary C. Etzkorn, pp. 297–302. Occasional Papers,, no. 3. Crow Canyon Archaeological Center, Cortez, Colorado.

———. 1994. *The Duckfoot Site*, vol. 2: *Archaeology of the House and Household*. Occasional Papers,, no. 4. Crow Canyon Archaeological Center, Cortez, Colorado.

Lightfoot, Ricky R., and Kristin A. Kuckelman. 2001. A Case of Warfare in the Mesa Verde Region. In *Deadly Landscapes: Case Studies in Prehistoric Southwestern Warfare*, edited by Glen E. Rice and Steven A. LeBlanc, pp. 51–64. University of Utah Press, Salt Lake City.

Lindsay, Alexander J., Jr. 1961. The Beaver Creek Agricultural Community on the San Juan River, Utah. *American Antiquity* 27:174–187.

———. 1969. *The Tsegi Phase of the Kayenta Cultural Tradition in Northeastern Arizona*. PhD dissertation, Department of Anthropology, University of Arizona, Tucson. University Microfilms International, Ann Arbor.

———. 1987. Anasazi Population Movements to Southeastern Arizona. *American Archeology* 6:190–198.

———. 1992. Tucson Polychrome: History, Dating, Distribution, and Design. In *Proceedings of the Second Salado Conference*, edited by Richard C. Lange and Stephen Germick, pp. 230–237. Arizona Archaeological Society.

Lindsay, Alexander J., Jr., J. Richard Ambler, Mary Anne Stein, and Philip M. Hobler. 1968. *Survey and Excavations North and East of Navajo Mountain, Utah, 1959–1962*. Museum of Northern Arizona Bulletin, no. 45, Glen Canyon Series, no. 8. Museum of Northern Arizona, Flagstaff.

Lindsay, Alexander J., and Jeffrey S. Dean. 1983. The Kayenta Anasazi at AD 1250: Prelude to a Migration. In *Proceedings of the Anasazi Symposium 1981*, edited by Jack E. Smith, pp. 163–168. Mesa Verde National Park, Cortez, Colorado.

Lindsay, La Mar W. 1986. Fremont Fragmentation. In *Anthropology of the Desert West: Essays in Honor of Jesse D. Jennings*, edited by Carol J. Condie and Don D. Fowler, pp. 229–251. Anthropological Papers, no. 110. University of Utah, Salt Lake City.

Linton, Ralph. 1944. Nomad Raids and Fortified Pueblos. *American Antiquity* 10:28–32.

Lipe, William D. 1970. Anasazi Communities in the Red Rock Plateau, Southeastern Utah. In *Reconstructing Prehistoric Pueblo Societies*, edited by William A. Longacre, pp. 83–139. A School of American Research Book. University of New Mexico Press, Albuquerque.

———. 1989. Social Scale of Mesa Verde Anasazi Kivas. In *The Architecture of Social Integration in Prehistoric Pueblos*, edited by William D. Lipe and Michelle Hegmon, pp. 53–71. Occasional Paper no. 1. Crow Canyon Archaeological Center, Cortez, Colorado.

———. 1992. Introduction. In *The Sand Canyon Archaeological Project: A Progress Report*, edited by William D. Lipe, pp. 1–10. Occasional Paper no. 2. Crow Canyon Archaeological Center, Cortez, Colorado.

———. 1995. The Depopulation of the Northern San Juan: Conditions in the Turbulent 1200s. *Journal of Anthropological Archaeology* 14:143–169.

Lipe, William D. 1999a. National Register of Historic Places Registration Form for Bass Site Complex (5MT136). Submitted by the Crow Canyon Archaeological Center, Cortez, Colorado. Colorado Historical Society, Denver.

————. 1999b. National Register of Historic Places Registration Form for Cannonball Ruins (5MT338). Submitted by the Crow Canyon Archaeological Center, Cortez, Colorado. Colorado Historical Society, Denver.

————. 2002. Social Power in the Central Mesa Verde Region, AD 1150–1290. In *Seeking the Center Place: Archaeology and Ancient Communities in the Mesa Verde Region,* edited by Mark D. Varien and Richard H. Wilshusen, pp. 203–232. University of Utah Press, Salt Lake City.

————. 2006. Notes from the North. In *The Archaeology of Chaco Canyon: An 11th Century Regional Center,* edited by Stephen Lekson, pp. 261–313. School of American Research Press, Santa Fe, New Mexico.

————. 2007a. Where Did the Mesa Verde People Go? Public lecture, Denver Museum of Nature and Science, Denver, CO.

————. 2007b. Can Archaeology Track Migrations? Presented at "Ben Rouse's Legacy," a symposium honoring Irving Rouse's contributions to world prehistory. Yale University, New Haven, Connecticut.

Lipe, William D., Timothy A. Kohler, Mark D. Varien, James N. Morris, and Ricky Lightfoot. 1988. Synthesis. In *Anasazi Communities at Dolores: Grass Mesa Village,* compiled by William D. Lipe, James N. Morris, and Timothy A. Kohler, pp. 1213–1276. U.S. Bureau of Reclamation, Engineering and Research Center, Denver.

Lipe, William D., and Stephen Lekson. 2001. Mesa Verde Pueblo Migrations and Cultural Transformations, AD 1250–1350. Paper presented at the sixty-sixth annual meeting of the Society for American Archaeology, New Orleans.

Lipe, William D., and Scott G. Ortman. 2000. Spatial Patterning in Northern San Juan Villages, AD 1050–1300. *Kiva* 66:91–122.

Lipe, William D., and Mark D. Varien. 1999a. Pueblo II (AD 900–1150). In *Colorado Prehistory: A Context for the Southern Colorado River Basin,* edited by William D. Lipe, Mark D. Varien, and Richard H. Wilshusen, pp. 242–289. Colorado Council of Professional Archaeologists, Denver.

————. 1999b. Pueblo III (AD 1150–1300). In *Colorado Prehistory: A Context for the Southern Colorado River Basin,* edited by William D. Lipe, Mark D. Varien, and Richard H. Wilshusen, pp. 290–352. Colorado Council of Professional Archaeologists, Colorado Historical Society, Denver.

Litton, Cliff D., and Caitlin E. Buck. 1996. An Archaeological Example: Radiocarbon Dating. In *Markov Chain Monte Carlo in Practice,* edited by Walter R. Gilks, Sylvia Richardson, and David J. Spiegelhalter, pp. 465–480. Chapman and Hall, London.

Loose, Ann A. 1974. *Archeological Excavations near Arroyo Hondo, Carson National Forest, New Mexico.* Archeological Report no. 4. USDA Forest Service, Southwestern Region, Albuquerque.

Lorenz, Joseph G., and David Glenn Smith. 1996. Distribution of Four Founding mtDNA Haplogroups among Native North Americans. *American Journal of Physical Anthropology* 101:307–323.

Lowell, Julia C. 2007. Women and Men in Warfare and Migration: Implications of Gender Imbalance in the Grasshopper Region of Arizona. *American Antiquity* 72:95–124.

Luchetta, Sarah. 2005. Soza Phase Sites in the Lower San Pedro Valley, Arizona. Unpublished master's thesis, Department of Anthropology, University of Arizona, Tucson.

Luebben, Ralph A., and Paul R. Nickens. 1982. A Mass Interment in an Early Pueblo III Kiva in Southwestern Colorado. *Journal of Intermountain Archeology* 1:66–79.

Lyneis, Margaret M. 1986. A Spatial Analysis of Anasazi Architecture, AD 950–1150, Moapa Valley, Nevada. *Kiva* 52:53–74.

———. 1992. *The Main Ridge Community at Lost City: Virgin Anasazi Architecture, Ceramics, and Burials*. Anthropological Papers, no. 117. University of Utah, Salt Lake City.

———. 1995. The Virgin Anasazi, Far Western Puebloans. *Journal of World Prehistory* 9(2): 199–241.

———. 1996. Pueblo II-Pueblo III Change in Southwestern Utah, the Arizona Strip, and Southern Nevada. In *The Prehistoric Pueblo World, AD 1150–1300*, edited by Michael A. Adler, pp. 11–28. University of Arizona Press, Tucson.

Lyons, Patrick D. 2003. *Ancestral Hopi Migrations*. Anthropological Papers of the University of Arizona, no. 68. University of Arizona Press, Tucson.

Lyons, Patrick D., J. Brett Hill, and Jeffery J. Clark. 2005. Demography, Social Power, and the Dynamics of Identity among Ancient Immigrants. Paper presented at the seventieth annual meeting of the Society for American Archaeology, Salt Lake City.

———. 2008. Demography, Agricultural Potential, and Identity among Ancient Immigrants, In *The Social Construction of Communities in the Ancient Southwest*, edited by Mark D. Varien and James M. Potter, pp. 191–213. AltaMira Press, Lanham, Maryland.

Lyons, Patrick D., and Alexander J. Lindsay Jr. 2006. Perforated Plates and the Salado Phenomenon. *Kiva* 72:5–54.

MacDonald, Glen M., and Roslyn A. Case. 2005. Variations in the Pacific Decadal Oscillation over the Past Millennium. *Geophysical Research Letters* 32(L08703): 1–4.

Mace, Ruth. 2008. Reproducing in Cities. *Science* 319:764–766.

Mackey, James. 1977. A Multivariate, Osteological Approach to Towa Culture History. *American Journal of Physical Anthropology* 44:477–482.

———. 1980. Arroyo Hondo Population Affinities. In *Pueblo Population and Society: The Arroyo Hondo Skeletal and Mortuary Remains*, by Ann M. Palkovich, pp. 171–181. Arroyo Hondo Archaeological Series, vol. 3. School of American Research Press, Santa Fe.

Madsen, David B., and La Mar W. Lindsay. 1977. *Backhoe Village*. Antiquities Section Selected Papers vol. 9, no. 12. Utah State Historical Society, Salt Lake City.

Maguire, Don. 1894. Report of the Department of Ethnology, Utah World's Fair Commission. In *Utah at the World's Columbian Exposition*, pp. 105–110. Salt Lake Lithographing Co., Salt Lake City.

Mahoney, Nancy M. Michael A. Adler, and James W. Kendrick. 2000. The Changing Scale and Configuration of Mesa Verde Communities. *Kiva* 66:67–90.

Mallory, J. P. 1989. *In Search of the Indo-Europeans*. Thames and Hudson, London.

Malouf, Carling. 1944. Thoughts on Utah Archaeology. *American Antiquity* 9:319–328.

Mann, Michael E., Raymond S. Bradley, and Malcolm K. Hughes. 1998. Global-Scale Temperature Patterns and Climate Forcing over the Past Six Centuries. *Nature* 392:779–787.

Mantua, Nathan J., Steven R. Hare, Yuan Zhang, John M. Wallace, and Robert C. Francis. 1997. A Pacific Interdecadal Climate Oscillation with Impacts on Salmon Production. *Bulletin of the American Meteorological Society* 78:1069–1079.

Marshall, Michael P. 1982. Bis Sa'Ani Pueblo: An Example of Late Bonito-Phase, Great House Architecture. In *Bis Sa'Ani: A Late Bonito Phase Community on Escavada Wash, Northwest New Mexico*, vol. 2, pt. 1, edited by Cory Dale Breternitz, David E. Doyel, and Michael P. Marshall, pp. 169–358. Navajo Nation Papers in Anthropology 14, Window Rock, Arizona.

Marshall, Michael P., John R. Stein, Richard W. Loose, and Judith E. Novotny. 1979. *Anasazi Communities of the San Juan Basin*. Public Service Company of New Mexico and New Mexico Historic Preservation Bureau, Albuquerque and Santa Fe.

Marshall, Michael P., and Henry Walt. 2007. *The Eastern Homeland of San Juan Pueblo: Tewa Land and Water Use in the Santa Cruz and Truchas Watersheds; An Archaeological and Ethnogeographic Study*. Prepared for Ohkay Owingeh (San Juan) Pueblo. Cibola Research Consultants Report no. 432. Corrales, New Mexico.

Martin, Debra L. 1994. Patterns of Health and Disease: Stress Profiles for the Prehistoric Southwest. In *Themes in Southwest Prehistory*, edited by George J. Gumerman, pp. 87–108. School of American Research Press, Santa Fe.

———. 1997. Violence against Women in the La Plata River Valley (AD 1000–1300). In *Troubled Times: Violence and Warfare in the Past*, edited by Debra L. Martin and David W. Frayer, pp. 45–75. Gordon and Breach Publishers, Amsterdam.

———. 2008. Ripped Flesh and Torn Souls: Skeletal Evidence for Captivity and Slavery from the La Plata Valley, New Mexico (AD 1100–1300). In *Invisible Citizens: Captives and Their Consequences*, edited by Catherine M. Cameron, pp. 159–180. University of Utah Press, Salt Lake City.

Martin, Paul S., and William Byers. 1965. Pollen and Archaeology at Wetherill Mesa. In *Contributions of the Wetherill Mesa Archaeological Project*, assembled by Douglas Osborne, pp. 122–135. Society of American Archaeology Memoirs, no. 19. Salt Lake City.

Martin, Steve L. 1999. Virgin Anasazi Diet as Demonstrated through the Analysis of Stable Carbon and Nitrogen Isotopes. *Kiva* 64:495–514.

Martinez, Esther. 1982. *San Juan Pueblo Tewa Dictionary*. San Juan Pueblo Bilingual Program, San Juan Pueblo, NM.

Marwitt, John P. 1970. *Median Village and Fremont Culture Regional Variation*. Anthropological Papers, no. 95. University of Utah, Salt Lake City.

Matson, R. G. 1991. *The Origins of Southwestern Agriculture*. University of Arizona Press, Tucson.

———. 2003. The Spread of Maize Agriculture into the U.S. Southwest. In *Examining the Farming/Language Dispersal Hypothesis*, edited by Peter Bellwood and Colin Renfrew, pp. 341–356. McDonald Institute for Archaeological Research, University of Cambridge, Cambridge.

Matson, R. G., and Brian Chisholm. 1991. Basketmaker II Subsistence: Carbon Isotope and Other Dietary Indicators from Cedar Mesa, Utah. *American Antiquity* 56:444–459.

Matson, R. G., William D. Lipe, and W. R. Haase IV. 1988. Adaptational Continuities and Occupational Discontinuities: The Cedar Mesa Anasazi. *Journal of Field Archaeology* 15:245–264.

Maxwell, Timothy D. 1994. Prehistoric Population Change in the Lower Rio Chama Valley, Northwestern New Mexico. Paper presented in the symposium "Big Changes in Big Sites on the Big River: Regional Variability in Classic and Protohistoric Sites of the Northern Rio Grande, New Mexico" at the fifty-ninth annual meeting of the Society for American Archaeology, Anaheim, California.

———. 2000. *Looking for Adaptation: Engineering Analysis of Prehistoric Agricultural Technologies and Techniques in the Southwest*. Unpublished PhD dissertation, Department of Anthropology, University of New Mexico, Albuquerque.

McCabe, Gregory J., Julio L. Betancourt, and Hugo G. Hidalgo. 2007. Associations of Decadal to Multidecadal Sea-Surface Temperature Variability with Upper Colorado River Flow. *Journal of the American Water Resources Association* 43(1): 1–10.

McCabe, Gregory J., Michael A. Palecki, and Julio L. Betancourt. 2004. Pacific and Atlantic Ocean Influences on Multidecadal Drought Frequency in the United States. *Proceedings of the National Academy of Sciences* 101:4136–4141.

McDonnell, Mac, David E. Doyel, and Elinor Large. 1995. Plain Ware, Red Ware, and Other Ceramic Artifacts. In *Archaeological Excavations at Pueblo Blanco: The MCDOT Alma School Road Project*, edited by David E. Doyel, Andrew T. Black, and Barbara S. Macnider, pp. 187–250. Cultural Resources Report no. 90. Archaeological Consulting Services, Ltd., Tempe, Arizona.

McGregor, John C. 1941. *Southwestern Archaeology*. John Wiley and Sons, New York.

McKenna, Peter J., and Marcia L. Truell. 1986. *Small Site Architecture of Chaco Canyon*. Publications in Archeology 18D, Chaco Canyon Studies. National Park Service, Santa Fe.

McLellan, George E. 1969. *The Origin, Development, and Typology of Anasazi Kivas and Great Kivas*. Unpublished PhD dissertation, Department of Anthropology, University of Colorado, Boulder.

McNutt, Charles H. 1969. *Early Puebloan Occupations at Tesuque By-Pass and in the Upper Rio Grande Valley*. Museum of Anthropology, University of Michigan, Anthropological Papers, no. 40. Ann Arbor.

Meighan, Clement W. 1956. Excavations at Paragonah: A Summary. In *Archeological Excavations in Iron County, Utah*, by Clement W. Meighan, Norman E. Coles, Frank D. Davis, Geraldine M. Greenwood, William M. Harrison, and E. Heath MacBain, pp. 1–22. Anthropological Papers, no. 25. University of Utah, Salt Lake City.

Meighan, Clement W., Norman E. Coles, Frank D. Davis, Geraldine M. Greenwood, William M. Harrison, and E. Heath MacBain. 1956. *Archeological Excavations in Iron County, Utah*. Anthropological Papers, no. 25. University of Utah, Salt Lake City.

Mera, H. P. 1935. *Ceramic Clues to the Prehistory of North Central New Mexico*. Laboratory of Anthropology Technical Series, Bulletin 8. Laboratory of Anthropology, Santa Fe.

———. 1939. *Style Trends of Pueblo Pottery in the Rio Grande and Little Colorado Cultural Areas from the 16th to the 19th Century*. Memoirs of the Laboratory of Anthropology 3. Museum of New Mexico, Santa Fe.

Miller, Wick R., and Irvine Davis. 1963. Proto-Keresan Phonology. *International Journal of American Linguistics* 29:310–330.

Mills, Barbara J. 1999. Ceramics and the Social Contexts of Food Consumption in the Northern Southwest. In *Pots and People: A Dynamic Interaction*, edited by James Skibo and Gary Feinman, pp. 99–114. University of Utah Press, Salt Lake City.

———. 2007. Performing the Feast: Visual Display and Suprahousehold Commensalism in the Puebloan Southwest. *American Antiquity* 72:210–239.

———. In press. Themes and Models for Understanding Migration in the Southwest. In *Changing Histories, Landscapes, and Perspectives: The 20th Anniversary Southwest Symposium*, edited by Margaret Nelson and Colleen Strawhacker. University Press of Colorado, Boulder.

Milo, Richard G. 1991. Corn Production on Chapin Mesa: Growing Season Variability, Field Rotation, and Settlement Shifts. In *Proceedings of the Anasazi Symposium 1991*, edited by Art Hutchinson and Jack E. Smith, pp. 35–50. Mesa Verde Museum Association, Inc., Mesa Verde National Park, Colorado.

Minnis, Paul E. 1996. Notes on Economic Uncertainty and Human Behavior in the Prehistoric North American Southwest. In *Evolving Complexity and Environmental Risk in the Prehistoric Southwest*, edited by Joseph Tainter and Bonnie Bagley Tainter, pp. 57–78. Santa Fe Institute Studies in the Sciences of Complexity, vol. 24. Addison-Wesley, Boston.

Molles, Manuel C., Jr., and Clifford N. Dahm. 1990. A Perspective on El Niño and La Niña: Global Implications for Stream Ecology. *Journal of the North American Benthological Society* 9(1): 68–76.

Moore, James L. 2008. Rethinking Thirteenth to Fourteenth Century Migration into the Northern Rio Grande. In *Chasing Chaco and the Southwest: Papers in Honor of Frances Joan Mathien*, edited by R. Wiseman, T. O'Laughlin, C. Snow, and C. Travis, pp. 117–132. Archaeological Society of New Mexico, no. 34. Albuquerque.

———. 2009. Exploring Ethnicity: A Comparison of the Northern Rio Grande and San Juan Regions during the Late Developmental Period. Paper presented in the symposium "Puebloan Prehistory: Research Themes in the Northern Rio Grande" during the New Mexico Archeological Council fall conference "The Middle and Northern Rio Grande," November 14, 2009. Maxwell Museum of Anthropology, University of New Mexico, Albuquerque.

———. In press. Projectile Point Typology and Analysis. In *Land, Settlement, and Community in the Southern Tewa Basin*, vol. 3, edited by J. L. Boyer and S. A. Lakatos. Office of Archaeological Studies, Museum of New Mexico, Santa Fe.

Moore, James L., and Eric Blinman. 2008. San Juan Migrations and the Northern Rio Grande. Paper circulated at the Amerind Foundation Seminar on Depopulation of the Northern San Juan Region, February 23–27, 2008. Amerind Foundation, Dragoon, Arizona.

Moore, James L., and Jeffrey L. Boyer. 2009. Too Many People: How Tanoan Social Organization Coped with Late Prehistoric Village Aggregation. In *Between the Mountains, Beyond the Mountains: Papers in Honor of Paul Williams*, edited by Emily J. Brown, Karen Armstrong, David M. Brugge, and Carol J. Condie, pp. 125–138. Archaeological Society of New Mexico 35. Albuquerque.

Moore, Roger A. 1981. An Analytical and Stylistic Approach to Typology: The Projectile Point Sequence at Salmon Ruin, New Mexico. Unpublished MA thesis, Eastern New Mexico University, Portales.

Morley, Sylvanus G. 1908. The Excavation of the Cannonball Ruins in Southwestern Colorado. *American Anthropologist*, new series, 10:596–610.

Morris, Earl H. 1939. *Archaeological Studies in the La Plata District, Southwestern Colorado and Northwestern New Mexico*. Carnegie Institution of Washington Publication no. 519. Washington, DC.

Morris, Earl H., and Robert F. Burgh. 1954. *Basket Maker II Sites near Durango, Colorado*. Carnegie Institution of Washington Publication no. 604. Washington, DC.

Morris, James N. 1991. *Archaeological Excavations on the Hovenweep Laterals*. Complete Archaeological Service Associates, Cortez, Colorado.

Muenchrath, Deborah A., Maya Kuratomi, Jonathan A. Sandor, and Jeffrey A. Homburg. 2002. Observational Study of Maize Production Systems of Zuni Farmers in Semiarid New Mexico. *Journal of Ethnobiology* 22(1): 1–33.

Muir, Robert J. 2007. Faunal Remains. In *The Archaeology of Sand Canyon Pueblo: Intensive Excavations at a Late-Thirteenth-Century Village in Southwestern Colorado*, edited by K. A. Kuckelman. http://www.crowcanyon.org/sandcanyon (accessed February 2, 2008).

Muir, Robert J., and Jonathan C. Driver. 2002. Scale of Analysis and Zooarchaeological Interpretation: Pueblo III Faunal Variation in the Northern San Juan Region. *Journal of Anthropological Archaeology* 21:165–199.

————. 2004. Identifying Ritual Use of Animals in the Northern American Southwest. In *Behaviour Behind Bones: The Zooarchaeology of Ritual, Religion, Status and Identity*, edited by S. J. O'Day, W. Van Neer, and A. Ervynck, pp. 128–143. Proceedings of the ninth annual conference of the International Council of Archaeozoology, Durham, August 2002. Oxbow Books, Oxford, UK.

Munro, Natalie D. 1994. An Investigation of Anasazi Turkey Production in Southwestern Colorado. Unpublished MA thesis, Department of Archaeology, Simon Fraser University. Burnaby, British Columbia, Canada.

Naranjo, Tessie. 2006. We Came from the South, We Came from the North: Some Tewa Origin Stories. In *The Mesa Verde World*, edited by David Grant Noble, pp. 49–57. School of American Research Press, Santa Fe.

National Commission for Women. 2005. *Water and Women*. Research Foundation for Science, Technology, and Ecology. New Delhi, India.

Nauman, Alissa. 2007. Learning Frameworks and Technological Traditions: Pottery Manufacture in a Chaco Period Great House Community on the Southern Colorado Plateau. Unpublished master's thesis, Department of Anthropology, Washington State University, Pullman.

Nelson, Ben A., and Steven A. LeBlanc. 1986. *Short-Term Sedentism in the American Southwest: The Mimbres Valley Salado*. Maxwell Museum of Anthropology and University of New Mexico Press, Albuquerque.

Nelson, Margaret C. 2000. *Mimbres during the Twelfth Century: Abandonment, Continuity, and Reorganization*. University of Arizona Press, Tucson.

Neuzil, Anna. 2008. *In the Aftermath of Migration: Renegotiating Ancient Identity in Southeastern Arizona*. Anthropological Papers of the University of Arizona,, no. 73. University of Arizona Press, Tucson.

Newberry, J. S. 1876. *Report of the Exploring Expedition from Santa Fe, New Mexico, to the Junction of the Grand and Green Rivers of the Great Colorado of the West, in 1859, Under the Command of Capt. J. N. Macomb, Corps of Topographical Engineers; with Geological Report*. Government Printing Office, Washington, DC.

Ni, Fenbiao, Tereza Cavazos, Malcolm K. Hughes, Andrew C. Comrie, and Gary Funkhouser. 2002. Cool-Season Precipitation in the Southwestern USA since AD 1000: Comparison of Linear and Nonlinear Techniques for Reconstruction. *International Journal of Climatology* 22:1645–1662.

Nials, Fred L., David A. Gregory, and Donald A. Graybill. 1989. Salt River Streamflow and Hohokam Irrigation Systems. In *The 1982–1984 Excavations at Las Colinas: Environment and Subsistence*, by Donald A. Graybill, David A. Gregory, Fred L. Nials, Suzanne K. Fish, Robert E. Gasser, Charles Miksicek, and Christine R. Szuter, pp. 59–78. Arizona State Museum Archaeological Series, no. 165(5). Arizona State Museum, University of Arizona, Tucson.

Nickens, Paul R. 1975. The 1974 Johnson–Lion Canyon Project: Report of Investigation I. Mesa Verde Research Center, Department of Anthropology, University of Colorado, Boulder.

Nordby, Larry V. 2001. *Prelude to Tapestries in Stone: Understanding Cliff Palace Architecture*. Mesa Verde National Park Archeological Research Series, Architectural Studies, no. 4.

Mesa Verde National Park Division of Research and Resource Management. Mesa Verde National Park, Colorado.

Nordenskiöld, Gustaf. [1893] 1979. *The Cliff Dwellers of the Mesa Verde, Southwestern Colorado: Their Pottery and Implements.* Translated by D. Lloyd Morgan. Rio Grande Press, Glorieta, NM.

Odling-Smee, John, Kevin N. Laland, and Marcus W. Feldman. 2003. *Niche Construction: The Neglected Process in Evolution.* Princeton University Press, Princeton.

Odum, Eugene P. 1971. *Fundamentals of Ecology.* 3d ed. W. B. Saunders, Philadelphia.

Oliver, Theodore J. 2001. Warfare in the Tonto Basin. In *Deadly Landscapes: Case Studies in Prehistoric Southwestern Warfare*, edited by G. Rice and S. LeBlanc, pp. 195–217. University of Utah Press, Salt Lake City.

Oliver-Smith, Anthony. 1996. Anthropological Research on Hazards and Disasters. *Annual Review of Anthropology* 25:303–328.

Oppelt, Norman T. 1989. The Mesa Verde Style Mug: Description and Development of a Distinctive Prehistoric Pottery Form. *Southwestern Lore* 55(2): 11–32.

Orcutt, Janet D. 1999. Demography, Settlement, and Agriculture. In *The Bandelier Archaeological Survey*, vol. 1, edited by Robert P. Powers and Janet D. Orcutt, pp. 219–308. Intermountain Cultural Resource Management Professional Paper 57. Santa Fe.

O'Rourke, Dennis H., Ryan L. Parr, and Shawn W. Carlyle. 1999. Molecular Genetic Variation in Prehistoric Inhabitants of the Eastern Great Basin. In *Prehistoric Lifeways in the Great Basin Wetlands: Bioarchaeological Reconstruction and Interpretation*, edited by Brian E. Hemphill and Clark Spencer Larsen, pp. 84–102. University of Utah Press, Salt Lake City.

Ortiz, Alfonso. 1969. *The Tewa World: Space, Time, Being, and Becoming in a Pueblo Society.* University of Chicago Press, Chicago.

———. 1972. Ritual Drama and the Pueblo World View. In *New Perspectives on the Pueblos*, edited by Alfonso Ortiz, pp. 135–162. University of New Mexico Press, Albuquerque.

———. 1979. San Juan Pueblo. In *Handbook of North American Indians*, vol. 9: *Southwest*, edited by A. Ortiz, pp. 278–295. Smithsonian Institution, Washington, DC.

———. n.d. A Sacred Symbol through the Ages. Unpublished manuscript in possession of William D. Lipe, Department of Anthropology, Washington State University, Pullman.

Ortman, Scott G. 2000a. Artifacts. In *The Archaeology of Castle Rock Pueblo: A Thirteenth-Century Village in Southwestern Colorado*, edited by Kristin A. Kuckelman. http://www.crowcanyon.org/castlerock (accessed May 3, 2002).

———. 2000b. Conceptual Metaphor in the Archaeological Record: Methods and an Example from the American Southwest. *American Antiquity* 65:613–45.

———. 2002. Artifacts. In *The Archaeology of Woods Canyon Pueblo: A Canyon-rim Village in Southwestern Colorado*, edited by Melissa J. Churchill. http://www.crowcanyon.org/woodscanyon (accessed April 11, 2005).

———. 2003. Using Cognitive Semantics to Relate Mesa Verde Archaeology to Modern Pueblo Languages. Paper presented at the Fifth World Archaeological Congress, Washington, DC.

———. 2006. Ancient Pottery of the Mesa Verde Country: How Ancestral Pueblo People Made It, Used it, and Thought about It. In *The Mesa Verde World*, edited by David Grant Noble, pp. 101–110. School of American Research Press, Santa Fe.

———. 2007. Population Biology of the Four Corners to Rio Grande Migration. Paper presented in the symposium "New Light on the Thirteenth-Century Depopulation of the Northern Southwest," second annual meeting of the Society for American Archaeology, Austin.

———. 2008a. Architectural Metaphor and Chacoan Influence in the Northern San Juan. In *Archaeology without Borders: Contact, Commerce, and Change in the U.S. Southwest and Northwestern Mexico*, edited by Laurie Webster and Maxine McBrinn, pp. 227–255. Proceedings of the 2004 Southwest Symposium. University Press of Colorado, Boulder.

———. 2008b. Action, Place and Space in the Castle Rock Community. In *The Social Construction of Communities: Studies of Agency, Structure and Identity in the Southwestern U.S.*, edited by Mark D. Varien and James M. Potter, pp. 125–154. AltaMira Press, Lanham, MD.

———. 2008c. Bowls to Gardens: A History of Tewa Community Metaphors. Paper presented in the symposium "Tension and Transition: Religious Ideologies in the Pueblo Southwest, AD 1250–1450," at the seventy-third annual meeting of the Society for American Archaeology, Vancouver, British Columbia.

———. 2009. Genes, Language and Culture in Tewa Ethnogenesis, AD 1150–1400. Unpublished PhD dissertation, School of Human Evolution and Social Change, Arizona State University, Tempe.

Ortman, Scott G., and Bruce A. Bradley. 2002. Sand Canyon Pueblo: The Container in the Center. In *Seeking the Center Place: Archaeology and Ancient Communities in the Mesa Verde Region*, edited by Mark D. Varien and Richard H. Wilshusen, pp. 41–78. University of Utah Press, Salt Lake City.

Ortman, Scott G., and Catherine M. Cameron. In press. A Framework for Controlled Comparisons of Ancient Southwestern Movement. In *Changing Histories, Landscapes, and Perspectives: The 20th Anniversary Southwest Symposium*, edited by Margaret Nelson and Colleen Strawhacker. University Press of Colorado, Boulder.

Ortman, Scott G., Donna M. Glowacki, Melissa J. Churchill, and Kristin A. Kuckelman. 2000. Pattern and Variation in Northern San Juan Village Histories. *Kiva* 66:123–146.

Ortman, Scott G., and Mark D. Varien. 2007. Settlement Patterns in the McElmo Dome Study Area. In *The Archaeology of Sand Canyon Pueblo: Intensive Excavations at a Late-Thirteenth Century Village in Southwestern Colorado*, edited by Kristin Kuckelman. http://www.crowcanyon.org/sandcanyon (accessed August 10, 2008).

Ortman, Scott G., Mark D. Varien, and T. Lee Gripp. 2007. Empirical Bayesian Methods for Archaeological Survey Data: An Application from the Mesa Verde Region. *American Antiquity* 72:241–272.

Osborne, C. M. 2004. The Wetherill Collections and Perishable Items from Mesa Verde. Los Alamitos, California.

Palmer, Wayne C. 1965. *Meteorological Drought*. Research Paper no. 45. U.S. Department of Commerce, Weather Bureau, Washington, DC.

Parr, Ryan Lynn. 1998. Molecular Genetic Analysis of the Great Salt Lake Wetlands Fremont. Unpublished PhD dissertation, Department of Anthropology, University of Utah, Salt Lake City.

Parr, Ryan L., Shawn W. Carlyle, and Dennis H. O'Rourke. 1996. Ancient DNA Analysis of Fremont Amerindians of the Great Salt Lake Wetlands. *American Journal of Physical Anthropology* 99:507–518.

Parsons, Elsie Clews. 1939. *Pueblo Indian Religion*. Vol. 1. University of Nebraska Press, Lincoln.

———. 1994. *Tewa Tales*. University of Arizona Press, Tucson. Reprint of 1924 edition.

Peckham, Stewart. 1984. The Anasazi Culture of the Northern Rio Grande Rift. In *New Mexico Geological Society Guidebook, 35th Field Conference: Rio Grande Rift, Northern New Mexico*, pp. 275–281. New Mexico Bureau of Mines and Mineral Resources, Socorro.

Peckam, Stewart, and John P. Wilson. 1967. Archaeological Survey of the Chuska Valley and the Chaco Plateau, New Mexico. Part 2: Survey. Manuscript on file, Laboratory of Anthropology, Museum of New Mexico, Santa Fe.

Peregrine, Peter. 2006. Synchrony in the New World: An Example of Archaeoethnology. *Cross-Cultural Research* 40(1): 6–17.

Petersen, Kenneth L. 1988. *Climate and the Dolores River Anasazi: A Paleoenvironmental Reconstruction from a 10,000-Year Pollen Record, La Plata Mountains, Southwestern Colorado*. University of Utah Anthropological Papers, no. 113. University of Utah Press, Salt Lake City.

———. 1994. A Warm and Wet Little Climatic Optimum and a Cold and Dry Little Ice Age in the Southern Rocky Mountains, U.S.A. *Climatic Change* 26:243–269.

Petersen, Kenneth L., and Meredith H. Matthews. 1987. Man's Impact on the Landscape: A Prehistoric Example from the Dolores River Anasazi, Southwestern Colorado. *Journal of the West* 26(3): 4–16.

Phagan, Carl J. 1988. Projectile Point Analysis, Part I: Production of Statistical Types and Subtypes. In *Dolores Archaeological Program: Supporting Studies; Additive and Reductive Technologies*, compiled by Eric Blinman, Carl Phagan, and Richard Wilshusen, pp. 9–52. U.S. Department of the Interior, Bureau of Reclamation, Engineering and Research Center, Denver, Colorado.

Pippin, Lonnie C. 1987. *Prehistory and Paleoecology of Guadalupe Ruin, New Mexico*. University of Utah Anthropological Papers, 107. Salt Lake City.

Plog, Fred T. 1983. Political and Economic Alliances on the Colorado Plateaus, AD 400–1450. In *Advances in World Archaeology*, vol. 2, edited by Fred Wendorf and Angela E. Close, pp. 289–330. Academic Press, New York.

———. 1989. The Sinagua and Their Relations. In *Dynamics of Southwest Prehistory*, edited by L. S. Cordell and G. J. Gumerman, pp. 263–292. Smithsonian Institution Press, Washington, DC.

Plog, Stephen, and Julie P. Solometo. 1997. The Never-Changing and the Ever-Changing: The Evolution of Western Pueblo Ritual. *Cambridge Archaeological Journal* 7(2): 161–182.

Pollan, Michael. 2006. *The Omnivore's Dilemma: A Natural History of Four Meals*. Penguin, New York.

Poore, Richard Z., Milan J. Pavich, and Henry Grissino-Mayer. 2005. Record of North American Southwest Monsoon from Gulf of Mexico Sediment Cores. *Geology* 33:209–212.

Potter, James M. 1997. Communal Ritual and Faunal Remains: An Example from the Dolores Anasazi. *Journal of Field Archaeology* 24:353–364.

———. 2000. Pots, Parties, and Politics: Communal Feasting in the American Southwest. *American Antiquity* 65:471–492.

———. 2002. Community, Metaphor, and Gender: Technological Changes across the Pueblo III to Pueblo IV Transition in the El Morro Valley, New Mexico. In *Traditions, Transitions, and Technologies: Themes in Southwestern Archaeology*, edited by Sarah H. Schlanger, pp. 332–349. University Press of Colorado, Boulder.

———. 2004. The Creation of Person, the Creation of Place: Hunting Landscapes in the American Southwest. *American Antiquity* 69:322–338.

Potter, James M., and Jason Chuipka. 2007. Early Pueblo Communities and Cultural Diversity in the Durango Area. *Kiva* 72:407–429.

Potter, James M., and Scott G. Ortman. 2004. Community and Cuisine in the Prehispanic American Southwest. In *Identity, Feasting, and the Archaeology of the Greater Southwest,* edited by B. J. Mills, pp. 173–191. Proceedings of the 2002 Southwest Symposium. University Press of Colorado, Boulder.

Powell, Shirley. 1983. *Mobility and Adaptation: The Anasazi of Black Mesa, Arizona.* Southern Illinois University Press, Carbondale.

Powers, Robert P., William B. Gillespie, and Stephen H. Lekson. 1983. *The Outlier Survey: A Regional View of Settlement in the San Juan Basin.* National Park Service, Albuquerque.

Powers, Robert P., and Janet D. Orcutt. 1999. Summary and Conclusions. In *The Bandelier Archeological Survey,* vol. 2, edited by Robert P. Powers and Janet D. Orcutt, pp. 551–589. Intermountain Cultural Resources Management Professional Paper no. 57. U.S. Department of the Interior, Santa Fe, New Mexico.

Preston Blier, Susan. 1987. *The Anatomy of Architecture: Ontology and Metaphor in Batammaliba Architectural Expression.* University of Chicago Press, Chicago.

Prudden, T. Mitchell. 1903. The Prehistoric Ruins of the San Juan Watershed in Utah, Arizona, Colorado, and New Mexico. *American Anthropologist* 5:224–288.

Putsavage, Kathryn J. 2008. Mesa Verde Style Mugs: An Analysis of Domestic and Ritual Functions. Unpublished master's thesis, Department of Museum and Field Studies, University of Colorado, Boulder.

Quinn, William H., and Victor T. Neal. 1992. The Historical Record of El Niño Events. In *Climate since 1500,* edited by Raymond S. Bradley and Philip D. Jones, pp. 623–648. Routledge, London.

Rainey, Katharine D., and Karen R. Adams. 2004. Plant Use by Native Peoples of the American Southwest: Ethnographic Documentation. http://www.crowcanyon.org/plantuses (accessed December 12, 2007).

Rapoport, Amos. 1969. *House Form and Culture.* Prentice-Hall, Inc., Englewood Cliffs, NJ.

Rappaport, R. A. 1971. Ritual, Sanctity, and Cybernetics. *American Anthropologist* 73:59–76.

——. 1979. The Obvious Aspects of Ritual. In *Ecology, Meaning, and Religion,* by R. A. Rappaport, pp. 173–222. North Atlantic Books, Berkeley.

Rautman, Alison E. 1993. Resource Variability, Risk, and the Structure of Social Networks: An example from the prehistoric Southwest. *American Antiquity* 58:403–424.

——. 1996. Risk, Reciprocity, and the Operation of Social Networks. In *Evolving Complexity and Environmental Risk in the Prehistoric Southwest,* edited by Joseph A. Tainter and Bonnie Bagley Tainter, pp. 197–222. Santa Fe Institute Studies in the Sciences of Complexity, Proceedings, vol. 24. Addison-Wesley, Reading, MA.

Ravesloot, John C., J. Andrew Darling, and Michael R. Waters. 2009. Hohokam and Pima-Maricopa Irrigation Agriculturalists: Maladaptive or Resilient Societies? In *The Archaeology of Environmental Change: Socionatural Legacies of Degradation and Resilience,* edited by C. T. Fisher, J. B. Hill, and G. M. Feinman, pp. 232–245. University of Arizona Press, Tucson.

Rawlings, Tiffany. 2006. Faunal Analysis and Meat Procurement: Reconstructing the Sexual Division of Labor at Shields Pueblo, Colorado. Unpublished PhD dissertation, Department of Archaeology, Simon Fraser University. Burnaby, British Columbia.

Rawlings, Tiffany, and Jonathan Driver. 2006. Faunal Remains from Shields Pueblo. In Communities through Time: The Archaeology of Shields Pueblo (5MT3807), Montezuma

County, Colorado, edited by Andrew Duff and Susan Ryan. Manuscript on file, Crow Canyon Archaeological Center, Cortez.

Redman, Charles L. 1999. *Human Impact on Ancient Environments*. University of Arizona Press, Tucson.

Reed, Erik K. 1949. Sources of Rio Grande Culture and Population. *El Palacio* 56:163–184.

————. 1956. Types of Village-Plan Layouts in the Southwest. In *Prehistoric Settlement Patterns in the New World*, edited by Gordon R. Willey, pp. 11–17. Viking Fund Publications in Anthropology, no. 23. Wenner-Gren Foundation for Anthropological Research, Inc., New York.

————. 1958. *Excavations in Mancos Canyon, Colorado*. Anthropological Papers, no. 35. University of Utah, Salt Lake City.

Reid, J. Jefferson. 1989. A Grasshopper Perspective on the Mogollon of the Arizona Mountains. In *Dynamics of Southwest Prehistory*, edited by Linda S. Cordell, and George J. Gumerman, pp. 65–98. Smithsonian Institution Press, Washington, DC.

Reiter, Paul. 1938. *The Jemez Pueblo of Unshagi, New Mexico, with notes on the earlier excavations at "Amoxiumqua" and Giusewa*. Monographs of the School of American Research, nos. 5–6. University of New Mexico Press, Albuquerque.

Relethford, John H. 2003. Anthropometric Data and Population History. In *Human Biologists in the Archives: Demography, Health, Nutrition, and Genetics in Historical Populations*, edited by D. Anne Herring and Alan C. Swedlund, pp. 32–52. Cambridge University Press, Cambridge.

————. 2004. Global Patterns of Isolation by Distance Based on Genetic and Morphological Data. *Human Biology* 76:499–513.

Relethford, John H., and John Blangero. 1990. Detection of Differential Gene Flow from Patterns of Quantitative Variation. *Human Biology* 62:5–25.

Relethford, John H., Michael H. Crawford, and John Blangero. 1997. Genetic Drift and Gene Flow in Post-Famine Ireland. *Human Biology* 69:443–465.

Relethford, John H., and Francis C. Lees. 1982. The Use of Quantitative Traits in the Study of Human Population Structure. *Yearbook of Physical Anthropology* 25:113–132.

Rice, Glen E. 1998. War and Water: An Ecological Perspective on Hohokam Irrigation. *Kiva* 63(3): 263–301.

Richens, Lane D. 2000. Ceramics. In *Clear Creek Canyon Archaeological Project: Results and Synthesis*, by Joel C. Janetski, Deborah E. Newman, Lane D. Richens, and James D. Wilde, pp. 47–65. Museum of Peoples and Cultures, Occasional Papers, no. 7. Brigham Young University, Provo, UT.

Richerson, Peter J., Robert Boyd, and Robert L. Bettinger. 2001. Was Agriculture Impossible during the Pleistocene but Mandatory during the Holocene? A Climate Change Hypothesis. *American Antiquity* 66:387–411.

Ritchie, Steven W., John J. Hanway, and Garren O. Benson. 1992. *How a Corn Plant Develops*. Cooperative Extension Service Special Report no. 48. Iowa State University, Ames.

Robb, John. 2007. *The Early Mediterranean Village: Agency, Material Culture, and Social Change in Neolithic Italy*. Cambridge University Press, Cambridge.

Robbins, Wilfred William, John Peabody Harrington, and Barbara Freire-Marreco. 1916. *Ethnobotany of the Tewa Indians*. U.S. Government Printing Office, Washington, DC.

Robinson, Hugh L. 2005. Feasting, Exterior Bowl Design and Public Space in the Northern San Juan, AD 1240–1300. Unpublished master's thesis, Department of Anthropology, Washington State University, Pullman.

Rohn, Arthur H. 1965. Postulation of Socio-economic Groups from Archaeological Evidence. In *Contributions of the Wetherill Mesa Archeological Project*, assembled by Douglas Osborne, pp. 65–69. Society for American Archaeology, Memoirs, no. 19. Salt Lake City, Utah.

———. 1971. *Mug House, Mesa Verde National Park, Colorado*. National Park Service, Washington, DC.

———. 1989. Northern San Juan Prehistory. In *Dynamics of Southwestern Prehistory*, edited by Linda S. Cordell and George J. Gumerman, pp. 149–177. Smithsonian Institution Press, Washington, DC.

Roney, John R. 1995. Mesa Verde Manifestations South of the San Juan River. *Journal of Anthropological Archaeology* 14:170–183.

———. 1996. The Pueblo III Period in the Eastern San Juan Basin and Acoma-Laguna Areas. In *The Prehistoric Pueblo World, AD 1150–1350*, edited by Michael A. Adler, pp. 145–169. University of Arizona Press, Tucson.

Root, Matthew J. 1992. Casa del Rito, LA 3852. In *Bandelier Archaeological Excavation Project: Summer 1990 Excavations at Burnt Mesa Pueblo and Casa del Rito*, edited by Timothy A. Kohler and Matthew J. Root, pp. 5–36. Department of Anthropology Reports of Excavations, no. 64. Washington State University, Pullman.

Rose, Martin R., Jeffrey S. Dean, and William J. Robinson. 1981. *The Past Climate of Arroyo Hondo, New Mexico, Reconstructed from Tree-Rings*. Arroyo Hondo Archaeological Series 4. School of American Research Press, Santa Fe.

Rose, Martin R., William J. Robinson, and Jeffrey S. Dean. 1982. Dendroclimatic Reconstruction of the Southwestern Colorado Plateau. Manuscript on file at the Laboratory of Tree-Ring Research, University of Arizona, Tucson.

Ross, Malcolm. 1997. Social Networks and Kinds of Speech-Community Event. In *Archaeology and Language I: Theoretical and Methodological Orientations*, edited by Roger Blench and Matthew Spriggs, pp. 209–261. Routledge, London and New York.

Rouse, Irving B. 1958. The Inference of Migration from Anthropological Evidence. In *Migrations in New World Culture History*, edited by Raymond H. Thompson, pp. 63–68. Social Science Bulletin, no. 27. University of Arizona, Tucson.

Ruscavage-Barz, Samantha. 1999. Knowing Your Neighbor: Coalition Period Community Dynamics on the Pajarito Plateau, New Mexico. Unpublished PhD dissertation, Department of Anthropology, Washington State University, Pullman.

———. 2002. Understanding Santa Fe Black-on-white Style and Technology: An Example from the Pajarito Plateau, New Mexico. *Kiva* 67:249–268.

Ruscavage-Barz, Samantha, and Elizabeth A. Bagwell. 2006. Gathering Spaces and Bounded Places: The Religious Significance of Plaza-Oriented Communities in the Northern Rio Grande, New Mexico. In *Religion in the Prehispanic Southwest*, edited by Christine S. Vanpool, Todd L. Vanpool, and David A. Phillips Jr., pp. 81–101. AltaMira Press, Lanham, MD.

Russell, Frank. 1908. The Pima Indians. In *Twenty-Sixth Annual Report of the Bureau of American Ethnology, 1904–1905*, pp. 3–389. U.S. Government Printing Office, Washington, DC.

Ryan, Dennis John. 1977. *The Paleopathology and Paleoepidemiology of the Kayenta Anasazi Indians in Northeastern Arizona*. PhD dissertation, Department of Anthropology, Arizona State University, Tempe. University Microfilms International, Ann Arbor.

Ryan, Susan C. 2000. Late Pueblo III Kiva "Shrines" at Shields Pueblo (5MT3807). Poster presented at the seventy-third annual Pecos Conference, Dolores, Colorado.

Ryan, Susan C. 2008. Environmental Change, Population Movement, and the Post-Chaco Transition at Albert Porter Pueblo. Manuscript submitted for review, *Kiva*.

Ryan, Susan C., Karen R. Adams, and Andrew I. Duff. 2007. Long-Term Plant Use and Human Impact to the Environment at Shields Pueblo. Paper presented at the seventy-second annual meeting of the Society for American Archaeology, Austin.

Salzer, Matthew W. 2000a. *Dendroclimatology in the San Fransisco Peaks Region of Northern Arizona, USA*. PhD dissertation, Department of Geosciences, University of Arizona. University Microfilms International, Ann Arbor.

————. 2000b. Temperature Variability and the Northern Anasazi. *Kiva* 65:295–318.

Salzer, Matthew W., and Kurt F. Kipfmueller. 2005. Reconstructed Temperature and Precipitation on a Millennial Timescale from Tree-Rings in the Southern Colorado Plateau, U.S.A. *Climatic Change* 70:465–487.

Sanchez, Joseph P. 2006. The Franciscan Search for Mythical Teguayo: New Mexico and Utah between 1678 and 1778. In *They Came to El Llano Estacado*, edited by Felix D. Almaraz Jr., pp. 91–109. University of Texas, San Antonio.

Sapir, Edward. 1916. *Time Perspective in Aboriginal American Culture: A Study in Method*. Anthropological Series 13. Memoirs of the Canadian Geographical Society 90, Ottawa.

Sauer, Carl O. 1954. Comments to: Gatherers and Farmers in the Greater Southwest. *American Anthropologist* 56:529–560.

Saxton, Dean, Lucille Saxton, and Susie Enos. 1983. *Dictionary: Tohono O'odham/Pima to English, English to Tohono O'odham/Pima*. 2d ed., edited by R. L. Cherry. University of Arizona Press, Tucson.

Schaafsma, Polly. 1992. *Rock Art in New Mexico*. Rev. ed. Museum of New Mexico Press, Santa Fe.

————. 2000. *Warrior, Shield, and Star: Imagery and Ideology of Pueblo Warfare*. Western Edge Press, Santa Fe.

Schaafsma, Polly, and Curtis F. Schaafsma. 1974. Evidence for the Origins of the Pueblo Katchina Cult as Suggested by Southwestern Rock Art. *American Antiquity* 39:535–545.

Scheick, Cherie L. 2007. The Late Developmental and Early Coalition of the Northern Middle Rio Grande: Time or Process? *Kiva* 73:131–154.

Scherer, Andrew K. 2007. Population Structure of the Classic Period Maya. *American Journal of Physical Anthropology* 132:367–380.

Schillaci, Michael A. 2003. The Development of Population Diversity at Chaco Canyon. *Kiva* 68:221–245.

Schillaci, Michael A., Erik G. Ozolins, and Thomas C. Windes. 2001. Multivariate Assessment of Biological Relationships among Prehistoric Southwest Amerindian Populations. In *Following Through: Papers in Honor of Phyllis S. Davis*, edited by Regge N. Wiseman, Thomas C. O'Laughlin, and Cordelia T. Snow, pp. 133–149. Papers of the Archaeological Society of New Mexico, vol. 27. Albuquerque.

Schillaci, Michael A., and Christopher M. Stojanowski. 2005. Craniometric Variation and Population History of the Prehistoric Tewa. *American Journal of Physical Anthropology* 126:404–412.

Schlanger, Sarah H. 1987. Population Measurement, Size, and Change: AD 600–1175. In *Dolores Archaeological Program: Supporting Studies: Settlement and Environment*, edited by K. L. Peterson and J. D. Orcutt, pp. 569–616. U.S. Bureau of Reclamation, Engineering and Research Center, Denver.

Schmader, Matthew F. 1994. Early Puebloan Site Structure and Technological Organization in the Middle Rio Grande Valley, New Mexico. Unpublished PhD dissertation, Department of Anthropology, University of New Mexico, Albuquerque.

Schmidt, Kari M. 2006. *Excavations at a Coalition Period Pueblo (LA 4618) on Mesita del Buey, Los Alamos National Laboratory*. Report prepared for U.S. Department of Energy, National Nuclear Security Administration, Los Alamos Site Office. Los Alamos National Laboratory, Los Alamos, NM.

―――. 2007. Coalition Period Subsistence on the Pajarito Plateau: Faunal Remains from Five Room Block Sites. *Kiva* 73:155–172.

Schroeder, Albert H. 1979. Pueblos Abandoned in Historic Times. In *Handbook of North American Indians*, vol. 9: *Southwest*, edited by Alfonso Ortiz, pp. 236–254. Smithsonian Institution, Washington, DC.

Schubert, Siegfried D., Max J. Suarez, Philip J. Pegion, Randal D. Koster, and Julio T. Bacmeister. 2004. On the Cause of the 1930s Dust Bowl. *Science* 303:1855–1859.

Schweingruber, Fritz H. 1988. *Tree Rings: Basics and Application of Dendrochronology*. D. Reidel, Dordrecht, Netherlands.

Scott, Ralph C. 1991. *Essentials of Physical Geography*. West Publishing, New York.

Scuderi, Louis A. 1993. A 2000-Year Tree Ring Record of Annual Temperature in the Sierra Nevada Mountains. *Science* 259:1433–1436.

Sebastian, Lynne. 1992. *The Chaco Anasazi: Sociopolitical Evolution in the American Southwest*. Cambridge University Press, Cambridge.

Seddon, Matthew T. 2001. *Excavations and Data Analysis at the Utah Army National Guard Vehicle Maintenance Facility within Backhoe Village (42SV662) in Richfield, Sevier County, Utah*. Archaeological Report, no. 00-27. SWCA Environmental Consultants, Salt Lake City.

Sekaquaptewa, Emory, and Dorothy Washburn. 2004. They Go along Singing: Reconstructing the Past from Ritual Metaphors in Song and Image. *American Antiquity* 69:457–486.

Sellers, William D., and Richard H. Hill. 1974. *Arizona Climate, 1931–1972*. 2d ed. University of Arizona Press, Tucson.

Sharrock, Floyd W., and John P. Marwitt. 1967. *Excavations at Nephi, Utah, 1965–1966*. Anthropological Papers, no. 88. University of Utah, Salt Lake City.

Shaul, David L., and Jane H. Hill. 1998. Tepimans, Yumans, and Other Hohokam. *American Antiquity* 63:375–396.

Shaw, Robert H. 1988. Climate Requirement. In *Corn and Corn Improvement*, edited by George F. Sprague and John W. Dudley, pp. 609–638. American Society of Agronomy, Agronomy Monograph no. 18. Madison, WI.

Sheppard, Paul R., Andrew C. Comrie, Gregory D. Packin, Kurt Angersbach, and Malcolm K. Hughes. 2002. The Climate of the US Southwest. *Climate Research* 21:219–238.

Sheridan, Susan Guise. 2003. Childhood Health as an Indicator of Biological Stress. In *Centuries of Decline during the Hohokam Classic Period at Pueblo Grande*, edited by David R. Abbott, pp. 82–106. University of Arizona Press, Tucson.

Shimada, Izumi, Crystal Barker Schaaf, Lonnie G. Thompson, and Ellen Mosley-Thompson. 1991. Cultural Impacts of Severe Droughts in the Prehistoric Andes: Application of a 1,500-Year Ice Core Precipitation Record. *World Archaeology* 22:247–270.

Simms, Steven R., Jason R. Bright, and Andrew Ugan. 1997. Plain-Ware Ceramics and Residential Mobility: A Case Study from the Great Basin. *Journal of Archaeological Science* 24:779–792.

Simms, Steven R., and Kathleen M. Heath. 1990. Site Structure of the Orbit Inn: An Application of Ethnoarchaeology. *American Antiquity* 55:797–812.

Simpson, Derrick E. 2008. Architectural Patterning in Residential Structures of the Gallina Phase of Northwestern New Mexico. Unpublished master's thesis, Prescott College, Prescott, Arizona.

Smiley, Terah L. 1961. Evidence of Climatic Fluctuations in Southwestern Prehistory. In *Solar Variations, Climatic Change, and Related Geophysical Problems*, edited by Rhodes W. Fairbridge, pp. 697–704. Annals of the New York Academy of Sciences, no. 95 (Art. 1). New York.

Smiley, Terah L., Stanley A. Stubbs, and Bryant Bannister. 1953. *A Foundation for the Dating of Some Late Archaeological Sites in the Rio Grande Area, New Mexico.* Laboratory of Tree-Ring Research, Bulletin no. 6. University of Arizona, Tucson.

Smith, Rachel L. 1998. Kivas of the Northern San Juan and the Northern Rio Grande Regions, AD 1150–1350: A Comparative Analysis. Unpublished master's thesis, Washington State University, Pullman.

Smith, Watson. 1971. *Painted Ceramics of the Western Mound at Awatovi.* Papers of the Peabody Museum of American Archaeology and Ethnology, Harvard University, vol. 38. Cambridge.

Snead, James E. 1995. Beyond Pueblo Walls: Community and Competition in the Northern Rio Grande, AD 1300–1400. Unpublished PhD dissertation, Department of Anthropology, University of California, Los Angeles.

———. 2008a. *Ancestral Landscapes of the Pueblo World.* University of Arizona Press, Tucson.

———. 2008b. History, Place, and Social Power in the Galisteo Basin, AD 1250–1325. In *The Social Construction of Communities: Agency, Structure, and Identity*, edited by Mark D. Varien and James M. Potter, pp. 155–167. AltaMira Press, Lanham, MD.

Snead, James E., Winifred Creamer, and Tineke Van Zandt. 2004. "Ruins of Our Forefathers": Large Sites and Site Clusters in the Northern Rio Grande. In *The Protohistoric Pueblo World, AD 1275–1600*, edited by E. Charles Adams and Andrew I. Duff, pp. 26–34. University of Arizona Press, Tucson.

Snow, David H. 1971. *Excavations at Cochiti Dam, New Mexico, 1964–1966 Seasons* Vol. 1. Laboratory of Anthropology, Museum of New Mexico, Santa Fe.

———. 1976. *Archaeological Excavations at Pueblo del Encierro, LA 70, Cochiti Dam Salvage Project, New Mexico, Final Report: 1964–1965 Field Seasons.* Laboratory of Anthropology Notes 78. Museum of New Mexico, Santa Fe.

Spangler, Jerry D. 2000a. Radiocarbon Dates, Acquired Wisdom, and the Search for Temporal Order in the Uinta Basin. In *Intermountain Archaeology*, edited by David B. Madsen and Michael D. Metcalf, pp. 48–68. Anthropological Papers, no. 122. University of Utah, Salt Lake City.

———. 2000b. One-Pot Pithouses and Fremont Paradoxes: Formative Stage Adaptations in the Tavaputs Plateau Region of Northeastern Utah. In *Intermountain Archaeology*, edited by David B. Madsen and Michael D. Metcalf, pp. 25–38. University of Utah, Salt Lake City.

Sparks, Corey S., and Richard L. Jantz. 2002. A Reassessment of Cranial Plasticity: Boas Revisited. *Proceedings of the National Academy of Sciences* 99:14636–14639.

Speirs, Randall H. 1966. Some Aspects of the Structure of Rio Grande Tewa. Unpublished PhD dissertation, Department of Language and Literature, State University of New York at Buffalo.

Speirs, Randall H. 1979. Nambe Pueblo. In *Handbook of North American Indians*, vol. 9: *Southwest*, edited by A. Ortiz, pp. 317–323. Smithsonian Institution, Washington, DC.

Spielmann, Katherine. 2004. Communal Feasting, Ceramics, and Exchange. In *Identity, Feasting, and the Archaeology of the Greater Southwest*, edited by Barbara Mills, pp. 210–232. University of Colorado Press, Boulder.

Spielmann, Katherine A., and Eric A. Angstadt-Leto. 1996. Hunting, Gathering, and Health in the Prehistoric Southwest. In *Evolving Complexity and Environmental Risk in the Prehistoric Southwest*, edited by Joseph A. Tainter and Bonnie B. Tainter, pp. 79–106. Addison-Wesley Publishing Company, Reading, MA.

Spielmann, Katherine A., Margaret Nelson, Scott Ingram, and Matthew A. Peeples. In press. Mitigating Environmental Risk in the U.S. Southwest. In *Sustainable Lifeways: Cultural Persistence in an Ever-Changing Environment*, edited by Naomi F. Miller, Katherine M. Moore, and Kathleen Ryan. University of Pennsylvania Museum of Archaeology and Anthropology, Philadelphia.

Spielmann, Katherine A., M. J. Schoeninger, and K. Moore. 1990. Plains-Pueblo Interdependency and Human Diet at Pecos Pueblo, New Mexico. *American Antiquity* 55:745–765.

Stahle, David W., Edward R. Cook, Malcolm K. Cleaveland, Matthew D. Therrell, David M. Meko, Henri D. Grissino-Mayer, Emma Watson, and Brian H. Luckman. 2000. Tree-Ring Data Document 16th Century Megadrought Over North America. *EOS: Transactions of the American Geophysical Union* 81(12): 121–125.

Stanislawski, Michael B. 1963. Wupatki Pueblo: A Study in Cultural Fusion and Change in Sinagua and Hopi Prehistory. Unpublished PhD dissertation, Department of Anthropology, University of Arizona, Tucson.

Stark, Miriam T., Jeffery J. Clark, and Mark D. Elson. 1995. Causes and Consequences of Migration in the 13th Century Tonto Basin. *Journal of Anthropological Archaeology* 14:212–246.

Steadman, Dawnie Wolfe. 1998. The Population Shuffle in the Central Illinois Valley: A Diachronic Model of Mississippian Biocultural Interactions. *World Archaeology* 30:306–326.

———. 2001. Mississippians in Motion? A Population Genetic Analysis of Interregional Gene Flow in West-Central Illinois. *American Journal of Physical Anthropology* 114:61–63.

Steen, Charlie R. 1977. *Pajarito Plateau Archaeological Survey and Excavations*. Los Alamos Scientific Laboratory Report 77–4. Los Alamos.

Stein, John R., and Andrew P. Fowler. 1996. Looking beyond Chaco in the San Juan Basin and Its Peripheries. In *The Prehistoric Pueblo World, AD 1150–1350*, edited by M. A. Adler, pp. 114–130. University of Arizona Press, Tucson.

Sterner, Ray. 1997. Johns Hopkins University Applied Physics Laboratory. http://fermi.jhuapl.edu/states/maps_bw/nm_bw.gif (accessed July 18, 2008).

Stiger, Mark A. 1979. Mesa Verde Subsistence Patterns from Basketmaker to Pueblo III. *Kiva* 44:133–144.

Stodder, Ann Lucy. 1987. The Physical Anthropology and Mortuary Practice of the Dolores Anasazi: An Early Pueblo Population in Local and Regional Context. In *Dolores Archaeological Program: Supporting Studies: Settlement and Environment*, compiled by K. L. Petersen and J. D. Orcutt, pp. 339–504. Bureau of Reclamation, Engineering and Research Center, Denver.

Stojanowski, Christopher M. 2005. *Biocultural Histories in La Florida: A Bioarchaeological Perspective*. University of Alabama Press, Tuscaloosa.

Stone, Glen D., and Cristian E. Downum. 1999. Non-Boserupian Ecology and Agricultural Risk: Ethnic Politics and Land Control in the Arid Southwest. *American Anthropologist* 101:113–128.

Stone, Tammy. 2003. Social Identity and Ethnic Interaction in the Western Pueblos of the American Southwest. *Journal of Archaeological Method and Theory* 10:31–67.

Stone, Tammy, and William D. Lipe. In press. Standing Out Versus Blending In: Pueblo Migrations and Ethnic Marking. In *Changing Histories, Landscapes, and Perspectives: The 20th Anniversary Southwest Symposium*, edited by Margaret Nelson and Colleen Strawhacker. University Press of Colorado, Boulder.

Stuart, David E., and Rory P. Gauthier. 1981. *Prehistoric New Mexico: Background for Survey*. Historic Preservation Bureau, Santa Fe.

Stubbs, Stanley A. 1950. *Bird's-Eye View of the Pueblos*. University of Oklahoma Press, Norman.

———. 1954. Summary Report on an Early Pueblo Site in the Tesuque Valley, New Mexico. *El Palacio* 61:43–45.

Stubbs, Stanley A., and W. S. Stallings Jr. 1953. *The Excavation of Pindi Pueblo, New Mexico*. Monographs of the School for American Research and the Laboratory of Anthropology, no. 18. Santa Fe.

Stuiver, Minze E., and T. F. Brazunias. 1988. The Solar Component of the Atmospheric ^{14}C Record. In *Secular Solar and Geomagnetic Variations in the Last 10,000 Years*, edited by F. R. Stephenson and A. W. Wofendale, pp. 246–266. Klewer, Dordrecht, Netherlands.

Suina, Joseph H. 2002. The Persistence of the Corn Mothers. In *Archaeologies of the Pueblo Revolt: Identity, Meaning, and Renewal in the Pueblo World*, edited by Robert W. Preucel, pp. 212–216. University of New Mexico Press, Albuquerque.

Sweetser, Eve. 1990. *From Etymology to Pragmatics: Metaphorical and Cultural Aspects of Semantic Structure*. Cambridge University Press, Cambridge.

Swentzell, Rena. 1988. Bupingeh: The Pueblo Plaza. *El Palacio* 94(2): 14–19.

Syngg, J., and Thomas C. Windes. 1998. Long, Wide Roads and Great Kiva Roofs. *Kiva* 64:7–25.

Szuter, Christine R., and Frank E. Bayham. 1989. Sedentism and Prehistoric Animal Procurement among Desert Horticulturalists of the North American Southwest. In *Farmers as Hunters: The Implications of Sedentism*, edited by Susan Kent, pp. 80–95. Cambridge University Press, Cambridge.

Tainter, Joseph A. 1988. *The Collapse of Complex Societies*. New Studies in Archaeology. Cambridge University Press, Cambridge.

Tainter, Joseph A., and Bonnie B. Tainter. 1991. The Towers of Hovenweep. Paper presented at the fifty-sixth annual meeting of the Society for American Archaeology, New Orleans, Louisiana.

Talbot, Richard K. 2000a. Fremont Settlement Patterns and Demography. In *Clear Creek Canyon Archaeological Project: Results and Synthesis*, by Joel C. Janetski, Deborah E. Newman, Lane D. Richens, and James D. Wilde, pp. 201–230. Museum of Peoples and Cultures, Occasional Papers, no. 7. Brigham Young University, Provo, UT.

———. 2000b. Fremont Architecture. In *Clear Creek Canyon Archaeological Project: Results and Synthesis*, by Joel C. Janetski, Deborah E. Newman, Lane D. Richens, and James D. Wilde, pp. 131–184. Museum of Peoples and Cultures, Occasional Papers, no. 7. Brigham Young University, Provo, UT.

Talbot, Richard K., Shane A. Baker, and Lane D. Richens. 2004. *The Right Place: Fremont and Early Pioneer Archaeology in Salt Lake City*. Museum of Peoples and Cultures, Technical Series no. 03–07. Brigham Young University, Provo, UT.

Talbot, Richard K., and Lane D. Richens. 1993. *Archaeological Investigations at Richfield and Vicinity*. Museum of Peoples and Cultures, Technical Series, no. 93-15. Brigham Young University, Provo, Utah.

Talbot, Richard K., Lane D. Richens, James D. Wilde, Joel C. Janetski, and Deborah E. Newman. 2000. *Excavations at Five Finger Ridge, Clear Creek Canyon, Central Utah*. Museum of Peoples and Cultures, Occasional Papers, no. 5. Brigham Young University, Provo, UT.

Talbot, Richard K., and James D. Wilde. 1989. Giving Form to the Formative: Shifting Settlement Patterns in the Eastern Great Basin and Northern Colorado Plateau. *Utah Archaeology* 2(1): 3–18.

Thompson, Ian, Mark Varien, Susan Kenzle, and Rina Swentzell. 1997. Prehistoric Architecture with Unknown Function. In *Anasazi Architecture and American Design*, edited by Baker H. Morrow and V. B. Price, pp. 149–158. University of New Mexico Press, Albuquerque.

Till, Jonathan D., and Scott G. Ortman. 2007. Artifacts. In *The Archaeology of Sand Canyon Pueblo: Intensive Excavations at a Late-Thirteenth-Century Village in Southwestern Colorado*, edited by Kristin A. Kuckelman. http://www.crowcanyon.org/sandcanyon (accessed September 15, 2008).

Tilley, Christopher. 1999. *Metaphor and Material Culture*. Blackwell Publishers, Oxford and London.

Tivy, Joy. 1990. *Agricultural Ecology*. Longman Scientific and Technical, John Wiley, New York.

Torrence, Robin, and John Grattan. 2002. The Archaeology of Disasters: Past and Future Trends. In *Natural Disasters and Cultural Change*, edited by Robin Torrence and John Grattan, pp. 1–18. Routledge, London.

Trager, George L. 1942. The Historical Phonology of the Tiwa Languages. *Studies in Linguistics* 1(5): 1–10.

———. 1946. An Outline of Taos Grammar. In *Linguistic Structures of Native America*, edited by Harry Hoijer et al., pp. 184–221. Viking Fund Publications in Anthropology 6, New York.

———. 1967. The Tanoan Settlement of the Rio Grande Area: A Possible Chronology. In *Studies in Southwestern Ethnolinguistics*, edited by Dell H. Hymes and William E. Bittle, pp. 335–350. Mouton, The Hague.

Trenberth, Kevin E., and Timothy J. Hoar. 1996. El Niño–Southern Oscillation Event: Longest on Record. *Geophysical Research Letters* 23:57–60.

———. 1997. El Niño and Climate Change. *Geophysical Research Letters* 24:3057–3060.

Trierweiler, William N. 1990. *Prehistoric Tewa Economy: Modeling Subsistence Production on the Pajarito Plateau*. Garland Publishing, New York.

Trigger, Bruce G. 1976. *The Children of Aataentsic I: A History of the Huron People to 1660*. McGill-Queen's University Press, Montreal.

Turner, Christy G., II, and Jacqueline A. Turner. 1999. *Man Corn: Cannibalism and Violence in the Prehistoric American Southwest*. University of Utah Press, Salt Lake City.

Twitchell, Ralph Emerson. 1914. *The Spanish Archives of New Mexico*. Vol. 2. Torch Press, Cedar Rapids, Iowa.

Tyler, S. Lyman. 1952. The Myth of the Lake of Copala and Land of Teguayo. *Utah Historical Quarterly* 20(4): 313–329.

Underhill, Ruth M. 1946. *Papago Indian Religion.* Columbia University Contributions to Anthropology, no. 33. Columbia University Press, New York.

van der Leeuw, Sander E. 2009. What is an "Environmental Crisis" to an Archaeologist? In *The Archaeology of Environmental Change: Socionatural Legacies of Degradation and Resilience,* edited by Christopher T. Fisher, J. Brett Hill, and Gary M. Feinman, pp. 40–61. University of Arizona Press, Tucson.

Vanderpool, Tim. 2008. What Became of the Hohokam? *American Archaeology* 12(3): 32–37.

Van Gerven, Dennis P., and Susan Guise Sheridan (editors). 1994. *The Pueblo Grande Project,* vol. 6: *The Bioethnography of a Classic Period Hohokam Population.* Soil Systems Publications in Archaeology, no. 20(6). Soil Systems, Inc., Phoenix.

Van Pool, Christine S., Todd L. Van Pool, and David A. Phillips Jr. (editors). 2007. *Religion in the Prehispanic Southwest.* AltaMira Press, Walnut Creek, CA.

Van West, Carla R. 1994. *Modeling Prehistoric Agricultural Productivity in Southwestern Colorado: A GIS Approach.* Reports of Investigations, no. 67. Department of Anthropology, Washington State University, Pullman; and Crow Canyon Archaeological Center, Cortez, Colorado.

———. 1996. The Heuristic Value of Estimates of Prehistoric Agricultural Production: A Case Study from Southwestern Colorado. In *The Prehistoric Pueblo World, AD 1150–1350,* edited by Michael A. Adler, pp. 133–145. University of Arizona Press, Tucson.

Van West, Carla R., and Jeffrey S. Dean. 2000. Environmental Characteristics of the AD 900–1300 Period in the Central Mesa Verde Region. *Kiva* 66:19–44.

Van West, Carla R., and Timothy A. Kohler. 1995. A Time to Rend, A Time to Sew: New Perspectives on Northern Anasazi Sociopolitical Development in Later Prehistory. In *Anthropology, Space, and Geographic Information Systems,* edited by Mark Aldenderfer and Herbert D. G. Maschner, pp. 112–139. Oxford University Press, Oxford.

Van West, Carla R., and William D. Lipe. 1992. Modeling Prehistoric Climate and Agriculture in Southwestern Colorado. In *The Sand Canyon Archaeological Project: A Progress Report,* edited by William D. Lipe, pp. 105–119. Crow Canyon Archaeological Center, Occasional Paper no. 2. Cortez, Colorado.

Varien, Mark D. 1999a. *Sedentism and Mobility in a Social Landscape: Mesa Verde and Beyond.* University of Arizona Press, Tucson.

———. 1999b. Dating Summary. In *The Sand Canyon Archaeological Project: Site Testing,* edited by M. Varien, chap. 20. Crow Canyon Archaeological Center, Cortez, Colorado. http://www.crowcanyon.org/ResearchReports/SiteTesting/start.asp (accessed July 15, 2008).

———. 1999c. Regional Context: Architecture, Settlement Patterns, and Abandonment. In *The Sand Canyon Archaeological Project: Site Testing,* edited by Mark D. Varien, chapter 21. http://www.crowcanyon.org/sitetesting (accessed July 15, 2008).

———. 2000. Introduction. *Kiva* 66:5–18.

———. 2002. Persistent Communities and Mobile Households: Population Movement in the Central Mesa Verde Region, AD 950–1290. In *Seeking the Center Place: Archaeology and Ancient Communities in the Mesa Verde Region,* edited by Mark D. Varien and Richard H. Wilshusen, pp. 163–184. University of Utah Press, Salt Lake City.

Varien, Mark D. (editor). 1999b. *The Sand Canyon Archaeological Project: Site Testing.* Crow Canyon Archaeological Center, Cortez, Colorado. http://www.crowcanyon.org/ResearchReports/SiteTesting/start.asp (accessed July 7, 2008).

Varien, Mark D., and Kristin Kuckelman. 1999. Introduction. In *The Sand Canyon Archaeological Project: Site Testing*, edited by M. Varien, chap. 1. Crow Canyon Archaeological Center, Cortez, Colorado. http://www.crowcanyon.org/ResearchReports/SiteTesting/start.asp (accessed July 7, 2008).

Varien, Mark D., William D. Lipe, Michael A. Adler, Ian M. Thompson, and Bruce A. Bradley. 1996. Southwestern Colorado and Southeastern Utah Settlement Patterns: AD 1100–1300. In *The Prehistoric Pueblo World, AD 1150–1350*, edited by Michael A. Adler, pp. 86–113. University of Arizona Press, Tucson.

Varien, Mark D., and Barbara J. Mills. 1997. Accumulations Research: Problems and Prospects for Estimating Site Occupation Span. *Journal of Archaeological Method and Theory* 4:141–191.

Varien, Mark D., Scott G. Ortman. 2005. Accumulations Research in the Southwest United States: Middle Range Theory for Big-Picture Problems. *World Archaeology* 37:132–155.

Varien, Mark D., Scott G. Ortman, Timothy A. Kohler, Donna M. Glowacki, and C. David Johnson. 2007. Historical Ecology in the Mesa Verde Region: Results from the Village Ecodynamics Project. *American Antiquity* 72:273–300.

Varien, Mark D., Carla R. Van West, and G. Stuart Patterson. 2000. Competition, Cooperation, and Conflict: Agricultural Production and Community Catchments in the Central Mesa Verde Region. *Kiva* 66:45–65.

Varien, Mark D., and Richard H. Wilshusen. 2002. A Partnership for Understanding the Past: Crow Canyon Research in the Central Mesa Verde Region. In *Seeking the Center Place: Archaeology and Ancient Communities in the Mesa Verde Region*, edited by Mark D. Varien and Richard H. Wilshusen, pp. 3–23. University of Utah Press, Salt Lake City.

Vickery, Lucretia D. 1969. *Excavations at TA-26, A Small Pueblo Site near Taos, New Mexico*. Unpublished master's thesis, Department of Anthropology, Wichita State University, Wichita, Kansas.

Vicsek, Tamas. 2002. The Bigger Picture. *Nature* 418:131.

Vierra, Bradley J., and Richard I. Ford. 2006. Early Maize Agriculture in the Northern Rio Grande Valley, New Mexico. In *Histories of Maize*, edited by John E. Staller, Robert H. Tykot, and Bruce F. Benz, pp. 497–510. Elsevier, Amsterdam.

Vierra, Bradley J., Jennifer E. Nisengard, Brian C. Harmon, Beverly M. Larson, Diane C. Curewitz, Kari M. Schmidt, Pamela J. McBride, Susan J. Smith, and Timothy L. Binzen. 2002. *Excavations at a Coalition Period Pueblo (LA 4618) on Mesita del Buey, Los Alamos National Laboratory*. Report prepared for U.S. Department of Energy, National Nuclear Security Administration, Los Alamos Site Office. Los Alamos National Laboratory, Los Alamos, NM.

Vivian, R. Gordon. 1959. *The Hubbard Site and Other Tri-wall Structures in New Mexico and Colorado*. Archaeological Research Series no. 5. U.S. Department of the Interior, National Park Service. Washington, DC.

Wallace, Anthony. 1956. Revitalization Movements. *American Anthropologist* 58:264–281.

Wallace, Henry D., and William H. Doelle. 2001. Classic Period Warfare in Southern Arizona. In *Deadly Landscapes: Case Studies in Prehistoric Southwestern Warfare*, edited by G. Rice and S. LeBlanc, pp. 239–287. University of Utah Press, Salt Lake City.

Walling, Barbara A., and Richard A. Thompson. 1991. *An Interim Report of the Excavations at the Corngrower Site, AZ B:1:102 (BLM), Colorado City, Arizona*. Report on file, Bureau of Land Management Arizona Strip District Office, Saint George, UT.

Walling, Barbara A., and Richard A. Thompson. 1992. *The Second Interim Report of the Excavations at the Corngrower Site, AZ B:1:102 (BLM), Colorado City, Arizona.* Report on file, Bureau of Land Management Arizona Strip District Office, Saint George, UT.

———. 1993. *Third Interim Report: The 1992 SUU Field School Excavations at the Corngrower Site, AZ B:1:102 (BLM), Colorado City, Arizona.* Report on file, Bureau of Land Management Arizona Strip District Office, Saint George, UT.

———. 1995. *Fourth Interim Report: 1993 Southern Utah University Field School Excavations at the Corngrower Site, AZ B:1:102 (BLM), Colorado City, Arizona.* Report on file, Bureau of Land Management Arizona Strip District Office, Saint George, UT.

Walling, Barbara A., Richard A. Thompson, Gardiner F. Dalley, and Dennis G. Weder. 1986. *Excavations at Quail Creek.* Cultural Resource Series, no. 20. U.S. Department of the Interior, Bureau of Land Management, Salt Lake City.

Ward, Christine. 1997. The 1997 Field Season at Shields Complex (5MT3807), Montezuma County, Colorado. Crow Canyon Archaeological Center, Cortez, CO. Report submitted to the Bureau of Land Management, San Juan Resource Area Office, Durango, Colorado.

Ware, John A. 2008. Draft chapters from *Pueblo Social History,* in possession of the author.

Ware, John A., and Eric Blinman. 2000. Cultural Collapse and Reorganization: Origin and Spread of Pueblo Ritual Sodalities. In *The Archaeology of Regional Interaction: Religion, Warfare, and Exchange across the American Southwest and Beyond,* pp. 381–409. University Press of Colorado, Boulder.

Warner, Ted J. (editor). 1995. *The Dominguez-Escalante Journal: Their Expedition through Colorado, Utah, Arizona, and New Mexico in 1776.* Translated by Fray Angelico Chavez. University of Utah Press, Salt Lake City.

Wasley, William W. 1962. A Ceremonial Cave on Bonita Creek, Arizona. *American Antiquity* 27:380–394.

Waters, Michael R., and John C. Ravesloot. 2001. Landscape Change and the Cultural Evolution of the Hohokam along the Middle Gila River and Other River Valleys in South-Central Arizona. *American Antiquity* 66:285–299.

Watkins, Laurel. 1984. *A Grammar of Kiowa.* Studies in the Anthropology of North American Indians. University of Nebraska Press, Lincoln.

Wendorf, Fred. 1954. A Reconstruction of Northern Rio Grande Prehistory. *American Antiquity* 56:200–227.

Wendorf, Fred, and Erik K. Reed. 1955. An Alternative Reconstruction of Northern Rio Grande Prehistory. *El Palacio* 62(5–6): 131–173.

Wetherington, Ronald K. 1968. *Excavations at Pot Creek Pueblo.* Fort Burgwin Research Center, Publication no. 6. Taos, NM.

White, Timothy D. 1992. *Prehistoric Cannibalism at Mancos 5MTUMR-2346.* Princeton University Press, Princeton.

Whiteley, Peter M. 1988. *Deliberate Acts: Changing Hopi Culture through the Oraibi Split.* University of Arizona Press, Tucson.

Whitley, David S. 2008. Archaeological Evidence for Conceptual Metaphors as Enduring Knowledge Structures. *Time & Mind* 1(1): 7–30.

Wilcox, David R., William H. Doelle, J. Brett Hill, and James P. Holmlund. 2003. Coalescent Communities GIS Database: Museum of Northern Arizona, Center for Desert Archaeology, Geo-Map Inc. On file, Center for Desert Archaeology, Tucson.

Wilcox, David R., David A. Gregory, and J. Brett Hill. 2007. Zuni in the Puebloan and Southwestern Worlds. In *Zuni Origins: Toward a New Synthesis of Southwestern Archaeology,* edited by David A. Gregory and David R. Wilcox, pp. 165–209. University of Arizona Press, Tucson.

Wilcox, David R., Gerald Robertson Jr., and J. Scott Wood. 2001. Organized for War: The Perry Mesa Settlement System and Its Central Arizona Neighbors. In *Deadly Landscapes: Case Studies in Prehistoric Southwestern Warfare*, edited by Glen E. Rice and Steven A. LeBlanc, pp. 109–140. University of Utah Press, Salt Lake City.

Wilde, James D. 1992. Finding a Date: Some Thoughts on Radiocarbon Dating and the Baker Fremont Site in Eastern Nevada. *Utah Archaeology* 5(1): 39–53.

Wilde, James D., and Reed A. Soper. 1999. *Baker Village: Report of Excavations, 1990–1994*. Museum of Peoples and Cultures, Technical Series, no. 99-12. Brigham Young University, Provo, UT.

Wills, W. H. 2001. Pithouse Architecture and the Economics of Household Formation in the Prehistoric Southwest. *Human Ecology* 29:477–500.

Wilshusen, Richard H. 1986. The Relationship between Abandonment Mode and Ritual Use in Pueblo I Anasazi Protokivas. *Journal of Field Archaeology* 13:245–254.

———. 1988. Architectural Trends in Prehistoric Anasazi Sites during AD 600 to 1200. In *Dolores Archaeological Program, Supporting Studies: Additive and Reductive Technologies*, compiled by Eric Blinman, Carl Fagan, and Richard Wilshusen, pp. 599–634. U.S. Department of the Interior, Bureau of Reclamation, Denver.

———. 2002. Estimating Population in the Central Mesa Verde Region. In *Seeking the Center Place: Archaeology and Ancient Communities in the Mesa Verde Region*, edited by Mark D. Varien and Richard H. Wilshusen, pp. 101–122. University of Utah Press, Salt Lake City.

———. 2010. The Diné at the Edge of History: Navajo Ethnogenesis in the Northern Southwest, 1500–1750. In *Across the Great Divide: Continuity and Change in Native North American Societies, AD 1400–1900*, edited by Mark D. Mitchell and Laura L. Scheiber, 192–211. University of Arizona Press, Tucson.

Wilshusen, Richard H., and Ruth M. Van Dyke. 2006. Chaco's Beginnings: The Collapse of Pueblo I Villages and the Origins of the Chaco System. In *The Archaeology of Chaco Canyon: An Eleventh-Century Pueblo Regional Center*, edited by Stephen H. Lekson, pp. 211–259. School of American Research Press, Santa Fe.

Wilson, C. Dean. 1998. Ormand Ceramic Analysis Part I: Methodology and Categories. In *The Ormand Village: Final Report of the 1965–1966 Excavation*, edited by Laurel T. Wallace, pp. 195–251. Office of Archaeological Studies Archaeology Notes 229. Museum of New Mexico, Santa Fe.

———. 2003. A Reappraisal of the Nature and Significance of Spatial Distributions of Pottery from Sites in the Northern Southwest. In *Anasazi Archaeology at the Millenium: Proceedings of the Sixth Occasional Anasazi Symposium*, edited by P. Reed, pp. 129–136. Center for Desert Archaeology, Tucson.

———. 2008. Examination of Trends for Galisteo Black-on-white. In *Chasing Chaco and the Southwest: Papers in Honor of Frances Joan Mathien*, edited by R. Wiseman, T. O'Laughlin, C. Snow, and C. Travis, pp. 207–215. Archaeological Society of New Mexico, no. 34. Albuquerque.

Wilson, C. Dean, and Eric Blinman. 1995. Ceramic Types of the Mesa Verde Region. In *Archaeological Pottery of Colorado: Ceramic Clues to the Prehistoric and Protohistoric Lives of the State's Native Peoples*, edited by Bruce Bradley and Susan M. Chandler, pp. 33–88. Colorado Council of Professional Archaeologists, Denver.

Windes, Thomas C. 2007. Growing Up and Piling On. In *The Architecture of Chaco Canyon, New Mexico*, edited by S. Lekson, pp. 45–92. University of Utah Press, Salt Lake City.

Windes, Thomas C., and Dabney Ford. 1996. The Chaco Wood Project: The Chronometric Reappraisal of Pueblo Bonito. *American Antiquity* 61:295–310.

Windes, Thomas C., and Peter J. McKenna. 2001. Going against the Grain: Wood Production in Chacoan Society. *American Antiquity* 66:119–140.

Wiseman, Regge N. 1995. Reassessment of the Dating of the Pojoaque Grant Site (LA 835), a Key Site of the Rio Grande Developmental Period. In *Of Pots and Rocks: Papers in Honor of A. Helene Warren*, edited by Meliha S. Duran and David T. Kirkpatrick, pp. 237–248. Papers of the Archaeological Society of New Mexico, vol. 21. Albuquerque.

Wiseman, Regge N., and Bart Olinger. 1991. Initial Production of Painted Pottery in the Rio Grande: The Perspective from LA 835, The Pojoaque Grant Site. In *Puebloan Past and Present: Papers in Honor of Stewart Peckham*, edited by M. Duran and D. Kirkpatrick, pp. 209–217. Papers of the Archaeological Society of New Mexico, vol. 17. Albuquerque.

————. 2007. On the Relationship between the Largo-Gallina and the Jemez. In *Texas and Points West: Papers in Honor of John A. Hedrick and Carol P. Hedrick*, edited by R. N. Wiseman, T. C. O'Laughlin, C. T. Snow, and C. Travis. Archaeological Society of New Mexico 33. Albuquerque.

Wolley, A. M. 1988. Prehistoric Zinc Nutrition: Archaeological, Ethographic, Skeletal and Chemical Evidence. Unpublished master's thesis, Department of Anthropology, University of Nebraska, Lincoln.

Woodbury, Richard B. 1954. *Prehistoric Stone Implements of Northeastern Arizona*. Papers of the Peabody Museum of American Archaeology and Ethnology, vol. 34, no. 6. Harvard University, Cambridge.

————. 1961. Climatic Changes and Prehistoric Agriculture in the Southwestern United States. In *Solar Variations, Climatic Change, and Related Geophysical Problems*, edited by Rhodes W. Fairbridge, pp. 705–709. Annals of the New York Academy of Sciences, no. 95 (art. 1). New York.

Woodhouse, Connie A. 1997. Winter Climate and Atmospheric Circulation Patterns in the Sonoran Desert Region, USA. *International Journal of Climatology* 17:859–873.

Woodson, M. Kyle. 1999. Migrations in Late Anasazi Prehistory: The Evidence from the Goat Hill Site. *Kiva* 65:63–84.

Worman, Frederick C. V. 1967. *Archaeological Salvage Excavations on the Mesita del Buey, Los Alamos County, New Mexico*. Report LA-3636. Los Alamos Scientific Laboratory, Los Alamos, NM.

Wozniack, Frank E., and Michael P. Marshall. 1991. *The Prehistoric Cebolla Canyon Community: An Archaeological Class III Inventory of 320 Acres of BLM Land at the Mouth of Cebolla Canyon*. Office of Contract Archaeology, University of New Mexico, Albuquerque.

Wright, Aaron M. 2006. A Low-Frequency Paleoclimatic Reconstruction from the La Plata Mountains, Colorado, and Its Implications for Agricultural Paleoproductivity in the Mesa Verde Region. Unpublished master's thesis, Department of Anthropology, Washington State University, Pullman.

————. 2008. Mesa Verdean Migrations and Climate Change in Broader Context. Discussion paper for the Amerind Foundation Seminar "New Light on the Thirteenth-Century Depopulation of the Northern Southwest," February 23–27.

Yava, Albert. 1978. *Big Falling Snow: A Tewa-Hopi Indian's Life and Time, and the History and Traditions of His People*. University of New Mexico Press, Albuquerque.

Yoffee, Norman. 1988. Orienting Collapse. In *The Collapse of Ancient States and Civilizations*, edited by Norman Yoffee and George L. Cowgill, pp. 1–19. University of Arizona Press, Tucson.

Yumitani, Yukihiro. 1998. A Phonology and Morphology of Jemez Towa. Unpublished PhD dissertation, Department of Linguistics, University of Kansas, Lawrence.

Zier, Anne H. 1982. Architecture. In *Bandelier: Excavations in the Flood Pool of Cochiti Lake, New Mexico*, edited by L. Hubbell and D. Traylor, pp. 33–112. National Park Service Southwest Cultural Resources Center, Santa Fe.

About the Contributors

KAREN R. ADAMS trained in both anthropology and biology to acquire background as a southwestern United States archaeobotanist. For four decades, she has analyzed and reported on plant remains from archaeological sites in all major southwestern prehispanic culture areas, in addition to in northern Mexico. She has published widely on maize (*Zea mays*) and other domesticates, as well as on the range of wild plants utilized by prehispanic groups. She has also synthesized the archaeological records of specific wild plants (tobacco, beeweed, reedgrass), regional areas, and the Greater American Southwest.

NANCY J. AKINS is an archaeologist and director of the osteological laboratory for the Office of Archaeological Studies in Santa Fe. Her work has primarily been in the middle and upper Rio Grande and Chaco Canyon and includes both field investigations and laboratory analysis. Her interests include applying bioarchaeological and zooarchaeological data to broader issues relating to social organization, mobility, and subsistence.

JAMES R. ALLISON is an assistant professor in the Department of Anthropology at Brigham Young University. He received his PhD from Arizona State University in 2000. His primary research interests are the small-scale societies of the northern Southwest, quantitative methods, ceramic analysis, and archaeological theory, and he has conducted archaeological research in northern Utah, the Virgin region, and the Four Corners area.

LARRY V. BENSON is a senior scientist with the National Research Program of the U.S. Geological Survey and is chief of the Arid Regions Climate Project. Much of his research is focused on the creation of records of past climate change, including lake-sediment-based records of change in the hydrologic balances of Great Basin surface-water systems. His research also includes cosmogenic dating of glacial features in the Front Range and south-central Colorado. Most recently, his research has focused on the response of southwestern Native Americans and midwestern Mississippian Cahokians to climate change via their dependence on a maize-based subsistence base.

MICHAEL S. BERRY completed the requirements for a PhD in anthropology from the University of Utah in 1980. Throughout the 1980s and 1990s, he held positions as a database programmer and network-systems engineer, working primarily with Fortune 500 companies. He is currently regional archeologist for the Bureau of Reclamation in Salt Lake City, Utah.

ERIC BLINMAN is director of the Office of Archaeological Studies at the Museum of New Mexico, New Mexico Department of Cultural Affairs. He received his MA and PhD in anthropology from Washington State University after completing his undergraduate degree at the University of California, Berkeley. His interests include ceramic and textile technologies of the Southwest, archaeomagnetic dating, past environmental change, and the social history of Puebloan peoples. Eric has authored or coauthored more than 150 articles, book chapters, reviews, contract reports, and professional papers. In 2007, he participated in a colloquium on Past Climate Change: Human Survival Strategies that was convened by King Carl XVI Gustaf of Sweden in Narsaq, Greenland. He serves as an outside member of several graduate committees at the University of New Mexico, and he is an instructor in Native American studies for Colgate University's Santa Fe Study Group. He has also authored or coauthored nine popular articles and delivers between fifteen and twenty-five public presentations or demonstrations each year as part of the Education Outreach Program of the Office of Archaeological Studies.

JEFFREY L. BOYER grew up with an historian in Taos, New Mexico, and had little choice but to go into some profession that studies the past. Between 1982 and 1987, he was curator of anthropology and director of the Contract Archaeology Program for what was then the Kit Carson Memorial Foundation, an historic preservation institution and public museum in north-central New Mexico. Since 1987, he has been a supervisory archaeologist/project director with the Museum of New Mexico's Office of Archaeological Studies in Santa Fe. Boyer's analytical interests lie in Euroamerican artifacts, earthen building materials, and geomorphology. His research interests are wide ranging but focus, at least for the moment, on early Pueblo community development and organization in the northern Rio Grande, ritual form and organization, Pueblo and Euroamerican frontiers, and comparative archaeological manifestations of Puebloan and Euroamerican worldviews.

CATHERINE M. CAMERON is professor in the Department of Anthropology at the University of Colorado. She works in the northern American Southwest, especially on the Chaco and post-Chaco eras (AD 900–1300). Her research interests include migration, understanding the evolution of complex societies through the study of regional social and political systems, methods for identifying social boundaries in the past, and prehistoric architecture. Since 1995, she has worked in southeastern Utah at the Bluff Great House, a Chacoan site, and in nearby Comb Wash, publishing a monograph on this research in 2009 (*Chaco and After in the Northern San Juan*, University of Arizona Press). She also studies captives in prehistory, especially their role in cultural transmission. She published an edited volume on this topic in 2008 (*Invisible Citizens, Captives and Their Consequences*, University of Utah Press). She has coedited the *Journal of Archaeological Method and Theory* since 2000.

JEFFERY J. CLARK received his PhD (1997) and MA (1990) from the University of Arizona and his BA (1983) from Cornell University. Dr. Clark has spent the past twenty years conducting research in the Tonto basin, the San Pedro Valley, and the Safford basin of central and southern Arizona. During the 1990s, he supervised large contract projects funded by the Bureau of Reclamation and the Arizona Department of Transportation in the Tonto basin as a project director for Desert Archaeology, Inc. In addition to working in the American Southwest, he has worked extensively in Southwest Asia, participating in excavations in Israel, Syria, and Iraq. Dr. Clark's research has focused on assessing the scale and impact of human migration. He is currently a preservation archaeologist for the Center for Desert Archaeology, a nonprofit organization in Tucson.

JEFFREY S. DEAN is an Agnese and Emil W. Haury professor of archaeological dendrochronology in the Laboratory of Tree-Ring Research, as well as professor of anthropology and curator of archaeology (for the Arizona State Museum) at the University of Arizona, Tucson. His long-term research interests include dendroarchaeology, archaeological chronometry, paleoenvironmental reconstruction, human-environment interaction, and the archaeology of the American Southwest.

WILLIAM H. DOELLE received his PhD from the University of Arizona in 1980. He is currently president of Desert Archaeology, Inc., and president and chief executive operator of the nonprofit Center for Desert Archaeology. His research interests are the large-scale demographic and cultural changes of the American Southwest and Mexican Northwest from AD 1200 to 1700. Preservation of archaeological sites and sharing research results with the public are his other professional priorities.

ANDREW I. DUFF is an associate professor of anthropology at Washington State University. He earned his MA (1993) and PhD (1999) in anthropology at Arizona State University, pursuing interests in transitions in southwestern social and community organization. He served as project director for the Shields Pueblo excavation project from 1998 to 2001 while at Crow Canyon Archaeological Center. This project sought to better understand the nature and timing of aggregation into community centers and the impact populations had on their surrounding natural environment, the topic of his coauthored contribution to this volume. Since 2002, he has been exploring many of these same questions in the context of Chacoan-period communities along the southern frontier of the Chacoan regional system. Recent publications include "Becoming Central, Organizational Transformations in the Emergence of Zuni" (with Gregson Schachner, in *Hinterlands and Regional Dynamics in the Ancient Southwest*, edited by Alan Sullivan and James Bayman, University of Arizona Press, 2007) and "History and Process in Village Formation: Context and Contrasts from the Northern Southwest" (with Catherine Cameron, *American Antiquity* vol. 73, 2008).

DONNA M. GLOWACKI received her PhD from Arizona State University in 2006 and is the John Cardinal O'Hara CSC assistant professor of anthropology at the University of Notre Dame, a senior researcher on the Village Ecodynamics Project, and a long-time research associate with Crow Canyon Archaeological Center. Her current research focuses on village formation and understanding the social circumstances leading up to the regional abandonment of Mesa Verde by the end of the 1200s. She has conducted fieldwork at sixty-three of the largest sites in the Mesa Verde region and is currently involved in fieldwork at Spruce Tree House cliff dwelling and other large sites in the backcountry at Mesa Verde National Park.

J. BRETT HILL received his PhD from Arizona State University in 2002 and is currently a research associate at the Center for Desert Archaeology and assistant professor at Hendrix College in Conway, Arkansas. He has participated in research projects in the American Southwest, the Near East, and Europe; and his current interests focus on human ecology in desert environments since the transition to agricultural economies. He is involved with multiple ongoing projects in Arizona, New Mexico, and Jordan using large archaeological databases and geographic information systems to study demography and human impacts on ancient environments at regional scales.

TIMOTHY A. KOHLER is a regents' professor in the Department of Anthropology at Washington State University, Pullman, and the senior principal investigator on the Village Ecodynamics Project. Although he started his professional career as a southeasternist after receiving his PhD from the University of Florida in 1978, for the past thirty years he has been working on problems of historical ecology, cooperation, and conflict, often with a modeling bent, in the U.S. Southwest. He is an external professor at the Santa Fe Institute, a research associate at Crow Canyon Archaeological Center, and edited *American Antiquity* from 2000 to 2004. He is interested in socionatural processes in Neolithic societies around the world.

KRISTIN A. KUCKELMAN is senior research archaeologist at the Crow Canyon Archaeological Center near Cortez, Colorado. She has conducted field research in the western United States for thirty years, the results of which have been published in numerous volume-length reports; in journals such as *Kiva*, *American Antiquity*, *American Scientist*, and *Polish Contributions in New World Archaeology*; and in many volumes on the archaeology of the American Southwest. She helped pioneer the publication of site reports and research databases on the Internet and currently serves as president of the Colorado Council of Professional Archaeologists. Her research interests include field methods, violence and warfare, anthropophagy, architectural patterning, environmental impacts on societal decision making, and the thirteenth-century depopulation of the Mesa Verde region.

STEVEN A. LAKATOS is a project director at the Office of Archaeological Studies in Santa Fe, New Mexico. Steven has worked in the American Southwest for more than twenty years in survey, excavation, and public-outreach projects. His field experience includes investigations of Paleo-Indian and Archaic manifestations in southeast New Mexico, Basketmaker and ethnohistoric Navajo occupations in the southern Chuska Valley, and Depression-era households in the Santa Fe area. Currently, his research interest is the archaeology of the northern Rio Grande Valley—particularly the Developmental Period—exploring cultural continuity through diachronic and synchronic comparisons in architectural design with the San Juan Anasazi regions of northwestern New Mexico and southwestern Colorado. Related research topics include examining demographic trends and community formation as populations grew and expanded in the northern Rio Grande Valley during this and subsequent periods.

WILLIAM D. LIPE is professor emeritus of anthropology at Washington State University. His archaeological research has focused on Basketmaker- and Pueblo-period community organization, demography, and population movements in the Glen Canyon and Cedar Mesa areas of southeastern Utah and the Dolores and Cortez areas of southwestern Colorado. His long-term interests in archaeological conservation and public archaeology are reflected in several publications. From 1985 to 1992, he served part time as the director of research at the Crow Canyon Archaeological Center in Cortez, and he remains a member of the center's board of trustees. Lipe was president of the Society for American Archaeology from 1995 to 1997.

PATRICK D. LYONS is head of collections and associate curator of anthropology at the Arizona State Museum, as well as an assistant professor of anthropology at the University of Arizona. He earned his PhD in anthropology at the University of Arizona, where he was awarded an Emil W. Haury Graduate Fellowship. Before joining the University of Arizona faculty, he spent six years as a preservation archaeologist at the Center for Desert Archaeology. His research interests include the late prehispanic and protohistoric archaeology of the American Southwest and northwestern Mexico; Hopi ethnography, history, and ethnohistory; ceramic decorative and technological style; ceramic compositional analysis; migration, diaspora, and identity; and the use of tribal oral tradition in archaeological research.

JAMES L. MOORE received his MA from the University of New Mexico in 1981 and has been a project director at the Office of Archaeological Studies since 1987. He has worked in the Southwest for more than thirty-six years, mostly focusing on northern New Mexico. Moore's long-term primary interests include prehistoric agricultural systems, population movement and migration, chipped-stone technology, and Spanish Colonial economics. For many years, he has been studying the effects of population movement in the Pueblo region and how it shaped the modern Pueblos, both archaeologically and culturally.

SCOTT G. ORTMAN received his PhD in anthropology from Arizona State University in 2009 and is director of research at the Crow Canyon Archaeological Center. He is also a fellow of the American Council of Learned Societies / Andrew W. Mellon Foundation, and a senior researcher on the Village Ecodynamics Project. He has conducted archaeological research in the American Southwest since 1990, initially in the Zuni and Mesa Verde regions but increasingly in the Rio Grande region as well. His research interests include historical anthropology, evolutionary theory, archaeology and linguistics, material-culture studies, and quantitative methods. Among his honors are the Society for American Archaeology Student Presentation Award and the Firestone Medal for Excellence in Undergraduate Research from Stanford University.

SUSAN C. RYAN received her MA from New Mexico State University in 1998 and is currently a PhD student at the University of Arizona. She has worked as a research archaeologist for Crow Canyon Archaeological

Center since 1998. Her major research interests include the Chaco to post-Chaco transition in the northern San Juan region, the built environment, and social memory.

MARK D. VARIEN is vice president of programs at the Crow Canyon Archaeological Center in Cortez, Colorado, where he and his colleagues seek to further the center's mission of archaeological research, public education, and American Indian involvement. He received a PhD from Arizona State University in 1997 and is a co-principal investigator on the Village Ecodynamics Project. He has published articles in many journals, including *American Antiquity*, the *Journal of Archaeological Method and Theory*, *Kiva*, *Ancient Mesoamerica*, and *World Archaeology*. His most recent book is the edited volume *The Social Construction of Communities: Agency, Structure, and Identity in the Prehispanic Southwest*. Among his research interests are household and community organization, patterns of sedentism and mobility, formation of cultural landscapes, human impact on the environment, and public education and American Indian involvement in archaeology.

C. DEAN WILSON (MA, Eastern New Mexico University, 1985) is the director of the Pottery Analysis Laboratory of the Office of Archaeological Studies, Museum of New Mexico, New Mexico Department of Cultural Affairs, in Santa Fe. He has been working with pottery from the Southwest for three decades, with special expertise in the central Mesa Verde and northern Rio Grande regions.

AARON M. WRIGHT is a PhD candidate in anthropology at Washington State University and a preservation fellow with the Center for Desert Archaeology in Tucson. He has participated in numerous survey and excavation projects in New Mexico, Arizona, Oklahoma, California, and Ohio. His prior graduate studies focused on the effect of climate change on Ancestral Puebloan demographic patterns in southwestern Colorado. His current research centers on Hohokam rock art and associated ritual features in the Salt river valley. His long-term research interests include paleoclimate reconstruction, analysis of ritual practice, the control and transmission of ritual knowledge, and the relationship between ideology and social power in the prehispanic Greater Southwest.